The Dalai Lama's Secret
and Other Reporting Adventures

THE DALAI LAMA'S SECRET

AND OTHER REPORTING ADVENTURES

Stories from a Cold War Correspondent

HENRY S. BRADSHER

Louisiana State University Press
Baton Rouge

Published by Louisiana State University Press

Manufactured in the United States of America
First printing

DESIGNER: Michelle A. Neustrom
TYPEFACE: Chaparral Pro
PRINTER: McNaughton & Gunn, Inc.
BINDER: Dekker Bookbinding

CARTOGRAPHER: Monica Bradsher

LIBRARY OF CONGRESS CATALOGING-IN-PUBLICATION DATA

Bradsher, Henry S. (Henry St. Amant), 1931–
The Dalai Lama's Secret and Other Reporting Adventures : Stories from a Cold War Correspondent / Henry S. Bradsher.
pages cm
Includes bibliographical references and index.
ISBN 978-0-8071-5050-4 (cloth : alk. paper) — ISBN 978-0-8071-5051-1 (pdf) — ISBN 978-0-8071-5052-8 (epub) — ISBN 978-0-8071-5053-5 (mobi) 1. Bradsher, Henry S. (Henry St. Amant), 1931– 2. Foreign correspondents—United States—Biography. I. Title.
PN4874.B6618A3 2013
070.4'332092—dc23
[B]

2012039371

The paper in this book meets the guidelines for permanence and durability
of the Committee on Production Guidelines for Book Longevity
of the Council on Library Resources. ♾

With respect, for journalists—foreign correspondents and also local reporters worldwide—who accept the difficulties and often dangers of providing the information vital for good and honest government.

CONTENTS

PREFACE *ix*

1. A Gubernatorial Push *1*
2. Riding the Buses in Montgomery *7*
3. Killing the Long-Haired Lama *20*
4. The Dalai Lama's Treasure *32*
5. Behind the Himalayas *41*
6. Climbing Cho Oyu *51*
7. Stumbling Over a Policeman's Severed Head *58*
8. Counting Crowds *63*
9. Into Bhutan by Mule *71*
10. Mail from the Nagas *88*
11. Left Off the Earth *101*
12. Tiger Hunting with Queen Elizabeth *108*
13. Punitive Expedition *117*
14. Of Royalty and Royal Weddings *132*
15. One Horse, Many Horses *145*
16. Denying Khrushchev *157*
17. Wrecking Receiving Lines *164*
18. Blocking Blackmail *169*
19. Stabbed in the Back *175*
20. Bombed in Moscow *183*

21. China's Most Despicable 203
22. Birth of a Nation 220
23. Reporting Vietnam 244
24. Riding the Dangerous Roads 255
25. Shoeshines at Jaffa Gate 266
26. Hazards of Journalism 277

Postscript 287

NOTES 291
INDEX 299

Photographs follow page 100

PREFACE

ANYONE WHO HAS WANDERED AROUND THE WORLD WATCHING INTERESTING events as a journalist accumulates lots of stories to tell. Here are some stories from twenty-seven years in journalism.

Most of them focus on specific events that I reported—or was otherwise involved in, such as thwarting a Soviet blackmail scheme. A few are more sweeping accounts of times and places, such as reporting parts of several wars with only a few forays into being a jungle-slogging war correspondent. These pieces were written over many years as stand-alone "anecdotes," so there is a little overlap.

However, this is not intended to be a comprehensive diary of my career as a reporter. Lots of things that engaged me are left out, such as being shot at by Communists trying to take control of Portugal, hoping an aging Lao helicopter was not really as hazardous as it sounded, interviewing President Gerald R. Ford on Air Force One while Henry A. Kissinger dozed off, witnessing the hardships of Vietnamese "boat people," talking with African guerrillas, and examining some South American politics. The collection includes almost nothing on reporting from Afghanistan, about which I wrote two books.

Most of the anecdotes here are from the longer periods of my career spent in South Asia, the Soviet Union, and East Asia. Without having a Soviet-style five-year plan, I ended up spending approximately five years in each of these areas—long enough to develop some background understanding of factors behind the news. Times have changed since then. Fewer American news organizations maintain correspondents abroad. Unfortunately, many organizations now depend on "parachute journalism"—dropping their stars briefly into hot spots about which they know little.

Improved communications have contributed to this change. From remote areas, I had to get to the nearest telegraph office to slap a typewritten report on the counter and hope it would soon be transmitted, or later, as communications improved, punch my story into Telex tape and try to get a connection to my newspaper. By the early twenty-first century my elder son, a *New York Times* correspondent, could get breaking stories from remote parts of Asia into his paper's late editions by cell phone dictation to a editor in Manhattan or typing into a smart phone.

Times have changed. My times were good.

Most spellings and names in use at the time of events described here have been changed to twenty-first-century usage. For example, Peking has become Beijing, Dacca is now Dhaka, and Chou En-lai is Zhou Enlai. A few unfamiliar changes, such as Calcutta to Kolkata, have been ignored, however.

The Dalai Lama's Secret
and Other Reporting Adventures

1

A GUBERNATORIAL PUSH

A BOYHOOD FASCINATION WITH WORLD WAR II STARTED MY INTEREST in world affairs that turned into a desire to become a foreign correspondent. It seemed to be an exciting world out there. So it proved to be. Before I became a foreign correspondent, however, my journalism got a push from a governor of Louisiana—an angry, not a friendly, push.

In third grade in the Louisiana State University "lab school," those youngsters who were doing well in various subjects were sometimes allowed to read quietly in a corner by open windows—this was before air conditioning. I was reading one morning when newsboys came by outside shouting, "Extra!" It was May 10, 1940, and Nazi Germany had invaded the Low Countries. That is my first recollection of the war, one day before my ninth birthday.

By the time the United States entered the war following the Pearl Harbor attack a year and a half later, I was working after school four times a week down the street at my grandfather's plant nursery. I was supposed to learn something about horticulture from the elderly German émigré who ran the nursery. With money thus earned, I subscribed to *Life* magazine for its graphic war coverage.

In the sixth grade at Highland School, Miss Lillian Kennedy used the war as part of her social studies and geography material. Students were asked to report every morning on the latest news. I gradually became the main reporter, recounting to the class the American troop landings in North Africa in November 1942 and other developments. I was hooked on reporting the news.

In a junior high school class that tried to focus students on what careers they might want to follow and how to prepare for them, I did my report on reporting. Work on my high school newspaper and yearbook seemed a logical part of becoming a journalist, although hardly useful preparation. The question was where to go to college. LSU had a good journalism school. Attending it would be the cheapest possibility, but the father of a friend urged me to go to his alma mater, the University of Missouri's School of Journalism, founded in 1908 as the world's first journalism school and still one of the most respected in the United States. He was C. P. Liter, the top editor for both of the locally owned morning and evening newspapers. This was endorsed by a close friend of my mother since childhood, Margaret Dixon, although she was an LSU graduate. She had become the top reporter for one of these papers, the *Morning Advocate.*

So, after a freshman year at LSU and spending the summer of 1949 bicycling and hitchhiking around Western Europe, I went in September to the University of Missouri, where my father had graduated. One of the courses that I took that sophomore year was "Recent U.S. History," taught by Dr. Irvin G. Wyllie. Covering the half-century from the Spanish-American War through World War II, it was a requirement for all journalism students and widely popular with other students. After I had earned an "E" in the course, Missouri's equivalent of an "A," and let it be known that I was looking for student employment, Wyllie asked me to grade the class papers. Throughout my junior and senior years, I spent most Friday and Saturday evenings reading the longhand answers to tests that Wyllie gave every Friday to the 150 or so students who took his course each semester. Grading the papers made me well-known to my fellow journalism students, many of whom did not seem to appreciate that I was just doing a job to help pay for my education.

Journalism school started off slowly. I soon realized that earning a Bachelor of Journalism required too many trade-type courses and not enough general education. I wanted a broad perspective with more history, economics, and other subjects. Early in that junior year, I decided to try to earn a Bachelor of Arts in history parallel with the BJ. This would require the equivalent of five years of college credits.

At the end of my sophomore year in the spring of 1950—a month before the Korean War started—I had "pre-enrolled" to enter in the autumn the advanced program of the Reserve Officers Training Corps, following the example of three uncles who served in World War II. Advanced ROTC students were normally required to spend the summer between their junior and senior years in military camp training. Fortunately for me, however, the crush of training active duty personnel for the Korean War caused the summer ROTC program to be cancelled in 1951. This enabled me to go to summer school and complete the BJ by February 1952 and the BA in May.

It required a heavy course load. I stayed very busy with classes, grading papers, and such extracurricular activities as debate, oratory, heading a World

Student Services fund drive to help foreign students, and other things. The journalism school setup helped. Missouri's J-School was unusual in publishing a full-scale town newspaper, not a student newspaper. The *Columbia Missourian* included community news reported by students under faculty supervision, news agency reports, and the whole range of typical newspaper contents. Those such as myself in the reporting curriculum—other curricula included news photography, radio, and advertising—had to do two semesters of covering reporting beats. Beat coverage took a lot of daily time that I could not spare while doing so many other things during regular semesters. The answer was "intersessions." To keep the paper publishing during university vacations, the J-School ran reporting and editing courses during these gaps. By six weeks of full-time reporting during the August 1951 break between summer school and the fall semester plus reporting over the Thanksgiving and Christmas holidays, I was able to fulfill the requirement.

More than just busy, I got overextended. While doing a massive research project to earn an BA with "distinction in history"[1] and writing press releases for Missouri contractors, I was offered another job. The graduate student who was the Columbia stringer (part-time reporter) for the United Press news agency's bureau in Kansas City was going off to Korean War military service. I probably should not have taken the job because I really did not have the time to do it properly. But I needed the extra money to hire a student's wife to type up the final version of the 311-page distinction paper. (The money ran out before the paper was fully typed, and I finished the typing myself.)

The UP job led to a major embarrassment. In the spring of 1952 a fad swept many college campuses of "panty raids"—shouting mobs of male students breaking into women's housing, or sometimes let in by squealing girls, to grab feminine underwear. At Missouri, it started one April evening on sorority row, at the other side of the campus from where I was in my room studying. Alerted but lacking a car or even a bicycle, I finally caught up with many hundreds of young men as they moved on to two private women's colleges near my side of the university. These college girls used mops and other things to try to repel the invaders. I phoned disjointed information to UP Kansas City, including second- and third-hand reports from sorority row.

The panty raids ended too late at night for comprehensive coverage in the next morning's papers. But the *St. Louis Post-Dispatch,* an afternoon paper that circulated in Columbia, published a graphic account—from UP. UP had always been noted for writing that sometimes was more flashy than accurate. Its afternoon version of the story, under my byline, had been rewritten in Chicago to make the raids sound more exciting than I had tried to describe. Some sorority girls whom I knew from J-School and elsewhere got mad at me over the UP story's saying the sororities had encouraged the raiders, rather than fighting back the way the girls at the women's colleges did. I was never sure how much truth there was in the encouragement report, although the situation probably varied from one sorority house to the next.

With the Korean War on, upon graduation I was ordered to report for active duty in mid-August. The J-School hired me between May and August at the lowest faculty rung, assistant instructor, to help supervise students in putting out the *Missourian.* Then I became an Air Force intelligence officer.

When I got out in May 1955, I intended to apply to the Associated Press for a job. After all, as editor of my 1948 high school yearbook I had written my own class prediction for 1960: "Henry S. Bradsher, foreign correspondent for Associated Press, has just returned from an extended assignment in India." While waiting for the AP to hire me, which came four months later, I applied for a job at the *Advocate,* where Maggie Dixon had by then become managing editor. She and Liter were willing to hire me at minimum wage on the understanding that I would leave as soon as I got an AP job.

In addition to getting the good experience of a wide variety of general assignment reporting jobs, I had some interesting stories. Shortly before I started at the *Advocate,* Dr. Jonas Salk had announced the first effective vaccine for polio. A public vaccination campaign was launched a week or two after I started at the paper. With the hope of a way to prevent the feared disease, the question arose nationwide of whether doctors would participate in mass vaccinations for little or no pay, or would give vaccinations as part of their regular office practices. Hearing that Baton Rouge's doctors were divided on this, I began inquiring around. I learned that doctors accredited at the main hospital in town planned to meet there to discuss what to do. So I phoned the head of the local medical association to ask him if the meeting was open. He said it was not advertised as a public meeting but was not closed.

I went to the hospital and, after lingering in a hall until everyone seemed to be inside a meeting room, went in and stood in the back. No one questioned me. An argument developed between those doctors who saw free public inoculations as a civic duty and those who felt their training and office expenses entitled them to give polio shots at their regular fees. Avoiding pulling out a pad to take notes for fear of having someone ask who I was, I listened intently. Then I went back to the newsroom to write about the debate, which was not resolved.

The next morning I got a call at home from an angry doctor. Even though I had not identified any doctors by name, many were embarrassed to have argued for regular fees at a time of heightened public anxiety over getting polio shots. The caller contended that I had improperly reported a private meeting. I told him I had asked ahead of time and was told it was not closed, and I had not misrepresented myself to anyone. Some doctors later volunteered their services for mass inoculations, but many did not.

In the early summer, the Pentagon announced plans for Exercise Sagebrush, maneuvers by eighty-five thousand army troops, to be staged from Camp Polk in impoverished, rural west-central Louisiana. The camp had been built in 1941 for the army's World War II buildup, closed after the war, reopened in 1950 to train troops for the Korean War, and closed again in June 1954. Sagebrush would reactivate it a year later for soldiers and their armored vehicles to fight mock battles in the surrounding pine forests and fields. The forestry industry became concerned that mechanized military equipment would interfere with logging and damage trees in the area. It opposed state government efforts to obtain permission from landowners for the army to use property that was contracted for tree farms and other forestry use.

Led by Governor Robert F. Kennon, the state government argued that Louisiana needed the money that the maneuvers would bring into the state and that the forestry damage would not be significant. In particular, officials contended that letting the maneuvers go ahead could mean the Pentagon would turn Camp Polk into a permanent installation, Fort Polk, with long-term economic benefits for the state.

Hearing the forestry side of this from the father of a friend, I began looking into it. I managed to talk Mrs. Dixon and Liter into assigning me to spend several days in the maneuver area talking to landowners, military people, forestry men, and others. Many of the landowners were skeptical about possible damage but eager to earn the small amount that the army would pay for crossing their property. My articles heated up the debate.

After my articles appeared, Kennon's spokesmen claimed that he had a promise from the Eisenhower administration to make Polk permanent after the maneuvers. Skeptical, I arranged for the *Advocate*'s Washington correspondent to check with the Pentagon on this. He was told flatly that the Defense Department had not made any commitment to make Polk a fort in return for being able to hold the maneuvers.

The day that the Pentagon's disavowal appeared in the *Advocate,* I went to the governor's suite in the Huey Long-built state capitol to seek comment.

Waiting for a press spokesman, I was standing by a secretary's desk in an outer office when Kennon came out of his private office on some other business. I had not expected to talk to him personally, but, taking advantage of the opportunity, I introduced myself and began to ask him a question. Before I could finish, he became angry, obviously recognizing my name from the newspaper stories. "I'm not going to talk to you," he said. Sticking his face up close to mine, he added more loudly, "You're just causing trouble." Then he grabbed me by the shoulder and pushed me backward. Stumbling a little, I managed to turn, and he then pushed me again toward the door. I left.

Maggie Dixon, who dealt with the governor on a regular basis as Louisiana's most-respected political reporter in addition to her editing role, was leery of my reporting this incident. Finally, she agreed to a cursory mention down in my story about new developments on the maneuvers.

The maneuvers were held. In the autumn, when I had begun working for the AP in Atlanta, someone in Baton Rouge sent me an unsigned postcard to which had been pasted a small newspaper item saying Polk had been converted into a permanent fort. This taunting turned out to be inaccurate, however. Polk was closed again in June 1959. With the Vietnam War heating up, it was opened yet again in September 1961—and stayed open. Not until October 1968 did the Defense Department declare it permanent. Fort Polk became a major infantry training center for the U.S. Army, where troops were prepared for fighting in Vietnam, Iraq, Afghanistan, and other parts of the world.

The *Advocate* was an enjoyable introduction to full-time journalism. After almost four months there, I left for the AP. I was off to Atlanta, Montgomery, New York, and fulfilling my sixth-grade ambition of becoming a foreign correspondent.

2

RIDING THE BUSES IN MONTGOMERY

THE PHONE IN MY LITTLE GARAGE APARTMENT WOKE ME UP ABOUT 4:30 on Sunday morning. I recognized the voice of an acquaintance who sold insurance in Montgomery, Alabama, but was somewhat of a local character because of his insomniac habit of cruising around town in the wee hours listening to the police radio. He also liked to hang around with reporters and had been nice to me the few times we had met. All he said was, "There's a bomb at King's house."

It was January 28, 1957. A month earlier a boycott of Montgomery city buses had been ended by those residents who at the time identified themselves as Negroes. The boycott to protest racial segregation practices on the buses had been led by the Rev. Dr. Martin Luther King Jr. A federal court order had forced the city to abandon bus segregation. A lot of white people were still angry.

As soon as the acquaintance hung up, I phoned Rex Thomas, my boss in the Associated Press bureau in Montgomery. His line was busy. By the time I had finished hurriedly dressing, the line was free. Rex had received a call from a friend in the police department about the bomb. It had not exploded. But other bombs had just exploded at a home and a service station owned by African Americans. We agreed that I should go to King's house while Rex went to the office. I would phone information for him to use along with police reports and other material in writing stories to file on the AP's Teletype wire.

King's white clapboard house was only a mile or so from my garage apartment. When I arrived, a large bundle of dynamite sticks with a defective fuse was lying near the top of the front steps, about a dozen feet across the porch from the master bedroom. A few police were already there and a crowd was beginning to gather, most of them angry African Americans. Tension was building.

They had reason to be angry. Two and a half weeks earlier, on January 10, 1957, three Baptist churches with black congregations had been bombed—one of them as I was passing a block away—along with the homes of two ministers.

Against the background of mounting violence directed at Montgomery's black leaders, this attempt to bomb King's home had created what police, journalists, and civic leaders from both sides of the racial divide would later call the angriest mood yet in the black community. Outside King's house in the small hours of that Sunday morning, the doctrine of nonviolence that he had preached throughout the bus boycott was being put to its most critical test. The possibility of a riot hung in the heavy night air as I talked with King, his aides, police, and people muttering on the street.

The situation in Montgomery had developed out of the work not of King but of a little-known son of an African American sharecropper and a number of other members of the city's black middle class. Edgar Daniel Nixon and the others had been planning and waiting for an opportunity to claim some of the rights inherent in the Supreme Court's 1954 decision in *Brown vs. Board of Education* that public school segregation was unconstitutional. Nixon, known to the world as E. D. Nixon and to his friends in the black church community as Brother Nick, was an acknowledged leader of the fifty thousand African Americans of Montgomery. He had organized and now headed the local chapter of the National Association for the Advancement of Colored People. As a Pullman car porter, one of the most prestigious jobs open to African Americans when he became a porter in 1923, he had also organized and now headed the Montgomery chapter of the Brotherhood of Sleeping Car Porters. The NAACP and the Brotherhood were the two most important national organizations working for African American rights in the early 1950s.

After the school decision, Nixon tried in the autumn of 1954 to enroll black children in a white elementary school near their homes. Montgomery city police turned them back. While court proceedings would be slow, Nixon realized that the economic power of the black half of the city's population was its best weapon.

Many African Americans, especially those who kept downtown stores clean and did the cooking and cleaning and babysitting in white homes, got to work on city buses. As was common in the South, they had to sit in the back of the bus while whites sat in front. As more whites boarded, blacks had to give up seats in the middle to them and stand in the back. The system in Montgomery was particularly onerous. Blacks were required to pay their fares at the front door, then get off and reboard at the back door, rain or shine. Bus drivers, all of them white, were often abusive. Sometimes they drove off as blacks who had paid their fares were making their way to the rear door.

By the summer of 1955, Nixon and others in Montgomery's black middle class had decided that the bus system should be targeted by a boycott to demand equal treatment. There was a precedent. In Baton Rouge, Louisiana, an eight-day bus boycott led by the Rev. T. J. Jemison in 1953 had won small improvements in conditions for black bus riders. All Nixon and his colleagues needed was an incident to try to build on that example. He rejected several incidents during the autumn of 1955 because the people involved had too many personal weaknesses to stand up to the media scrutiny that would result.

On Thursday, December 1, 1955, a forty-two-year-old black seamstress named Rosa L. Parks refused a bus driver's order to get up and move back so a newly boarded white passenger could sit down. She was tired after a hard day's work, she said later, and her feet hurt. The driver stopped the bus and summoned police. They took her off and charged her at the Montgomery jail with violating an Alabama segregation law. Nixon bailed her out.

Although her refusal to move had not been planned in advance, Mrs. Parks was not just another tired black woman. She was a member of Montgomery's well-educated black middle class despite her seamstress job that paid only $23 a week. She had been the secretary of the NAACP's local chapter, and at the time of her arrest she was training members of the organization's youth group in civil disobedience. And she was working as a volunteer with twenty-four-year-old Fred Gray, who had recently returned home with a law degree from Ohio (no Alabama school would educate African Americans to be lawyers) determined to fight for his people's rights. On several earlier occasions Mrs. Parks had been evicted from buses for refusing to obey drivers' instructions but had not been arrested.

That night she agreed to become a test case of bus segregation. Action began at once. A network of black activists sprang to life, and by the next morning leaflets were appearing calling for a bus boycott on the day of Mrs. Parks's court appearance. Nixon played a leading organizational role. First he called the Rev. Ralph D. Abernathy, the secretary of the Baptist Ministers Alliance of black pastors and a prominent voice in Montgomery's black church establishment. Next he called the older Rev. H. H. Hubbard, the alliance president. Both agreed to support a boycott. Then Nixon called a twenty-six-year-old minister who had arrived in Montgomery a year earlier to become pastor of the Dexter Avenue Baptist Church.

This tall, old, red brick building housed one of the most prestigious African American congregations in the South. It stood amid white-owned businesses and a few homes on the south side of the avenue that leads half a mile east from the business center of Montgomery up a gentle hill to the state capitol. In this town that proudly called itself "the cradle of the Confederacy" and that steered tourists to Jefferson Davis's "first White House," where he lived in 1861 just south of the capitol, the Confederate flag still flew above the capitol dome in 1955. The Dexter Avenue Baptist Church had the socially elite congregation of a black community that had always gotten along well with the white power structure by accommodating to its rules. The community had up to the 1950s accepted the restrictions of a town in which segregation was a way of life virtually unchanged since Reconstruction.

The new minister, Martin Luther King Jr., understood the situation. He had grown up in the comfortable black middle class of Atlanta, where his father was the pastor of the prominent Ebenezer Baptist Church. Sent to good schools, he had finished course work toward a doctorate in theology from Boston University. Then he had been called to the pastorate on Dexter Avenue. There he finished writing his dissertation, which years later became involved in controversy over his use of some sources.

According to Nixon, when he first phoned King, the young pastor asked for time to think about supporting a boycott. King, whose version differed somewhat, did not know Rosa Parks, and he apparently wanted to consult others on what was happening. By the time Nixon called him back, Nixon had already told some forty black leaders, more than half of whom were ministers, to meet that night at the Dexter Avenue Baptist Church. King concurred in this. After some argument at this December 2 meeting, the leaders agreed unanimously to call for a boycott of buses beginning the following Monday, December 5. Blacks began walking to work that chilly morning or using hastily improvised car pools, set up with advice that King got by telephoning Jemison in Baton Rouge.

That afternoon the black leadership met to establish an organization to keep the boycott going. They named it the Montgomery Improvement Association. Nixon became the MIA's treasurer, but he did not seek its leadership. His railroad job kept him out of town too much. Besides, he said later with great modesty about the role he had already played, a better-educated person was needed who could deal with all levels of society. Such a person was Rufus Lewis, a former teacher and football coach at Montgomery's historically black college, now named Alabama State University. Lewis, who had since the 1940s been leading a drive to register black voters, was considered by some to be a rival of Nixon's for leadership among black activists. Neither man wanted the other to lead the MIA.

Instead, the meeting decided a minister would make the best leader, for two reasons: the black community focused on its churches and looked to the pastors for leadership, and a minister would be less vulnerable to white economic pressure than a wage earner or businessman. Those black ministers long established in the community were caught up in personal rivalries and bickering, however, making it impossible to agree on Abernathy, Hubbard, or one of the other older men. In addition, some of them were considered to have been compromised by earlier dealings with the white community. So the meeting turned to the well-educated young newcomer, Dr. King, to take a job that he did not seek.

King had not been a social activist in his first year in Montgomery. Just a month before the boycott started he had declined to be nominated for the presidency of the local NAACP chapter. But now, backed by Nixon, Lewis, and many others, he rose to the occasion magnificently. His oratory inspired. His slowly developing sense of nonviolent assertion, in which he consciously drew from Gandhi and Thoreau, provided a theme for the boycott while steering it away from a confrontation with the white establishment that both sides feared might erupt into violence.

The campaign focused on black churches. The churches had historically preached acceptance of southern slavery—or, at least, not challenged it—and after slavery's abolition they accepted the segregated, second-class status of freed men. Churches had consoled blacks in their role in a white-dominated society. Now churches were used on a rotating basis for MIA meetings twice a week to rally and reinforce the community's increasingly difficult dedication to a break with the past. While King was often the featured speaker at these meetings, other black ministers and civic leaders also encouraged people to maintain the arduous boycott. Yet it was King who set the tone of firm, nonviolent resistance to white efforts to dissuade poor, suffering household maids, manual laborers, and others from continuing a quiet, humble, but proud defiance.

I went to some of these church meetings in order to report on the speeches on those occasions when the leadership sought endorsements for policy decisions. The powerful appeal of the meetings was built around Christianity. In my youth in Louisiana I had attended baptisms and other black church events as a spectator, so I was familiar with the intense emotions that such church meetings can generate. In Montgomery, the inspirational strength of a revival was mixed with the enthusiasm of claiming long-denied constitutional rights. The crescendo of the minister's oratory, the fervently shouted "Amens" to his biblical assertions and rhetorical questions, the massed power of the hymns, and the virtual religious trance that the congregation sometimes worked itself into—all these had to be experienced to be appreciated. Nothing I had seen in

Louisiana matched the sense of danger, defiance, and dedication in the Montgomery churches.

The danger was real. As the boycott persisted despite efforts by white civic leaders and employers to cajole or coerce blacks to abandon it, a small bomb exploded at King's house. He was leading a MIA meeting at a church while his wife and ten-week-old first child were at home that evening of January 30, 1956. The bomb did not hurt them and did little damage. If it was intended as a warning, it failed. Instead of intimidating King and the movement, it helped call outside attention to what was happening in Montgomery. So did legal actions by the city to try to break the boycott as an illegal conspiracy.

In the next few months the bus boycott became world news. At the age of twenty-seven, King was becoming an internationally known leader. Media attention focused on Montgomery. National and foreign journalists visited the city to write about the phenomenon. Then they left. Rex Thomas's AP bureau was under the pressure of maintaining constant coverage of a racially divided city, of providing the day-in and day-out reporting of the boycott that world media depended on, despite the sporadic presence of out-of-town reporters. Rex and the AP's Atlanta bureau, which supervised Alabama, decided one of the two reporters working for Rex could not handle the increasingly demanding job. They looked around for a replacement.

I had been hired in September 1955 by the AP's Atlanta bureau. After some general reporting and rewrite work, I was asked if I would like to go to Montgomery. I arrived there about May 1, 1956. The fourteen months that I spent there were not only professionally rewarding but also—with time for tennis, swimming, water skiing, and golf—enjoyable.

Rex Thomas was the kind of person who has always been the backbone of solid, reliable American journalism. As the AP's Montgomery bureau chief for more than a dozen years when I arrived, he was virtually an institution in Alabama politics because small-town papers around the state depended on AP coverage of the capital. He knew everyone from Governor "Kissin' Jim" Folsom on down. Rex's idea of how to use spare time was riding the highways with state police in their patrol cars swapping stories, or playing poker with a few old beer-drinking buddies. A little sensitive about having only a high school education because he had not been able to afford college during the Depression, he had a broad range of practical knowledge and a bearish precision on the use of words. Having read in my personnel file about a Phi Beta Kappa key, he made a few snide cracks when I arrived about that and the limited value of college educations. Then he set out to teach me. I learned a lot about journalism from him. He was a good boss, demanding but considerate.

At the three-newsman AP bureau in a corner of the newsroom of the local newspaper, the *Montgomery Advertiser,* Rex and Lynn Brannon worked during the day. I had the shift from 4 P.M. to 12:30 A.M., or whenever after that the work was done. One of the first things I learned was to operate the Teletype, because the fourth person in the bureau, a Teletype operator (and golfing buddy), went home at 6. Learning to punch articles into Teletype tape faster than the sixty words a minute at which it was transmitted was a skill of later value to me in Moscow, around Asia, and elsewhere. So were other things Rex encouraged me to learn, such as the ability to rush away from an event with only a few rough notes and immediately dictate a well-phrased, comprehensive news story to someone at the other end of a telephone.

Rex wanted me to have broad experience as well as skills. Although he kept me away from Alabama legislative sessions, which he and Lynn covered, he sent me out on a variety of stories. For years he had personally covered all the executions in the electric chair at the state prison near Montgomery, but he entrusted me with the dual job of being an official witness and reporting the AP's stories on the two executions that occurred while I was in his bureau.

I got out of the office to some black church meetings and some rallies of the White Citizens' Council, a slightly upscale version of the Ku Klux Klan with a name intended to be less inflammatory. The KKK, more prone to violence, loomed in the background. Most of my coverage was of necessity by telephone, often talking to people on both sides of the racial struggle whom I had not met personally. It soon turned out that I had a minor advantage. Those who talked to me could not quite place my accent. Although I had grown up in Baton Rouge, I had become accustomed to people's thinking that I was from somewhere more Midwestern—and to women's telling me that I sounded like Jimmy Stewart (who was from western Pennsylvania). Some months into working in Montgomery, one of the black leaders told me he had become willing to talk to me because I did not sound like a southerner—the unstated implication being that he assumed I could be objective. On the other hand, Citizens' Council leaders were a little suspicious of me until I learned to accentuate a "good ol' boy" drawl.

The Montgomery Improvement Association went through some difficult times while I was there. Financial pressures on the black community were intense, despite contributions from around the United States. The city's legal efforts to break up car pools and otherwise hamper the boycott were constantly being fought by Fred Gray and other young black attorneys with the support of a few local white lawyers and distant backing from the NAACP's national headquarters and some white organizations. Internal rivalries created tensions within the MIA. King's leadership had become so indispensable that he was not personally challenged, but his growing celebrity status did cause resentments. These were tricky stories to handle. Both sides in the conflict were constantly looking for bias in the reporting, and supporters of the boycott in distant American cities jumped critically on anything that suggested disunity or weakness within the association. The *New York Post,* then a bastion of American liberalism, got so alarmed by one of my late-night stories about MIA troubles that it began phoning black leaders in Montgomery with a "say it ain't so" attitude. Rex said to be more circumspect in the future.

When Rosa Parks was charged with violating a local segregation ordinance, MIA leaders assumed on the basis of *Brown vs. Board of Education* that a court case on her behalf would lead to a Supreme Court decision that segregation on buses was unconstitutional. But the leaders soon realized that the white establishment could stall the case in Alabama courts indefinitely—and the black community could not be expected to keep the bus boycott going forever. The MIA therefore paid Mrs. Parks's $10 fine and $4 in court costs to close her case. Her lawyer, Fred Gray, put together a separate case by four—later three—black women. They filed a civil suit in federal court charging that they had been mistreated on a Montgomery bus. A three-judge panel headed by the federal district judge in Montgomery, Frank M. Johnson Jr., heard arguments on May 11, 1956. A lawyer from the NAACP's national office argued on behalf of the MIA that the *Brown* ruling against the long-standing southern doctrine of separate but equal facilities for blacks in schools should also apply to Montgomery's bus system. The city's lawyers argued that abolishing segregation would turn Montgomery into a bloody battleground.

The federal panel ruled on June 4 that the municipal bus segregation ordinance was unconstitutional. The city appealed. The Supreme Court rejected the appeal on November 13. By then city officials were fighting a last-ditch battle to break the MIA's car pool operations by legal harassment based on car registrations, taxi regulations, and other subterfuges. But the war had been lost.

Still, the city commission grudgingly refused to abandon bus segregation until formally served with a federal order conveying the Supreme Court action. The white establishment did nothing to prepare the city's white residents for the impending change, nothing to urge restraint in the unprecedented new circumstances. In contrast, King and other MIA leaders stressed at continuing mass meetings and in visits to black schools the need for nonviolence in the face of possible trouble—for turning the other cheek if provoked or even if attacked—when blacks resumed riding buses under conditions of racial integration.

The federal order finally reached Judge Johnson's court on the afternoon of December 20. He called in city officials to convey it formally. I was at the court waiting to phone Rex. All I had to do was confirm the formalities and add the few remarks made by generally tight-lipped participants. In his thorough, well-prepared way, Rex had already talked privately with Johnson to be sure he had a complete, accurate picture of what would happen, and earlier AP stories had laid out the basic facts.

Early the next morning I was on the downtown street corner where King and Nixon planned to board the first bus. They had little to say. Rex was in the office, and I phoned him. This was before glass-walled or open pay phones on the streets, much less cell phones, so it was necessary to run inside a drugstore to call, temporarily losing sight of the principals. I got back in time to get on a bus with the MIA leaders, along with several other reporters and a few cameramen. The white bus driver said a polite "Good morning" to King, Nixon, Abernathy, and a white Methodist minister from Texas who had advised King throughout the boycott, Glenn E. Smiley. We rode uneventfully through some suburbs, changed buses where two lines crossed, and came back downtown. Elsewhere in Montgomery, bricks were thrown at some other buses carrying blacks, but bus integration passed fairly quietly.

Then came the bombs.

It was an unusual coincidence that I was driving by, only a block from the first one to go off at a church early on the morning of January 10, 1957. I seldom drove to work. Parking downtown was difficult or expensive or both, and, besides, I liked to walk. I usually rode the almost empty city buses to work—as a practical matter, not a political statement. Then I would walk home, a distance of slightly under two miles, after midnight. But I happened to drive to work the afternoon before the church bombings. After work, I went out with a few people from the *Advertiser* for pie and coffee. As I was driving home by an atypical route around 2 A.M. I heard an explosion nearby. I turned toward it and found smoke still lingering over the damaged steps and entranceway of a large Baptist church with a black congregation—not King's church. No one was in sight. As I stood there surveying the scene, I heard several other explosions in the distance. So I drove back to open up the office. After waking Rex up at home, I phoned the police and began getting out a story. In addition to three churches, bombs had gone off at the homes of Abernathy and of a white Lutheran pastor of a black congregation, the Rev. Robert Graetz, whose home had been bombed once before. No one was hurt, and the police said they could not find any witnesses. *Newsweek*'s Montgomery stringer (part-time correspondent) was the city editor of the *Advertiser.* He interviewed me, and the magazine led its story of the bombings by quoting me as the nearest thing to a witness.

Before police had made any arrests in the church bombings, and therefore while the black community still had no evidence that white officials cared to uphold the law when it came to racial matters, the bomb was placed at King's house on January 28.

Shortly after I got to his house early on that Sunday morning, an assistant state toxicologist arrived and decided that the fuse had been lit but inexplicably had gone out. Police were keeping everyone off King's lawn, but, muttering "AP" or "press," I walked by them and went up to join the explosives expert and other officials in examining the bomb. It was sixteen large sticks of dynamite taped into a bulky square, enough to devastate the house. A burnt fuse stuck out of one end. Later, police started to peel the bundle apart, taking off one four-stick layer before deciding not to go any further there on the steps. A local television station's crew then appeared and filmed the bomb. On Sunday afternoon the station's news director phoned Rex in a friendly way to say the AP's story was wrong in saying sixteen sticks of dynamite. His crew's film showed only twelve. I explained to Rex that I had personally examined sixteen sticks, and that the television people had gotten there after four had been removed. Rex stuck with my version, although I have since noticed the number given as twelve in a history of the Montgomery events.

A few MIA workers were in King's living room to protect him while also discouraging him from going out and talking to the crowd. There was fear of further trouble, perhaps someone's taking a shot at him from the darkness. I was allowed into the living room to talk with King briefly. He had little to say, other than disclosing that for safety reasons his family had not been living in the house for some time. He had only just arrived when told of the bomb. Outside the mood was getting uglier. Finally, King went outside to calm the crowd, telling them that "violence is not the answer to our problems."

Some black youths standing in the crowd near King's house began criticizing the white police for failing to halt the bombings. After I had gone back onto the street, there was a brief scuffle and the police arrested two blacks. This made the situation even more inflammatory. But MIA workers circulated in the crowd, urging people to go home. After a while, they did. By then it was nearing 6 A.M. King's early Sunday sermon at the Dexter Avenue Baptist Church was scheduled for only a few hours later.

He was there, and so was I—and some police. He delivered a magnificent sermon, obviously extemporaneous to deal with the situation, but calm, measured, truly Christian in its charity toward those who sought to provoke the black community. King did not dwell on the intended threat to his own family. Instead, he talked about the importance of love, of understanding, of healing in a divided city. He talked about perseverance in the difficulties that were sure to keep coming even with the boycott over. King declared, apparently for the first time, that he had had a vision telling him to lead the boycott "against segregation without fear." The movement had to be nonviolent, he said, "because our oppressors control the police, the National Guard even, and, if they send the federal government in here, that will be white folks, too. . . . Let us not get our guns because that will not solve our problems. Through our suffering, we are going to transform the hearts of those who are cowardly enough to throw bombs and shoot pistols." The circumstances made it a memorable occasion, but the oratory was memorable too.

The county prosecutor later said, "We were on the very edge of racial rioting" before the police arrested four white men on January 30 for the church bombings. The arrests had a limited calming effect, but there was some later violence against blacks, although none of it directed at leaders of the MIA. Two of the arrested men, nineteen and twenty-seven years old, were put on trial in a little, high-ceilinged courtroom in a small red brick building being used while a new county courthouse was under construction. An all-white jury acquitted them on May 30.

These and other events kept the AP bureau busy. But, with the boycott over, Montgomery was beginning to fade from national and international attention. In nearby Tuskegee, Alabama, an attempt was made to emulate Montgomery's example of economic pressure against segregation practices. Black leaders there were grouped around the Tuskegee Institute, where at the turn of the century Booker T. Washington had been the nation's preeminent spokesman for the economic progress of colored people, as his race was then known. The leaders organized a boycott of white-owned stores because of mistreatment of black customers. I drove over to Tuskegee several times to cover that boycott. But the effort lacked the organizational determination of an E. D. Nixon or the inspiring leadership of a Martin Luther King Jr. The Tuskegee boycott never attracted much attention, and it achieved only limited success.

As Montgomery returned to the relative obscurity typical of southern state capitals, albeit with a famous African American pastor on Dexter Avenue, the AP was looking for newsmen who had proven themselves in domestic coverage and wanted to go overseas. I left Montgomery in early July 1957 to work on the AP's foreign desk in New York until something opened up abroad.

The last time I saw King was in India in March 1959. On a grant from a Quaker foundation, he and his wife were visiting the land of Mohandas K. Gandhi, the apostle of nonviolent pressure on a perceivedly oppressive system, whose writings had influenced the bus boycott. I covered the Kings' tour of the Gandhi museum in New Delhi. King recognized me, and we chatted briefly, but there was not much of a news story beyond the fact of his being there. His activities did not automatically make the newspapers at that time.

That was during a period when neither King nor other black leaders were sure what to do with the power of a boycott or the legal precedent set in Montgomery. The federal courts' rejection of that city's bus segregation had not nullified such ordinances in other southern cities. Little had changed. King organized the Southern Christian Leadership Conference in Atlanta, but it was slow to do anything. Not until the early 1960s did the Montgomery bus boycott prove to be not an isolated incident but the harbinger of greater change. Then King began a new phase of leadership that led to his evocative 1963 letter from the Birmingham jail and later that year to the march on Washington and his "I Have a Dream" speech at the Lincoln Memorial, to the 1964 Nobel Peace Prize, to the 1965 Selma march—and in 1968 to his death in Memphis.

Rex never answered my notes on Christmas cards, and eventually I quit writing to him. But when, in January 1989, I was invited to speak on the Afghanistan war at the Air University at Maxwell Air Force Base just outside Montgomery, I went to see him. Rex had remained the AP's bureau chief and a reporter respected throughout Alabama until his retirement in the early 1970s. When I drove out to his house, he was in his late seventies and in frail health. But he had lost none of his spark in the thirty-two years since last I'd seen him. I had written ahead that I was going to be in town to speak at the Air University but had not explained how or why. He had gotten on the phone with his old persistence and learned from Air University officers where I now worked and what my topic would be.

I thanked Rex for all he had taught me, all he had done for my career in journalism and, indirectly, in foreign affairs. He had kept up with my journalistic career. He was warm and gracious, glad to be remembered. He died a year or two later.

3

KILLING THE LONG-HAIRED LAMA

THE CABLES FROM LONDON WERE ANGRY. THE FIRST ONE CAME IN THE wee hours of the morning of Saturday, March 21, 1959. The overnight messenger who dozed in the New Delhi bureau of the Associated Press received a phone call from the Indian government communications office, and he pedaled his bicycle over to Eastern Court to pick up the cable. Then he woke Rangaswamy Satakopan, the AP's invaluable reporter who lived with his wife and their nephew in rooms off one side of the office. Swamy read the cable and started calling Indian journalist friends, seeking information, but could get little at that hour.

Another rocket from London, the control and relay point for most of the eastern hemisphere for the AP's headquarters in New York. A "rocket" is an angry or unhappy message from headquarters to a foreign correspondent, typically asking why some news has not been reported. Cables were the only reliable form of communications, because telephone calls were slow, erratic, and often impossible, while other things such as Telex and fax were either nonexistent in South Asia or still unknown.

Satakopan phoned Watson S. Sims, the AP bureau chief. Wally was responsible for dealing with a problem. Reuters, our main competition in providing news from South Asia to the world media, was reporting that Tibetans had risen in revolt against Chinese Communist troops stationed in Lhasa. There was fighting on "the roof of the world." The AP had no reports on it.

It was about 8 A.M. when I got to work at the AP's ground-floor office at 19 Narendra Place. By then Satakopan had read the morning newspapers and tapped some of his numerous Indian government sources to produce a story. It was about as cursory as the Reuters one—more background and color on Tibet than facts on the fighting.

As the morning wore on, we learned that initial public reports of the fighting had come from Darjeeling, a Himalayan hill station close to the mule trails that carried commerce out of Tibet. The *Statesman* had published one report, but, unfortunately, in an economy move the AP had recently quit paying a tipster in the newsroom of the newspaper's Delhi edition to alert us to such stories the night before they were published. Reuters was tied into India's national news agency, from which it had learned of the Tibetan uprising, while the AP lacked any domestic news agency access. We had a stringer in Darjeeling, but he was hard to reach and only mailed in occasional feature stories.

At the question period that opened Parliament at noon, Prime Minister Jawaharlal Nehru made a brief statement about fighting in Lhasa. India had inherited the old British Indian consulate there and maintained a small staff

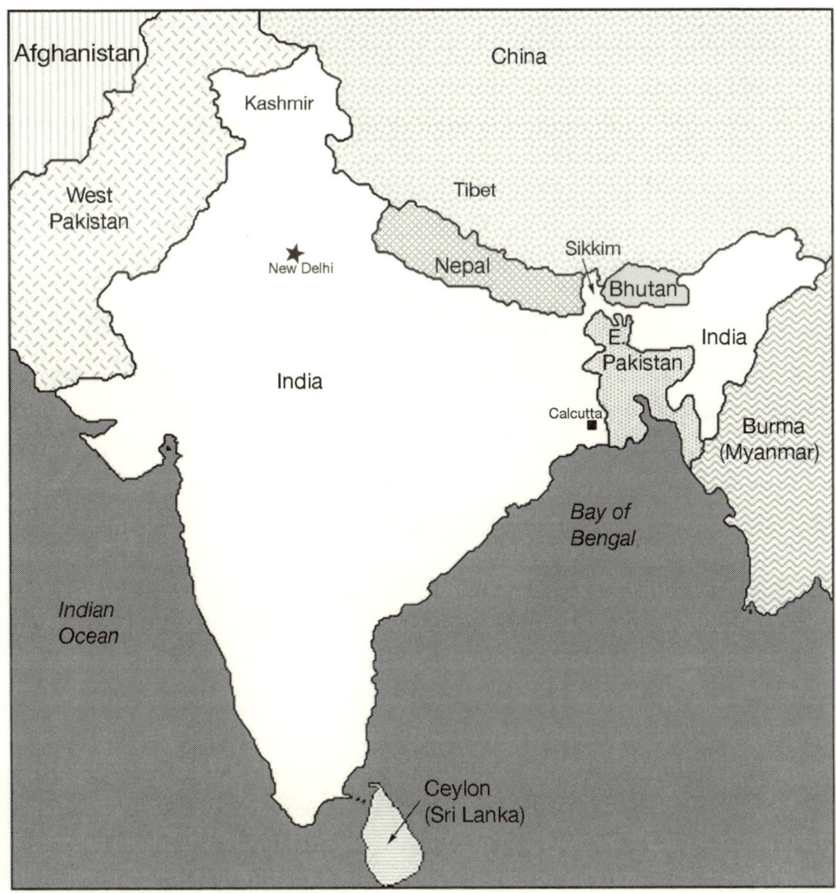

with a telegraph line and a radio transmitter. Nehru cautiously said little, but this was obviously a major news story.

There had been vague reports of guerrilla resistance since a few years after China invaded Tibet in the autumn of 1950, snuffing out almost four decades of de facto independence. Nehru's government, reluctant to let anything mar its relations with China, had tried to play down the reports reaching northeastern India. It even secretly stopped cables about the resistance sent to the *Daily Telegraph* in London by George Patterson. George, a British resident in Darjeeling who had once been a Scottish missionary in eastern Tibet for a small evangelical Christian sect, still had good Tibetan connections.

But now the reports of trouble in Tibet could not be ignored. The world wanted to know more about what was going on in the mysterious, alluring land ruled by Red China, as it was then known in the West.

Only three weeks earlier, on February 27, I had arrived in New Delhi to begin my career as an AP foreign correspondent. I was still learning my way around the Indian capital, working with Wally Sims, for the next two years the best boss of my entire journalism career, and with Swamy Satakopan, a wise and generous counselor. I had little expectation of traveling for some time. But, after Nehru's statement about the Lhasa situation, I was on that evening's flight to Calcutta, en route to Darjeeling.

The AP's stringer in Calcutta (now known as Kolkata), a deputy editor of that city's edition of the *Statesman,* met me at Dum Dum airport. That was my first exposure to Calcutta, an overcrowded, decaying industrial and port city where I would spend a lot of journalistic time in the next dozen years. It was late enough at night that most of the multitudes who lived on the sidewalks had let their little cooking fires go out and wrapped themselves in thin cloth to go to sleep on the hard pavement, looking like corpses laid out in disorderly array.

Early the next morning I flew north to Siliguri. There I hired a taxi to take me from the north edge of the plains up the twisting road to Darjeeling. A summer resort escape from Calcutta's steamy heat, Darjeeling lies along a ridgeline seven thousand feet high in the foothills of the Himalayas. It was what had been built in British colonial times as a "hill station."

The AP's Darjeeling stringer, Delip Bose, was a pleasant middle-aged man who had been a child star in Calcutta's large Bengali-language movie industry and was living a comfortable life of semi-retirement. Journalism was for him an amusement, but one he practiced with high enough standards to distinguish between facts and rumors. He tried to be helpful, providing the scant available facts, filling me in on the numerous rumors, and introducing me to a few people. I gave the telegraph office a few minor stories to cable to the AP in London. But it quickly became apparent that Darjeeling was not the best place to get information. After a few days I hired a taxi and moved eastward to Kalimpong: down to the Teesta River on a road so steep that there was a parking place halfway along where everyone stopped to let their vehicles' brakes cool, across the Coronation Bridge, and then twisting back up other Himalayan foothills.

While Darjeeling was a faded old resort with some residual distinction, Kalimpong was a grimy working town. Stretching along a slightly lower ridgeline, it was the terminus for mule trains that carried trade with Tibet. The mules came, bells jangling and owners' flags flying from head harnesses, over the 14,390-foot-high Jelap La ("la" means "pass" in Tibetan) from the Chumbi Valley of southern Tibet, across the southeastern corner of Sikkim, to dark old warehouses and smelly feed lots at Kalimpong. Wool, yak's hair, hides, musk, and other Tibetan exports were unloaded. Products of the industrial world, made in India or shipped from overseas to Calcutta's congested river port and taken by train and then truck to Kalimpong, were loaded onto the mules for their month-long return plod to Lhasa, or to other parts of Tibet.

In Kalimpong I did a lot of walking around (occasionally in brief rain showers that hit the hills unexpectedly), seeking news sources. The first full day I was there turned out to be Holi, a Hindu holiday when reveling youths douse people with colored water. Innocently unaware, I got thoroughly drenched. This amused Vicky Macdonald, who soon had my washable summer suit looking good again. The proprietress of the Himalayan Hotel, Vicky explained to me that the word used for a mountain in Nepali and several other mountain languages is "himal," with the accent on the second syllable, and Himalayas simply meant "the mountains." The correct pronunciation, therefore, she and others insisted, was Hi-MAL-a-yas, not the British corruption to Hi-ma-LAY-as.

As the first Western correspondent to arrive in Kalimpong, I soon attracted attention from India's Intelligence Bureau, the country's internal security organization. Kalimpong had long been known as a center of intrigue involving Tibet, Sikkim, and also Bhutan, the small Himalayan state to the east. Nehru had more than once told Parliament that Kalimpong was a hotbed of agitators and spies who were stirring up the kind of trouble in Tibet that he wished would go away. Two Intelligence Bureau officers came to the hotel to interview me about my purpose there. They eventually seemed to be satisfied that I was accredited to the government as a journalist in Delhi.

Within a week, the little Himalayan Hotel was full of reporters, all chasing rumors. Vicky entertained us with recollections of the last time her hotel had attracted so many journalists, when the Chinese invaded Tibet in the autumn of 1950. After reports of the modern Chinese Army's capturing some towns in extreme eastern Tibet from local people armed with nothing much better than flintlocks, there was little or no further news of military movements for some time. Most journalists left Kalimpong. But Vicky amusedly told of a British correspondent who sat in his hotel room with a map on which he measured off so many miles a day and then filed graphic accounts of the Chinese capturing such-and-such a Tibetan place on the way to Lhasa.

I interviewed several prominent Tibetans who had in earlier years gone into exile rather than have to work for the Chinese Communists. They included W. D. Shakabpa, a former Tibetan finance minister, and one of the Pandatshang brothers from the eastern Tibetan province of Kham. The Pandatshangs and their followers had been in revolt against the Chinese since 1955, and the name of their regional people, the Khampas, later became synonymous with anti-Communist guerrillas from all parts of Tibet. These were dramatic-looking men in colorful hand-woven, wrap-around *kho* robes with very full sleeves, some with daggers in their belts, most wearing jade earrings in their left ears at a time when men did not yet wear earrings in the West. They gave me a lot of background on Tibet, its geography, people, and politics. It was fascinatingly educational, but they had little current information on what was happening in Lhasa. And they could not shed light on what had become of the Dalai Lama, twenty-three-year-old Tenzin Gyatso. According to reports leaking out of the Indian government in Delhi, he was not in Lhasa after the uprising.

So I hired a car and driver to make the long, twisting trip down to the Teesta River and then follow the river's course up to Gangtok, capital of India's protectorate state of Sikkim. At fifty-five hundred feet, this was another town that straggled along ridgelines overlooking green sloping hills and forests. I went to talk with the relay man for news from the Indian consulate in Lhasa, India's political officer Apa Pant.

A gracious, sophisticated man, Pant came from a line of hereditary *dewans,* or prime ministers, for *maharajas* in British India, and was a senior civil servant of independent India. He had assumed the multiple jobs established for the senior British Indian civil servant in Gangtok of virtually running the government of Sikkim. This he did with the title of adviser to the *chogyal,* the little protectorate's king, while also supervising Indian consular and trade officers in Tibet and maintaining India's contacts with Bhutan. Pant had arranged by telephone for me to get the permission that foreigners needed to enter Sikkim, which was behind the "inner line" originally established by the British to keep outside influences from sensitive frontier areas. In an interview, he gave me some fresh information about the origins of the Lhasa uprising and the sporadic fighting that was continuing there, as well as some gloomy predictions about long-term prospects for the Tibetan people under a tightened Chinese rule.[1] But he was unwilling to go beyond saying that the Dalai Lama had been reported to have fled his capital.

It was a frustrating time. Few of the Western journalists who arrived in Kalimpong after I did could get permission to go up to Gangtok, and there was no news of the DL, as we came to refer to the Dalai Lama. Then, after I had been in Kalimpong more than a week, All-India Radio reported that Nehru had told Parliament that the Dalai Lama had crossed the border into India's North-East Frontier Agency (NEFA), east of Bhutan. Only much later was it revealed that the DL and his senior officials had fled Lhasa because they believed he was under threat of kidnapping by Chinese troops for resisting Beijing's control. Rather than risk the closely guarded main trade route southwest toward India, the group headed over mountains to the southeast. Several days later, they met Tibetan guerrillas who had been trained by the United States' Central Intelligence Agency. The guerrillas escorted them into a rugged area southeast of Lhasa toward the nearest border with India.

The DL's group was pursued into the Tibetan Himalayas by Chinese troops and planes as it fled along rough trails and across passes deep in snow. The guerrillas included a radio team. This put the DL's escort in contact with the CIA and, through U.S. government relays, the Indian government. They cautiously kept secret the DL's situation until he had safely crossed into NEFA. This Himalayan tribal area north of the Assam plains was closed by government decree not only to foreigners but also to most Indians to prevent commercial exploitation of unsophisticated peoples and their natural resources. The Chinese ended their pursuit at the de facto border.

When Nehru announced the border crossing, the DL was slowly making his way under Indian military escort along steep, jungled trails by mule and foot, and later by jeep along recently carved military roads, toward the plains. With great difficulty, I managed to get a poor phone connection from Kalimpong to Wally Sims in Delhi. Shouting to be understood, we agreed that I should get as quickly as possible to the area of Assam where the DL was first expected to cross the "inner line" out of NEFA and be accessible to the press. Within a day or two via Calcutta, I arrived in Tezpur, a dusty, sweaty little tea planters' town on the north bank of the Brahmaputra River. Thus began a hectic period that became known to the mounting numbers of journalists as "waiting for the Dalai Lama."

As the first correspondent in Tezpur, which was too small an Indian trading center to have a Western-style hotel, I found accommodation in one of four barren little rooms with metal frame beds and thin mattresses in a small concrete barracks behind the Planters' Club. The rundown little club near the river had seen its best days early in the twentieth century, when British planters flourished by growing lowland tea, cheaper and less sweet but more plentiful than the high-grown Darjeeling variety, on large plantations known as "tea gardens." By 1959 most of the big London-based tea companies had been bought out by Indian businessmen in Calcutta, and British managers of the gardens were beginning to be replaced with Indians.

The cook and bartender at the normally deserted club were glad for my business. They became less glad as more journalists poured into town, some of them sleeping on club sofas, while late arrivals ended up boarding with missionaries and tea planters. The very simple club menu, mostly eggs, greasy potatoes, and mutton chops, became pretty boring.

Shortly after I got there, another early arrival in Tezpur was Noel Barber, a roving correspondent of London's *Daily Mail*. In the 1950s the *Mail* and another popular London paper, the *Daily Express*, were the primary competitors in first-person, "I was there" journalism, which was intended to give British blue-collar workers a feeling of vicariously participating in exciting events around the world. The sarcastic joke among more serious journalists was that someone of Barber's ilk would send his office from the location of some dramatic event a cable that said only, "Awestruck, I watched as . . . uppick [news] agencies [accounts]," and go off to the nearest bar, leaving the rest to rewrite men on his copy desk.

But Barber had the reputation of being a hard-driving type. He had been wounded in the head in Budapest during the 1956 Hungarian "freedom fighters" uprising and later had been stabbed in a Moroccan bazaar during trouble over independence from France. And he was a friendly, personally likeable sort, whatever his journalistic ethics. In Tezpur, he became the ringleader as three or four of us talked one evening about the possibility of sneaking across the "inner line" at night in order to go into NEFA and meet the DL before other journalists could see him. I had my doubts about this mainly because I did not want to lose touch with the outside world via the primitive little Morse-key telegraph office in Tezpur. Anyway, the idea quickly fell through when efforts to find a guide turned up the information that the jungled foothills along the line were inhabited by tigers, poisonous snakes, and other dangers and that travel along the single road would be stopped by military guard posts.

A British planter had a copy of a book by one of the first British officials to visit Tawang, a Tibetan Buddhist monastery high in NEFA near the de facto Tibetan border and along the DL's route. The book described the elaborate religious ceremony, punctuated echoingly by ten-foot-long mountain horns, with which the official had been received by colorfully dressed lamas and monks of Tawang almost half a century earlier. Barber got hold of the book and proceeded to write a graphic, virtually eye-witness, description of the DL's arrival in Tawang, complete with ceremony and horns. He cabled this great scoop to the *Mail.* Unfortunately, he got a cable back that Tawang had already been reported. The *Mail*'s India stringer, an Anglo-Indian named Larry Atkinson, had been dispatched from Delhi to cover the story from the administrative center for NEFA, a hill station in Assam named Shillong. Atkinson had apparently found the book first. Knowing what his paper wanted, Atkinson had already cabled his own graphic fabrication of the religious homage with which the DL had been received in Tawang. But Atkinson did not try to match Barber's totally spurious but colorfully graphic claim of having flown over NEFA and seen the DL's party slowly wending its way down mountain trails.

World excitement over the DL was mounting. There was little else happening in this relatively peaceful period to compete with the Tibetan story. Wally Sims joined me in Tezpur, leaving coverage of Delhi in Satakopan's very capable hands. Don Royle, an AP photographer from London, also arrived. The first statement from India by the DL, and the first photographs of him to become available in several years, would make his arrival in Tezpur a major news event. The phones out of there were unreliable, and communications satellites had yet to be invented. To get news out, we were dependent on the slow, limited capacity of the Morse key at the little thatched-roof telegraph office, which obviously was going to be overloaded once all the journalists in town began filing stories. The nearest point equipped to transmit radiophotos abroad was the telegraph office in Calcutta.

Nehru sent a senior diplomat, Sarendranath Sen, to Tezpur to try to bring order out of the growing administrative confusion and media circus there. Just on Nehru's oral authority, rather than through bureaucratic paperwork, the smooth, sophisticated Sen effectively took control of everything in both civil and military administration in the area that could be related to the DL. He arranged that journalists could be bused in an escorted group to see the DL drive early one morning across the "inner line" at a jungle outpost named Foothills. This would be the world's first glimpse of the holy man since the Lhasa uprising had made him an object of intense interest. When he got to Tezpur, the DL was scheduled to drive to the circuit house, a small, simple state guest house built in a wooded area at a time when British administrators made regular circuits of their territories. There he would rest before going to a soccer field to grant to an assembled crowd *darshan,* a Buddhist and Hindu concept of people's gaining grace by being in the presence of a holy person. And then he would board a special train to a temporary exile residence at Mussoorie in the Indian Himalayas north of Delhi. The DL would not give a news conference in Tezpur nor make a speech at the soccer field, but he might issue a statement, Sen's aides said.

Wally decided that he would go to Foothills. We arranged that he would print out by hand the first parts of a report on the bus while returning to Tezpur and put them in a tobacco tin. I would be waiting by the road at the outskirts of Tezpur for him to throw me the tin, and I would then race to the telegraph office to file his cables before others on the bus had reached its destination and been able to find their way to the telegraph office. Of such stratagems is news agency competition made; being first with a story is important.

The day arrived, Saturday, April 18, 1959. Wally set out at dawn while I stayed near the Indian command center in Tezpur, which was in radio communications with Foothills and the DL's escort. Just in case anything went wrong along the way, I listened to radio reports of the progress of the DL and the press party back toward Tezpur, a ride of well over an hour, while waiting for the right moment to go out to the agreed point on the road just a few minutes away to catch the tobacco tin. Then, suddenly, there was the press bus disgorging reporters, including Wally. He was not the kind of person who screamed and shouted, but he was fuming as we jumped into my standby taxi and roared off to the telegraph office behind several others. It turned out that radio reports about the movements of the DL's convoy had been deliberately falsified for security reasons, causing me to miss the roadside rendezvous.

That got us off to a bad start that day, but we did elbow our way up to the telegraph office window and push Wally's story through. Wally described the calm, smiling young Dalai Lama, wearing the red robe of his religion, bare armed, with his head shaved in traditional Tibetan lamistic style.

Then I went to the circuit house to see about a statement from the Dalai Lama. The DL himself was resting and did not appear there, but several monks in his party came out on the porch. For the benefit of reporters, photographers, and a few newsreel and television cameras, one of the young monks in a red robe with crewcut hair read the DL's statement first in Tibetan and then in English. It was a strong statement, accusing the Chinese government of having broken its 1951 promise to permit full autonomy for Tibet and not to interfere in its religion, customs, and internal administration. Much later, it became known that Sen and other Indian officials had played a large part in writing the statement, which outlined events leading up to the DL's flight from Lhasa and expressed his appreciation of Indian sanctuary.

Indian officials had orchestrated the occasion so well that reporters were given copies in English of the statement after the monk finished reading it. Once we had grabbed copies in the usual feeding frenzy of reporters who fear they will miss out—which startled the peaceful monks—there was a mad dash to the telegraph office, writing on the way in bouncing taxis. At the telegraph office many of us fought to cram through the little window to the harried clerk inside new leads to the earlier stories, telling of the DL's accusations. But with the Morse key operator still tapping out a stack of Foothills descriptions, there was no guarantee when this new, more important news would get out.

The remaining event was the *darshan,* a good photo opportunity of the DL's blessing a reverent crowd. Neither Reuters nor another world news agency, Agence France Presse, dealt in photos in those days; AP's picture competition worldwide was United Press International. UPI's vice president for Asia, Ernie Hobrecht, who had been on a tour of Southeast Asia from his Tokyo base, turned up in Tezpur a few days before the DL. Hobrecht had chartered his own C-47 from one of the several companies at Dum Dum airport that served tea planters. He wanted UPI photographers to be able to get to Calcutta quickly to transmit radiophotos from the government telegraph office there. Wally had by then arranged to share a charter of another C-47 with one of the American television networks and other journalists so we, too, could get to Calcutta as soon as possible.

The others on our charter wanted to stay through the *darshan* before leaving, but on April 17 we heard rumors that Hobrecht planned to leave as soon as he got the first good picture of the DL. That meant he would beat us to the Calcutta telegraph office, and UPI would be the first to distribute pictures of the DL worldwide. So Wally and I cooked up a plan. I had gotten to know Sen pretty well by then. We went to him and said we had heard that some of the five or six charter planes standing by at the Tezpur airstrip planned to overfly the *darshan* taking pictures, which could be dangerous. Sen picked up the point and ordered that no planes be allowed to take off until the DL's train had pulled out. When an angered Hobrecht found out about this, he argued with Sen to no avail.

Wally and Don Royle were on our shared charter as it maneuvered for take-off position along with Hobrecht's plane, waiting for permission to leave. As the cleanup man, I had bought a seat on another, later press charter to Calcutta. Nonscheduled flights were supposed to follow an Indian air route from Tezpur to Calcutta that went west toward Siliguri and then south, covering two sides of a triangle in order to avoid overflying East Pakistan (now Bangladesh). But both Wally's and Hobrecht's planes, their pilots urged on by the photo competition and probably some extra money, took illegal routes directly across East Pakistan to Calcutta while filing false position reports and flying low in hope of avoiding detection and possible interception.

We had had our Calcutta stringer set up a temporary photo lab in a hanger at Dum Dum airport. Royle processed the Tezpur pictures there before racing into town to hand them across the telegraph office counter for radiophoto transmission to London. But Hobrecht's plane landed at Dum Dum first, and it turned out that he had organized a darkroom on his privately chartered plane. UPI got to the telegraph office before us. Knowing that international radiophoto transmission was a slow business—at best four pictures an hour and often only one or two, depending on atmospheric effects on radio signals—UPI filed multiple copies of their DL pictures. Since photos were sent by Calcutta's single transmitter in the order received, this would block our photos from getting to London for a long time. Royle realized he had suffered a grievous loss in the constant war between photo agencies to deliver important pictures first to newspapers.

By the time I arrived in downtown Calcutta an hour or two later, Wally and Don and one or two friends from other media organizations were sitting gloomily in the dark on the screened verandah of a friendly U.S. Information Agency man, sipping *nimbu pani* (lemonade) or something stronger. Don had cabled London that the photos had been filed. London cabled back, via the stringer who was relaying messages to us, that it had not seen them. Don went back down to the telegraph office and tried to bribe a clerk to move some of his pictures up in the stack of those waiting to be sent, but his 100-rupee notes—each of them then worth about $19, probably several weeks' wages for the clerk—were rebuffed.

Then the rockets really began to land. London cabled that UPI was distributing to newspapers pictures of the DL, and AP still had none in sight. It was a terse cable, ending abruptly, as such "service messages" of journalistic business usually did.

The night wore on. The group on the verandah became more gloomy. London cabled that afternoon newspapers there—five and a half hours behind India time—were on the street with pictures of the DL from "Unipress," which meant UPI photos were also in print in other papers around the world that had been near deadline. Our pictures were still unsighted, London said. It was a clear defeat for AP.

Finally, near midnight Calcutta time—which was nearly 6:30 P.M. in London, 1:30 P.M. in New York, meaning our photos had also missed the early Saturday deadlines of many U.S. afternoon newspapers—we got a cable saying our first pictures had at long last come through. But AP's London photo editors were perplexed. Referring to UPI and what they had seen in the local papers, the cable asked, "Howcome opposition Dalai Lama got long hair ours none query."

We immediately realized what had happened. UPI had distributed to newspapers a picture of the crew-cut monk reading the DL's statement at the circuit house, because the statement was the big news of the day. It had misidentified that monk as the shaven-headed Dalai Lama.

Before there was time for our explanatory reply to get through the telegraph office to London, another cable arrived. "Unipress killed long-haired lama," London said. "[Newspaper] editors much displeased. Regards."

UPI had issued a "kill" on their pictures, the journalistic term for telling editors not to publish erroneous material. But many had already published it. It was a major black eye for the competition. Their great triumph had turned to ashes. That "Regards" was the first kind word Wally and I had heard in all that long day.

It had turned out to be a good day after all. And a satisfying end to an exciting four weeks for a new correspondent in India.

4

THE DALAI LAMA'S TREASURE

THE 26TH OF JANUARY IS ONE OF INDIA'S GRANDEST HOLIDAYS.

This is not to be confused with the anniversary of the end of British rule. That is celebrated on August 15, the date in 1947 when Jawaharlal Nehru proclaimed that India had made "a tryst with destiny. . . . At the stroke of the midnight hour, when the world sleeps, India will awake to life and freedom." On each subsequent August 15, in the coolness just after dawn before another blistering day, the current prime minister mounts the parapet of Moghul emperor Shah Jahan's seventeenth-century Red Fort in old Delhi. The prime minister repeats Nehru's unfurling there on the first day of independence of the green, white, and orange national flag before a crowd stretching back into Chandi Chauk, the main street of the ancient city.

But August is too hot and sticky for proper celebrations. By delightful contrast, winter on the north Indian plain is a glorious time of 70-degree daytime temperatures, 40 or 50 at night, not a cloud in the sky for months, and multitudes of flowers in bloom. So when, on January 26, 1950, India adopted a constitution that broke its last legal ties to the British Crown, replacing King George VI's governor-general with a president as the chief of state, that date was proclaimed to be the main annual national day, Republic Day.

Republic Day involves several days of celebrations. These culminate in two events. One is the spectacular "beating retreat" of military bands on January 25. Keeping up the best traditions of the British empire, the bands perform—perfectly timed slow-step marches, trumpets blaring, bagpipes skirling, drums rattling between flourishing twirls of the drumsticks—as the sun sinks behind the army camel corps lining the walled backdrop of the massive central secretariat buildings that the British built on Raisina Hill in the 1920s. These office blocks of pink sandstone with Moghul trimming became the administrative center of the replacement for Calcutta as the capital of imperial India, New Delhi.

The other event is the parade on Republic Day itself, January 26. Men march, tanks rumble, the camel corps sways, and many others pass by, while jets flying low overhead stream out clouds of the flag's three colors. The parade goes down the central vista of the British empire's Indian jewel, the old King's Way that is now renamed Rajpath (government way). It runs between vast lawns and up Raisina Hill to the central secretariat and, beyond it, Rashtrapati Bhavan (President's House), the great palace built for British viceroys and now occupied by India's figurehead presidents.

This is a time when senior officials from all over India seek excuses to be in New Delhi, ostensibly for consultations but primarily to enjoy the social life and renew acquaintances. So it was in 1960 that, upon asking around, I learned that Apa Pant would be in town for Republic Day from his post in Gangtok, where he was India's civil servant supervising Sikkim's government.

After the Dalai Lama fled from Tibet and settled in exile in north India in April 1959, the Tibetan story had continued to be important. The following month, I had gone back to Tezpur, to interview refugees who followed him across the Himalayas.

They were a pitiful people. Most were poor but devout Buddhists who had fled their homes with only a few personal possessions, especially sacred objects that they later had to sell in order to eat. Clothed in heavy woolens appropriate for the eleven thousand-foot altitude to which they were accustomed, they sweated in Assam's tropical heat and oppressive humidity. Even worse, diseases that had been retarded by the thin air and dry climate of Tibet suddenly exploded into major medical problems for many. Goiter was one, and health workers found rampant venereal diseases and many other complaints.

Most of my interviews were conducted with the help of an Assamese lad of about fourteen years who spoke Tibetan and Hindi, plus one of the Indian Army officers responsible for building and managing refugee camps of split bamboo huts who spoke Hindi and English. Exact quotes this double translation did not produce, but the refugees' vivid statements of hardship and abuse by the Chinese were put in quotation marks anyway.

After the first wave of Tibetan refugees—some one hundred thousand fled within a year or so of the Lhasa uprising—there was little news from "the roof of the world." China had clamped a lid on Tibet, broken only by its propagandistic assertions of how happy the peasants were to be relieved of the crushing oppression of rule by the Buddhist lama hierarchy. Rumors of continuing unrest that circulated in such Indian border towns as Darjeeling and Kalimpong were believable but unreliable. So, as Republic Day came in January 1960 I was eager to talk with Pant in hope of picking up some fresh news from Tibet.

While in New Delhi, Pant was busily rushing from official meetings to appointments with old friends in the elite of Indian bureaucracy, and on to dinner parties. This made him hard to contact. I left messages. Finally, a day or two after Republic Day, he phoned back. He was taking the evening plane to Calcutta on the way back to Gangtok, and he was busy all afternoon. But, he said, if I wanted to drive out to Delhi's airport he would talk with me while waiting for his flight.

I found him in the airport coffee shop sitting with a distinguished-looking friend. Pant invited me to join them and ask him questions. I asked about Tibet. My questions were general, exploratory, because I had little specific information with which to prime him. Pant told me something of his understanding of the current situation in Tibet.

Then, as my questions slowed, he asked—I don't remember the transition—if I were referring to the movement of the Dalai Lama's treasure. I wasn't, because I knew nothing about a treasure or its movement, but that seemed to be only Pant's way of opening up the subject, possibly to justify his discussion of it for his friend. Pant proceeded to tell me a fascinating story.

The background was already familiar. In the autumn of 1950, after consolidating Communist power over eastern China, Mao Zedong sent an army into Tibet to establish a degree of control that successive Chinese central governments had for centuries pretended to have but never really exercised. Facing a small Tibetan army with little training or even knowledge of modern warfare, an army equipped only with antique weapons, the battle-hardened Communist victors in China's long civil war against Chiang Kai-shek quickly captured eastern Tibet. In this emergency, regents for the fourteenth Dalai Lama, fifteen-year-old Tenzin Gyatso, decided to invest him with full power for the spiritual and temporal guidance of Tibet even though he had not reached his majority. They advised him to flee the massive Potala palace in Lhasa, just as his predecessor, "the Great Thirteenth," had fled to India in 1910 to escape a Manchu army coming to assert greater Chinese control—until the Manchu dynasty collapsed in 1912.

On December 20, 1950, the Dalai Lama and a small group of senior officials left Lhasa by horseback and mule. Following the main trade route southwest from Lhasa, they arrived on January 2 in Yatung (now written Yadong), in the Chumbi Valley of southern Tibet just across the 14,750-foot-high Nathu La ("pass of the listening ear") from Gangtok. There he spent the winter within easy distance of escape to India should the Chinese make a move toward capturing him.

After much disagreement and difficulty, and under extreme psychological pressure, a team of Tibetan negotiators signed with the Chinese Communist government in Beijing on May 23, 1951, what became known as the Seventeen-Point Agreement. It said China's "central authorities will not alter the existing political system in Tibet," would maintain "the established status, functions, and powers of the Dalai Lama," and the "local government of Tibet should carry out reforms of its own accord" only if the Tibetan people demanded them and only after consultation with "the leading personnel of Tibet."

There was great uncertainty and controversy among the Dalai Lama's advisers in Yatung over accepting the agreement because of some vague wording as well as rumors of secret side arrangements that exceeded the negotiators' authority. But, finally, in July 1951 he left Yatung to return to Lhasa at the urging of his elderly advisers. Less than eight years later, he fled into lasting exile in India with a sharp denunciation in Tezpur of the Chinese for having violated their commitment to respect Tibet's internal autonomy.[1]

Pant only briefly alluded to this background. What had been a secret, he now told me, was that when the Dalai Lama went to Yatung in 1950 he took as much of the centuries-long accumulation of treasure from the Potala as his lengthy mule train could carry. There were numerous boxes of gold, silver, and jewels, some in the form of Buddhist religious objects, some bullion and loose stones. When he returned to Lhasa half a year later, this treasure did not go back. Fearful of what might happen under Chinese rule and therefore preparing for future trouble, Tibetan officials decided to hide the treasure out of Beijing's reach. The boxes were loaded onto mules again and taken over the Nathu La to Gangtok.

The ostensible ruler of Sikkim—the *maharaja* as Indians referred to him in the British tradition, but the *chogyal* in his own language—came from a small ethnic group traceable to eastern Tibet. These Bhutia peoples were lamaist Buddhist, but from the Nyingmapa sect, known as the Red Hats, rather than the Dalai Lama's Gelugpa or Yellow Hat sect that had appeared in fourteenth-century reforms. Nonetheless, Himalayan Buddhists of all sects accepted the Dalai Lama as their spiritual leader. The *chogyal*'s second son, Palden Thondup Namgyal, had, in a happenstance that seemed to occur among Himalayan royalty and Tibetan nobility with much more than statistical probability, been discovered in his childhood to be an incarnation of a Buddhist lama. This, conveniently, gave Sikkim's royal family a special sanctity and extra claim to authority.

Thondup had been sent to a Nyingmapa monastery in Tibet to be educated for a life of religious devotion. During World War II, however, the elder son and heir apparent had been killed in a training accident while serving with the British military in India. Thondup was therefore ordered to abjure the monastery life of Buddhist prayer and chastity. (According to stories told around Gangtok, Darjeeling, and Calcutta, he gave up the latter restriction with great enthusiasm.) Leaving his monastery and preparing to succeed his father, he married a daughter of the Tibetan nobility, started a family to carry on the royal line, and studied British-style administration. He became, in the terminology then in use for a *maharaja*'s heir, the *maharajkumar* of Sikkim.

It was to the trustedly devout, although playboy, *maharajkumar* that the treasure boxes were sent in 1951 across the Nathu La under Tibetan and Indian guard to be hidden in Gangtok. Pant did not mention one detail that I learned later. The boxes were buried by lantern light under the floor of Gangtok's royal stables. There they rested for more than eight years.

When the Dalai Lama went into exile in 1959, Prime Minister Jawaharlal Nehru assumed on behalf of India a responsibility for his maintenance. This gave the Indian government some degree of control over the Dalai Lama's political activities, which Delhi feared might complicate its efforts to maintain good relations with China—until their 1962 border war. But Nehru perhaps also felt an obligation to the young monk arising from what had happened in 1956.

On an official visit to India then, the twenty-one-year-old Dalai Lama had privately lamented to the sixty-seven-year-old Nehru that living under Chinese occupation in Tibet was not working out, that the Chinese were ignoring their promises of internal autonomy, that Tibet was being treated like a country under military occupation. Ethnic Chinese migrants were taking over key government jobs and beginning to dominate commerce, treating Tibetans like colonial subjects. The Dalai Lama did not want to return to Lhasa and be further reduced toward a figurehead for ethnic Chinese, Communist rule. In his best avuncular manner, Nehru talked him into giving the Chinese another chance. This was at the mid-1950s peak of "*Hindi-Chini bai-bai*" ("Indians and Chinese are brothers"), an oft-repeated slogan as Nehru, the world-respected leader of nonalignment, and Chinese Premier Zhou Enlai were professing undying friendship between their two countries. Nehru wanted nothing to spoil it. So, reluctantly, the Dalai Lama went back to the Potala.

When the Dalai Lama fled into exile, Nehru borrowed from the Birla family of Indian industrialists a mansion in the Himalayan hill station of Mussoorie for the Dalai Lama's temporary residence. Between my visits to Tezpur in April and again in May 1959, I drove from Delhi up to Mussoorie to report Nehru's first meeting with the Dalai Lama after the flight from Lhasa. I also went to Mussoorie later in 1959 to cover the Dalai Lama's testimony on Chinese oppression and human rights abuses in Tibet before a delegation from the International Commission of Jurists. Later, India set the Dalai Lama up permanently at another hill station, Dharamsala, where I interviewed him in October 1960.

With what Nehru called a charitable obligation, the Indian government also assumed responsibility for the Tibetan refugees. Slowly, it moved them from temporary camps to permanent colonies. Some were in Himalayan hill stations such as Dharamsala, some in jungled areas of south India that they cleared to live on agriculture and handicrafts while supporting religious studies.

Despite Indian hospitality, the Dalai Lama needed money for his personal entourage and religious activities. The decision was made in late 1959 to dig up the Gangtok stable floor and convert the treasure into bank accounts. Pant told me that in January 1960, not long before our conversation, a secret operation had been carried out. Under cover of darkness and of Indian police and military guards, the treasure boxes were trucked down from Gangtok and put into a Calcutta branch of the State Bank of India. The bullion and jewels were now being sold off, Pant said. When I asked him how much it was all worth, he said no one was sure, but probably several million dollars. No better estimate ever became public, but speculation ran wildly to much more than several million.

Although I don't recall our specifically discussing how I might write this story, Pant and I were both professionals. He understood that, in telling me, he knew I would publish something about the treasure, but I would protect my source. I therefore waited for three days, giving him time to get back to Gangtok, before cabling a story to AP that only vaguely alluded to official sources.

Before writing it, I phoned the Indian official responsible for relations with China and for Tibetan affairs. Jagat Mehta, whose title was additional secretary in the External Affairs Ministry, was a bright young protégé of Nehru's whom I had gotten to know fairly well from numerous interviews. We remained friends for decades, but he was less than friendly when I phoned to ask questions about the Dalai Lama's treasure. What was I talking about? He professed to know nothing about it, in a sharp tone. It was obvious that I had touched a sensitive subject. Already vulnerable to criticism for helping Tibetans more than poverty-stricken Indians, Nehru obviously did not want it known that the Dalai Lama had some money of his own.

At the time, the *Times of India,* a major paper with its main edition in Bombay and separately edited editions in Delhi and several other cities, ran an in-house news service to link the editions. Using this subterfuge of a news service to get around a government restriction on foreign news agencies, it subscribed to AP's radioteletype transmissions. The paper's Bombay edition published my treasure story in full, credited to the AP but without my byline. The Delhi edition ran an edited-down version, with AP credit, on an inside page.

Outside India the story attracted little attention because world interest in Tibet arising from the Lhasa uprising and the Dalai Lama's flight had faded. Even in India, there was little immediate response to the story, somewhat to my surprise. I took the precaution of sending a note to the AP's new stringer in Calcutta. Summarizing the treasure story for him, emphasizing the Calcutta bank angle, I asked him to be alert for any followup that might develop there.

Then I got a surprising response in Delhi. Someone from Inland Revenue, the Indian version of America's Internal Revenue Service, phoned for an appointment with me at the AP bureau. Two men came to interview me on the treasure. What did I know about this apparently unauthorized, and therefore illegal, import of valuables into India without customs duties or taxes being paid? Who was responsible? Under what name was the treasure being held in Calcutta? And so on. Their part of the government obviously had not been informed about what another part had done. I politely refused to tell them anything. Instead, I suggested that they might want to talk to Jagat Mehta or someone else at the External Affairs Ministry. They went away unhappy.

I doubted that the treasure was ever taxed directly. There might, however, have been some tax derived from an Indian businessman's pipe manufacturing venture in which Tibetan officials working for the Dalai Lama invested some of the treasure's yield. The venture failed, and the Dalai Lama lost a lot of money. Rumors in Calcutta suggested that naive Tibetan officials had been victimized by the sharp dealings of a somewhat dubious businessman.

Mehta never again asked me where I had learned of the treasure. I found out later that a number of officials had been questioned about the leak, presumably including Pant. Although we met again a number of times, Pant and I never discussed the subject. I was, however, asked for my sources by one of the Dalai Lama's older brothers, Gyalo Thondup. Shortly after the Chinese invasion of Tibet, Gyalo Thondup had secretly left Lhasa, taking the same route southeast toward Tezpur that the DL followed in 1959. In India he became a private channel for communications outside Chinese control between Tibet's leadership and the Indian government. Articles that began appearing in the Western press around 1970 disclosed that he had also become the Tibetan leadership's contact man with the CIA. Working through him, starting about 1957, the CIA had begun training Tibetan guerrillas, who were already fighting the Chinese, and it later helped subsidize the Tibetan exile movement.

By the time I wrote the treasure story, I had gotten to know Gyalo Thondup fairly well. He was then living in Delhi most of the time as the Dalai Lama's personal representative and troubleshooter. Thondup was politely aggrieved with me when next we met after the treasure story had appeared, and he tried unsuccessfully to cajole my sources out of me. Nonetheless, he remained a friend.

After about ten days of Indian media silence on the treasure following my story's obscure appearance in the *Times of India,* one of that paper's main competitors, the *Statesman,* prominently published a long, colorful story on the subject. It was written from Calcutta by Desmond Doig, a World War II British officer with the tough Gurkha soldiers recruited in the Himalayas of Nepal. Doig had stayed on in India and become a journalist, developing into a notable character who specialized in writing about mountain areas. While much of his reporting was solid, original coverage of the region, he also specialized in the kind of imaginatively detailed stories for which some of his British press colleagues were famous, or infamous.

Our stringer told me later that he had discussed the treasure story with his friend Doig after getting my message about it, apparently alerting Doig to it. Doig's *Statesman* account had no facts that I had not had—the State Bank of India and others were not talking—but it was embroidered in such picturesque ways as describing the treasure-carrying mule train, bells jingling, small flags flying from harnesses, and the royal stable. Displayed by the *Statesman*'s editions in both Calcutta and Delhi, it was news to those who had not noticed my story in the *Times of India,* and its embroidery made it good reading for everyone.

A week or so later, several foreign correspondents based in Delhi went down to Calcutta on the early morning flight to cover a visit there by one of the numerous important foreign leaders who trooped through India in the heyday of nonalignment. As we were standing around Dum Dum airport waiting for the visitor to arrive, I fell into conversation with Don Connery, *Time* magazine's Delhi correspondent. I expressed surprise that he would bother to come cover such a visit. The AP had to cover them all, but this visitor was hardly worth space in *Time*. Well, Don explained, he was partly interested in the visitor, but he had also come to Calcutta to write a story on the colorful Himalayan expert Desmond Doig for *Time*'s press section. The peg, or justification for doing a story at the time, was going to be the way Doig had revealed to the world the interesting tale of the treasure.

Ah, well, I said as modestly as possible, actually I broke that story. Doig was only picking up my facts. Don expressed disbelief. Ask your Bombay stringer to check the files of the *Times of India,* I suggested. Don never mentioned the subject again. *Time* never published a story on Doig.

5

BEHIND THE HIMALAYAS

THE TRAIL WAS NARROW AND TWISTING, OFTEN DISAPPEARING INTO areas of landslides, where travelers had to pick their way over loose stones on steep slopes high above the Kali Gandak River. It was so difficult and dangerous that even sure-footed mules that carried freight in other rugged parts of the Himalayas—in Tibet, Bhutan, India, and here in Nepal—could not use this trail. Only human porters carried cooking oil, matches, kerosene, and other products of the industrial world to people eking out near-subsistence livelihoods beyond where the river slashed between two of the world's highest peaks. These barefoot men returned, their heavy packs rising high off their backs, with wool, rock salt, yak skins, and other products of the Tibetan frontier.

Yet, despite the steepness and difficulty, there near the top of a deep gorge, at an uninhabited point where anyone entering the frontier region had to pass, was a surprise. Rounding a turn on the twisting trail, I came upon three men sitting on the ground by a little folding table. As surprised as I was, they jumped up and silently eyed me as I waved to them and continued on my way north toward Nepal's border with Tibet. The men clearly were Tibetan, looking unlike the various Nepali ethnic groups of the region.

Before rounding the next turn, I looked back. One of the men was scampering through the brush down the steep slope below their table.

This was the first sign that I had found what I was looking for on a two-week trek into a part of Nepal normally closed to foreigners: Tibetan guerrillas operating from an area that the royal government in the capital, Kathmandu, did not control. Perhaps the American Central Intelligence Agency was supporting Tibetans there for strikes across the Nepali border against Chinese Communists in their homeland.

It was early October 1961. Two and a half years earlier an uprising against tightening Chinese control in Tibet's capital, Lhasa, had caused the Dalai Lama

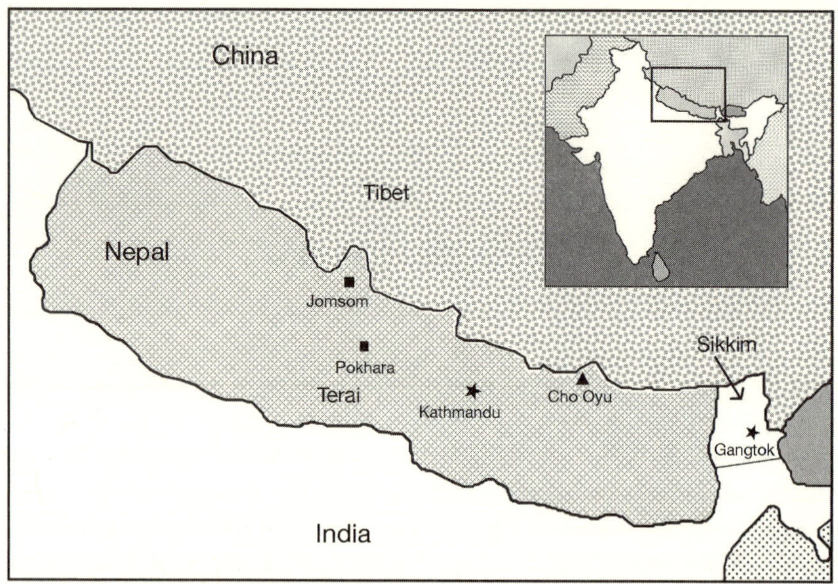

to flee into exile in India. The Chinese had cracked down savagely on Tibetan resistance to their rule. The CIA-trained guerrillas who had been fighting inside Tibet had been killed, captured, or driven across the borders into India or Nepal. Now, some were reported to have moved into a remote, almost inaccessible area of Nepal.

This was an area on the northern, Tibetan side of the main Himalayan peaks, the side less known than the southern slopes facing India. Walking into the region was one of the more arduous yet interesting of my trips into the mountains above India. I had ridden a mule into the eastern Himalayas of Bhutan in May 1960. The first trek on my own was a vacation expedition in October of that year, when I walked from the lush, 6,400-foot-high Kulu Valley through a rugged crack in the western Himalayas, the 14,009-foot Hampta La, to India's Lahaul and Spiti areas of ethnic Tibetan Buddhists. A year later, I looked for another interesting vacation destination.

I consulted Nepal's ambassador to India, Nar Pratap Thapa. He had become a friend on my visits to Kathmandu when he was Nepal's foreign secretary. He immediately had an idea. He described rumors about a Tibetan guerrilla force up the Kali Gandak near the Tibetan border. But, he said, his government did not have any real control of the area—as was true at the time of many remote parts of Nepal difficult of access—and was not sure what was going on there. Thapa suggested that I walk up there to see.

But such frontier areas are closed to foreigners, I knew. Thapa had a way around that. He knew that King Mahendra Bir Bikram Shah Dev was scheduled to make a state visit to China in early October, when I proposed to go trekking. Thapa's successor as foreign secretary would accompany Mahendra. That meant a young man who had been Thapa's protégé would be left in charge of the foreign office, and it was the foreign office that had to issue permits for foreigners to enter frontier areas. Thapa said he would send a note to the protégé telling him to give me a permit to visit the famous Hindu shrine at Muktinath, as many pilgrims from India did. This seemed like a legitimate destination for a trek, but it was in the area where the Tibetans were rumored to be. The rumors said they were in Mustang, a small, bleak, semi-independent principality more than twelve thousand feet high that makes a bulge of Nepal's border into Tibet. Many of them turned out to be lower on the Kali Gandak, in Thakkhola district, where the valley opened up a little, with Muktinath high up its eastern slope.

Thapa's plan worked. Taking vacation, I flew to Kathmandu and went to see the acting foreign secretary. He readily gave me an official-looking piece of paper saying I could walk up to Muktinath. Nepali friends knew a currently unemployed man who had acted as a guide and government representative on a number of mountain-climbing expeditions. K. B. Rana, a genial person who spoke competent English, was happy to get the job of accompanying me to Muktinath.

Rana and I flew over to the grass airstrip at Pokhara, 125 miles west-northwest of Kathmandu at an altitude of twenty-nine hundred feet. The little farming center, where Nepal's royal family had originated in the eighteenth century, has in clear weather a magnificent view of the Annapurna range of the Himalayas. During an overnight stay in the nearest thing the little town had to a hotel, consisting of some canvas shelters and an open-air kitchen near the airstrip, we hired two porters. They carried canned Australian cheese, a little jam, a change of clothes, a sleeping bag, and other supplies that I had brought from Delhi, plus their own food, while I carried my camera, binoculars, and other things in a rucksack. Somehow, I was convinced by Rana that I needed to rent a large old canvas tent in case we needed to camp in an open area, especially if we encountered snow at higher altitudes. A third porter was required just to carry it. It was never used.

Making our way along narrow paths atop dikes separating rice fields, dried up after monsoon rains had ended and the crops mostly harvested by October, the five of us headed west. The route led up over steep spurs coming down from the Annapurna massif, crossing one at 9,186 feet. As darkness descended, the pattern for the trek was established. Rana would approach a farmhouse and ask if we could buy some food and sleep on its dirt or mat-covered floor. The isolated farmers, leading bare subsistence lives, were always happy for outside money. The houses were usually simple one-room thatched structures with low roofs and shutters for windows, tidy and neat. The available food usually consisted of potatoes and eggs, sometimes rough homemade bread, occasionally chicken or goat meat. I supplemented this with cheese and a bit of jam.

The second day, going up the second spur, we passed through little clusters of farmhouses where children followed us, cheerfully chattering in local languages. Occasionally, men came out to talk in English. They were former Gurkha soldiers of the British or Indian armies, now back in the areas from which they had been recruited, living on modest pensions and some farming. On the third day we reached the Kali (Black) Gandak, which flows southward into India as a tributary of the Ganges River, at Tatopani ("warm water," from a spring), only thirty-nine hundred feet high. On the trail near there my permit passed inspection by a curious official.

From Tatopani we began to ascend the Kali Gandak as it slashed through mountain defiles. This is one of five rivers that cut directly through the Himalayas, in contrast to streams in other parts of the world that flow away from mountains. This oddity long puzzled geographers and geologists. The reason was only understood later in the 1960s as the geology of plate tectonics, or continental drift, began to be understood. When peninsula India began plowing into Asia more than 35 million years ago, the rivers were already there draining the continental highlands. The collision between the peninsula and the continent squeezed the mountains up like toothpaste from a tube, in earthquake-jolted bumps, with an average rate of an inch or two a year. The rivers were able to erode their courses as fast as the Himalayas were pushed up, so they held their approximate positions, cutting down into the uplifting mountains.

Several hours' walk upstream from Tatopani we picked our way hazardously across the twisted girders of a steel bridge built over the Kali Gandak several decades earlier—one of the few signs of modern construction in the region, showing the importance of the trade route up the river. The bridge had been wrecked by a flood unleashed by the breaching of a natural dam created somewhere upstream by a landslide, or possibly a collapsing glacier, that had temporarily blocked the flow. Snaking around steep slopes, the trail often virtually disappeared into rocky areas of recent landslides, where picking our way over loose stones was difficult. Occasionally we passed men with large loads on their backs braced with straps across their foreheads. These sweaty porters were crudely dressed, and their bare feet had deep cracks in thick calluses.

It was here, in this narrowest, steepest part of the trail, that I came upon the three men and their folding table. But I was still looking for more evidence of Tibetan guerrillas.

The scenery was spectacular. At an altitude of 8,136 feet, where a few farmers grew corn, potatoes, and vegetables, was a twenty-mile gap between the peaks of the world's seventh and tenth highest mountains, the blockish, abrupt 26,795-foot Dhaulagiri to its west and the long, rambling 26,545-foot Annapurna massif to its east. The 360-degree view from this gorge—at more than three and a half miles, the world's deepest—is wooded slopes rising sharply into gray rocky tumults topped by immense fields of snow and glaciers. Beyond the gorge, where the river widened into a meandering course lined with sloping barley fields, was the Thakkhola region. The peaks created ethnic, religious, and agricultural divisions between Nepali Hinduism in lower, well-watered areas and Tibetan Buddhism in the bleaker highlands seldom reached by monsoon rains.

At one point, away from the river, a Buddhist prayer wall stood in the trail, which split so that travelers always passed it on their right, as is the custom throughout Tibetan cultural areas. In the wall were a few prayer wheels for passersby to spin, thus wafting upward good thoughts that might benefit them in this life or some subsequent incarnation. The whitewashed stone wall was topped by a number of loose stones carved in Tibetan script with the prayer "Om Mani Padme Hume." This mantra, "Blessed Is the Jewel in the Lotus," refers to the Buddha, who is often depicted sitting cross-legged in the lovely flower that grows from nasty muck at the bottom of ponds, signifying that beauty and good thoughts can come from bad things.

After several other villages, we walked into Jomsom. It sits eighty-nine hundred feet high in a wide enough place beside the Kali Gandak for a rocky airstrip accessible to STOL aircraft (Short Take-Off and Landing). At the time, only sparse flights of these special mountain planes came and went on official business, flying up the gorge when visibility was good. The village was also the site of an Indian Army radio team. This was one of several teams stationed in the upper parts of Nepal, close to the Tibetan border. Several years earlier, India, worried about the Chinese Army's presence in Tibet, had talked Nepal into permitting observers in frontier areas facing Tibet that Nepal itself lacked the resources to monitor.

As I walked into Jomsom, an Indian Army sergeant asked politely who I was and what I was doing there. I told him I was a tourist on my way to Muktinath. That, unsurprisingly, did not seem to satisfy him. After all, this area was closed to foreigners and I didn't look like a Hindu or Buddhist pilgrim. He probably radioed to his headquarters an assumption that I was a CIA officer.

The village had what passed in those days for a hotel, consisting of a large mud-plastered, one-room building. Along its one open side were tables for a teahouse and beer hall, and in the dark rear was floor space where I slept that night. After I had put down my rucksack and sleeping bag, I went back to the tables for dinner.

Eating there and drinking beer were four large, hearty-looking Tibetan men dressed in fairly new, trim uniforms made of military camouflage material and wearing .45 pistols on their web belts. The uniforms and pistols looked like some variety of U.S. Army issue but had no insignia. Pretending to ignore them, although intensely curious, I sat down to order a steak from the simple menu offered orally by the aged Nepali woman who seemed to be in charge, with translation help from Rana. One of the uniformed Tibetans then approached me and tried to open a conversation as his friends watched. On discovering that I did not speak Tibetan, he began using a little broken English. Our difficulty in keeping up a conversation did not discourage him. He seemed to make a point of letting me see his expensive gold wristwatch under a loose sleeve. I repeated my story of being a tourist on the way to Muktinath, nothing more. Eventually, he returned to his friends and they loudly enjoyed their meal and beer, with occasional smiles and gestures in my direction.

This seemed to be what I had been looking for. These men were very unlike the indigenous people of Thakkhola, although many locals were of Tibetan heritage. The men's uniforms and pistols clearly indicated outside connections, and the watch suggested ample funding. Perhaps the man who approached me was Gyen Yeshe or one of his deputies. Perhaps he had been alerted by a radio message a couple of days earlier from that man who scampered down the slope after I passed the folding table in the gorge, an obvious checkpoint for raising an alert about whoever came up into this region. Perhaps this Jomsom encounter was not accidental. Perhaps the Tibetans had been waiting to try to find out who I was.

Yeshe was the leader of the Tibetan guerrilla force in the region. A Buddhist monk, he had turned to fighting in 1956 when the Chinese bombed his monastery in Kham, the eastern edge of the ethnic and religious Tibetan area where uprisings against Chinese Communist rule of Tibet began. The name for the area's fierce warriors, Khampas, later became a generic term for all Tibetan resistance fighters. The 1956 revolt caused the United States, still stinging from its bitter conflict with the Chinese Communists in Korea, to decide to help the Tibetan resistance. Washington had made secret contacts with the Dalai Lama in 1951 and again in 1956 on the possibility of his leaving Tibet to oppose the Chinese Communists from abroad, but he had chosen to stay and try to work with them.

The CIA was assigned to help the resistance. It began working with the Dalai Lama's elder brother, Gyalo Thondup, who had gone into exile in India. In late 1956 or early 1957, Thondup selected six Tibetan exiles on India's northeastern frontier for CIA instruction in skills useful for guerrilla warfare and particularly in information gathering and communications techniques. After American training abroad, they began to be parachuted into Tibet from CIA planes. The first two contacted senior advisers of the Dalai Lama. When he fled from Lhasa in March 1959 in fear of a Chinese plot to seize him, CIA-trained Tibetan guerrillas operating southeast of the capital intercepted his party and protected it from Chinese troops as he reached the Indian border.

The Dalai Lama's dramatic escape energized the United States. Its government promised secret financial support for him in exile. And President Dwight D. Eisenhower authorized increased support for the Tibetan resistance. More guerrillas parachuted into Tibet were unable to withstand pressure from China's People's Liberation Army (PLA), however. They never scored any significant military victories. Of forty-nine men dropped by the CIA in Tibet between 1957 and 1960, only twelve survived. A CIA officer involved in the program wrote decades later, "The Tibetans surely had played their part bravely. But the concept of sustaining a large-scale guerrilla movement by air in Tibet had proven a painful failure."[1]

Even before the hope of keeping up resistance in eastern and central Tibet had been lost, guerrilla operations from the Mustang area had been proposed. The CIA accepted a guerrilla leader's idea of recruiting twenty-one hundred Tibetans who had sought refuge in India to operate from the Mustang area without asking permission from the government of Nepal. The U.S. government was confident that Kathmandu would not know, or, if it came to know, would not feel able to complain, about guerrillas in an area over which it had little if any control. In June 1960 a clash between soldiers of the PLA and Nepalis occurred along the poorly defined Nepali-Tibetan border at Mustang.[2] This caused concern back at CIA headquarters as well as in Kathmandu but did not affect plans for the guerrilla force.

By the time I reached the area in 1961, according to revelations decades later, the Tibetan force was well established, with its headquarters about five miles southeast of Jomsom. Companies of up to one hundred guerrillas each were scattered at sites extending from there some thirty miles up into Mustang.

In September 1961, this force made a first small foray into Tibet, ambushing a Chinese patrol. Then, probably about the time I was in the area, Yeshe planned for forty men to attack vehicles on the main highway running west from Lhasa along the north bank of the Tsangpo River. On October 25, by which time I was back in India, they shot up a PLA command car, killing a colonel and six others. They looted from the wreckage a leather case with sixteen hundred pages of secret documents. These turned out to give the most valuable information ever obtained by Washington on morale and problems in the PLA, famine in China after the failure of Mao Zedong's "Great Leap Forward," and other current reports of intense interest to CIA analysts. This success enabled supporters of the Mustang force to fend off critics in Washington, but the guerrillas never achieved more than minor harassment of China's strong grip on Tibet.

By 1962, the future of the force was in question. Even though some Tibetan guerrillas were recruited by India after its 1962 border war with China, Mustang became a sideshow. The 2,030 Tibetan guerrillas there, up to half of them without weapons, were mostly inactive by early 1963. They repeatedly refused to relocate into Tibet. Finally, pushed to prove their worth, they sent thirty-five men on horseback to raid into Tibet in the spring of 1966. The PLA ambushed them, killing six. The force was then ordered to limit itself to passive intelligence collection in order not to provoke a Chinese attack into Nepal. Its war was effectively over.

The morning after my encounter with the armed Tibetans in the Jomsom teahouse, Rana, the porters, and I walked on up the Kali Gandak to Kagbeni, an old walled village at ninety-two hundred feet. We stopped at a teahouse's little stools in the invigoratingly cool air and bright sunshine. Soon, along came a caravan from the direction of Tibet. A grizzled old herder and several fierce-looking dogs were driving a few yaks and a herd of unshorn sheep, probably for sheering around Tukuche, a few miles downstream from Jomsom, and then slaughter. Slung under each sheep was a small packet of salt, and the yaks carried large loads on their backs.

The trail from Kagbeni went up the eastern slope of a side valley. After six days of walking from Pokhara, we were at Muktinath, 12,474 feet high on the mountainside. With an effect probably heightened by the effort of getting there, it struck me as one of the most beautiful places I had ever seen.

At a higher elevation than trees grew elsewhere in the region, poplars with leaves then yellowing in the chill autumn air clustered around a site sacred to both Hindus and Buddhists. At the center was a small temple with three pagoda-style roofs. Inside the temple, which I could not enter, being neither a Hindu nor a Buddhist, I could see the flickering of small fires at an altar decorated with symbols of both religions. Cut into the mountain on three sides around the temple was a wall from which projected 108 bull-faced gargoyles pouring icy water from a spring onto slate drains seven feet below. The backdrop to the south, standing boldly against a clear blue sky, was the snowy masses of Dhaulagiri and Annapurna. A magnificent picture.

Muktinath is one of two names. This Hindu one means "place of salvation." It is one of the eight most sacred shrines of the Vaishnava Hindus, those in the majority in India who consider the four-armed Vishnu to be the supreme god of the Hindu pantheon of gods. Its sanctity is based on the belief that it is the only place on earth where can be found together all five elements from which everything is made: fire, water, sky, earth, and air. The fire in the temple is the burning of natural gas seeping from the mountainside by the spring. The temple was built in 1815 by order of Nepali queen Subarna Prabha at a time when the kings of Nepal were considered to be incarnations of Vishnu, but Hindus had been worshipping there long before.

To Buddhists, the place is Chumig Gyatsa, or "hundred waters." They believe that a Buddhist holy man, Padma Sambhava, known as the Guru Rimpoche, meditated there in the eighth century on his way from Swat—now in northern Pakistan—to perform miracles that established Buddhism in Tibet and Bhutan. Buddhist nuns are the traditional caretakers of the site.

Numerous pilgrims and I spent two nights nearby in a small, squarish, mud-colored monastery building with a large, darkly gloomy central room, a few smaller rooms, and a place where the nuns lived. Then Rana, the porters, and I began the return trek. Being mostly downhill, and having adapted to the altitude, I found it easier. The one difference from the walk up was crossing the Kali Gandak. Rana and the porters decided against hazarding the broken bridge again. Instead, at a point between cliffs where the riverbed broadened into many streams at this low-flowing dry season, we forded the cold, swift water. This was not without hazard of its own. In the deepest part of the river, almost three feet deep, the current pushed rocks rapidly along the bottom, making footing difficult and risky. Finally across, we sloshed along in wet clothes and shoes until the chill air dried us.[3]

In Pokhara I returned the tent and paid the porters an agreed rate of about two U.S. dollars a day. Then Rana and I flew back to Kathmandu. One of those with whom I usually checked to find out what was going on in Kathmandu was Elizabeth Hawley. She was an American who settled there in 1960, saying she had gotten a grant in the United States to do academic and social research in Nepal for a couple of years. The grant was from the Knickerbocker Foundation, which *Ramparts* magazine listed in 1967 as a CIA front. When I went to see Hawley after the trek, before she started part-time work for Reuters news agency and therefore became a competitor of my AP work, she was as incredulous as everyone else I met in Kathmandu about my getting a permit to go up the Kali Gandak.

I told her about seeing the Tibetans. She said that was very interesting, and maybe the American embassy would be interested, too. She suggested that I talk with a particular person there, someone with a name of Baltic origin. I had never met him in my contacts with the U.S. ambassador, his deputy, the political and economic officers, or the press officer. She gave me a phone number. Sure, why not?—although I suspected that he was a CIA officer. I intended to publish everything I knew anyway. Maybe I could learn something from him. The young man was very interested in what I had seen but offered in return no information of use to me. I came away convinced of his CIA connection but didn't feel that I had lost anything.

As soon as I returned to Delhi, I wrote about the men at the little table in the gorge, the men in the Jomsom teahouse, and the rumors of the CIA's supporting a Tibetan guerrilla force in upper Nepal. It made a good story, albeit more suggestive than conclusive. I wrote under the dateline "Behind the Himalayas," but AP editors in New York changed this to a less romantic sounding Jomsom, Nepal, dateline.

And I invited Ambassador Thapa to lunch again to tell him what I'd found and to thank him for making possible such an enjoyable outing.

6

CLIMBING CHO OYU

THE HIMALAYAS HAVE ALWAYS FASCINATED MANKIND. THEIR LOFTY, snow-covered summits were considered in many of the ancient cultures that flourished and faded below them to be the abode of the gods.

About the time in the middle of the nineteenth century that young men from the English leisure class invented modern mountain climbing on vacations in the Alps, British surveyors and their Indian assistants discovered that European scientists had for two centuries been wrong in thinking that Chimborazo in Ecuador's Andes was the world's tallest mountain. Its dormant volcanic cone is only 6,310 meters (20,701 feet) high. The Survey of India found that a number of peaks in the Himalayas reached much farther above sea level. The survey eventually counted fourteen peaks in the Himalayas and connected ranges whose heights were more than 8,000 meters (26,246 feet), the metric measurement standard that came to be generally used by scientists and mountain climbers. Nowhere else on earth do mountains soar close to 8,000 meters above sea level.

These lofty lumps presented a challenge that British mountain climbers accepted after World War I. Some expeditions sought the grandest prize of all: getting to the top of Mount Everest. Why? The classic answer was by George Leigh Mallory: "Because it's there." Seven attempts from the Tibetan side between 1921 and 1938 failed—or, at least, the climbers failed to come back alive from the top.[1]

Nepal on the southern side was then virtually closed to foreigners, a "hermit kingdom." India sponsored a revolt by Nepal's figurehead king in November 1950, however, that ousted the dictatorial Ranas, a century-old line of hereditary prime ministers, and began opening the country up. This made possible a glorious decade of mountain climbing in which all of the eight thousand-meter peaks were ascended by all-male expeditions.

In 1959 a group of twelve women set out to make the first all-female ascent of an eight thousand-meter peak. Few had climbed in the Himalayas or anywhere else nearly so high, and they lacked experience working together. Most of them did not even know each other before their expedition.

The leader was blue-eyed Claude Kogan, a thirty-nine-year-old bathing suit designer from Nice on the French Riviera. Only four feet, ten inches tall, and weighing at most one hundred pounds, she was a tough, no-nonsense sort who had become a mountain climber after marrying Georges Kogan in 1944. He was killed in a climbing accident in 1951. She kept climbing, in the Alps, the Andes, and three times to the Himalayas before leading the "Expedition Feminine au Nepal." Four other members of the expedition were French, three British, and two were teenage daughters of Tenzing Norgay, the Nepali Sherpa conqueror of Everest. And there was Claudine van der Straten-Ponthoz, the daughter of a Belgian count. A twenty-six-year-old former skiing star, she was the only beauty in this hard-bitten bunch and, next to Kogan, the most respected climber.

This is the story of the journalistic aspects of their expedition. I had only a peripheral involvement in it, but the story is too good not to tell.

The women chose to climb the world's sixth-highest mountain, Cho Oyu, 8,201 meters (26,906 feet) high. It lies at the western end of the great thirty-mile-long Nepali-Tibetan border curve of jagged, jumbled blocks of snow, ice, and bare rock that includes Everest and Lhotse, and ends in the east with Makalu—all over eight thousand meters. Known as "the turquoise goddess" for its sometimes coloring at sunset, Cho Oyu was considered one of the toughest of the high Himalayas because of storms that frequently lashed its upper slopes. It had defeated a British team in 1952 and the Swiss in 1954. As part of the mostly male Swiss group, Kogan and Raymond Lambert had gotten to within fifteen hundred feet of the summit before being turned back by storms. Despite failing to reach the top, Kogan then set an altitude record for women climbers. Later in 1954 an Austrian expedition finally conquered Cho Oyu, and an Indian team ascended it in 1958.

There are two brief times of year when the fierce winds and snowstorms that usually envelop the high peaks might abate long enough for climbers to have a chance in the Nepali Himalayas. One is in the late spring, after most winter storms have ended but before the monsoon sweeps up from the south. It was in this period that Tenzing and Edmund Hillary made the first ascent of Everest, on May 29, 1953. But it was also in this period, on May 10 and 11, 1996, that a sudden storm added eight more names to the list of more than 140 climbers who had by then died on Everest.

The other brief break in Nepal's weather, in early October when the monsoon is over and winter has not yet set in, is the most glorious time in the Himalayas. Then, for a few weeks, the crisp mountain air is crystal clear and one can see forever. It was in early October that I took all three of my vacations for mountain treks: to Spiti and Lahul in India's western Himalayas in 1960, to the little Hindu shrine at Muktinath near Nepal's border with Tibet in 1961, and with Monica after marrying her in 1963 from Swat up beyond Kalam in the Kohistan part of Pakistani Kashmir.

The "all-women's expedition to Cho Oyu," as it was called in English, chose what in later space launch terminology was the 1959 autumn "window" for their climb. That meant starting out from the nearest airport and supply point, at Kathmandu, the capital of Nepal, amid August's monsoon rains to trek to a base camp. The route to Cho Oyu goes northeast from Kathmandu to the main settlement of the Sherpa people, Namche Bazaar. A few miles beyond, it turns left at the Sherpas' Thyangboche monastery of Tibetan Buddhist monks to go up the Ngozumpa glacier, instead of turning right and heading for the Khumbu glacier and the base camp area for Mount Everest. For a big expedition laden with tents, climbing equipment, food, and other necessities, the walk to Cho Oyu's base takes about three weeks, but a strong, unencumbered walker can make it back from Namche to Kathmandu in less than a week.

My AP boss in Delhi, Wally Sims, agreed that while the women were preparing their climb I should go look at the situation in Nepal since its first freely conducted parliamentary elections. To the aggrieved surprise of King Mahendra, who wanted credit for being somewhat democratic but had counted on a number of small political parties' splitting the vote so that he could play them off against each other, the Nepali Congress Party led by Bishweshwar Prasad Koirala had won a strong majority in Parliament. The new government made an interesting situation for me to explore in features and analytical stories. Our Kathmandu stringer was an Indian resident of Nepal named M. M. Gupta. He was no good for much more than brief stories on spot news developments—and we worried about his reliability even on those.

In addition, the United States was in the process of opening its first embassy in Nepal, after having handled diplomatic relations from the New Delhi embassy. L. Douglas Heck, a political officer acquaintance of mine from the U.S. embassy in Delhi, was in Kathmandu making arrangements for the new embassy. So I flew to Kathmandu with several story lines to pursue.

Sizing up Nepal's new government and talking to the Americans were easier than covering the women. The Americans, Heck, and especially people in a long-established U.S. aid mission were eager to have an American journalist take interest in a usually neglected land. Most Delhi-based correspondents went to Nepal once for the exotic flavor, wrote a story to justify their expense accounts, and never went back. Nepal's politicians were open, hospitable, and also eager to have international press attention. This included the Communists, whose little office up a rickety staircase had a lovely view of Kathmandu's main temple square.

Prime Minister Koirala was a charmingly polite, almost shy, man who spoke excellent English. He was so informal and hospitable that my first interview with him was conducted as we sat on the floor of a large bedroom in the old house that was his temporary official residence. As we talked, he was sorting masses of recently acquired governmental papers into stacks around himself. Among other things, he instructed me that the adjectival form of his country's name should be Ne-PAL-i. The old British form of Nep-a-LESE had the colonial connotation of a quaint, backward land, Koirala said, but he did not want Nepal to be thought of simply as an exotic tourist destination. He was looking ahead to economic growth and modernization.

Reporting on the women was an amusing problem. To raise money for their expedition, they had found various kinds of sponsorships: manufacturers of climbing gear, packaged food, and such. One sponsor was London's *Daily Express*, a tabloid then locked in a free-wheeling circulation war with the *Daily Mail*. Both papers were willing to exaggerate or even fabricate stories that might titillate a reader on the London Underground. In this case, however, the *Express* simply wanted to be sure it had exclusive rights to whatever facts and colorful sidelights developed from the climb. To write those facts and sidebars, the women were accompanied by an experienced *Express* reporter, Steve Harper. Later I learned that Harper already had a reputation as a difficult, sometimes nasty person. I quickly saw that side of him, although circumstances were as much to blame as personality.

Under their sponsorship agreement, the women were not supposed to give interviews to anyone except Harper. I was the only other foreign correspondent in Kathmandu at the time, and the city then had only one hotel catering to

Westerners. This was the Royal, a run-down and then sparingly rehabilitated old wooden ramble of rooms that had belonged to a member of the large Rana clan, hence giving it the cachet of being a palace. In a town then lacking restaurants that most Westerners would risk, there was no way that the women and I could avoid seeing each other around the hotel at mealtimes.

Harper was constantly skulking around trying to make sure expedition members did not talk to me or the local stringers for other news agencies and newspapers. Several of the women were friendly types, however, particularly an older woman who was the chief logistical organizer, Dorothea Gravina, the British wife of an Italian count, plus the attractive Claudine. So, when Harper was not looking I picked up some personal tidbits and comments to enliven stories about their readily visible preparations.

When the day came for the women to set out for Namche and the mountain, August 21, I went out with a large picnic party to see them off at the end of the road on the eastern side of the Kathmandu Valley. Harper was snarling as usual, but the women were relaxed and friendly and talked to me. And then they were gone, swinging up the trail amid their numerous porters.

A day or two later, my stories about Nepal also finished, I flew to Calcutta on the way to an exploratory visit to East Pakistan. Gupta was left to watch for any reportable developments on the women. Harper, after walking a day or two up the trail with them, returned to the Hotel Royal to begin waiting for their reports. He had arranged for them to send back messages by "runners"—actually fast walkers—that he could then turn into stories to cable to the *Express*.

Always peripheral, my involvement in the Cho Oyu story had ended. But, in the enjoyable annals of journalistic escapades, the best was yet to come. And for the women, the worst.

In Calcutta the AP's new stringer, Subhash Chakravarti, arranged for us to meet in a hotel bar with a couple of Irish brothers whose names I don't remember. They had become semiprofessional *yeti* hunters. As more mountaineering expeditions had gone into the Himalayas during the 1950s, stories had proliferated about *yeti,* legendary creatures also known as "abominable snowmen." Various mountain people and a few Western climbers claimed to have seen huge, hairy, half-man/half-ape creatures, usually by moonlight or in other visually dubious circumstances, and there were numerous reports of very large, ape-like tracks found in high-altitude snowfields. The Western world was intrigued. Some Texas oil millionaire had decided that he would win renown by sponsoring the capture of a *yeti* to be brought back alive for his local zoo.

Somehow, the oilman had engaged the Irish brothers to find him a *yeti*. They had already made several expeditions into the Himalayas but come back empty-handed. Now, they told me in the Calcutta bar, they were about to set out on another search. There was a touch of cynicism in their tale. They apparently enjoyed tramping around in the mountains, not only being paid for their time but maybe also pocketing some expense account money from the minimal costs of equipment and hiring porters. So long as they had someone to cover the bills, they intended to keep doing it. Chakravarti and I spent an interesting evening listening to them. Since they'd been around a while and had already failed, however, I did not think it was worth writing a story about their new plans. Better to save my notes and wait for results. They never found a *yeti*. No one has, and the large tracks in the snow have been explained as sun-melt expansions of small game spoor.

Some weeks later, about October 16, when I was somewhere away from Delhi—I believe that was when I was down in Ceylon (now Sri Lanka) reporting the aftermath of the assassination of the prime minister, whom I'd interviewed just a few months earlier—startling news came.

The *Daily Mail*, arch-rival of Harper's *Express*, had filled its front page with a screaming headline. It said something like, "Disaster on Cho Oyu; Women's Expedition Smashed by Blizzard on Himalayan Peak; Climbers Missing." Kogan and van der Straten-Ponthoz along with a Sherpa had been lost as they prepared for the assault on the peak.

The *Mail* had a graphic account of the tragedy. Starting from the base camp at nineteen thousand feet, five climbers had established an advance camp at twenty-three thousand feet on October 1. But two of the women had to be evacuated to the base camp because of altitude sickness, leaving Kogan, van der Straten-Ponthoz, and the Sherpa—a man with the supposedly all-women expedition—to attempt the summit. Then the weather closed in. For days the upper slopes of Cho Oyu were lashed by storms. Winds were estimated to be up to one hundred miles an hour. When the weather finally cleared, climbers went up from the base camp on October 10. They found nothing where the advance camp had been. The area had been swept clean by the blizzard and resulting avalanches. No trace of the three-person assault team was ever discovered.

The same day's *Express* had nothing from Nepal. The *Mail* had a journalistic scoop in the most sensational, freebooting old tradition of press wars. The explanation quickly spread around the journalistic fraternity in Delhi, where Larry Atkinson was the *Mail*'s well-known resident correspondent. Atkinson, a convivial Anglo-Indian (British father, Indian mother), and his bosses in London had set out to sabotage the *Express*'s exclusivity agreement with the expedition. They had succeeded spectacularly.

The *Mail* had secretly hired the *yeti*-hunting Irish brothers, rather than their usual Texas patron. Telling a cover story of following *yeti* spoor, they pitched their tents above Namche Bazaar on the trail up the Ngozumpa glacier toward Cho Oyu. As runners came down from the women's base camp, the brothers intercepted them and by some means—presumably bribery, with money probably reinforced by a warm meal—had learned the climbers' news before sending the runners on their way to Harper in Kathmandu. Then the brothers wrote out their own messages and gave them to *their* runners.

Instead of turning west at Jubing, below Namche Bazaar, on the trail to Kathmandu, their runners continued south, following an easier and therefore quicker trail down a river valley than the westerly route up and down over high Himalayan spurs. Their runners headed for a tea garden just across the Nepali border at the extreme northern edge of the Indian telephone network. Boarding there, waiting, was Larry Atkinson. When the news arrived, he telephoned a nephew who worked for a Calcutta newspaper and dictated a story. The nephew cabled it to the *Mail* in London.

Twenty-four hours later, after the AP and others had quoted the *Mail* on the women's disaster, the *Express* published Harper's account. Those of us who had met him took some guilty pleasure in his disgrace. But that did little to offset the thought of the gallant women and the devoted Sherpa.

7

STUMBLING OVER A POLICEMAN'S SEVERED HEAD

THE TWO MAIN RIVERS THAT DRAIN SPRING'S SNOW MELT AND SUMMER'S monsoon rains from the Himalayas and their foothills and carry this vast volume of water across the north Indian plains are the Ganges and the Brahmaputra. They mingle their waters in a shifting network of channels before reaching the Bay of Bengal. This large, fertile delta area and some adjacent plains, known collectively as Bengal, has supported many prosperous empires over the centuries. So it was natural that in 1696 English merchant adventurers of the East India Company set up a delta headquarters seventy miles up from the Bay of Bengal on the westernmost of the rivers' navigable channels, the Hooghly.

This became Calcutta, capital of India from 1833 to 1912, the Victorian heyday of the British empire. The British laid out an attractive new city, with imposing government buildings, spacious public gardens, and such fashionable streets as Chowringhi running along the east side the *maidan,* or main open park area. Both north of the city center and across the Hooghly on the west bank in the suburb of Howrah were factories where jute and other products of the delta were processed, tea from Assam and the Himalayan foothills sorted and packed, and manufacturing industries developed. As the economic as well as governmental hub of India, Calcutta grew into the empire's second largest city after London. At the beginning of the twentieth century, Calcutta was known as a relatively clean, well-run, wealthy city of Hindus and Muslims.

During World War II the city was swept by famine and violent clashes between Hindus and Muslims. When British India was partitioned in 1947 between predominately Hindu India and a separate nation for Muslims with the invented name of Pakistan, the city controversially went to India. Most of Calcutta's delta hinterland east of the city, however, became East Pakistan, because of the Muslim majority there. Hundreds of thousands of members of the Hindu minority in East Pakistan fled to Calcutta, turning parts of it into teeming slums while thousands lived on the streets. Others overwhelmed the housing, social services, sanitation system, and graciousness of Calcutta. As the postwar use of DDT to reduce malaria and other factors raised health standards, India's population grew rapidly. Uneducated and unskilled young men, unable to subsist on repeatedly subdivided family farmlands, poured into Calcutta from a vast semicircle to the west, seeking any kind of menial work. They drove down wages, eking out skeletal existences while sending as much money as possible home to families still in the villages. Many of them, too, survived on the streets. Or they settled into fetid slums without sanitation and just one water tap for thousands, aslush in mud during the monsoon.

By the time I first visited Calcutta in March 1959, it had become known worldwide as a symbol of poverty, overcrowding, pestilence, and urban decay. In this, it was simply ahead of its time. In the decades that I have been repeatedly in and out of cities from Cairo to Bangkok to Jakarta, with fewer glimpses of Mexico City, Sao Paulo, Shanghai, Beijing, and Lagos, all of them have become increasingly overcrowded and polluted, and sometimes chaotic and anarchic.

As I was driving in from Calcutta's airport to spend my first night there, the Associated Press's stringer regaled me with stories about the city. As we passed a large engineering works near the airport, he told how some months earlier Indian workers, angered by abusive treatment by British supervisors, had seized two bosses and tossed them screaming into the company's big industrial furnace. Calcutta was slipping toward anarchy. Worker protests and strikes were becoming more common.

A favorite form of labor action in 1959 was the *hartal,* a complete stoppage of all commercial activity in the city. Anyone who failed to join in this general strike was subjected to abuse or even violent attack. Indian businessmen, and the few old British companies whom they had not yet bought out, were by 1959 already beginning stealthily to move out of the Calcutta area by using profits and even some operating capital to build new factories in mostly union-free southern India. Calcutta, once the industrial heart of India, was starting to run down.

After several other visits over a busy period, in early September 1959 I was again in Calcutta on the way back to Delhi from East Pakistan. When I arrived there was trouble in the air. The Calcutta municipal government had just raised bus fares by a few *naiya paisa* (hundredths of a *rupee,* with the *rupee* then worth about 19 cents apiece). Its reason was to reduce the city's large subsidy for public transportation. The raise incensed the city's strong labor unions. Many of them were controlled by India's then undivided but somewhat bourgeois Communist Party. It was spoiling for a fight with the municipal and state governments, which at the time were controlled by Prime Minister Jawaharlal Nehru's Congress Party, in order to enhance the Communist appeal to Calcutta's multitude of poor.

On the advice of the AP stringer, Subhash Chakravarti, I did not head to my usual hotel in Calcutta, the Grand on Chowringhi, which was still the city's best but was so run-down by then that it would have rated as a fourth-class hotel in the West, at most. Instead, I went to a dark, dank little hotel that had the advantage of being just across the street from the government-run central telegraph office. The unions had called a *hartal* for the following day. That meant all transportation would be halted and it would be slow if not impossible to get the mile and a half or so from the Grand to the telegraph office to cable stories to AP London.

The next morning the *hartal* began, with violence. The worst was in Howrah, which had by 1959 become a crowded slum. After a skirmish whose origins were unclear, demonstrators attacked a Howrah police station. Some policemen who were caught outside on the street trying to block the attack were set upon. One was beheaded with a crude sword. As the police then barricaded themselves inside the station, the rioting mob tossed bombs made out of coconut shells filled with gunpowder, metal bolts, and a wick.

Elsewhere in town, several other policemen and demonstrators were killed. In some places police tried to clear roads with what were known in India as "*lathi* charges," using their long, heavy, metal-tipped staves named *lathis* to beat back demonstrators. These and other clashes led in some places to "police firings," meaning police opened gunfire on hostile crowds. In theory, a "police firing" was the last resort by police to avoid being overwhelmed, but I had already seen in south India's Kerala state in June and July 1959 that political circumstances often loosened the old British restrictions on conditions under which guns could be used on unarmed mobs.

The press was theoretically exempt from the demonstrators' ban on any vehicular movement. Chakravarti found the driver of a tiny, Indian-made taxi who was willing, for a good price and with hand-lettered "press" signs in his windows, to carry him, two other Indian journalists, and me to survey the situation in the city. Crammed into the taxi, we didn't get far. On a broad thoroughfare filled with demonstrators and curious pedestrians, a gang of youths set upon our little vehicle despite our cries of "press" in English and Bengali.

Had they been really angry, they would have immediately begun swinging iron bars to break the windows and then dragged us out, as I saw happen to another car later in the day. But instead, in a spirit of youthful exuberance, they began rocking the taxi and seemed likely to turn it over. Fortunately, the driver kept his head and somehow managed to accelerate through a momentary opening in front and escape, followed by jeers. After that experience, there was no question of getting across the river to Howrah, some miles away across a decrepit-looking and normally traffic-jammed bridge, to check personally on the worst of the trouble.

By that afternoon the West Bengal state government had taken over from the faltering municipal administration. That meant Dr. B. C. Roy was in charge. Bidhan Chandra Roy, a physician who was widely respected as a colleague of the *mahatma,* Mohandas K. Gandhi, in India's independence struggle, had been chief minister, or head of the state government, since 1948. A strong—some said reactionary—figure in the Congress Party, Roy was accustomed to command. Chakravarti and I walked through nearly deserted streets to Roy's morning and afternoon news conferences for updates on the situation.

For me, the news conferences were not only informative but also amusing because of the linguistic situation. Roy and the local journalists whom he was briefing—I was the only foreign correspondent on the scene—were bilingual in English and Bengali. Roy would usually start talking in English, but if he came to a term such as *hartal* that was never translated into English, he would unconsciously switch to speaking Bengali and continue without a break. Until, that is, he came to a term such as "law and order" that even Bengali speakers always used in English, whereupon he would fluidly switch back to speaking in English. Fortunately, I was able to fill in the Bengali parts from Chakravarti or others among the always friendly and helpful local press.

After a couple of days, the heat went out of the protest and order began to return after Roy got the municipal administration to cut the bus fare increase in half as a compromise.

Early one evening after calm had returned and I was planning to leave for Delhi the next morning, I was in the telegraph office sending a final story when I unexpectedly bumped into Noel Barber. We greeted each other as old friends because we had been together the previous April in Tezpur waiting for the Dalai Lama to appear. Barber was a world-roving correspondent of the London *Daily Mail* who specialized in the "I was there" kind of graphic journalism about exciting events that sold newspapers to British blue-collar workers. I had seen in Tezpur his tendency to dress up or even fabricate stories, but he was a genial and likeable person despite his adherence to the low journalistic ethics of the London tabloid press. It was not until the following year that his Tezpur escapades were publicized in a way that forced him into early retirement from daily journalism.

Barber said he had just flown into Calcutta to report on the riots—several days late. In the tradition of journalism among people who are not directly competing in the same market—the more remote or troubled the location, the stronger the brotherhood of journalists—he asked me for a fill-in on what had been happening. I readily began describing for him the nature of the *hartal* and the violence, including the Howrah trouble, the coconut bombs, and the police firings.

He listened for a while and then asked where I was staying. Across the street, I said. Would I mind if he came over and used my telephone, Barber asked, because he had not yet checked into a hotel? He wanted to call his office in London, where a deadline for his paper's afternoon edition was nearing. He assured me he would reverse the charges. You'll probably not get through, I said, because phone connections to Europe are very uncertain. Never mind, he'd like to try.

So we went up to my room and, to my surprise, he soon got a connection to the *Daily Mail*. "Give me dictation," he shouted in best B-movie style. He began dictating.

"By Noel Barber Calcutta fullstop. I turned a corner in the ghastly Howrah slum and stumbled over the still-bleeding head of a policeman as the howling mob receded down the littered street fullstop." Without notes, he dictated more personalized details of the days-earlier attack on the police station, including some colorful points that I had not told him, had never heard, and doubted were true.

Then he came to mention of the homemade bombs. Turning to me as I sat on the bed listening, fascinated, he asked as an aside, "How did you say they made those bombs?" I told him again, and he turned back to continue dictating his first-person account.

At that time I had been a foreign correspondent for half a year. I was getting a quick education running around the South Asian subcontinent on a succession of interesting stories. But this was one kind of journalistic education that didn't seem very useful.

8

COUNTING CROWDS

THE DISTINGUISHED-LOOKING, BUT AT THE SAME TIME OBVIOUSLY FIT and tough, Secret Service agent was clearly harried and a little distressed. He was also impressed. Nothing in a lot of years spent protecting presidents of the United States had quite prepared him for this. "I've never seen a crowd like this," said the head of Dwight D. Eisenhower's security detail, James Rowley. He was looking out at the multitude of Indians gathered at the Ram Lila grounds, an open space named from Hindu mythology, where British-built New Delhi adjoined the old Moghul city of Delhi.

Eisenhower and his daughter, Barbara, who had accompanied him to India in place of his wife, had an even better view of the crowd. They, together with their host, Prime Minister Jawaharlal Nehru, and Nehru's daughter, Indira Gandhi, were seated about twelve feet above the crowd on a white concrete speakers' pavilion some sixteen feet square, with stairs up the back and a canopy overhead.

In front of them stretched a mass of Indians. Some were well dressed in light-weight gray and brown woolen Western-style clothes, others wore farmers' white *dhotis* and jackets or *saris* and shawls in the warm autumnal sunshine of December 1959. Most sat close together on the dusty ground between double lines of posts with metal pipe railings that divided up sections of spectators and were intended to keep the crowd from rushing toward the pavilion. Indian policemen, carrying the heavy, metal-tipped staves called *lathis* used to batter at unruly mobs, manned the narrow alleys between the pipe fences. Out beyond the divided Ram Lila area, people stood pressed together seeking a better look, spilling out into the streets on either side of the grounds. Other people edged the roofs of every building within distant view. It was a lot of people.

How many? The American journalists accompanying Eisenhower, who were milling around, stirring up dust behind the pavilion while waiting for the speeches, wanted a figure that they could use in their stories. Indian officials, reluctant to commit themselves, were no help. So the reporters turned to the Secret Service's Rowley. He was supposed to be experienced in dealing with presidential crowds, so he should have a good estimate.

Eisenhower had been drawing large crowds since he reached the Indian subcontinent six days earlier. His first landing was on December 7 at Karachi. The Associated Press bureau in New Delhi was responsible for coverage in Pakistan and the rest of South Asia. The bureau chief, Wally Sims, decided he should stay in Delhi to perfect coverage arrangements there rather than risk getting stuck in Karachi and being late for the more-important Delhi visit. Wally sent me down to Karachi to handle arrangements there. That meant setting up a temporary newsroom and darkroom with the help of our Karachi stringer, Zamir Siddiqi, close to a temporary cable office.

The office naturally was equipped with typewriters, but I quickly discovered that the AP's chief White House correspondent, Marvin L. Arrowsmith, did not know how to use one. He had for so many years been phoning his stories in to the AP bureau in Washington that his typing skills had atrophied. I ended up having to have him pace up and down with his notes dictating to me as I typed out his stories on cable forms.

Crowds turned out to see Eisenhower in Karachi. It was in 1959 a city of something over a million persons. The crowds were sizeable but manageable. They presented no problem in movements around Karachi by Eisenhower and his host, President Mohammad Ayub Khan, a general who had seized control of Pakistan in 1958 from squabbling, corrupt, and ineffective politicians.

After two nights and a day in Karachi, Eisenhower flew off on December 9 to a brief stop in Afghanistan and then to New Delhi, where I arrived just before him. As I rushed in to the AP bureau to man the phones, I saw huge crowds along the road that eclipsed the turnout in Karachi. The Indian government, which preached a sometimes moderately pro-Soviet form of nonalignment but had greatly benefited from American economic aid throughout the 1950s, had made a stronger effort to turn out welcoming crowds than had Pakistan, a military ally of the United States. Free buses were provided to bring in Indian villagers from a wide radius around New Delhi. But the lure of seeing the leader of a distant, rich, almost fabled America was enough to attract many Indians to turn out without the encouragement of free transportation. Many farmers drove their bullock carts to the route through the countryside from the airport into the city and parked beside the road to picnic with their families. By the time Nehru welcomed Eisenhower, police were barely able to keep open that single road from the airport into town as eager, happy crowds awaited a chance to see their motorcade pass. As soon as the two leaders passed along the road to shouts of *zindabad* ("long life") and other enthusiastic welcomes, the crowd surged into the road, closing it. Lesser Indian officials, diplomats, and others who had participated in the airport arrival ceremonies took hours to make their way through the slowly dispersing congestion and reach the city.

The planned route for Eisenhower's motorcade went around Connaught Place, a large circular plaza that was the commercial center of New Delhi. Crowds were so densely packed there—on the pavement, on the grass, atop the buildings, even spilling into the street despite the best efforts of *lathi*-wielding police—that it took a long time for an ever-smiling Eisenhower and an increasingly irritated Nehru to circumnavigate the plaza. In all, it took them two hours and ten minutes to cover the thirteen-mile route from the airport to Rashtrapati Bhavan, the Indian president's massively imposing residence. Nehru later said two and a half million people had turned out to welcome Eisenhower. The basis for that figure was never explained, and it probably was a gross exaggeration.

So the crowd at the Ram Lila grounds two days later came as no surprise. But how huge was the turnout? Rowley was reluctant to estimate. American reporters pressed him.

Finally, he committed himself. "Must be at least a million, maybe more," he declared. That was the figure that was reported: a million or more Indians had turned out to see Eisenhower, some said, while the more cautious wrote "nearly a million." But it bothered me as I stood there with the other reporters.

I had already had some problems with crowd estimates while reporting from south India's Kerala state the previous June and July. Tropical Kerala had in 1957 become the world's first significant-sized political entity to bring a Communist government to power through free, fair elections. In 1959, Nehru's Congress Party that controlled most other states as well as the national government began accusing the Kerala government of illegal and corrupt practices. Most independent political observers thought the problem was not so much illegality or corruption—the Congress Party certainly had its share—as it was concern that the Communist Party was governing so effectively that the Kerala Congress Party would not be able to oust it in a fair vote at the next election, due by 1962.

The Congress Party began a civil unrest movement intended to make Kerala ungovernable. Its goal was to provide an excuse for the national government to step in, dissolve the Communist regime, and put the state under "president's rule" by Congress-influenced civil servants until another election could be held ahead of schedule. This was a clearly unconstitutional exercise of power by Congress under the recently and nepotistically selected party president, Nehru's daughter, Indira, who was just beginning to show the political toughness displayed in her later career as prime minister. Nonetheless, Nehru's national government did dissolve the Kerala Communist government on July 31, 1959, and impose direct rule.

Reporting the many political rallies, torchlight parades, and occasional flare-ups of violence in Kerala in which Communist-controlled police fired on crowds of demonstrators—once, beneath palm trees on an Arabian Sea beach—I heard a lot of crowd estimates. Whether it was a crowd chanting *KPCC zindabad, KPSS murdabad* ("long live the KPCC [Kerala state Congress Committee], death to the KPSS [Kerala state Communist Party]") or one chanting the reverse, some partisan organizer would always appear at my elbow to offer a crowd estimate. "At least a *lakh*," he would usually tell me.

Even when speaking English, Indians use the organizational concepts of the Hindu counting system. The word *lakh* means one hundred thousand; there is no concept or usage of a million, ten *lakhs* being used instead; and the next round term or unit of measurement is a *crore*, which is 10 million. As Western linguists have found, language shapes our thinking. In China, a *li*, which is ten thousand (as in "one picture is worth ten thousand words," often misquoted as "a thousand words"), crops up in numerous situations where a count would show far fewer. In India, the nice, round concept of a *lakh* was easy to use.

But in situations that were static enough to give me a chance, I would begin mentally sectioning off the Kerala crowds that were listening to Malayalam-language speeches. I would make quick, rough counts by twos of the number of persons in sample sections—or, if time allowed, all the sections—and then multiply for a very approximate total. I seldom found a crowd that I could count as more than ten thousand—far short of a *lakh*, but still a lot of people, especially when they were excited under the flickering light of torches on a warm, tropical evening.

The Secret Service man at the Ram Lila grounds did not, as an Indian might have, offer an estimate of ten *lakhs*. Rowley thought in nice round Western concepts of millions, which were easier than trying to be precise in hundreds of thousands. And he was a quotable source with his figure of a million. In 1959 the press in the United States and elsewhere had not yet focused much analytical effort on crowd estimates. Instead, reporters usually turned to a senior police official on the spot and took whatever guess he made. Who better here than an experienced old Secret Service man? Anyway, Arrowsmith was writing the main story that played up the size of the crowd as well as the content of the speeches. I expressed my doubts to him. This had no effect. Even the Indian press picked up Rowley's estimate.

After it was all over, after Eisenhower had flown away from India following his time in New Delhi and the visitors' virtually mandatory quick look at the Taj Mahal 110 miles to the south in Agra, I began doing a little checking.

I learned from reference books that the Ram Lila grounds are seventeen acres in size. An acre is 43,560 square feet. I calculated that a human being—even a poorly fed Indian—occupies at least two square feet when standing and at least four square feet when sitting down. Even in the press of the most closely compacted crowd, the required individual area would be a bit more. This meant there were unlikely to have been more than eleven thousand persons an acre sitting in front of Eisenhower, or 187,000 total. The next time I was passing the Ram Lila grounds, I stopped to make a visual estimate of the area of streets, sidewalks, and adjacent areas outside the grounds themselves that I had seen also packed with standing people. This area I calculated at one person per two square feet. A generous estimate was added for people on rooftops. Still, there was no way the figure could come to much more than three and a half *lakhs*: 350,000 persons. A lot, but not a million.

Within the next few years, and particularly during the late 1960s demonstrations against the Vietnam War, the American media made a greater effort to pin down crowd estimates. Too many police officers had just been making guesses, usually influenced by earlier but unproven guesses for similar crowds in similar locations. Too many organizers of demonstrations had been offering the press their own selfishly motivated estimates of how many they had succeeded in calling out. The best method turned out to be kind of thing I'd done: the measurement, or at least the approximation, of the area occupied by a crowd combined with an estimate of the crowd's density to yield a rough multiple. The U.S. Park Service eventually developed this to the point of having helicopters photograph crowds on the Washington Mall and then placing a grid over the pictures to derive the area and crowd density of each grid square. This did not, however, absolve the Park Service of controversy with aggrieved crowd organizers, and it eventually quit offering estimates.

But something was needed in India. I began practicing estimating areas. Fourteen months of early morning golf in Montgomery, Alabama, had taught me a little about estimating how many yards it was to a golf green. Estimating the distance to some object while walking around New Delhi, and then counting my yard-long paces to it, helped improve my concept of sizes and distances.

The next time India staged a "public meeting" at the Ram Lila grounds for a foreign dignitary, I was ready. At other locations I usually felt more confident about my own crowd estimates than any I might have been able to solicit from Indian officials, who seldom were willing to make any. With journalistic reticence, however, I used my estimates in reporting only as a check on what could be drawn out of reticent officials.

The real test came in January 1961, when Queen Elizabeth II toured the Indian subcontinent. British journalists accompanying her, particularly those from the London tabloids, were keenly aware of the record crowds that had turned out for Eisenhower in New Delhi. They acted as if national pride required their queen to evoke larger crowds in the country ruled until 1947 by her king-emperor father than had turned out for that upstart, "have a nice day" sort of leader of a former colony.

Delhi was disappointing. The Indian government made some effort to turn out crowds for the queen, but apparently not so much effort as for Eisenhower. After all, Britain was not in a position to give much aid to India compared to what the United States had provided and could provide in the future. A second road had hurriedly been built through the countryside as an alternate link from the airport to the city to avoid the 1959 traffic jam, but even the main route was not so crowded for the queen's motorcade. Connaught Place was crowded, but not so much that her motorcade was obstructed. There was no Ram Lila grounds gathering.

Ah, the British journalists said, but wait for Calcutta. That huge, congested city had far more people than the Delhi metropolis. Surely the crowds turning out to see Queen Elizabeth there would set records unseen anywhere in India, perhaps the world. As I traveled around India and East Pakistan reporting on the queen, the British journalists talked themselves into greater and greater expectations for crowds on the long drive in from Dum Dum airport to the old British governor-general's mansion in downtown Calcutta. But, I asked several of the reporters, how will we be able to get a reliable crowd estimate? Their replies were vague. I began to think out a strategy. It was based on the fact that, as the representative of a major world news agency, I was usually able to watch events from fairly close up, placed by officials in motorcades only four or five vehicles behind the queen.

When we landed at Dum Dum on February 17, 1961, I was glad to see that my assigned vehicle was a jeep without a top but with handrails, enabling me to ride standing up and to see not only the crowds but also the driver's dashboard. I shared the jeep with two British reporters. I briefed them on my plans because I wanted witnesses. I particularly made the point to them that a person fills about two feet of linear distance along a sidewalk unless pressed very uncomfortably against his neighbor. They did not disagree.

As the jeep started off in the motorcade, I noted aloud to my colleagues the dashboard's odometer reading down to tenths of a mile and wrote this in my notebook. Then I began surveying the crowd lining the streets inside the airport grounds, making repeated spot counts, and saying, "Looks like [the people are standing] about six deep [on each side] here," writing this down. As people thinned out at the edge of the airport, I sounded off the odometer reading—so many tenths of a mile covered, so many people, which I also wrote down. This continued as we went along toward town: "About three deep here for four-tenths of a mile," and so on. As we got into the city, the spot counts rose to ten, sometimes twelve, even fifteen deep for so many tenths of a mile. I tried to compensate for extra people spilling back into cross streets and looking down from buildings, explaining to my colleagues that the depth count was being raised above what we actually saw on the sidewalks and lining the edges of the streets along the route. In some places the average estimate for a block got as high as twenty-five persons deep on each side of the street. At the end of the eight-mile route from the airport, the crowd was so dense that the street had to be cleared for the queen to reach the stately old governor-general's mansion.

The AP's stringer had already cabled short stories on the queen's landing at Dum Dum, her brief remarks there, and her arrival downtown, so I was not too rushed when I reached the press center. I sat down with my notebook and began multiplying crowd depth estimates with tenths of miles, times two for both sides of the streets. The result came to around 450,000 persons. On top of my earlier generosity with the depth estimates as I had written them down, I added some more to call it a crowd of half a million. This seemed far short of Eisenhower's Delhi arrival crowd. It would have topped an accurate Ram Lila figure, but a sober assessment after the fact naturally never caught up with the Rowley estimate.

The British press was meanwhile badgering Calcutta officials manning the press center to get them an official crowd estimate. The officials were uncomfortable, lacking experience with such estimates but aware that London newspapers wanted something grandiose. A senior policeman was brought in. "About a million," he hesitantly guessed. The British journalists booed him down. It had to be more than that. They had never seen such crowds, so it must be 2 or 3 million, they insisted. After all, this was Calcutta, a big and notoriously crowded city. Facing hostility and trying to maintain a good atmosphere for the queen's visit, the Indian police official was accommodating. "Maybe," he said, "it was 2 million." Some British journalists reported 3 million, a record, the largest crowd ever seen in India, maybe anywhere.

I showed my calculations to my fellow jeep travelers. They were not interested. Did they have any problem with my methodology? No, they simply did not care. What I had done was not politically correct, to use later terminology. Thus, it could be ignored.

So I sat down and knocked out a story saying that Queen Elizabeth had arrived in Calcutta to a tremendous outpouring of people, who crowded the downtown area. Down in the story I gave an estimate of half a million people and then spent three paragraphs explaining how that figure was derived. So far as I know, that story was not very widely published. The only print or broadcast media really interested in the story were in Britain, and therefore represented by their own correspondents, or in a few Commonwealth countries that usually used dispatches on royalty from the London-based Reuters news agency.

And then there was the *New York Times*. It published a one-paragraph item from its Calcutta stringer that began, "About 1.5 million" persons welcomed Queen Elizabeth II to Calcutta. No source was given for this estimate, which was no doubt intended to be a conservative downgrading of the higher figures being tossed about. But, unsourced, it is now part of history because it appeared in "the newspaper of record."

The failure of my counting efforts to win attention did not surprise me. I did not delude myself into thinking that anything could have been allowed to dim the luster of the queen's royal procession. Crowd figures are usually too politically important for those who bandy them about to permit the intrusion of an attempt to apply some scientific method.

9

INTO BHUTAN BY MULE

AS EACH ARCHER TOOK HIS POSITION AND BEGAN TO BEND HIS LONG bow with great effort, leaning forward so that his knee-length, wrap-around *gho* drooped from its dagger-carrying belt, the singing girls launched into their smiling songs. Intended to rattle opposing teams' archers by good-naturedly denigrating their sexual prowess and more intimate physical attributes—in terms that local officials considered too embarrassing to translate for visitors—the lilting songs by local beauties in *kiras* with bright homespun aprons were part of the festive atmosphere of the contest. Arrows whispered in high trajectories and came down some 150 yards away on the circular target with impressive accuracy. Applause rose from the crowd by the trees just across the Pachu, or Paro River ("chu" means river), from a tall-looming, massive whitewashed stone *dzong*. Here was the government of Bhutan temporarily located in this fortress monastery at Paro, high in a Himalayan valley.

The next event on this special holiday was clearly a humorous Western concept. Some Bhutanese official probably had picked it up while being educated at government expense at a boys' school in British India. Organizers invited pairs from the crowd of several thousand gathered in the meadow to participate in a three-legged race, each man tied by his left leg to a woman's right leg. A number of couples volunteered and began practicing to general amusement.

One man who had been mingling with the spectators, chatting easily with a wide variety of people, wanted a partner. The *druk gyalpo,* Jigme Dorje Wangchuck, walked along the front of the crowd, smiling and talking, until he came to an old woman who, to be charitable, might be described as not the best-looking or swiftest potential partner. Apparently a poor peasant, she was dressed in what was probably her finest outfit with long skirt and the colorful apron of horizontal stripes found throughout the Tibetan ethnic area.

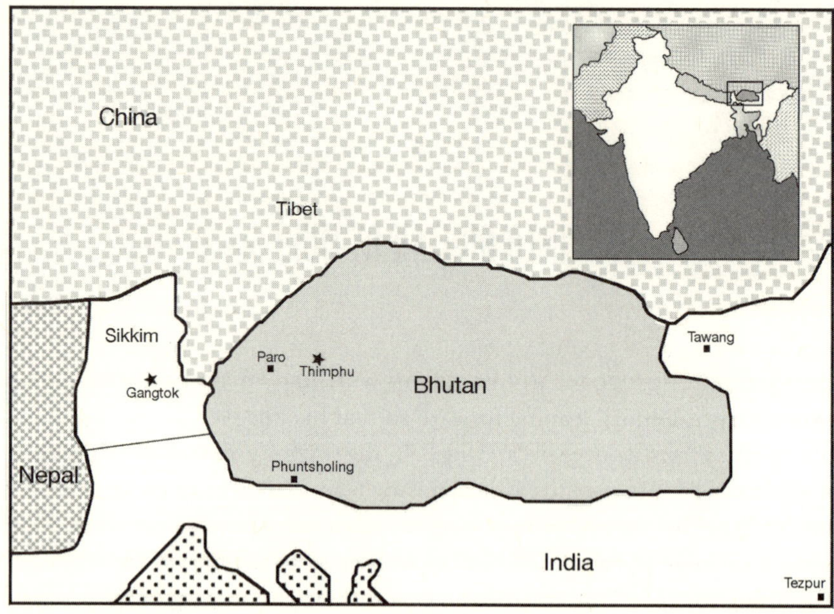

Come on, the *druk gyalpo* smilingly said to her in Dzongkha, the lingua franca of the little Himalayan land that he ruled as absolute monarch. Greatly embarrassed, she hesitated, but the crowd laughingly encouraged her, so she came forward. An aide tied the king's and his subject's legs with a bright woven cloth. Their efforts to practice walking together were awkward, while younger couples were learning to be adept at it. Then the race began. The king and his subject made a determined if clumsy effort, coming in close to last. The crowd roared in approval.

The festival's climax was dances by the *dzong*'s Tibetan Buddhist lamas. The holy men pranced and swirled and leaped in enactment of Himalayan religious tales. One was the dance of the lords of the cremation grounds, wearing white skull masks, and another, the dance of the judgment of the dead.

The most popular and best-known one was the "Black Hat Dance." It told the story of a stranger in a black hat and black cloak riding a black horse. In 842 A.D., he rode into Lhasa and began a mesmerizing dance for the forty-second in a line of Tibetan kings stretching back into legend. This evil king, Lang Darma, was suppressing Buddhism, trying to turn his people back from two centuries of that religion to Tibet's earlier animistic faith, known as *bön*. Gradually dancing closer, the stranger, a Buddhist monk named Pelgyi Dorje, drew a bow and arrow from his cloak and assassinated the king. Jumping back on his horse, he escaped pursuers by reversing his hat and cloak to their white sides and dashing through a stream to wash the charcoal off his white horse.

In this triumph of good over evil, two lama dancers impersonated Pelgyi Dorje and Lang Darma, while others wore fantastic masks and bright costumes of demons and saintly incarnations, of cadavers and spirits.[1] Mountain horns of polished bronze, some stretching out ten feet across the grass in front of the musicians, added distinctive timbre to the music of stringed instruments, large drums, and cymbals.

Archery, races, and dancing were highlights of a festive day in May 1960 in Paro. The day celebrated the meeting there of Bhutan's *tsongdu,* or consultative assembly, and the visit by two foreign delegations to the closed mountain kingdom. During the day, the *druk gyalpo,* whose title can be translated as "precious ruler of the dragon people," spent hours walking around talking to ordinary people. A warm rapport between king and subjects was evident in the relaxed, friendly manner on both sides. It was a rapport so strong that the *druk gyalpo*'s efforts to introduce elements of popular participation in government, voluntarily relinquishing some of his absolute powers, found little acceptance among a pastoral people who were long accustomed to a paternalistic monarchy.

Jigme Dorje Wangchuck had begun moving gradually toward elements of democracy about seven years earlier. Later, he also began trying to make the world aware of Bhutan's existence. To the very limited extent that the outside world knew of Bhutan, most people thought of it as being somehow part of neighboring India. This was a concept that Indian officials did little to contradict and, indeed, often seemed to encourage, although Bhutan was linked only by treaty to New Delhi. At the same time, many in the other land bordering Bhutan, Tibet, still considered it to be a provincial extension of their area, based on geography, history, religion, and language. This was a concept that Chinese officials did not assert, although since the Communist consolidation of control of Tibet in 1951 they were not on record as denying it, either.

The *druk gyalpo*'s effort to acquaint the world with his country, to be sure it had a separate identity, was the reason I attended that festival at Paro. Along with two other Western correspondents and four Indian journalists, I had been invited as an Associated Press correspondent to visit Bhutan as a guest of its monarch. So had a delegation from India's Parliament.

In 1960, the only way to get there was to ride a mule from the Indian border up through densely jungled Himalayan foothills to the high central valleys of the little kingdom. The delegations spent five days on mules from the border of India's Assam state into the valley heartland of a primitive but pleasant country. The trip up narrow, twisting, vine-saturated jungle trails lined with orchids and other wildflowers, fording mountain torrents, turned from steamy to Alpine pleasant as we went higher and jungle gave way to pines and rhododendrons.

By the time we started back after ten days in the Paro area, however, the monsoon had moved inland from the Bay of Bengal. Intermittent but frequent rains soaked us on now-slippery trails down through the jungle and made the streams more dangerous to cross. It was difficult to avoid leeches that waited on leaves to brush off on passing warm-blooded creatures. Despite protective measures, including puttees wrapped from the tops of canvas boots up around trouser legs, some leeches managed to penetrate. When discovered at the end of the day, their blood-bloated bodies had to be carefully detached from feet, legs, sometimes arms and other areas. Too much pulling risked getting only their bodies, tearing off heads that remained embedded and pumping blood. The heat of a cigarette was the best way to get the whole leach to withdraw, leaving a wound oozing blood because of the anticoagulant that it had injected.

Until just a year earlier, an easier, more healthy mule route had been used to reach central Bhutan from India at altitudes that avoided jungles. That route had two starting points. One was at the end of the road at Gangtok, the mountain-ridge capital of Sikkim, a neighboring Himalayan state closely tied to India. The other began nearby in India at Kalimpong, the terminus near the end of the Indian rail system for mule-carried trade with Tibet and the limited traffic into Bhutan. From Kalimpong, mules labored up an altitude change of some two miles to cross a spur of the Himalayas at the 14,390-foot-high Jelep La ("lonely, level pass"), and from Gangtok to the higher Nathu La, two saddles in the mountains only three miles apart. Beyond them, the trails joined to switchback down into a tongue of Tibet projecting southward between Sikkim and Bhutan, the Chumbi Valley. There the trail descending from the passes split, uphill north to Lhasa in Tibet or downstream southeast to Paro in Bhutan.

With permission of the Chinese authorities in Tibet, Prime Minister Jawaharlal Nehru of India had used the Chumbi Valley route from Gangtok over the Nathu La on a mule-ride visit to Paro in September 1958. However, the Lhasa uprising of Tibetans against Chinese Communist rule in March 1959, the flight of the Dalai Lama to exile in India, and the subsequent Chinese tightening of control in Tibet had led to the closure of that route.

The result of events in Tibet was a change that brought Bhutan out of centuries of deliberate isolation from the world. Cautiously, it emerged into the family of nations while trying to protect its distinctive character. I reported the beginning of that change.

Shortly after I arrived in New Delhi in late February 1959, the man referred to in the outside world as the prime minister of Bhutan visited the Indian capital for consultations with the government. He was Jigme Palden Dorje, the then forty-year-old member of an aristocratic Bhutanese family that had supplied three generations of kings with their chief advisers. Jigme Dorje's younger sister was one of two wives of the *druk gyalpo,* thus one of Bhutan's two queens. Jigme Dorje and the future *druk gyalpo* had both studied in British India, and as youths they had learned of a broader world by spending six months together in Scotland with the family of a botanist who had explored Bhutan. As a result, Jigme Dorje, who frequently left the country on business while the *druk gyalpo* stayed home, moved easily and confidently between his closed kingdom and the Western world.

When I asked for an interview in Delhi, Jigme Dorje kindly and patiently gave me an introductory education on his little country as well as cautiously discussing his fairly routine business with India. In a quiet news period, the interview made an interesting feature story about a closed, roadless land where the only wheels were Tibetan Buddhist prayer wheels, but a few small hydroelectric power plants were planned that would put wheels in mountain streams. In its rectangular eighteen thousand square miles, about a third the size of Louisiana, from near sea level in the south to peaks up to twenty-four thousand feet along the northern border, it then had perhaps six hundred thousand people.[2]

Virtually all of Bhutan's trade in early March 1959 was either with Tibet across their Himalayan passes or with India, crossing Tibet's Chumbi Valley on the round-about route up from the nearest big city and seaport, Calcutta. Jungle trails directly from the border of India into Bhutan's high central valleys were too difficult and unhealthy to sustain extensive commerce. Long trains of mules carried the trade via Tibet, the lead mule wearing a bell-jingling harness to wave the bright flag of the caravan's owner.

While there were both economic and political reasons for Bhutan to be oriented toward India, its much weaker other neighbor, Tibet, maintained a strong attraction. Bhutan had emerged from the dimness of unrecorded history as an extension of the Tibetan Buddhist system of religious government. The country was unified in the seventeenth century under a lama whose religious title was *shabdrung*. The theocracy used a lay official taking guidance from successive *shabdrungs* to administer secular affairs. These officials gradually became more powerful amid wars between Bhutan's valleys. From sporadic conflict emerged in the nineteenth century, by way of violence and treachery, one dominant official who named his younger son, Ugyen Wangchuck, as governor at Paro, the main monastery center in western Bhutan. In 1885, at the age of twenty-three, Wangchuck won what proved to be Bhutan's last civil war. In 1907, Wangchuck assumed the title of king, while the spiritual role of a *shabdrung* was deliberately assigned to obscurity.

The British in the lowlands south of Bhutan began dealing with it through a distant cousin of Wangchuck's, Ugyen Dorje. His grandson was the prime minister who arranged my visit to Bhutan; my host, *druk gyalpo* Jigme Dorje Wangchuck, was the grandson of Ugyen Wangchuck; and one of the *druk gyalpo*'s wives was a granddaughter of Ugyen Dorje as well as the prime minister's sister, as mentioned.

In 1907 and 1908, the representative of the Chinese emperor in Lhasa, whose power there was more imaginary than real, gave indications that Bhutan was considered under Chinese authority. Reacting, the British proposed a treaty with the new king, sweetening the proposal by increasing a subsidy started after nineteenth-century battles to define the British-Bhutanese border. The treaty's key clause said, "The British government undertakes to exercise no interference in the internal administration of Bhutan. On its part, the Bhutanese Government agrees to be guided by the advice of the British Government in regard to its external relations." The Bhutanese signed this without any qualms in January 1910. They wanted only to be let alone in their mountains, without concern for external relations. The treaty fell far short of those forced on the many *maharajas* on the Indian plains, who came under effective British control in most aspects of their rule.

After India became independent in 1947, it signed on August 8, 1949, a new treaty with Bhutan that contained the same clause on internal autonomy and external advice, only substituting India for Britain. India also promised to help in the defense of Bhutan and to continue subsidies to the small mountain nation with a primitive subsistence economy lacking modern sources of income.

The second *druk gyalpo*, Jigme Wangchuck, began to contemplate changes in the customary law and medieval administration practices that his father had left in place. Shortly after his son, Jigme Dorje Wangchuck, became *druk gyalpo* in 1952, he began cautious steps toward modernizing the system of absolute government. In 1953 he established by decree the *tsongdu* as a consultative body and conveyor of policies to the public. In 1956 he decreed the abolition of slavery, which had existed for generations of people captured from the Indian plains and used mostly as household servants. He did not, however, change the feudal system of villagers' being conscripted to carry out such work as maintaining trails, restoring flood-damaged bridges, and rebuilding fire-vulnerable *dzongs*.

This, then, was the situation when I met Jigme Dorje in March 1959. Within a week, Bhutan's situation began to change. The cause was the uprising in Lhasa against China's violation of its 1951 agreement to leave the Dalai Lama in control of Tibetan internal affairs.

The uprising and the unknown status of the Dalai Lama sent me up to the frontier seeking information. Moving between Darjeeling, Gangtok, and Kalimpong, I found Jigme Dorje in Kalimpong at Bhutan House, the lovely old stone home and office suite that his grandfather had built in his trading days. Jigme Dorje provided a few tidbits of information and generally useful background. The next time I saw him was in Calcutta the following August. The AP's new stringer, Subhash Chakravarti, had heard that Jigme Dorje was in town. We went to the apartment that he maintained there to interview him, me for the AP and Chakravarti for his primary employer, the *Times of India*. Our hope was to pick up fresh information about the Tibetan situation.

Jigme Dorje had little on that subject, but we came away with a better story. He told us that, as a result of the Chinese crackdown in Tibet following the Dalai Lama's flight, Bhutan had decided to close its northern border with Tibet. It had halted sales to Tibet of rice, wheat, vegetable dyes, brass utensils, and the other meager Bhutanese exports. Instead, it had accepted an Indian offer to build roads into the isolated kingdom from the south.

The decision, made by the *druk gyalpo* and agreed to by the *tsongdu* at a recent session, was a radical one. For decades, Bhutan had refused offers from British India to build roads up from the plains to the central valley heartland of the country. It feared disruptive Indian influences that roads would bring to a subsistence economy and sheltered cultural system. It also feared that land-hungry farmers would try to use roads enter the kingdom's sparsely populated southern regions. But now it was more fearful of the threat of Communist control from a China that had long claimed some historic authority over Bhutan and had destroyed the Buddhist governing system of Tibet. Chakravarti and I wrote articles disclosing the reorientation of Bhutan. Supplementing difficult mule trails with roads to India did not mean, however, that the kingdom was really opening its long-closed doors.

I kept in touch with Jigme Dorje later that year and early in 1960, seeing him whenever he came to New Delhi. As a result, when the *druk gyalpo* decided to invite a few journalists to publicize Bhutan's independent status, Jigme Dorje informed me as the first Westerner to hear about the trip. I told the *Times* of London correspondent based in Delhi, my good friend Neville Maxwell, and suggested that he ask to go. Paul Grimes of the *New York Times* was also invited as the third Delhi-based foreign correspondent. A few Indian journalists were also invited. The Bhutanese also invited a delegation from India's Parliament to visit Paro. Some five parliamentarians made the mule trip separately a day or two behind us and were in Paro most of the same days.

At the end of April, Neville, Paul, and I flew to a grass airstrip near Hassimara, a few miles inside India from the Bhutanese settlement of Phuntsholing. The settlement had just been established, with barracks-like buildings and a few open-front shops, to be the terminus for the first road that was beginning to be built into Bhutan. It sat just inside Bhutan, where the plains of rural north India met the Himalayan foothills.

A deputy of Jigme Dorje's showed us where the road was already being cut the first mile or two up into the "front range" of hills. Engineers from the Indian Army's Border Roads Organization were in charge, and they operated some earth-moving equipment, but much of the work was being done by hand. This involved conscripted Bhutanese villagers, the men wielding shovels, the women sitting by piles of stones hammering them into gravel. Some of the women had babies tied to their backs, some had toddlers playing in the dirt nearby. This use of peasant women was a common sight on road projects throughout India. But here in the hills, cutting roads was more difficult than in other areas for reasons that went beyond the gradient. The Himalayas are geologically new mountains and therefore unstable and subject to rapid erosion and landslides. Earthquakes occasionally shake the area as peninsula India continues to push into continental Asia, the tectonic movement that competes with erosion to thrust the Himalayas even higher. Building roads that snake into Bhutan, and then keeping them open despite erosion and landslides caused by monsoon downpours or earthquakes, plus other problems, was going to be a difficult job.

In Phuntsholing we became guests of the *druk gyalpo*. After a night in a barracks, we were driven early the next morning to a point where a number of mules and their handlers were waiting. Each of us was assigned a mule, our small, tin trunks were loaded onto other mules, and we were off, ascending into the jungle.

The mule is a stoic beast, seldom complaining as it labors up jungle trails. Passengers sit on simple saddles as the mules plod along. In the steepest places, trails switchback to maintain an acceptable gradient. Passengers ride up. But, when coming down a steep place, the rule is that passengers get off and walk, to ease the burden on the mule and ensure that it can keep its footing. Passengers usually take shortcuts straight downhill while the mule stays on the sloped trail. Our English-speaking guides were reluctant to translate some of the things the Bhutanese mule handlers said to their charges, especially those used when the mules were uncooperative, but we learned a few words of encouragement for the animals.

The Bhutanese government had a system of shelters one day's mule ride apart. We spent the first night in a jungle camp with a large open-air but screened wooden shelter, lit by kerosene pressure lamps. It was not until the end of the second day that we began to see signs of human habitation, including numerous Tibetan Buddhist prayer flags wafting good thoughts upward with every breeze. That was Chhukha Dzong, a small fortress on the river that drained down from Paro, with a small village and little terraced farming fields around it. It is only twenty miles as the Himalayan raven flies to the northeast of Phuntsholing, but by mule trail much farther. We slept in a bare room in the stone-walled old *dzong*. Its toilet consisted of a small space projecting out over the top of the wall that had a hole in the floor.

The next stop was another *dzong* at Kyapcha, and the final night on the trail was a camp at a place called Confluence, where came together rivers from Paro to the northwest and one from the northeast. By now we were above the jungle and into alpine terrain of conifers, flowering bushes, and some open meadows where cattle and yaks grazed.

Riding up the Paro River on the fifth day, we came upon a hundred or so people waiting in a meadow to greet us. They were led by Bhutanese officials in bright *ghos,* the wrap-around robes with very full arms, belted waists, and skirts going down to about the knees—the official dress of men in the kingdom. Some officials wore colorful boots up to their knees, some wore Western-style shoes and knee-length stockings, some were barefoot. Accompanying them was an honor guard in nineteenth-century uniforms of striped *ghos,* boots, metal helmets with topknots and cloth drapery that hid the ears and neck, swords, and shields of rhino leather with four metal studs and a sun and moon symbol. The welcoming party was completed by several dozen schoolchildren who sang national and greeting songs in Dzongkha. Each of the journalists was draped with a white scarf, the Tibetan Buddhist form of greeting.

The Paro *dzong*—formally, it is the Rinpung Dzong at Paro—was a massive rectangular stone building, 250 or more feet long by some 200 feet wide. Its whitewashed wall, sloped slightly inward like such buildings throughout the Himalayas, rose blankly for two tall stories of granaries and storerooms before a higher three stories have windows for monastery inhabitants. Inside was a large courtyard surrounded by carved wooden balconies. From the courtyard rose a central castle-like keep that stood another three stories higher than the wall, plus a shorter building near the entrance. The *dzong*'s back loomed forbiddingly one hundred feet or more above the river to the west. On the east side, the single entrance behind a moat and drawbridge that looked like it had not been raised in a long time faced uphill toward a small separate citadel on the skyline. The *dzong* dominated a seven thousand-foot-high valley of terraced fields perhaps three-quarters of a mile wide and curving irregularly for some eight or ten miles, typical of the fertile upper valleys that are the heart of Bhutan.

Down a trail below the southwest corner of the *dzong* was a cantilevered, covered wooden bridge across the river, named the Nyamai Zampa bridge. It had small fortified stone blockhouses at either end through which the trail passes. Just as the *dzong* we saw was a version rebuilt after a 1906 fire, the bridge that was there in 1960 was washed away in a flood nine years after our visit and a new, similar one was built. Few bridges in the high Himalayas last for the centuries that they look built to survive. Torrents of water from the breaking upstream of temporary dams, created by earthquakes or crumbling glaciers, are a regular hazard in the valleys, although also beneficial in coating fields with fertile mud.

A sizeable house, brightly painted with Buddhist symbolism, stood just outside and on the south side of the *dzong* entrance. It was the residence of the *druk gyalpo* when there with one or both of his wives. Women are not allowed to spend the night in the *dzong* because of its monastery status. Below the *dzong* and across the river on the bottomland was another building, the four-story, pagoda-looking Ugyen Pelri Palace built about 1930 by a grandson of Ugyen Wangchuck who was at the time the Paro governor.

Staggered downhill near the north side of the *dzong* entrance were six or seven houses, the nearest thing to a village in the valley. Made of stone, they had wooden shingled roofs with large flat rocks atop them to hold the shingles down in windy weather. Scattered around the valley were other houses, each situated amid its farm fields in the dispersed manner found in many parts of the Himalayas, where residences do not congregate into villages. These farmhouses were all two stories high. The ground levels served as barns to shelter livestock in the winter, their body heat helping keep the family warm on the second level—as well as providing interesting smells to which residents were obviously accustomed. The second floor in the houses we visited were all fairly bare, single rooms with areas for a cooking fire, bedrolls stored along walls, a few curtained-off corners, and simple Buddhist art.

Men were plowing small, separately terraced fields after the winter wheat crop had been harvested. In the two-crop system that made these valleys prosperous in a simple, subsistence form of agriculture, women were beginning to plant rice seedlings. Bending over, they thrust the shoots into the mud in those fields that had already been flooded with river water in preparation for the soon-arriving summer monsoon rain.

In this simple economy without towns, there was no spare space for visitors, no hotels or guest houses. Instead, the government ordered the valley people to build a special camp for the journalists and parliamentarians at the edge of the meadow across the bridge from the *dzong*. The temporary huts were made of woven bamboo strips, a common structural style. It was an ingenious area of clean, neat little buildings, comfortable in the pleasantly cool weather.

Nor did the economy produce goods for anything other than minimal personal needs. Such sparse imports as matches, tea, and kerosene for lamps were sold in a few open-front stalls open occasionally, but regular stores were lacking. When we visitors expressed interest in acquiring examples of local handiwork and other souvenirs, Jigme Dorje's attractive wife, Tessla, put out the word to valley people. Anyone who had homemade cloth, jewelry, or other items that they wanted to sell was invited to an impromptu bazaar that was set up near the *dzong* on our last full day there. This produced a nice selection of items. Tessla, the daughter of a Tibetan nobleman, also included in the bazaar craftsmen who showed how they worked silver, painted Buddhist icons, wove cloth, and made other local handicrafts.

In addition to casual meetings at the holiday of games and lama dances and on other occasions in the informal atmosphere of Paro, Jigme Dorje Wangchuck, the *druk gyalpo,* met with the journalists in the *dzong* for what might be called a press conference. First we exchanged the traditional Buddhist white silk scarves with him. Then, in fluent English, he discussed his nation's economic and political situation in realistic terms. His hopes for bringing Bhutan into the benefits of the modern world, while warily seeking to avoid the many problems of modernization, were stated eloquently. He was setting a clear direction but moving toward it with slow caution in order not to upset a still-isolated, scarcely educated populace, nor to allow exploitation of Bhutanese ignorance by outsiders.

The monarch's servants served us Tibetan-style tea, an essential element of good hospitality in these mountains. It is made with Chinese brick tea, lots of yak butter, a dash of salt, and a bit of soda. Nutritious, healthy, even enjoyable for people living at high altitude, it is—to put it politely—an acquired taste. Anyone drinking it for the first time should sip carefully, partly because it is usually served very hot, but mainly to avoid a tendency to gag or even to vomit. After stemming that initial reaction, I actually developed a taste for it.

At that time, Bhutan did not have a fixed capital. Following centuries of shifting leadership, the capital was wherever the *shabdrung* or later the current strongman was. The location of Paro in western Bhutan made it the most convenient place for foreign visitors to reach, so it became the temporary capital when appropriate. Modernization was going to require a more fixed address for administrative facilities, however. As part of India's aid for Bhutan to begin its first five-year development plan in 1961, Indian engineers started in 1962 surveying the eight thousand-foot-high valley around Thimphu, east of Paro by some fifteen miles as the raven flies, for the construction of a permanent capital. Partly built in traditional Bhutanese style, government buildings looking similar to old *dzongs,* it grew into a town similar to many in north India.

The *tsongdu* usually met sometime in late spring or early summer. A meeting seemed to have been scheduled while we were in Paro in order to show off the monarch's efforts to dilute his absolute rule by consulting representatives of the people. Both journalist and Parliament visitors were invited to attend a session.

The main hall of the Paro *dzong,* where the monastery's monks daily chanted their prayers, was used for *tsongdu* sessions. The members sat cross-legged on the long, low, rug-covered benches. They looked different from the monks that one sees at prayer in Tibetan monasteries because of their dress of brightly colored *ghos* instead of dull red religious robes, but somehow they also looked bigger, sturdier, and more weather-beaten. After all, these were the bosses of the many little valleys of Bhutan. Most of them had earned their right to be there not only by family ties but also by being tough outdoorsmen.

According to a translator, the discussion that morning was about expanding education and improving health care—no doubt, subjects carefully selected to give visitors good impressions. The *druk gyalpo* and his prime minister had a plan to use economic aid from India to replace monasteries' religious education with village schools offering basic reading, writing, and arithmetic skills, to spread health workers across the valleys, and to begin vaccinations. Schooling in Dzongkha or local dialects would be accompanied by the teaching from primary grades of English, which was considered the language of modernization.

In connection with the *tsongdu* session and our talks with the *druk gyalpo*, Jigme Dorje, and others, we learned of some general concerns of Bhutanese officials. One was the already-evident concern about developments in Tibet. Bhutanese officials were aware of old historic claims by Tibet to have some sort of suzerainty over their land and, in turn, Chinese claims of suzerainty over Tibet. In New Delhi, people had been muttering about rumors that the Chinese in Lhasa were talking about this. The border between Tibet and Bhutan had never been fixed in modern terms. Not until April 1984 did Bhutan and China hold direct talks on their border, but decades later nothing had been concluded.

These direct talks were part of Bhutan's emergence as a clearly recognized separate nation, no longer tied to India's apron strings. The process that Jigme Dorje had begun in 1960 on behalf of the *druk gyalpo* of winning international recognition for Bhutan proceeded slowly. India played the role of introducing Bhutan into the family of nations. It first sponsored Bhutan for membership in 1962 in the Colombo Plan, a British-led economic aid grouping for Asia. Then Bhutan joined the International Postal Union. Finally, in 1971, it became a member of the United Nations. India came, somewhat reluctantly, to accept Bhutan's interpretation of the 1949 treaty that seeking Indian advice on foreign relations did not obligate it to accept that advice.

Another concern was the growing number of Nepali Hindus living in the jungles of southern Bhutan and their increasing political assertiveness. Unlike the highland Bhutanese Buddhists, whose population apparently had remained fairly stable for centuries, the people of Nepal had a high birth rate and rapidly rising total numbers that caused them to expand eastward. When Ugyen Dorje became Ugyen Wangchuck's agent for southern Bhutan in 1900, he was given responsibility for settling Nepalis in southern Bhutan and levying taxes on them. They apparently were considered an economic asset. But by 1928 the second *druk gyalpo* had become aware of difficulties. The Bhutanese government seemed to have lost control over the combined influx of land-hungry migrants and the natural population increase of those already there. In 1958, the *tsongdu* granted citizenship to Nepalis already settled in Bhutan, who were known as *Lhotshampas*. The following year, further immigration was prohibited.

While we were in Paro, we heard vague references to a Bhutan National Congress, in a country that lacked political parties. It was circulating leaflets from an office in Siliguri, in India just southwest of Bhutan. The leaflets complained about the lack of rights for Nepali settlers and called for abolition of the 1959 prohibition of immigration. They also expressed resentment over conscription of Nepalis for road construction gangs, as Bhutanese villages were assigned quotas to provide road workers.

In addition to observing a *tsongdu* session in the *dzong*, we were given an extensive tour of the massive monastery-fort. From the courtyard opened simply furnished rooms in which monks worked and lived. A large, dim, smelly communal kitchen contained vast vats set atop stone fireplaces, with young apprentices at work preparing vegetables and doing other boring work under the supervision of grizzled old men. In the Tibetan system used there, youths often live for years in monasteries but then return to their farms rather than becoming monks. Those who stay divide into several categories, ranging from the more learned Buddhist teaching monks down through skilled artisans to simple support staff.

It was the artisans and the senior monks who were responsible for the many chapels that we visited. Most of these stuffy little rooms were dimly lit by candles or bowls of burning yak butter. Each had a theme of devotion to one aspect of the Buddha, who in the Tibetan form of the religion is manifested in many ways, some benign, some more militant or even threatening. One particularly gloomy chapel, for example, was devoted to a ferocious-looking form of Hevajra with his three bulging eyes and his crown of human skulls. Such statues incorporate a strong element of Tibet's pre-Buddhist *bön* beliefs.

Our hosts also arranged a mule trip up the Pa River valley to visit on a side ravine the most famous and most photographed monastery in the country. This is Taksang, a small group of buildings hugging narrow ledges high up a sheer cliff face, seeming almost to grow out of the cliff. Padma Sambhava, the legendary eighth-century Guru Rimpoche who consolidated Buddhism in the Tibetan region, was believed to have meditated in a tiny cave in the cliff face behind the buildings, getting there on the back of a winged tigress. One could see how a winged tigress would be an advantage for reaching the sheer wall. Leaving our mules in the valley, we climbed a hazardously narrow path cut up and around the cliff face to reach the dusty, deserted, and bare little rooms of the four-story monastery and its shaky little associated buildings.[3]

Jigme Dorje and his wife, Tessla, invited us one evening to dinner at his spacious bungalow that faced the Paro *dzong* from up the hillside on the opposite side of the valley. As the sun went down behind the hill back of the *dzong* and the sparse light of lanterns and candles came on in farm homes scattered along the valley, the pleasantly rural scene dominated by the castle-like *dzong* had a beautifully medieval air of meditative Buddhist calm.

After busy days in the Paro area, we started back to the Indian border. The monsoon rains had begun regularly to soak the lower jungles and us, and the leeches were out in hungry profusion. Whatever the difficulties, however, it had been a fascinating look at a medieval land on the eve of entering the modern world.

POSTSCRIPT

By the time I returned to Bhutan as a tourist in 2005, much had changed.

The meditative calm had not always remained. In April 1964, while Jigme Dorje was in Phuntsholing on business, someone fired a shot from nighttime darkness through a window. It killed the prime minister who had played a key role in beginning to bring Bhutan into the modern world. Four members of the small army being trained by India were tried and executed for the murder, but its roots ran deep into tensions within the royal family and resentment by some old-line officials over modernization.

An attempt to assassinate the *druk gyalpo* was made in July 1965 for murky reasons apparently involving his queens and a mistress. In 1972 heart trouble killed him. His seventeen-year-old son, Jigme Senge Wangchuck, succeeded him on July 24. The fourth *druk gyalpo* continued policies begun by his father. One was the cautious modernization of Bhutan in a way that emphasizes "gross national happiness." This modified Western economists' gross national product measurement of progress by output. Instead, Bhutan pays more attention to such things as literacy, immunization rates and availability of health care, infant mortality, protection from natural disasters, and other factors of importance to a still rural, agricultural people living in new towns and villages or on isolated farms.

Ensuring that Bhutan's traditional life is not warped by modernization, the government cautiously keeps out too many foreigners. The country has benefited from the help of a small number of foreign experts in fields ranging from medicine and education to forestry and dairy farming. But, while wanting to earn money from those who would like to visit its magnificent scenery and friendly people, it has been mindful of "tourist pollution" and problems with doped-up hippies that have afflicted such colorfully attractive countries as Afghanistan and Nepal. So it has limited visas to only about three thousand affluent tourists a year.

Jigme Senge Wangchuck furthered the devolution of power to the people, taking gradual steps into democracy at his own initiative. There was no public pressure, and changes were not greeted with enthusiasm by officials long accustomed to cooperatively following the lead of their popular ruler. The *druk gyalpo* worked with advisers to write a new constitution that established a constitutional monarchy, giving the *tsongdu* power to impeach the *druk gyalpo* and requiring him to retire at the age of sixty-five. It provided for a democratic two-party political system as the basis for an elected *tsongdu* of two houses.

In December 2005, at the age of fifty, Jigme Senge Wangchuck abdicated the throne to his son, Jigme Khesar Namgyel Wangchuck, for a fresh approach to the new governmental system. After parliamentary elections, the fifth *druk gyalpo* ratified the constitution in July 2008. The democratic instincts of our host in 1960 had been carried to completion.

The Nepali settlers came to be seen as a major problem. A key element was India's support for agitation by the growing majority of Nepalis in neighboring Sikkim against its traditional people, leading in 1975 to India's annexation of the little state. Although by then protected by its United Nations membership and other aspects of separate nationhood, Bhutan took this precedent as a warning of what might happen if the number of Nepalis continued to grow and eventually outnumbered the ethnic Bhutanese. After a 1988 census, Bhutan's government began requiring all inhabitants of the country to speak Dzhongka, to wear Bhutanese national dress, and to adopt other national customs. Nepali settlers began agitating against these rules in September 1990. What happened next is disputed, but the end result was that tens of thousands of Nepalis fled Bhutan. Some ninety thousand people ended up in eastern Nepal in seven camps run by the United Nations Office of the High Commissioner for Refugees (UNHCR). Most were still there decades later.

In October 2005, my wife and I flew into Bhutan's only airport, built in the 1980s in the Paro River meadow where the journalists had been welcomed in 1960. The valley had been extensively developed. Across the river from the Paro *dzong,* a town of some fifty shops, restaurants, car repair garages, and numerous houses now existed. On the hill across the valley from the *dzong,* where Jigme Dorje's house had stood in isolation, were a hospital, numerous houses, schools, and a few hotels.

As we drove to Thimphu, we could see that other areas once occupied only by farms and isolated houses now had villages. Thimphu itself is a busy town of some eighty thousand people. The first *shabdrung*'s old *dzong* presiding over a pastoral valley now faced the nucleus of a large government compound built in traditional Bhutanese style. Indeed, most houses outside Thimphu followed traditional designs as a result of the government's efforts to maintain the country's customs. But no longer were roofs made of multiple layers of wooden shingles held down by stones. As part of the official effort to maintain Bhutan's forests at more than 60 percent of total area, roofs are now decreed to be made of sheets of imported corrugated metal.

This determined effort to keep the traditions of Bhutan has enabled the Himalayan kingdom to maintain much of the charm that I had first seen forty-five years earlier.

10

MAIL FROM THE NAGAS

"HAS TODAY'S MAIL COME IN YET?"

The question asked privately among Western journalists did not have the usual meaning. No postman was expected to deliver letters to a group of foreign correspondents visiting the jungled hills of northeastern India where Naga tribes live.

This mail was a tragic record of the suffering of these people scattered along India's border with Burma (now called Myanmar). The mail was delivered surreptitiously at irregular intervals. It gave the correspondents an aspect of the story of Nagaland that we were not hearing from Indian officials on a tour that they conducted, or from the Naga spokesmen whom they delegated to speak to us while they monitored what was said.

This aspect was the cost to Nagaland's people of India's long efforts to suppress their guerrilla resistance to Indian rule. It was a disjointed account of their suffering in trying to reestablish the separation from lowland Hindus that they had enjoyed before the British, ignoring their objections, made their hilly homeland a part of India when London's Indian empire became independent in 1947.

The first mail delivery was made on our first afternoon there in December 1960. We were driving slowly in caravan through pedestrians in the crowded bazaar in Kohima, the hilltop capital of Nagaland. I was sitting in the right-hand front seat of an old jeep from World War II. Unexpectedly, someone thrust into my lap a cloth-wrapped package and melted into the crowd before I could turn around and get a good look at the messenger. I glanced at the Indian Army enlisted man driving the jeep, but he was too busy avoiding people in the street to have noticed. So I said nothing and covered the package with my jacket.

After dinner that evening, in one of the spartan rooms of the small military camp where we were being housed, I and a couple of the other foreign correspondents opened the package. It contained typed pages listing villages in Nagaland and names of people with the dates on which they had been brutalized or killed. Some poor-quality photos of burned huts and of simple wooden grave markers were included. The limited explanatory material indicated that these villagers were victims of the Indian Army in its campaign against the guerrillas.

Other mail deliveries elaborated on this suffering. Some of the Nagas presented by Indian officials as presumably loyal spokesmen made clear in only politely veiled terms their displeasure with the political status imposed by New Delhi.

The Indian government had long sought to hide or deny the way it was trying to suppress the guerrilla war and the public hostility that supported it. It prohibited foreigners from entering the closed area of Nagaland, which at

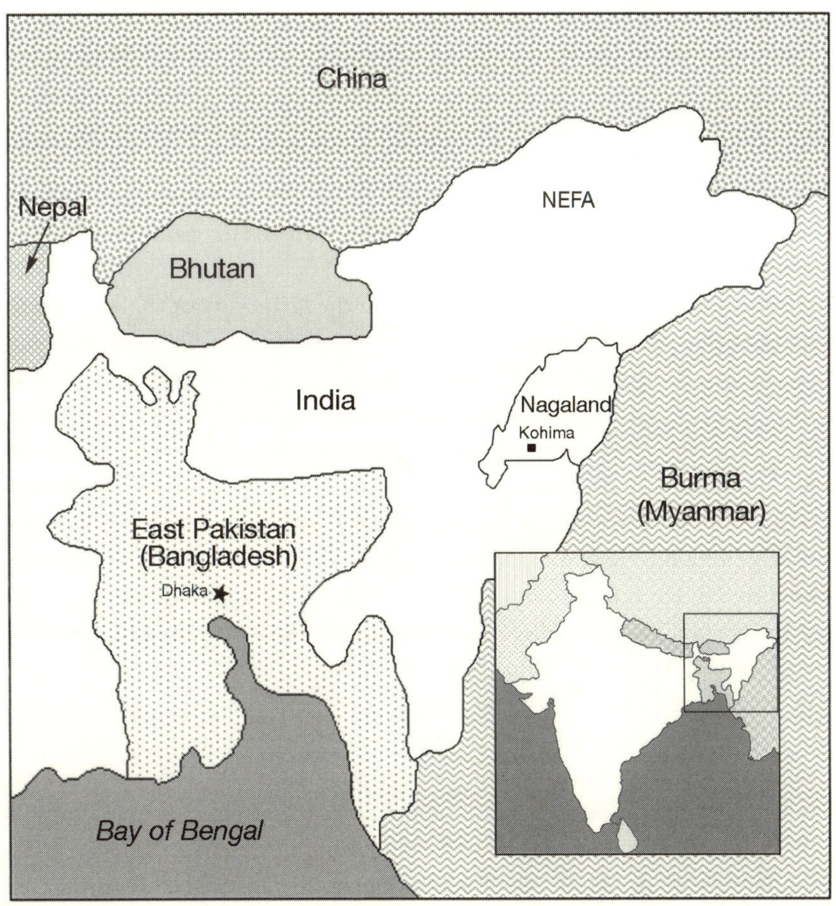

sixty-four hundred square miles is a bit larger than Connecticut. In the vacuum of independent news from the area, Naga spokesmen abroad charged that the government was guilty of human rights violations and atrocities in putting down the festering rebellion. Rumors that circulated in northeast India supported the general charge of brutality. Some reports of human rights violations were voiced in Parliament in New Delhi. Denials by officials there won little credence from outside observers.

In December 1960, the Indian government decided that the situation was sufficiently under control for it to invite some journalists on a conducted tour of Nagaland. The idea was that we would see how peaceful the area had become and would find that the Naga people accepted their role in the Republic of India. The visit was clearly intended to counter accusations circulated by Naga spokesmen abroad.

But the irregular mail and various episodes during our visit failed to serve the government's intended purpose. On the contrary, they tended to substantiate the accusations and rumors of human rights violations, to prove that armed resistance to Indian rule was going on, to show that the Naga people remained restive. They still do: more than half a century later, the tragedy of Nagaland that began in the middle of the twentieth century continues into the twenty-first.

Descendants of tribal people who had in the latter part of the nineteenth century been converted by missionaries from animism to Christianity—and had, mostly, been convinced to give up head-hunting—still wanted to escape control of the predominately Hindu government of India. They also hoped to block what they consider to be economic exploitation by lowlanders allowed into Nagaland as part of integration with India. Despite the very doubtful viability of their little landlocked and economically backward area as an independent nation, an immeasurable but significant number of Nagas sought to be set free.

The Naga hills rise in discordant folds from the lush plains of Assam to heights along the wildly rugged border with northwestern Burma that at one peak touches 12,600 feet. From farmed fields and lower jungles climbing steeply but irregularly into sub-Alpine forests, the difficult landscape has a defiant beauty. To the natural vegetation of Southeast Asia—majestic bamboo and stately palms and towering teak trees and sinuous vines and almost innumerable other varieties of rooted life—have been added imported fruit trees and other useful plants, plus poinsettias. When we were there the week before Christmas, poinsettias were in profuse blaze, their stalks festooned in seasonal glory with bright red leaves standing six or eight feet high around little hilltop villages. Most Naga villages are three thousand or four thousand feet above sea level.

Naga[1] is a collective name for fourteen or more Indo-Mongoloid tribal groups speaking mutually unintelligible Tibeto-Burman languages who live in a territory defined by British India. There are Aos and Angamis, Semas and Konyaks, Lothas and other distinct peoples, perhaps half a million of them. Anthropologists have found it impossible to distinguish Naga tribes from many other tribes in adjacent mountain areas of India and Burma. It is their history that in the past has separated them from others, now compounded by their demand for independence.

For centuries various Naga tribal war parties descended upon the Assamese plains to pillage and lop off heads. The heads from the plains, as well as those from warfare in the hills, were displayed in their longhouses as prizes of manly military virtue, and they possibly also had pre-Christian religious significance. The Nagas' reputation as headhunters had long made them feared among more peacefully sedentary plains farmers. But aggression was not all one-sided. At least one ethnic group from the Brahmaputra River plains below the Naga hills occasionally raided into the hills to capture slaves for agricultural work. Other than those raids, however, the wild and uninviting Naga hills were through history beyond the frontier of India's many Buddhist, Muslim, and Hindu empires.

Then came the British. Their East India Company began in the eighteenth century to build a business empire radiating from its headquarters at Calcutta. Commercial interests of the British in Bengal were early in the nineteenth century threatened by warfare upstream in Assam and by Burmese military attacks there. So, in the 1820s the British moved in to pacify the rich Brahmaputra River plains of Assam and add the region to their expanding Indian empire.

Imperial rulers in Calcutta and their bosses in London saw no commercial benefit in trying to extend control up into the hills east of Assam. What they needed, however, was to protect the lowlands from raids out of the Naga hills. Between 1832 and 1851, the British colonial government sent eleven punitive expeditions into the hills, only to be harassed by sustained and effective guerrilla attacks. The raiding continued. Here was a classic colonial situation: no matter how far imperial power advanced, trouble on a wild, unadministered frontier seemed to demand yet another advance in order to deal with the trouble, so an empire expanded virtually automatically until it finally butted against some other colonial power or consolidated state.[2]

The British decided that raiding by the Angami Nagas required the extension of colonial control to their part of the hills. But when, by 1878, they had been pacified and begun to pay taxes, they became vulnerable to attacks by the adjacent tribe of Sema Nagas, who were their historic enemies. So the British had to subdue the Semas, too. This process continued sporadically until British rule had been extended by 1890 over most of what is now Nagaland and some adjacent parts of India also inhabited by Naga tribes but now in other Indian states. As part of trying to check fighting, the British outlawed headhunting without eliminating it. Christian missionaries, primarily American Baptists, who began working in the hills in the 1830s were successful in converting most Nagas to Christianity, but not in stopping all headhunting.

British officials soon came to respect the independent, straightforward character of the Nagas. This was part of a colonial tendency to hold a higher regard for many of the hill peoples in such places as Nepal and Afghanistan than for most ethnic and linguistic groups on the plains of India, who were looked down upon as being more servile. Recognizing the militant hostility between the Nagas and plainsmen below their hills, the British administered Nagaland as virtually a closed area. They banned the lowland merchants and speculators who had spread behind British administrators into exploitive positions in much of India, modernizing economies in previously primitively agricultural societies at the cost of their economic independence.

The British also kept out of Nagaland the newly qualified Indians who helped the small cadre of colonial officials from the United Kingdom to run the empire. British officials and both British and American missionaries were the outsiders with whom Nagas became familiar and, eventually, comfortable. When the end of the British *raj* appeared on the horizon in the late 1920s, the Nagas began to worry about being placed under lowlanders' control in an independent India. A Naga spokesman reportedly told the British, "You are the only people who have ever conquered us. When you go, we should be as we were," that is, separate and independent. In London's grant to India of limited self-rule in 1937, Nagaland was left separate under direct British administration.

But as self-rule failed to satisfy the Indian independence movement, decisions had to be made in the rush to set India free in 1947 as two nations, predominately Hindu India and Muslim Pakistan. The British decided that landlocked little Nagaland, lacking much more than a subsistence agricultural economy, was not viable as a separate and independent nation. Nor was its independence likely to be accepted by Indians, who expected to inherit the whole span of empire not assigned to Pakistan. India's independence leaders, Mohandas K. Gandhi and Jawaharlal Nehru, had talked before 1947 of the right of peoples to choose whether to stay in India. In the confusion of independence, however, Nehru was determined to ensure that big, important states, such as Hindu-ruled but predominately Muslim Kashmir and Muslim-ruled but predominately Hindu Hyderabad, were part of India. The idea of a secessionist choice disappeared for them and for little Nagaland.

Naga aspirations of avoiding control by Hindu lowlanders came to be expressed by the Naga National Council (NNC), headed by Angami Zapu Phizo. On May 16, 1951, the NNC organized a plebiscite that, it claimed, showed 99.98 percent popular support for independence. This led to a showdown meeting between Phizo and Nehru in 1952. Reportedly angry, Nehru flatly rejected independence. India tightened its administrative control. In 1955, it expelled foreign missionaries, whom it accused of supporting a separatist conspiracy.

By 1955 Indian efforts to replace locally chosen councils of NNC supporters led to the beginning of violent resistance. The government's paramilitary Assam Rifles were sent into the hills, soon followed by regular Indian Army units. The whole Naga area was described as "disturbed" in January 1956, and shortly after that the army was put in charge of suppressing rebellion. This provoked the NNC into proclaiming on March 22, 1956, the establishment of a Federal Government of Nagaland for "a people's sovereign republic." It formed a Naga Home Guard. A sporadic guerrilla war was on.

Reports began to reach New Delhi of what one member of Parliament called "an orgy of murder" by security forces. Other reports told of crops being destroyed, villages burned, and people forcibly moved into what critics described as concentration camps in an effort to deny support to guerrillas. These reports obviously bothered Nehru's government. He frequently criticized Western nations that still hung on to overseas territories. Accusations that his government was conducting its own little colonial policy by bloody means in the Naga hills stung him.

By the end of the 1950s, Indian officials estimated that some fifteen thousand Naga guerrillas were opposing them. This was primarily based on counts of people missing from their villages. But the few Nagas with whom we foreign correspondents were able to discuss this subject laughed at the figure. They said the number of guerrillas was much lower, with supporters in administrative and logistic roles. Most independent observers agreed—but were unable to document—that Pakistan was helping Naga guerrillas in retaliation for India's refusal to negotiate the status of disputed Kashmir.

The costs to the Naga people of the guerrilla war in suffering and blood began to raise doubts about the possibility of shaking Indian control by fighting it. This led in the late 1950s to the creation of a Naga People's Convention (NPC) that could talk to the Indian government in a way the outlawed NNC and its leader Phizo, self-exiled to London, no longer could. The NPC, which also wanted a separate Nagaland, thus became the legal face of the NNC, with which it apparently was in contact. In 1960, in an effort to pacify the situation, New Delhi agreed to make Nagaland a separate state in the Indian union—its smallest and least populous. Statehood was formally established in 1963, after delays for constitutional and administrative changes.

Following the 1960 agreement on statehood, New Delhi seemed to believe that the Naga situation was sufficiently under control that it could disprove atrocity accusations and allay criticism from the few foreigners who were aware of the Nagaland situation.

In a public relations move, Nehru's government—and Nehru himself was always closely involved in such things—decided to allow independent observers, made up of a small group of Delhi-based foreign correspondents plus some Indian journalists, to visit the normally closed Nagaland. Indian officials clearly expected us to see that the Naga people accepted their role in India, and, at worst, only a small group of fanatics was still fighting a lost separatist cause. The foreign media were assured that we would be allowed to talk to anyone and see whatever we wanted, so that we could arrive at an objective judgment.

I was reporting in Nepal when my boss in Delhi, Wally Sims, got in touch to ask me to cover the Nagaland trip. That was fine. I was always eager to go look at new and different places. I flew to Jorhat on the Brahmaputra River in upper Assam. Indian and foreign journalists invited on the trip met there on December 14.

The other foreign correspondents were friends from the fairly close-knit Delhi press corps: Neville Maxwell of the *Times* of London,[3] Paul Grimes of the *New York Times,* Roger Bernheim of the Swiss *Neue Zürcher Zeitung,* and Rawle Knox of the *Observer* in London. Reuters news agency was also invited, but the British man-and-wife team running its Delhi bureau assigned their main Indian reporter, V. M. Nayar. Seven reporters for Indian media completed the press party.

The press party was conducted by the chief of press relations for the Indian government's Ministry of External Affairs in New Delhi, an unctuous man named P. N. Menon. He and Indian officials in Nagaland arranged a few meetings in Kohima with trusted people. These included some leaders of the Naga People's Convention, then headed by Dr. Imkongliba Ao. In the presence of guides, who were always at our elbows, NPC people quite expectably praised the impending arrangements for Nagaland's separate statehood and expressed appreciation for New Delhi's spending on roads and other infrastructure in their hills—sentiments for which the rebels of Phizo's Naga National Council had been denouncing them as quislings, traitors to the national cause.

In that first batch of documents thrust upon me in the bazaar, however, and in occasional muttered or whispered asides from people in crowded shops to the Western correspondents—not to the Indian journalists in our party—we began to sense hostility to the central government's rule. And, tellingly, we were not offered the opportunity to seek out people of our own choosing for private conversations, contrary to the assurances given in Delhi when the invitation was extended. Not only were we housed in a military area cut off from Kohima, so we could not walk around talking to people casually, but also our schedule for the entire visit was packed too tightly to permit time for seeking out private contacts. Several abrupt changes of plans from what we had been told were next days' schedules also suggested a desire of our hosts to block any plans to contact us by unauthorized individuals.

The first documents in the "mail" were carbon copies of carefully typed records of abuse at the hands of Indian troops. Identifying villages, dates, and usually the Indian military units involved, they gave numbered lists of names and ages of people with precise descriptions of beatings, torture, rape, and murder. Some villages had been burned. These did not seem to be protest memorandum prepared for the press. They were the documentation of Naga suffering prepared in order to remember a hard history, or perhaps to use if they ever attained a futilely hoped-for hearing at the United Nations.

We foreign correspondents let the Indian journalists with us see the documents that first night. We thought we were all there together for an independent investigation. We were soon disabused of this. It became obvious the next morning that one or more of the Indian journalists had reported the documents to our official hosts. This was the beginning of a split that led to some mild confrontations between the two groups of journalists, some arguments in the presence of officials and of Naga spokesmen to whom we were introduced, and to us foreigners no longer sharing the daily mail of documents with the Indian journalists.

After a day or two in Kohima, our guides took us out into the hills to meet leaders of some of the many tribes and to see ordinary people in some of the hilltop villages. We started along dusty roads slashed into mostly barren hills in a convoy of vehicles preceded and followed by truckloads of armed Indian troops. On the first of these trips, we had not gone many miles before the convoy halted at a place where the road slashed at an angle up a fairly open hillside. We could hear shooting ahead of us. We had been ambushed.

As we climbed higher into the increasingly jungled hills in the next few days, this happened several times. Every time, we would pile out of the vehicles, stand around by the side of the road for a while without seeking to take cover, then, when the shooting stopped, get back in and go on. No one seemed to be shooting directly at our vehicles, nor did the troops protecting us seem to find any targets off the road for return fire. Our hosts admitted neither to sustaining any casualties nor to having shot any attackers.

We foreign correspondents quickly concluded that the ambushes had been arranged by the NNC for our benefit. The NNC underground seemed to know our travel plans, presumably having been tipped off by some penetration of the Kohima administration. So they were able to stage noisy shows intended not to inflict casualties but to prove to us the existence of armed opposition that could harass Indian authorities with seeming impunity. The ambushes presumably were a second reason that our guides kept changing the itinerary.

At stops in the hills that obviously had been carefully arranged by the authorities, we met people who were introduced as leaders of various Naga tribes. With Indian officials looking on, they made short speeches of appreciation for the government's economic development efforts, such as linking isolated villages by motorable roads. But on the side, occasional whispered remarks to the Westerners indicated hostility toward our Indian hosts and their government's actions in Nagaland. And the mail continued to come in, small packets of material being handed on several occasions to one or another Westerner, usually me. Their main theme was the destruction of villages as people were concentrated in guarded areas—destruction often accompanied by rape and murder, the documents said—and the hardships of life in concentration camps a long walk from working farms. Photos showed burned villages and grave markers: white, wooden Christian crosses with names and dates on them.

Our escorts apparently had laid out a route that was intended to show us typical villages still existing on isolated hillsides amid regularly farmed fields or slash-and-burn areas of shifting cultivation. We could not, of course, tell just how typical these were. Several times, we were conducted on walks through villages. In one case, the convoy dropped us off on one side of a village and we were invited to walk through it to meet the vehicles at the other side, three-eighths or so of a mile away and several hundred feet lower. A smiling young Naga woman greeted us in English, but no one else was willing or allowed to speak to us. People just stood around watching as we walked. None invited us into their stilted, thatched homes, but Indian officials shepherded us through a couple of obviously preselected houses.

About halfway through this particular village, with poinsettias in tall red blaze, I had the bright idea—*I* thought it was a bright idea, anyway—of beginning to sing a Christmas carol. After all, it was just a few days before Christmas, and these people were all Baptists, courtesy of Western missionaries. The Naga villagers immediately picked up the song, singing in their own language as I sang in English. I began to feel like the Pied Piper as I strode through the village with an increasing following of people singing one carol after another in a medley of voices and languages. My Western colleagues were amused but did not join in. The Indian officials were not at all amused.

Their idea of keeping us busy was repeated shows of local culture, which varied from one tribal area to another. This meant tribal dances by men and women in the home-woven, distinctive bright color patterns of each different tribal group, and sampling of a weakly alcoholic home brew from rice known as *mudu,* the local version of beer.

Rawle Knox came up with a sarcastic poem to commemorate this way of diverting us from the promised opportunity to investigate local conditions and opinions:

> Dances and mudu, mudu and dances,
> That's how investigation advances.
> Mudu and dances, dances and mudu.
> Don't be obstreperous,
> Do as you should do.
> Mudu and dances, dances and mudu.

One of the more memorable of our tribal meetings was a nighttime gathering around a large campfire. Local leaders in the colorful garb of their tribe—woven shawls, short pants, and high stockings—were lined up along one side of the fire, other tribal members in a variety of clothes formed part of a large circle, and the journalists and Indian escorts were across the circle facing the leaders. In excellent English, a leader made a speech about how happy his people were to welcome such visitors. It was so nice to see white people again, he said, because his people had such good memories of the benefits that white men had brought to them. Now he wanted to honor the white men by giving them special tribal souvenirs of friendship.

This was a clear reference to we five Westerners, distinguishing us from the darker hued Indian journalists and officials. Embarrassed, none of the five moved, but Naga girls came forward to tug us out of the visiting group and urge us around the fire to their leaders. There, an aide handed the speaker elaborate bags hand-woven in that particular tribe's pattern. They contained samples of tribal crafts, he said, and he hung one around each of our necks.

Except that the one hung around my neck was surprisingly heavy. While the others had gotten crafts, I had also received a large delivery of the day's mail right in front of our unsuspecting Indian escorts. I straightened up without comment, we somewhat sheepishly thanked the leaders, and we walked back around the fire. After some tribal music, the function ended and we went to our vehicles. The Indian officials were muttering.

Two days later, after we had toured some other parts of the hills, meeting a variety of Indian-approved spokesmen, we passed back through the area of that firelight meeting. A delegation from the tribe was waiting at a dusty crossroads. When we stopped, our Indian escorts obviously knew what was about to happen. They gathered us around the tribesmen, who had a handful of woven bags similar to those that the Westerners had received. The same leader made another brief speech. He said that his tribe also appreciated their Indian visitors, meaning the journalists, and they wanted to give them souvenirs, too—as if they had just, somehow, been overlooked or forgotten in the darkness away from the campfire. It was an embarrassing moment for all. It seemed clear to us Westerners that the Indian authorities had read the riot act to the tribal leaders, coercing them to pretend that they appreciated Indian friendships as much as they did that of the British and missionaries.

The bundle of documents delivered surreptitiously at the campfire was the largest of all, but several others arrived in our remaining days in Nagaland. On almost all occasions, they were thrust on me. Why me, rather than one of my Western colleagues, was never clear. Perhaps it was because I was the tallest and therefore easiest to identify. The last mail came in shortly before we left Kohima, flying back to Jorhat and then Calcutta en route home to Delhi just in time for Christmas.

None of the journalists tried to transmit reports about the tour from the little Morse-key telegraph office in Kohima. We Westerners were a bit apprehensive about surveillance or even censorship in Nagaland, and even the Indian journalists waited until they had left to write accounts. Those I saw later in Indian newspapers mentioned signs of Naga unhappiness but did not make it sound as severe as had been my impression.

Overnighting at a hotel in Calcutta, I began writing my articles on the trip. In describing the materials recording the destruction of villages and the savage treatment of the Naga people, I referred in one article to my possession of records kept by Nagas. The reference to having documents was intended to substantiate my account, but it proved troublesome.

Early in the new year, after Indian embassies abroad had picked up the articles from various newspapers and cabled them to Delhi, Neville Maxwell told me that an official friend had told him the government was worried about what might become of the documents. They were thinking of taking legal action to get them from me. Rather than get into such a confrontation, and having already made as much use of the documents as I or the other four Westerners could in writing articles, Neville and I agreed that I should destroy them. I burned them in the tiny walled courtyard behind the AP office and passed word of their destruction back through Neville. I felt somewhat guilty in burning them, as if I were destroying something sacred to the embattled Nagas, but we had already done everything we could to publicize their situation.

The publicity embarrassed the Indian government. It probably led to some recriminations among the officials who had thought they would reap favorable reports from the foreign correspondents. If anything, the publicity reenergized spokesmen in Europe for the Naga independence cause. These included not only Phizo but also various human rights organizations and groups supporting ethnic and linguistic minorities in many countries.

The struggle continued. When Nagaland became a separate state of India in 1963, the head of its government, Chief Minister Shilo Ao, was soon assassinated. Those Nagas who staffed the new administration in Kohima were denounced by many as quislings. But the argument was made by some independent observers that such Naga participants in the new regime were simply patriotic realists, trying to make the best of Nagaland's difficult situation. Others suggested that some Naga civil servants may have been penetrations of the Indian-created regime to covertly aid the resistance

In following decades, Nagaland remained a disturbed area. Periodically, cease-fires occurred, and peace talks were held with the public face of the underground guerrillas. While guerrilla attacks became rare, public demonstrations and even riots against Indian control flared from time to time.

So the problem that we glimpsed in 1960 remained unresolved and, seemingly, unresolvable well into the next century. The Nagas have become one of many small peoples around the world, from Tibetans and Uighurs in China to several ethnic elements in Ethiopia to many others in many African countries and elsewhere, who to various degrees chaff at their status in larger states dominated by different peoples.

Indian Prime Minister Jawaharlal Nehru talking to the press during President Dwight D. Eisenhower's visit to New Delhi, India, December 1959; Bradsher, center, in bow tie.

Bradsher riding a mule into Bhutan, May 1960.

Foreign correspondents and Indian journalists with the *druk gyalpo* of Bhutan, Jigme Dorje Wangchuck, center, in Paro, Bhutan, May 1960; Bradsher on left end.

Bradsher trekking “behind the Himalayas” in Nepal, October 1961.

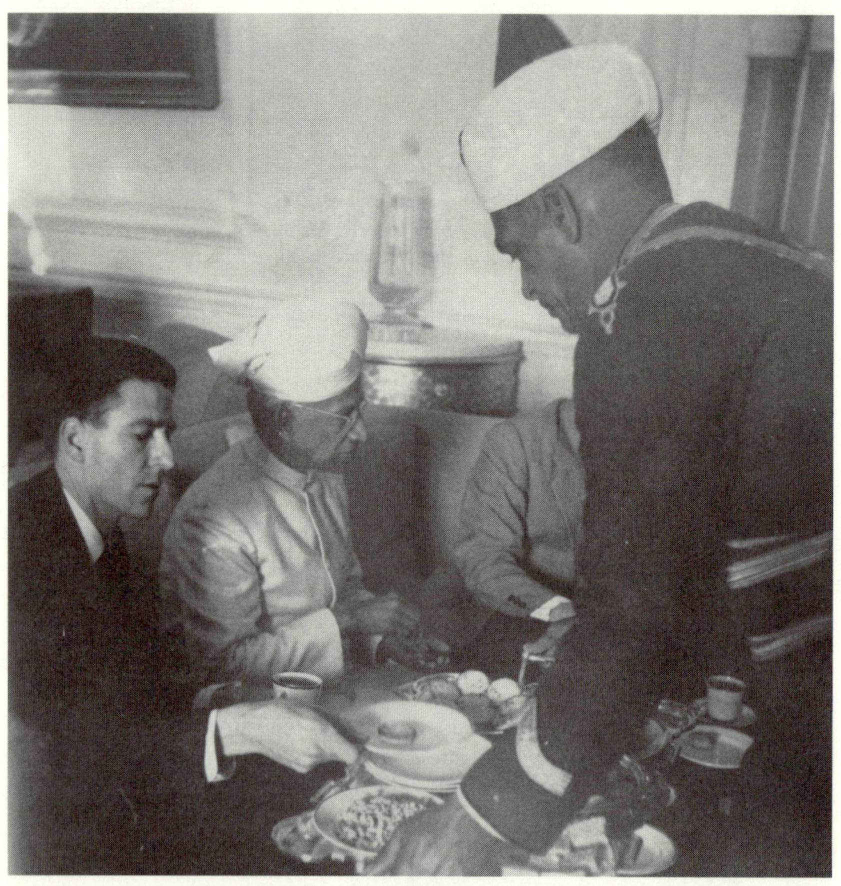

Having tea with Dr. Sarvepalli Radhakrishnan, president of India, while Bradsher was president of the Foreign Correspondents' Association in New Delhi, autumn 1962.

Wedding in old Delhi, India, July 25, 1963. Left to right: Delhi Administration's Deputy Commissioner for Housing (Loans) J. O. G. Russell, Mrs. Rangaswamy Satakopan, U.S. consular officer E. Paul Taylor, Bradsher, Monica Pannwitt Bradsher.

Monica with bodyguards assigned by the Wali of Swat, in Kalam, Swat, Pakistan, October 1963.

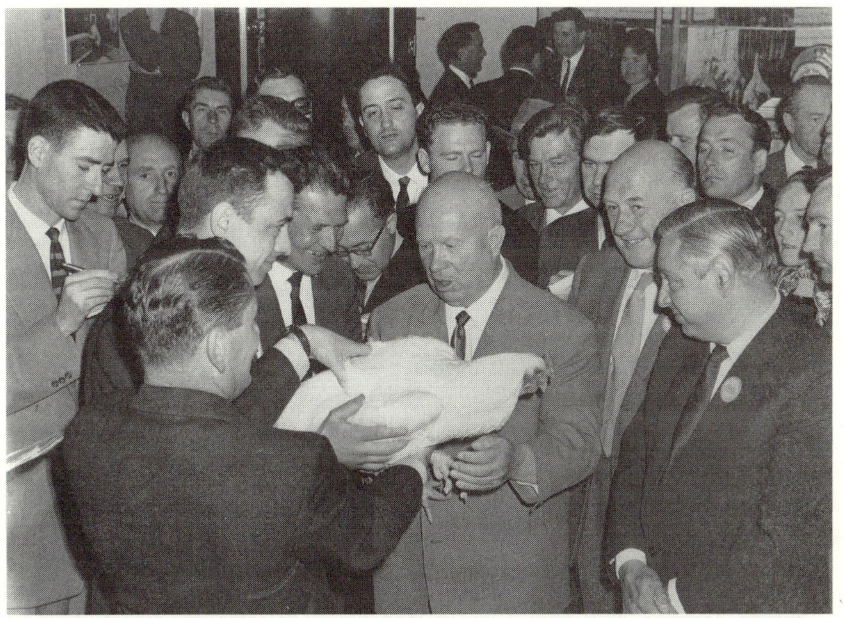

Soviet Premier Nikita S. Khrushchev at an American agricultural exhibition in Moscow, spring 1964; Bradsher taking notes at left.

Associated Press bureau staff in Red Square, Moscow, in winter 1965; Bradsher, hatless, in rear.

Visiting general manager of the Associated Press, Wes Gallagher, with Bradsher in Red Square, Moscow, winter 1965.

Bradsher, second from right, reporting Moscow airport welcome of British Prime Minister Harold Wilson, left, by Soviet Premier Alexei N. Kosygin, center, July 18, 1966.

Damage to Bradsher's Volkswagen caused by bomb that blew up under front right side, Moscow, December 25, 1967.

Bradsher shaking hands with Chinese Premier Zhou Enlai, Pokhara, Nepal, May 1960.

Bradsher on the Great Wall of China during President Richard M. Nixon's visit to the wall, February 1972.

Bradsher shaking hands with President Nixon in Hangzhou during his China visit, February 1972.

Bradsher and an Italian correspondent looking at downtown Saigon, South Vietnam, December 1972.

Current portrait of Bradsher.

11

LEFT OFF THE EARTH

AS THE LEADER OF THE UNITED NATIONAL PARTY, DUDLEY S. SENANAYAKE had just won a narrow victory in the March 1960 parliamentary elections, so I went to interview him on his plans as prime minister. A friendly, Westernized politician with whom I had talked several times while reporting the election campaign, he received me warmly at his bungalow on the outskirts of Colombo, capital of the Indian Ocean island then known as Ceylon.

Dudley, as everyone called him, and I talked about the prospects for his government with the UNP holding the most seats of any party in the 151-seat Parliament, but only fifty. Sitting across from him at an office desk, I noticed on it a small brass globe engraved with the outline of continents. When he excused himself briefly to take a telephone call, I examined the globe. To my surprise, its simple engraving did not include a number of islands—with Ceylon off the tip of India being one of those omitted. After his call, I mentioned this curiosity. Dudley laughed unconcernedly.

It was a relaxed country, sometimes. But Ceylon had endured turbulent times a few years before I began reporting from it in 1959 and even more bloody trouble after I left South Asia in 1964. On a return visit in 2007, I found that what was once a pleasantly sleepy Colombo had turned into an armed camp with barbed-wire defenses against suicide bombers, while politics had become increasingly intolerant. By then, the nation's name had been changed in 1972 from Ceylon, derived from a Portuguese explorers' word for "sky," to Sri Lanka, from the Sanskrit-derived words in the language of its Sinhalese majority people for "venerable island."

The people of the lovely tropical island about the size of West Virginia, rising from pristine beaches to jungled mountains, always seemed to me pleasantly hospitable. Almost three-quarters of the population are the world's only Sinhalese, most of them adherents of Theravada Buddhism, while some 7 percent of the islanders are Muslims and 8.5 percent are Hindu Tamils akin to the people of southeastern India. During my time there for the Associated Press, Ceylon had some impressive orators among its colorfully varied cast of politicians, good civil servants working for a democratic system, entrepreneurial merchants, and a solid economy based on exports of tea, rubber, and other crops, plus mining. Of all the lands given independence by European colonial powers after World War II, Ceylon was the first—and for several decades, only—one with an egalitarian-enough political system for governmental control peacefully to change hands through a fair election process.

Unlike on that little brass globe, the island was not omitted from the world known to the ancients. Its cinnamon reached Egypt as early as 1400 B.C., and King Solomon in the tenth century B.C. received its ivory and peacocks. Chinese trade goods passed through its ports long before the Portuguese entered the Indian Ocean in 1498 A.D. to take control of its coastal areas. By 1655 it became a colony of the Dutch, who lost it to the British in 1796. Under the British, Ceylon prospered. In the 1830s, the British instituted reforms that ensured the rule of law. They, along with American and other Protestant missionaries, began educating locals for administrative and professional work.

In 1931 Ceylonese citizens were granted the universal franchise, only three years after women began to vote in Britain and fifteen years before this was instituted in any other Asian colony. Local self-government prepared Ceylon for independence as a member of the British Commonwealth on February 4, 1948. After enjoying probably the highest living standards of any colony, it had the most modernized social and political system of any nation that became independent in the period after World War II, as well as an overall better-developed economy than other new nations.

Dudley's father, Don Stephen "D. S." Senanayake, was a leader of the island's independence movement. As the head of the United National Party, he became the free nation's first prime minister. When his father died after falling from a horse in 1952, forty-year-old Dudley succeeded him as prime minister for nineteen unsuccessful months before another UNP leader took over. But they represented the Westernized elite, and another party was able to marshal grassroots Sinhalese nationalism. This was the Sri Lanka Freedom Party, headed by Solomon West Ridgeway Dias Bandaranaike, who had defected from the UNP in 1951. In 1956, the SLFP led a coalition to victory in parliamentary elections, and Bandaranaike became prime minister.

Ceylon was run in the English language, which 95 percent of the population did not understand. The coalition campaigned for adoption of the Sinhalese language, Sinhala, which was used by 70 percent of the population, as the sole national language. This was quickly passed into law, to the disadvantage of the Tamil-speaking minority, although the government continued to operate primarily in English, which educated Tamils spoke. Rising ethnic tensions led in May 1958 to clashes between Sinhalese and Tamils in which some three hundred people, mostly Tamils, were killed. The Tamil language was then given some limited official use. However, lasting suspicion between the new nation's main peoples led two decades later to civil war—after my reporting time there, which proved to have been during a peaceful interlude.

From late May into July 1959, I made several trips from New Delhi to Kerala state at the southwest tip of India to report on agitation against the Communist government elected there in April 1957. During a lull in the Kerala trouble at the beginning of July, I went from there on my first visit to nearby Ceylon. At the time, a dockworkers' strike was causing trouble, and a long line of ships was stuck frustratingly and expensively at anchor off the port. The AP's stringer there was Denzil Peiris, the editor of the leading English-language newspaper, the *Observer,* and of a Sinhala magazine. Denzil gave me a good introduction to the complexities of Ceylonese affairs before I began interviewing people.

Two of them were civil servants whom I got to know well on repeated visits to Ceylon and who went on to major roles in the United Nations, testimony to the quality of the government's personnel. One was Hamilton Shirley Amerasinghe, a man known as Shirley who as a member of the nation's elite civil service wore many hats, including chairman of the government's Port (Cargo) Corporation seeking a solution to the strike. Another was an economist, Dr. Gamani Corea, who was then the secretary of the National Planning Council.

And I went to see Sir Oliver Goonetilleke. A civil servant who had worked with D. S. Senanayake for independence, he became in 1954 the first Ceylonese named as governor-general, Queen Elizabeth II's figurehead chief of state. A pudgy man with both a stutter and a lisp, he received me warmly in Queen's House at his desk with his back to the sea. We talked about reports of sporadic violence from the strike. He assured me that the situation was being brought under control. Then his phone rang. He picked it up, held it to his ear briefly, then stuttered and lisped, "They're defying the police? Rioting? We can't allow that. You must restore order. Crack down." After a brief pause as if listening, he added: "Shoot them." And he hung up. I was immediately suspicious. It was not the governor-general's role to give such orders. When I questioned Denzil later, he said there had not been any disorder while I was interviewing Goonetilleke. Denzil explained that the governor-general was known to have a button under his desk to make the phone ring in order to try to impress visitors with his decisive command of events.

Interviewing Prime Minister Bandaranaike took a bit more arranging. Finally, I was invited along with two other visiting foreign correspondents to meet him at his home. One was Tillman Durdin, an "old China hand" correspondent for the *New York Times* temporarily filling in at the paper's New Delhi bureau. The other was Cyril Dunn, the lean and scholarly Delhi correspondent for the respected London Sunday newspaper the *Observer.*

Bandaranaike, a somewhat craggy and ascetic-looking man wearing the simple cloths of a Ceylonese peasant, received us in a sparsely furnished room just off the front verandah of his private residence, Tintagel. We began asking questions about the strike and more general matters, such as the political situation as parliamentary elections approached and the nation's economic problems. The prime minister was somewhat evasive, somewhat windy in his answers, but the interview seemed to me to be about normal for a South Asian politician. Suddenly, Dunn jumped up abruptly, said he had to go, and rushed out. Bandaranaike was surprised, and Durdin and I were stunned. The interview continued without producing any significant news, but was worthwhile for a general overview of Ceylon's situation and a look at its leader. Durdin and I later ran into Dunn at a hotel. "He's mad," Cyril exploded. "Mad." Somehow, he had found Bandaranaike even more irritatingly evasive than we had.

On that visit and later ones, I came to know other political leaders. All were willing to receive a representative of the world's largest news agency, showing the hospitality of politicians that I found in other South Asia nations with a British tradition of open parliamentary systems. Two of them were the leader and deputy leader of the world's only active political party still proclaiming loyalty to the ideology of the old Bolshevik whom Stalin had had murdered in 1940, Leon Trotsky. Their Lanka Sama Samaja Paksava (Social Equality Party) was the island's first modern political party, founded in 1935 and becoming strong through trade union work for abused plantation laborers. The LSSP later split, some members becoming unquestioningly loyal to Moscow and becoming Ceylon's Communist Party, while the LSSP joined the Fourth International created by Trotsky in 1938. The LSSP leaders were Dr. N. M. Perera and Dr. Colvin R. de Silva. Both had imbibed Communism while obtaining higher educations in England. Both were spellbinding talkers, in both English and Sinhalese. Another leftist politician whom I met was Pieter Keuneman, who had become a Marxist at Cambridge and president of the Cambridge Union. He had become the Communist Party leader.[1]

The next time I was in Ceylon was different because of a saffron-clad Buddhist monk named Talduwe Somarama. On September 25, 1959, he waited patiently in a line on the verandah at Tintagel as Bandaranaike carried out the normal political duty of receiving constituents. When it came his turn, Somarama drew a pistol from beneath his robes and fatally shot the prime minister. Peiris gave the AP good reporting on this, but Wally Sims rushed down to Colombo to follow up on the story.

When Wally returned to Delhi, I went in early October to West Pakistan to report the beginning of the government's move from Karachi, planning to go to Rawalpindi, where it would be while a new capital was built nearby, Islamabad. But, after writing about the first officials' departures and consulting Wally, I flew from Karachi to Colombo. The question of how to handle Bandaranaike's murderer was exciting Ceylon. Bandaranaike had suspended capital punishment, but there was a strong popular demand for the execution of Somarama and of two senior Buddhist priests of a temple near Colombo who had put him up to the assassination. The priests reportedly were angry that the prime minister had refused to award business contracts to a company of theirs.

Members of the deceased's SLFP introduced legislation in Parliament to make the death penalty retroactive. This was controversial. From a perch high in the steep gallery overlooking the floor of Parliament, I covered the debate on the law, conducted according to British parliamentary tradition and almost entirely in English. In many parts of the world, capital punishment was by the mid-twentieth century evoking strong emotions and strong language for and against. In the debate, LSSP members were against the retroactive law on moral grounds. Speeches by Perera and de Silva reached some of the greatest heights of oratory that I had ever heard. Nonetheless, the law passed. Somarama was hanged in 1962, reportedly after converting to Christianity. The two senior priests were given life imprisonment after it was realized that sloppy legal drafting had made the law apply only to an assassin, not to those involved in conspiracy to assassinate.

While interviewing various politicians, I asked to see the new prime minister, a cabinet deputy of Bandaranaike's named Wijayananda Dahanayake. An assistant said he was very busy but would see me at 5:30 A.M. before driving south to his constituency in Galle. Getting up early, I did not find an impressive leader. But he lasted long enough to lead the SLFP into the March 1960 elections. Many party members preferred, however, to take advantage of the Bandaranaike name by rallying behind his politically inexperienced widow, Sirimavo Ratwatte Dias Bandaranaike, known as Sirimavo.

Covering the election on my third visit to Ceylon in eight months, I got to see something of the island outside Colombo. Neville Maxwell rented a car, and he and I took the lovely drive up into the mountains to Kandy to report on a political rally there. On my own, I went around interviewing the growing number of contacts in my Ceylon address book and adding new ones. Among the new ones was Junius Richard Jayewardene, known as J. R. Such keen observers of the Ceylonese political scene as Denzil credited J. R. with the grassroots rebuilding of the UNP while Dudley sulked after the SLFP victory in 1956. Talking with J. R., I got a better sense of Ceylon's problems and possibilities than I did from Dudley.

Together, they enabled the UNP to win the March 1960 elections with 29.4 percent of the popular vote to the SLFP's 20.9 percent, taking a third of the seats in the new Parliament. As British tradition required, Goonetilleke called on Dudley to form the new government. It did not last long. The disparate opposition parties—the SLFP, LSSP, Communists, and a Tamil-based party—quickly combined to overwhelm Dudley's minority government. As a result, another parliamentary election was held in July 1960, which Denzil covered for the AP because Wally and I were busy on other reporting. The UNP won a majority of the popular vote but, against an electoral combination of other parties, this yielded only thirty seats. The SLFP, now led by Sirimavo, won seventy-five.

She became the world's first woman prime minister. She was also the forerunner of at least six other Asian women about whom I later wrote who achieved national leadership because of their late husbands or fathers rather than earning it on their own.[2] After a marriage of two aristocratic old Sinhalese families, Sirimavo was primarily a housewife until her husband was assassinated. While her competence to run the country was widely questioned, the appeal of the two families and her husband's populism in courting rural Sinhalese voters, plus her own growing toughness in political infighting, made her an increasingly strong prime minister. Many of her policies, such as nationalizing key economic sectors, dropping English as an official language and ordering all government business to be conducted in Sinhala, and allying the SLFP with the LSSP, led to the fall of her government and the return to power of Dudley's UNP in 1965.

Several other visits to Ceylon during Sirimavo's premiership produced reporting on a variety of subjects. One that intrigued me was the island's rapid population growth as a result of good health programs. A population a bit under 7 million at the time of independence had grown to about 9 million when I wrote about the subject less than fifteen years later. Half a century after independence, it topped 20 million.

On another visit in August 1961, I drove around the island primarily to take color photographs requested by the AP's London bureau. Unfortunately, London photos reported that my cheap AP camera's light meter seemed to have been defective. Most of the photographs were not usable. It was a delightful trip, however, and yielded a few feature articles. And it left me with ideas two years later of where to go on part of my honeymoon. After I'd done a little reporting in early August 1963 on a new national budget and political matters, my bride and I drove around the island.

As Denzil had advised us to do, we arrived in Kandy in the central highlands for the full moon that signaled Esala Perahera, a festival combining a third century B.C. ritual to bring rain and a celebration of what is held sacred as a tooth of the Buddha. The tooth was said to have been saved from his funeral pyre in 543 B.C., smuggled to Ceylon in the fourth century A.D., and entombed in a Kandy temple, where its possession gave the king authority to rule the island. From the balcony of an old British merchants' club along Kandy's main road, we watched one night the torch-lit parade of some one hundred gaily decorated elephants escorted by fire dancers as the tooth was conducted ceremoniously through the town for public veneration on its only outing of the year.

That was my last reporting trip to Ceylon. After it had become Sri Lanka, it spiraled down into civil war as fanatical Tamils sought to carve out an independent state. The war was finally brought to a bloody end in 2009 by a government that became increasingly dictatorial. But during my time reporting there, a stimulating example of democracy in action was offered by a lovely island so easily left off globes of the earth.

12

TIGER HUNTING WITH QUEEN ELIZABETH

ONE OF THE HIGH POINTS OF KING GEORGE V'S VISIT TO HIS BRITISH Indian empire in 1911 was a side trip to hunt wild game. Accompanied by a large entourage, the king visited the separate, but British-influenced, nation of Nepal. He was a guest of the Rana family of hereditary prime ministers who controlled the Himalayan country while keeping its king as a figurehead.

George V spent two weeks in Nepal's Terai, the jungled area at the northern edge of the vast Indian plains just under the first folds of the upthrusting Himalayan mountains. In elaborate tent encampments in the wilderness, the royal party dined from fine china set on white linen. The king, a crack shot from atop an elephant or in a blind, bagged twenty-one Indian tigers, eight one-horned Asian rhinoceroses, a bear, and miscellaneous other game.[1] In those days, such game seemed plentiful, shooting them was considered the manly thing for European royalty and colonialists to do, and stuffed animals were prominent decorations of many palaces and upper-class homes.

Half a century later, George V's granddaughter went tiger hunting in Nepal. Her overnight trip to hunt in the Terai was one of the more interesting episodes in Queen Elizabeth II's 1961 tour of India, Pakistan, and Nepal.

During most of her six-week-long wanderings around South Asia, I traveled in the press group with this royal circus to report and, whenever possible, take photographs. The tour involved stultifying protocol sometimes relieved by casual conversation, boring set-piece formal occasions, some interesting sightseeing, a couple of trips to the racetrack, and a lot of dubious activities among journalists primarily from the London media.

More excitingly, it gave me a chance to participate in what was probably the last great royal hunt for some of the diminishing number of tigers in the world. A journalism colleague and I were atop the "press elephant," standing four or five elephants from the royal party in a circle of perhaps a hundred mounted pachyderms that trapped a doomed tiger. Behind us circulated a "bar elephant" so an attendant could refresh the hunters. Later we plunged through swamps atop our elephant to follow a hunt for the Asian one-horned rhinoceros. It made for an interesting day, and a controversial one.

Reporting tours of South Asia by foreign leaders was a routine requirement for the Associated Press. As the junior American correspondent in AP's New Delhi bureau from my arrival in February 1959 until I became bureau chief in December 1961, I got lots of experience and saw a lot of the region while following around such people as President Dwight D. Eisenhower, Vice President Lyndon B. Johnson, Soviet premier Nikita S. Khrushchev, Chinese prime minister Zhou Enlai, Indonesian president Sukarno, Egyptian president Gamal Abdel Nasser, then Japan's crown prince, later emperor, Akihito, and numerous other lesser lights.

Lyndon Johnson came to India and Pakistan from visits in Southeast Asia in May 1961, just four months after he had taken office as John F. Kennedy's vice president. At the time, the North Vietnamese effort to take over South Vietnam behind a veil of a supposedly indigenous southern insurgent force, the Viet Cong, was just a small cloud on the horizon of the new Kennedy administration. Johnson's trip was, secretly, primarily intended to evaluate the Vietnam situation and attitudes of other Asian countries toward it. His earlier stops in Southeast Asia had been accompanied by rumors that he was covertly seeking help from U.S. allies to bolster the Saigon government so that the United States' own involvement could be kept limited. Pakistan was an ally as a member of the Southeast Asia Treaty Organization (SEATO), established in 1955 to rally countries believed to be threatened by Communist dangers.

In Pakistan's main city, Karachi, Johnson talked with President Mohammad Ayub Khan, the career soldier who had seized control of Pakistan in 1958. At a reception for Johnson that night, a few of us reporters who knew the blunt-talking Ayub gathered around him in the garden of his official residence as Johnson stood nearby. What was the point of Johnson's visit, I asked. Was there a Vietnam angle? Ayub replied straightforwardly that Johnson had asked him to send Pakistani troops to South Vietnam to train, advise, bolster, and generally help improve the morale of Saigon's forces as part of SEATO support. But, Ayub added, he did not think this was a good idea, and Pakistan did not want to get involved in such an unclear, distant situation. Johnson, who had edged closer to hear this exchange, blanched noticeably. When we went to him for comment, the usually garrulous vice president refused to talk to us and went inside. But quoting Ayub to reveal the secret purpose of Johnson's trip—and the Pakistani rebuff—made an important story.

Queen Elizabeth was making the first monarchial visit since Britain divided its Indian empire into independent India and Pakistan in 1947, indeed, the first British royal visit to India since George V's. Three years after London relinquished power, India abandoned the Commonwealth system of using the British monarch as the formal head of state. It chose instead to have its own president as the figurehead for a parliamentary system then headed by Prime Minister Jawaharlal Nehru. But affection for the British royal family remained strong in India. In preparation for Elizabeth's visit, London journalists generated interviews with wizened old Indian villagers whom they quoted as believing Queen Victoria or some descendant of hers was still their ruler. So the visit was anticipated with great enthusiasm.

One place where both Eisenhower and Elizabeth drew crowds was Connaught Place, at the commercial center of New Delhi. Police had lost control of the crowds, which blocked the road around the large circle, when Ike arrived in December 1959. For Elizabeth thirteen months later, they kept the road open as multitudes cheered her motorcade. Riding in an open press car just a few vehicles behind the queen and her host, Prime Minister Jawaharlal Nehru, I had a good vantage point for taking photographs of them and the crowd that were widely used in British and other newspapers.

That was, however, the beginning of trouble over my taking photographs during the tour. As a reporter who also took some pictures, I was routinely assigned with the writers in motorcade vehicles and positions at various events, while the gaggle of photographers from London newspapers had their own separate vehicles and positions. Occasionally, as during the circling of Connaught Place, my location turned out to provide better vantage for pictures than the location of the photographers, who were usually not as close to the queen. They had fancy cameras with various lenses, while I had just a simple fixed-lens reflex camera, but, as in real estate, location was what counted. My Connaught Place pictures got better usage in some London newspapers than their own staff photographers' shots.

Among the number of photographers from London was a staff photographer for United Press International. In an unusual move intended to limit expenses in covering Elizabeth II's tour, he was working jointly for UPI and the AP, normally bitter competitors in news photographs as well as reporting. Any pictures I took were just supplemental to shared photos that AP got from the UPI professional. This gave the AP an edge of something extra and different. As the royal tour went on, anger grew among photographers from London newspapers because I was occasionally producing more interesting pictures. The UPI man valiantly supported my right to take pictures in addition to reporting. Nonetheless, I had to live with a lot of muttered hostility from London photographers, a few confrontations more direct and angry than merely muttered, and their occasional efforts to block my view or otherwise spoil my photos.

From its beginning in New Delhi, the royal tour made the standard tourist triangle trip. This meant a visit to the Taj Mahal in Agra, south of Delhi, and to Jaipur in the desert state of Rajasthan to the southwest. The Taj visit was the standard look at that magnificent white marble tomb that I visited repeatedly with foreign visitors. But the Jaipur visit was made special by a revival of the kind of spectacle that George V or earlier monarchs might have seen there. Atop an elephant, Elizabeth rode into the Ram Bagh Palace of the *maharaja,* Sir Sawai Man Singhji Bahadur the Second, up the long, sloping drive past servants wearing traditional past-century uniforms and holding torches at twilight, and through a huge gateway in the massive walls.

Another traditional way to entertain visiting royalty was a tiger hunt in the low, dry jungle terrain in eastern Rajasthan. Journalists were not allowed. We were briefed later that the queen's consort, Prince Philip, had shot a tiger, with pictures provided by a royal photographer. This raised a great hue and cry back in Britain from the increasingly large number of people criticizing blood sports. Not only was it a barbaric throwback to olden times to go out and shoot tigers, they protested, but also the number of tigers in India was declining rapidly. In fact, tigers were becoming an endangered species in Rajasthan, a result of a combination of outside hunters and a growing population's turning tiger terrain into farmland.

After a few other quick stops in north India, the queen went to Pakistan before coming back to see more of India. Her India visit was divided because of Pakistan's observation beginning February 16 of the Islamic religious period of Ramadan. This is a lunar month when all good Muslims are obligated to abstain from food, drink, and sexual activity from the time in the morning when it becomes light enough to distinguish between a white thread and a black one until evening when it becomes too dark any longer to distinguish. Since royal visits revolve around such social events as lunches and teas, it was not reasonable to schedule Elizabeth's visit to Pakistan during Ramadan. Therefore, after beginning in India, her tour took her to Pakistan just before Ramadan and then brought her back to finish seeing India and also visit Nepal while Pakistanis were fasting.

Although Wally Sims assigned me as the primary person to cover the tour, he chose to cover the West Pakistan part. Then I picked up the royal party in Dhaka, the capital of East Pakistan. From there we returned to India. In Calcutta, capital of Britain's Indian empire in its Victorian heyday, the highlight for the horse-loving queen was a visit to the racetrack. Then on to South India, beginning with Bangalore.

A Bangalore reception was held in the delightfully warm, dry, and sunny winter weather in a large garden studded with palm trees. While the queen sat at a table in the shade of a small pavilion, "toddy-tappers" demonstrated how they scurried barefoot up palm trees to make an incision and draw sap for fermentation into a popular, mildly alcoholic drink known as toddy. Standing off to one side, I noticed that under the table the queen has slipped her shoes off to rub her stocking feet together. I mentioned this in my report on the reception and later received a cable from AP's London photo desk asking for a picture of the queen with her shoes off. But the little reflex camera that was all the AP ever provided did not have the long lens needed for a closeup, so I had not tried to take a picture. The tour photographers had not noticed the shoeless feet.

From south India and a visit to Bombay, including its racetrack, the traveling circus went north to Nepal, its final stop. The queen became a guest of King Mahendra Bir Bikram Shah Dev. From Kathmandu, the royal party flew down to the Royal Chitwan National Park in the Terai jungle. Facilities in the jungle for the royal hunting party were limited, so the mob of journalists could not follow the queen there. British press officers accompanying the tour followed normal procedure in such situations by designating news agency correspondents who write for all media to handle "pool" coverage that would be made available to individual newspapers' and other media's correspondents. This meant that Sidney Weiland of Reuters and I, the only agency reporters on the whole tour, would go on the tiger hunt while other journalists remained in Kathmandu awaiting our reports as the basis for writing their accounts. Similarly, one photographer would take pictures that would be distributed to all the other photographers.

When the British photographers heard that I was going, they raised a fuss with the press officers. All their accumulated hostility to my opportunities to take photos that they missed came out at an angry meeting. I must not be allowed to take pictures on the hunt, they insisted, or that would break the pool arrangement. As the price for going, I had to agree to leave my camera behind when we flew to a grass runway in the national park.

A tented encampment had been erected there. Arrangements for the overnight stay in the jungle were even more elaborate for Queen Elizabeth II than for King George V. In addition to a bedroom tent, her enclosure included a flush toilet installed in an attached bathroom tent. Others had to make do with latrines. While the queen and Prince Philip slept, Nepali workers staked out a goat in an area of trees and high grass a mile or so way. The goat's bleating attracted at least one tiger, who enjoyed what was intended to be its last meal.

At dawn, the queen doubtlessly dined royally, while the rest of us enjoyed a substantial buffet in a dining tent. During breakfast, word spread that, unfortunately, Philip had accidentally cut himself sometime recently and was suffering from an infected trigger finger, or a boil, or something. He would not be able to shoot. When Philip turned up with the queen to mount their elephant, yes, remarkably, Philip had a large white bandage around his right hand and, just to be sure the point was clear, a sling to hold up his arm. Tough luck! But the more cynical of us assumed this misfortune had more to do with the reaction back home to his shooting the tiger in Rajasthan than any infection. The doctor in the royal party refused to shed any light on the prince's problem.

Instead of Philip, Sidney and I were told, the hunting honors would go to the senior British government official accompanying the royals. This was the foreign secretary, Sir Alexander Frederick Douglas-Home, the fourteenth Earl of Home, a rather effete-looking example of generations of English nobility's inbreeding.

We all mounted our assigned elephants. Sidney and I sat cross-legged on the small wooden howdah mounted on the press elephant behind its mahout, or driver. More than one hundred tame elephants, both the kind that haul timber from forests and do other jobs and those few especially used for hunting, had been rounded up for this occasion. Those on which the royal party was mounted ambled through yard-high grass to the area where beaters had driven at least one tiger and formed a large circle around the area, with a diameter of perhaps one hundred yards. The royal party was concentrated on one side of the circle, with elephants ridden only by their mahouts forming most of its circumference. Queen Elizabeth and Prince Philip's elephant, with an umbrella-shaded sofa on the howdah, was accompanied by a senior Nepali official to give explanations and translations. Lord Home was on an elephant that also carried a Royal Navy officer serving as his aide. Sidney and I were on their left with a good view of the proceedings.

The baited tiger, a large example of such carnivorous cats, had been trapped by the elephants, which tigers instinctively fear and will not challenge. But it was virtually invisible down in the brown grass, its striped coloring helping to camouflage it. Beaters on elephants inside the circle moved across the large space making noise, stirring the tiger up. The beast bounded across the circle, seeking to escape the beaters but halting when coming to a line of elephants. This gave the hunting party brief glimpses as it dashed back and forth, increasingly frenzied. But hitting a bounding tiger with a hunting rifle was not easy, as Lord Home quickly demonstrated.

A first-class cricket player in his youth, the foreign secretary was not a first-class shot. Time after time, the tiger was flushed into view, Home fired, and the unhit tiger disappeared again into the tall grass. After this happened an embarrassing seven or eight times, Philip signaled to an aide on another elephant to approach and said something to him. The aide rode over to Home's elephant and said something. The word was then passed to the press elephant that the treasurer of Philip's household, Rear Admiral Christopher Bonham-Carter, and the queen's private secretary, Sir Michael Adeane, would also participate.

The next time the tiger appeared, three shots rang out. The tiger fell. Home was officially given credit for killing it. While an elaborate buffet lunch was served in a shady spot nearby, we all got the obligatory opportunity to admire the tiger, if not the prowess of the foreign secretary who was photographed by it.

Then we mounted our elephants again for the afternoon hunt: "the greater Asian one-horned rhinoceros," also an endangered species. Poaching for the horns, believed by Chinese and some other East Asians to have aphrodisiac qualities, had reduced the number in Nepal to about one hundred at the time of the queen's hunt, although India had many more in a reserve in Assam that I had visited by elephant in 1959.

Vectored by Nepali gamekeepers on their own elephants, we swayed slowly and ponderously through a half mile or so of jungle to the edge of a swampy area. Whether a rhino had been somehow baited into the area was not clear, but, after some mucking about, one was found on low, marshy ground. Someone in the royal party of lesser rank than Lord Home managed to shoot it, rhinos not moving very fast and therefore being easier targets than bounding tigers.

The press elephant was close enough to this action for Sidney and me to see what was happening. What we also saw was that after the rhino toppled over dead, two young rhinos appeared from the brush somewhere nearby, went over to nuzzle the body, then fled squealing back into the undergrowth. The hunter had killed a mother rhino. The furor back in Britain over the killing of a tiger in Rajasthan was mild compared with the outrage of the anti-blood-sport crowd over the slaughter of a mother and the orphaning of its children.

The British press officers had arranged for a report on the day's hunting, written jointly by Sidney and me, to be transmitted to Kathmandu. We composed our dispatch back at the jungle camp. When it reached Kathmandu, it was turned over to the press party as raw material for them to write their own dispatches, as well as being cabled on our behalf to the AP and Reuters.

After the royal party flew back to Kathmandu, King Mahendra gave a formal dinner for the queen. At the time, he was the absolute ruler of Nepal. His father had, with India's help, overthrown Rana family rule a dozen years earlier. In the 1950s, Mahendra sought the appearance of democracy by allowing political parties to function, but he maneuvered the many squabbling parties into canceling each other out and leaving real power to himself. Apparently confident that this would continue, he held parliamentary elections in 1959. To general surprise, the Nepali Congress Party headed by B. P. Koirala won a strong majority in Parliament, and the king had no choice but to make him prime minister. Koirala quickly proved to be a dynamic leader whose efforts to revitalize the backward kingdom attracted world attention. The attention to Koirala lessened the perceived importance of the king, a poorly educated man who had been raised in the confines of the palace. Jealous of his prerogatives, the king staged a royal coup on December 15, 1960—two days after I had had another lengthy interview with Koirala and then left Nepal for Nagaland. Mahendra had Koirala locked up on vague and untrue charges of leading Nepal toward Communism.

Two months later, the formal dinner for Queen Elizabeth was given in Singha Durbar, the huge, rambling, four-story main government building with a few decorative public halls along the front and dingy, rundown, even nasty offices extending around two courtyards in the rear. According to the usual bureaucratic form, the queen's banquet speech had been written by the British career foreign service officer who was serving as Her Majesty's ambassador in Kathmandu, Leonard A. Scopes. In it, the queen praised Mahendra for leading his nation into democratic modernization. There was no hint of his having destroyed the only really democratic government that Nepal had ever had.

This quite rightly created a flap among journalists who knew that Koirala, the democratically elected prime minister, was sitting in a prison cell within earshot of Singha Durbar. Although I just laid out the facts with the required news agency objectivity, some British reporters with more latitude in what they wrote rightly blamed the ambassador for having been too eager to please Mahendra. They also blamed Lord Home for having failed to check the speech carefully. Nonetheless, on the lawn of the small British embassy building on a bright, pleasant afternoon before the banquet, Scopes had already knelt and been knighted by the queen for his services in arranging the visit.

At least the ambassador had not shot a mother rhino. His arrangements had made for a memorable visit that provided a brief look at what had once been the sporting life of empire.

13

PUNITIVE EXPEDITION

IT WAS ROUTINE JOURNALISM: GIVING A CURRENT ANGLE TO A LONG-running news story. The report was cabled from New Delhi to London for onward transmission to the Associated Press headquarters in New York for worldwide distribution. I began, "India rushed troops today to its northeast to reinforce its army as Chinese soldiers continued pushing down through the Himalayas toward the Assam plains."

Several Indian newspapers, as well as military sources talking to me and other foreign correspondents, had been reporting for several days that commercial airliners had been commandeered to fly troops to the threatened northeast. So there was nothing new in the lead of my story, which summarized the latest developments in the 1962 India-China border war.

But that "rushed troops today" came at a time when overly sensitive Indian officials were worried about leakage of military secrets. I was summoned to the Press Information Bureau down Parliament Street from the AP bureau for mild chastisement. By reporting that troops were being rushed on a particular day, a civilian bureaucrat asserted, I had disclosed a military secret. After politely protesting that Indian media had reported daily military flights, I promised not to do it again.

This came during a busy period. I was not only leading AP coverage of the war but also, as current president of the Foreign Correspondents' Association in Delhi, representing all overseas journalists trying to report conflict in the remote mountains. It was an unusual kind of conflict for the mid-twentieth century.

The annals of warfare are studded with military forces sent to punish an enemy and then withdrawn. By the twentieth century, such punitive expeditions had just about died out in a world of clearly recognized borders. But in 1962, China launched from Tibet what turned out to be an old-fashioned punitive expedition against India. Angered by Indian military efforts to assert

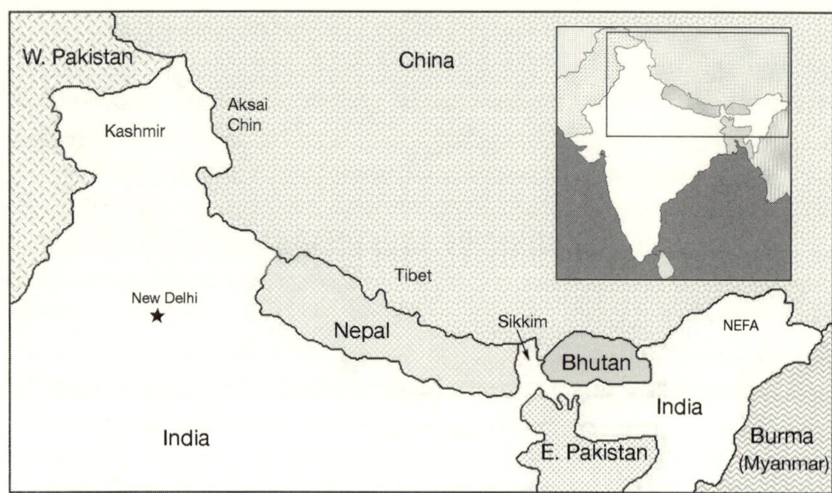

ownership of vaguely defined borderlands, China decided to halt those efforts. A panicked Indian government was slow to recognize China's limited intentions, however. Rapid Chinese military success in the Himalayas and adjacent mountains stirred unrealistic fears that China intended to march down onto the plains of North India in a full-scale invasion.

Those fears gripped India for many autumnal weeks. It made one of the more exciting and important news stories that I covered during five years in India. But it was a war that I reluctantly had to cover primarily from briefing rooms in New Delhi.

One reason was that, after almost three years as the AP's man on the spot for just about every interesting story anywhere in South Asia, I had become bureau chief ten months before this war. I had to stay in Delhi directing coverage of it. Amid long hours, my job led to problems with Indian authorities and lots of rushing around dealing with communications difficulties, as well as reporting news from Delhi, while I sent others out toward the action.

A second reason was that all the fighting took place in remote mountain regions where no journalist, Indian or foreign, had access to firsthand coverage, to actually seeing a little of what was happening. Unlike other wars, reporters could not accompany troops on the chaotic Indian side. The closest that reporters could get to the action was the scarcely talkative Indian military headquarters well behind the lines. On the Chinese side, the Tibetan region was completely closed off to any journalists except a few Chinese military correspondents posted to the headquarters of the People's Liberation Army, the PLA.

There was another complication, unfortunate for the common journalistic vanity of wanting one's reporting to get wide attention. When the India-China border war began, it was the top story in international news, rating big headlines around the world. It revived Western apprehensions of Chinese aggression left from the Korean War and China's 1958 shelling of coastal islands held by the Nationalist regime on Taiwan.

Just two days after the border war began, however, President John F. Kennedy disclosed the existence of Soviet missiles in Cuba, thus beginning the Cuban missile crisis. With the specter of nuclear war between the United States and the Soviet Union looming over the world, the limited war in our remote area was quickly eclipsed in world media. Some interest returned after the Cuban missile crisis was resolved in six harrowing days. But, after Beijing's surprise ending of its month-long drives into Indian-claimed territory and voluntary withdrawal of its troops, the world quickly lost interest—even though the border dispute remained unresolved decades afterward.

The border war was fought in one of the world's most forbidding terrains. The Himalayas and Karakorams to the north of the Indian subcontinent limited contact between the Tibetan highlands and the north Indian plains. Below the world's highest peaks, tigers, leeches, and malarial mosquitoes, among other hazards in jungled foothills, limited movement from the plains. The 1962 conflict arose from the combination of isolation and ruggedness in the mountain region with long lack of governmental concern about European concepts of national borders. None of the various peoples in primitive agricultural communities and religious establishments had, before the British pushed up into the mountains in the nineteenth century, attempted to define their territorial limits. Indeed, they lacked the power to control territory, being vulnerable to occasional marauding by armies from Tibet, China, the Gurkha tribal areas of Nepal, and other places. This left what was, by the concepts of international law that had evolved in Western Europe only relatively recently, an undefined region.

Long before arriving in India, I had been fascinated by this frontier region. One of the first Indian officials with whom I sought an interview upon arrival in Delhi was Jagat Mehta, the External Affairs Ministry's senior man handling relations with China. I remembered a 1957 report that Indian and Chinese maps disagreed on ownership of territory at the western end of Tibet. Beijing's maps had recently begun to show a road running across it from China's westernmost Xinjiang province into Tibet. This territory was Aksai Chin, a name meaning "desert of white stones." On this plateau some seventeen thousand feet high between the Karakoram and Kunlun mountains, nothing grew and no one lived permanently.

Interested in writing an article about the status of this highway and the dispute over ownership, I asked Mehta about the current situation. I also asked to see the ministry's collection of pertinent Chinese maps. He politely refused to discuss the subject or show me the maps. It was obviously a sensitive topic that his government did not want publicized.

Without publicity, the Indian government had after independence in 1947 been redrawing its maps to show as definite northern boundaries the maximum claims ever cartographically asserted by the British. In the northwest, the maximum line included Aksai Chin and some pastures high on the northeast, Xinjiang watershed side of the Karakorams where shepherds in summer took flocks from lower winter pastures on the Kashmir side. The war between India and Pakistan over Kashmir had stopped with a United Nations-negotiated cease-fire in 1948 that left Pakistan in control of the southwestern side of the Karakorams, where the shepherds wintered, while India kept Kashmir's easternmost Ladakh region that extended into Aksai Chin. India continued to assert its legal title to all of Kashmir, including the summer pastures. Chinese maps claimed Aksai Chin and the pastures.

In the northeast, north of the Brahmaputra River plains of Assam, India considered the border to be the McMahon Line. It had been drawn along Himalayan crests by the British in 1914 but never formally accepted by China. The central and eastern parts of the territory between the plains and the McMahon Line were inhabited by animistic tribes without any Buddhist attachment to Lhasa. But in the western part, adjacent to Bhutan, at ten thousand feet altitude, lay a great Buddhist monastery at Tawang affiliated with Lhasa. The monastery's influence extended down close to the plains.

Ignoring the 1914 drawing, Chinese maps showed the border as running along the edge of the plains, with Tibet extending down through the rugged foothills of the Himalayas. So did British Indian maps for another two decades, in effect acknowledging that China had never accepted the McMahon Line. Then in 1937 Delhi covertly backdated a key official reference to show the line as an accepted boundary, and newly published Indian government maps began using it. Thus were the foothills and mountains north of Assam incorporated into British thinking as part of India. Not until 1951, however, after Indian independence in 1947, did Delhi extend Indian administration to Tawang, expelling representatives of Lhasa's "mother monastery," Drepung. The reason was the beginning in the autumn of 1950 of the Chinese Communist invasion of Tibet to establish a firm grip on the region long claimed but rarely controlled by China. This caused the Indian government to try preemptively to consolidate its authority south of the McMahon Line. The area south of the line was then administered by Delhi as the North-East Frontier Agency (NEFA).

The areas of conflicting claims at both ends of the Indian-Tibetan frontier became known as the McMahon Line's eastern sector and Aksai Chin's western sector, while an area of minor disputes at Himalayan passes just west of Nepal was identified as the middle sector. These differences were clear on official maps left from British rule in India and Chiang Kai-shek's Nationalist period in China. The Nationalist government had told Delhi in 1948 that the border shown on maps of newly independent India was unacceptable, but neither Chiang, then losing his civil war with Mao Zedong, nor India paid much attention to the dispute.

In 1954, India complained to China that its maps were wrong and should be corrected. The Communist government said it had only reissued maps inherited from the Nationalists and had not had time to review them. In 1956, Chinese Prime Minister Zhou Enlai indicated a willingness to accept the McMahon Line but did not raise the Aksai Chin question.

In September 1957, Chinese media reported the completion of the road linking western Tibet with Xinjiang. A small map indicated that it went across Aksai Chin. When warm weather came in 1958, India sent two military patrols to investigate. One reported that the road ran across India's claimed territory. The other patrol disappeared. Delhi protested the road to Beijing—secretly, not admitting a problem publicly. The Chinese counter-protested the patrols' incursions into its territory. They released the second patrol, which they had captured. After the Lhasa uprising in March 1959 that caused the Dalai Lama to flee into exile in India, Mao told his comrades on April 23 that "Indian expansionists" wanted to "seize Tibet." This set the tone for later Chinese accounts of what followed. Studies published in Beijing in the 1990s said India wanted to turn Tibet into a colony or protectorate. This, they alleged, was the root cause of the border war.

In the 1950s, however, China took the position that its borders with India had never been negotiated or delimited, and now it was time for the two nations to sit down and discuss them. China conveyed its willingness to accept the McMahon Line in return for India's giving up its Aksai Chin claim. Zhou considered this a fair compromise. But Prime Minister Jawaharlal Nehru was obstinate. Referring to the areas shown on Chinese maps, Nehru wrote to Zhou in December 1958, "There can be no question of these large parts of India being anything but India, and there is no dispute about them."[1] Thus did the normally cool, rational Nehru, whose leadership set India firmly on a democratic road and whose preaching of international conciliation won world acclaim, allow nationalistic emotions to drag his nation into a situation that cast a depressing shadow over the end of his life.

In August 1959, the *Times of India* revealed the patrol findings and detention, which the government had been keeping secret. This stirred a furor in Delhi. But Nehru and his advisers had already set a policy of refusing to negotiate with China, of asserting a right to every inch of territory shown on Indian maps, of insisting that China should withdraw from Aksai Chin. Public opinion had not forced the government into this ultimately disastrous position. At the time the official Indian position hardened, there was no public knowledge of the situation, much less interest in it. Later, however, nationalistic emotions whipped up for political purposes made it seem politically impossible to back out of the dead end by compromising on a border settlement that would yield any of India's claimed territory. The mystical importance of the Himalayas in the Hindu religion, as an abode of the many gods and mythical heroes, contributed strongly to this impossibility.

These were busy times for foreign correspondents in Delhi, who had to depend on the government cable office to send their dispatches. Most important news developments came from statements in the Lok Sabha, the lower house of the Indian Parliament, usually made by Nehru himself. As soon as an important new bit of information had been disclosed—a clash between Indian and Chinese border patrols, for example—we correspondents would race down from the steep little press gallery overlooking the Lok Sabha floor, type up a news dispatch, and rush it to the cable office counter a mile away for transmission to home offices. In the AP's case, this meant cabling to London for entry in AP's Teletype system to New York and thence to worldwide distribution.

At that time, the cable office was across the street from my home at the balcony front of the utilitarian, government-owned Janpath Hotel. Wally Sims and I worked out a system to take advantage of this location. When an important announcement in Parliament was expected, I would go to the press gallery while Wally took up position in my room. Our office driver, Daniel, an Indian Christian, would wait on the ground beneath the fourth-floor room. On hearing the news, I raced to a phone at Parliament and dictated a few sentences of the key facts to Wally. He typed them out, put the paper in a weighted can, and dropped it to Daniel, who raced across the street to submit it at the cable counter. This was repeated several times as I continued dictating to make a complete story. Of such urgency is the worldwide competition between news agencies made.

Nehru's various statements dug India into a fixed political and diplomatic position. In exchanges of letters with Zhou, he refused to make any concessions while demanding that the Chinese withdraw from territory claimed by India. By late November 1959, pushed by jingoistic noises from some opposition political parties and some media to face a situation that his own obduracy had created, Nehru was talking of the possibility of war.

Zhou proposed talks with Nehru to try to work out the problem. Nehru stalled, but finally it was agreed that Zhou would come to New Delhi on April 19, 1960. In more than twenty hours of talks with Nehru, Zhou affirmed his willingness to accept the McMahon Line while keeping Aksai Chin. This would legalize the existing situation: China would give up claims to NEFA, while India would relinquish claims to the high, barren plateau that it did not control in the west. Nehru was adamant that this was unacceptable, and now-aroused Indian political and media opinion backed him strongly.

In a late-night news conference that Chinese officials arranged in Delhi—Indian officials had sought to keep the visit as unpublicized as possible—Zhou said that in their private talks Nehru had not accused China of aggression along the border. Zhou's statement provoked angry attacks in the Indian Parliament. The opposition accused Nehru of being too accommodating of his guest, too soft to uphold India's position. Responding heatedly, Nehru then flatly accused China of aggression in Aksai Chin. Asked about this at a news conference that I covered in Kathmandu, where Zhou had gone to visit Nepal, Zhou displayed controlled, perhaps calculated, anger. He charged Nehru with making an unjustified accusation that he had been unwilling to discuss directly with the Chinese leader. This led us journalists to make a mad dash, ignoring traffic rules, to the telegraph office there.

Zhou and Nehru were able to agree on having their experts do a joint study of the border's history. After several months, they produced a massive collection of documents and maps ancient and new that put the two countries' positions in clear contradiction. Nehru's government read it as reinforcing the Indian position. The lead Indian expert, Dr. Sarvepalli Gopal, asked me what I thought of India's case. I cautiously told him it seemed impressive. In fact, during this period both correspondents and diplomats in Delhi tended to believe that India was the aggrieved party, that its border claims were supported by history. The perception of an aggressive Communist China, linked in the Cold War to the Soviet Union, was strong in many minds, Asian as well as Western.

After Zhou's failed effort to work out a peaceful settlement, India began a "forward policy." Civilian officials assumed they could peacefully assert India's claim to Aksai Chin by sending military patrols into the bleak plateau to establish outposts between Chinese positions, without directly attacking those positions—sort of a chess game of control. They ignored Chinese implications that any challenge in Aksai Chin would be countered by challenges to the McMahon Line. They also ignored the poor condition of the Indian armed forces for such ventures. They were equipped and oriented toward another conflict with Pakistan after their 1947–1948 war over Kashmir. And the civilians ignored India's difficult logistical access to the high areas of contention. It lacked good roads and transport as well as adequate supply aircraft, while China had built up its own logistical assets with the always-important military advantage of holding the high ground by already being on the Tibetan plateau.

After some resistance by the unprepared army, overcome by political browbeating of the professional soldiers, the provocative "forward policy" was launched in secrecy. Despite continued political rumblings, the Indian government did not brag about efforts to assert its nationalistic claims. In September 1962, however, the army decided to invite six foreign correspondents to see how it was building up its forces in Leh, the capital of Ladakh and the forward base for Aksai Chin. By a lucky draw, I was one.

We saw Indian troops and supplies at the gravel airstrip that sloped down from Leh toward the Indus River but learned little about army activities. A brisk briefing by an Indian brigadier emphasized the supposed readiness and alertness of the army in Ladakh. But it was later revealed that the army had protested a year earlier that it had inadequate logistical support in Ladakh to push against the Chinese-claimed territory. There and in NEFA, Indian troop numbers were few, their equipment for high-altitude combat inadequate, their acclimatization to the altitudes scant, and their logistical support too poor for the deployments urged from Delhi.

By the time of our visit to Ladakh, however, a tense positional game was going on in the bleak, high mountains east of Leh. But it was in NEFA where the border dispute finally exploded. The Chinese had been content to observe the McMahon Line as the de facto border, although contending that it had never been legally agreed. India decided, however, that the 1914 map did not show a good borderline at the western end near the trijunction of India, Tibet, and Bhutan. A ridge three or four miles further north than the map's trijuncture coordinates was a militarily better position, Indian officers thought. In late 1959 they established a small army outpost just below the sixteen thousand-foot passes on Thag La ridge. This was a ridge too far, but the Chinese did not initially react. When another outpost was pushed closer to the ridgetop in 1962, PLA troops confronted it peacefully, in the same way that countermoves were being made in Ladakh.

India's defense minister was V. K. Krishna Menon, a militarily unqualified, acerbic, leftist colleague of Nehru who had earlier been India's controversial—to most Westerners, provocative—representative at the United Nations. He decided without full, considered governmental approval that the army should push the Chinese troops back to the revised border. The command structure ignored repeated reports from soldiers in the area that India had access only by rugged mountain trails and had few, poorly supplied troops there. They faced five or ten times as many Chinese troops operating from nearby truck roads.

By late September, Delhi media reported the intention to push the Chinese over Thag La ridge before winter set in a month or so later. The Chinese had ample warning. Chinese officials held a meeting, apparently on October 6, to plan a military effort to counter India's "forward policy." Mao told the meeting that the PLA needed to "knock Nehru to the negotiating table." But Nehru, deluded by Krishna Menon about the Indian Army's capabilities, had no intention of negotiating.

With the timetable for further Indian action uncertain, however, in early October I made a long-planned trip to Kabul to report on Afghan affairs. While I was there, a small-scale defeat of ill-equipped Indian troops as they moved up the ridge by a stronger, better-prepared Chinese force led Nehru publicly to reiterate India's determination to push the Chinese back. Beijing then decided to put an end to Indian provocations. On October 20, 1962, the day before I was scheduled to return to Delhi, it launched attacks along the McMahon Line in NEFA and also in Aksai Chin. The punitive expedition had begun.

Its course can be summarized briefly. In Aksai Chin, the PLA quickly overwhelmed the Indian outposts and moved to the border as shown on Chinese maps. In NEFA, the Indians were pushed back from the original McMahon Line. After their first attacks below Thag La, the Chinese paused before continuing in two main corridors toward their map claim, which included all of

NEFA ending at the edge of the Assam plains. Nowhere was the weak, unprepared Indian Army able to check the strong Chinese thrusts. It was a debacle for Delhi, militarily and politically. Within a month, the PLA controlled almost all the key roads and routes shown on Chinese maps in Ladakh and NEFA.

AP headquarters sent several reporters and photographers to supplement coverage by myself and the bureau's other two reporters. One of the two was our veteran mainstay, Rangaswamy Satakopan, a lawyer by training who had been a solid, hard-working, widely liked AP reporter for some two decades. The other was my successor as the junior American, Alan Kennedy. The AP, apparently enough intrigued by Kennedy's having studied Chinese in the U.S. Army to overlook his limited journalistic experience, had sent him out from New York on his first foreign assignment some six months earlier.

We three could handle the news coming out of Delhi, so New York's idea was to deploy the reinforcements to cover the fighting, or at least forward military headquarters. This was unrealistic because of the remoteness of the fighting and traditional Indian reluctance to expose the armed forces to firsthand media coverage. I was able to send one correspondent and a photographer, Don Royle, who had come to India for the Dalai Lama's arrival, to the army headquarters in Assam near NEFA. This was at Tezpur, the little tea planters' center on the Brahmaputra River where I had waited for the Dalai Lama in April 1959, and the following month I had used it as a base for interviewing Tibetan refugees who followed him into Indian exile. Another reporter, Dave Lancashire, was sent to Srinagar in Kashmir but was unable to reach Leh. Neither of these deployments yielded much news.

Most of the important news came from Nehru's midday statements in the Lok Sabha and from late afternoon diplomatic and military summaries given by the External Affairs Ministry spokesman. The military itself did not talk directly to the press. Midday news developments could be cabled with some assurance that they would reach London fairly promptly. By late afternoon, however, the cable office usually was backed up with traffic for London and reports got out slowly. So I invented a way around the blockage.

For three years, I had been moonlighting with occasional broadcasts for ABC Radio in New York. These voicecasts were made from the same Indian telegraph building where cables were filed. When ABC editors thought South Asian news important enough, they booked voicecasts and cabled to me a time to show up at the studio with a short script to read—actually, several scripts, because ABC wanted different versions of the same story to be used on different newscasts.

The Indian border war was important enough that AP in New York and London agreed to the expense of my booking voicecasts from Delhi to London. With the late afternoon briefings always over by about 6:30, after a mad car race competing news agency correspondents reached the cable office about 6:40 and began flinging over the counter short "takes" of stories hot from their typewriters. By 7 P.M. I was usually finished writing and then disappeared upstairs with my carbon copies. A voicecast was waiting for me at 7:10. I then dictated my story to the London desk. Within a few days, Sidney Weiland of Reuters began complaining that the BBC newscast at 7:30 always used my account of the latest news from the briefing. His, and other correspondents', was still stuck in the cable office backlog.

The logjam hurt some days later. Shortly before 8 P.M. on November 8, the government announced the resignation of Krishna Menon. Nehru had resisted blaming his close colleague—indeed, virtual soulmate—for the growing military disaster. With pressure building from his Congress Party, however, the prime minister had to sacrifice the controversial leftist who as defense minister was responsible for a poorly prepared army then being run by sycophants after the best professional fighting men had been pushed aside.[2]

Typewriter in hand, I hurried to the telegraph office. I began writing of the resignation and its background, tossing the takes across the counter, as many others were doing. Finished, I returned to the office. Within an hour a rocket landed—a complaint from editors. London cabled that the Soviet news agency, TASS, was reporting Krishna Menon's resignation. They lacked a report from us. Obviously, the Delhi to London circuits were jammed, and my story was waiting in a pile to be sent. All I could do was wait.

This gave us a valuable lesson, however. Circuits from Delhi to Moscow were little used and therefore copy moved quickly on them. I alerted AP Moscow to expect us to send duplicate copies of important stories to them to put on their Teletype circuit. I also ascertained that Delhi circuits to Tokyo were usually open, so I also alerted AP's Tokyo bureau to be prepared to relay stories. Although there were a few times when we did duplicate war reports to Moscow and Tokyo, both bureaus were slow to react, partly because of delays in receiving copy in those two places. Nonetheless, we did not suffer another embarrassment of being beaten by TASS.

In addition to stories from Parliament and the briefings, we had to do a roundup every morning that, because of the time difference, was the basis of AP stories for afternoon papers in the United States. It was one such story about troops being rushed to the northeast that got me into trouble.

Indian media authorities saw more of me in my role that year of president of the Foreign Correspondents' Association of South Asia, which made me the spokesman for foreign journalists in Delhi. I spent a lot of time trying to negotiate—with very little success—some access to the fronts, or at least to military headquarters for the eastern and western fronts, on behalf of all foreign correspondents. This included not only the score or so resident ones but also the numerous ones sent in to cover the war. Many of these "parachute" reporters, to use the later term for journalists who drop into hot spots about which they know little or nothing, turned up at the AP bureau for background information and various other kinds of help.

After the initial Chinese attacks, Zhou sent another proposal to Nehru on October 24. He reiterated the Chinese position since 1959, that both sides respect "the line of actual control" while a legally agreed border was worked out. That would, of course, mean continued control of Aksai Chin as Indian troops abandoned any "forward policy," but it would leave India in control of NEFA—up to the 1914 McMahon Line. Even more angrily unwilling to accept this than before China's punitive expedition began, Nehru scorned such a halt to the fighting. With political pressure strong behind him, he was unwilling to be seen as having conceded China's right to control any of India's claimed territory.

Where Nehru did make a major change of attitude was toward accepting foreign military aid. On October 29, as Indian troops were retreating from Tawang, U.S. ambassador John Kenneth Galbraith called on Nehru to offer American military equipment. The Indian cabinet immediately accepted. Mountain warfare weapons, cold weather gear, communications equipment, and others supplies began arriving by air five days later from U.S. stocks in Germany.

The situation in Ladakh quickly settled down to the PLA's holding almost all the territory claimed on Chinese maps and India's being unable to mount a significant counterattack. In NEFA the PLA halted after Chou's October 24 proposal. The Indian Army, however, built up its forces—flying them to the area, as I reported—and on November 14 launched offensives toward occupied Tawang and also in eastern NEFA. The PLA replied beginning November 18 with preplanned drives, pouring through virtually unguarded mountain passes to thrust toward the base of the Himalayan foothills, which their maps showed as the border. One of the two main thrusts through NEFA came along the route the Dalai Lama had followed three and a half years earlier through Tawang to Tezpur.

The Indian military command, weakened by years of Krishna Menon's promoting courtiers rather than experienced fighting men, collapsed into confusion. With NEFA's defenders killed, captured, or routed, panic developed in India. In Delhi there was wild talk of China's plunging on across the Assam plains to reach the Brahmaputra, perhaps even crossing it to cut off northeastern India from the rest of the country. Nehru appealed for the U.S. Air Force to attack the Chinese advancing toward Assam. In Tezpur on the Brahmaputra's north bank, people began on November 18 to try to flee. The local branch of the State Bank of India burned its stock of money. But Royle and the AP reporter with him stood fast and continued trying to send photos and news dispatches from the chaos.

Then, with India demoralized and Nehru talking gloomily as if the nation faced a long, painful war, suddenly the war stopped. By asserting control of all the disputed border regions, the punitive expedition had made its point.

China announced that at midnight on November 20–21, its "frontier guards" would cease fire along the entire border, and they would begin ten days later to withdraw twenty kilometers (twelve miles) behind the November 1959 "line of actual control." This meant India could reoccupy NEFA, from which it had been so disastrously driven. But India, too, China said, was expected to send only police within twenty kilometers of the line—the line that Zhou had repeatedly since 1959 urged India to observe while the border was negotiated. It also meant that China would keep control of Aksai Chin.

The Chinese withdrawal left Indians as perplexed as they were surprised. It seemed too good to be true. There must be some trick. Surrounded in Delhi by such doubts, I was reluctant to let Royle or the reporter leave Tezpur. Lancashire had already been pulled back from unproductive Srinagar. My reluctance was backed up by AP New York. Finally, however, as things remained quiet, I let everyone go home in time for Christmas. The AP operation in India was back to normal. India itself, and especially Nehru, were not.

The cease-fire made moot the request for American air attacks on the advancing Chinese. But Washington did send a squadron of C-130 transport planes to bolster the inadequate Indian ability to supply their troops in the mountains by air. In early January, I arranged to fly on one of their missions from Delhi to Leh. Instead of laboring perilously through a mountain pass, as a World War II surplus plane of the Indian Air Force had done when I went to Leh in September, the American turboprop soared easily over the western Himalayas to deliver tons of military supplies to Ladakh.

Later in January the government invited a handful of correspondents to visit Tawang. The date set was, perhaps coincidentally, Republic Day, India's national day on January 26. We set out from an airstrip near now-quiet Tezpur on a large, Soviet-made helicopter, heading to the north on a route to clear the first line of Himalayan ridges and then turning northwest. But clouds obscured the first ridges. The helicopter pilot returned to refuel, then set out again westward along the foothills, finally turning north up the Dangme River valley to overfly Bhutan and reach Tawang. The air was so thin there that in order to take off at the end of several hours at Tawang the pilot had to creep the helicopter to the edge of its pad and fall over the side into the river gorge to gain enough air speed for flying.

Indian civilian officials had returned to Tawang only five days earlier, with no army troops there. Showing us around the simple old Indian military buildings, the civilians pointed out the shallow trenches that PLA soldiers had dug in apparent apprehension of air raids. They accused the Chinese of leaving the place in a mess, with latrines not covered up and empty supply boxes littered about. It seemed a surprising attitude for a defeated nation to take under the circumstances. We walked over to the large monastery, a walled campus of solidly constructed stone temples, dormitories, and other buildings, and looked around. Few of the seven hundred Buddhist monks who had lived there had yet to return from fleeing the Chinese occupation.

The mood in Delhi was sour. India had been greatly embarrassed as well as defeated. The word on everyone's tongue was "humiliation." The politics-ridden army had been proven weak, although the war had the benefit of leading to reforms that replaced courtiers with qualified fighting commanders. Nehru, the acclaimed world leader of nonalignment in the 1950s, had been victimized by his failure to follow his preachings to others of the need for calm, rational negotiations of disputes. Visibly aged by the crisis and increasingly waspish, he never recovered the authority in his governing Congress Party or in the world that he had had before the border war. After decades of global greatness with a well-earned reputation as a statesman, he was a sad shadow of his former self by the time of his death on May 27, 1964, a year and a half after the war.

What to do now? Feeling themselves the victims of Chinese aggression, many angry Indian leaders wanted to build up the armed forces and retake every inch of land claimed on the maps. An intellectual leader of these militaristic hawks was Gopal, the mild-mannered historian. India will reclaim its territory, he assured me. We made a bet. He said that by the end of the decade the Indian Army would control the entire area claimed on its maps. I doubted it. The loser of the bet was to buy the winner a meal in the best restaurant in whatever city we first met after January 1, 1970.

While civilian hawks made defiantly anti-Chinese noises in Delhi, the army stayed fairly quiet. Its new leaders recognized the tremendous problem of finding resources for mountain warfare while keeping the main military forces in a posture to meet any trouble on the plains with Pakistan, the once and future enemy. Some new mountain units were developed and roads built up into the difficult, landslide-prone terrain, but the army never got the resources to mount offensives in the high Himalayas. The general public, which would have had to pay the price of diverting resources from economic development, showed little enthusiasm for an expensive military buildup. When I saw Gopal during a reporting trip back to Delhi in 1970, he bought me lunch in the simple cafeteria of the India International Center, where he maintained a small bachelor apartment.

Several limited border clashes occurred later. The largest erupted at the Nathu La, where an old mule route crossed from Sikkim into Tibet. In sporadic skirmishing between September 11 and 16, 1967, India lost 65 killed and 145 wounded while it estimated Chinese losses at a possibly exaggerated 400 killed or wounded.

Half a century after China's punitive expedition, the border remained quiet. The dispute, however, stayed unresolved despite numerous rounds of official talks between Delhi and Beijing. Political timidity had long kept Indian politicians from accepting the compromise suggested by China since 1956. Few politicians were willing to renounce the Indian territorial claim that Nehru had so unwisely made to Aksai Chin or the adjustment to the McMahon Line. Then China began hardening its position, its claims to the northeast becoming more vocal. Well into the twenty-first century, the India-China border dispute remained unresolved.

In India, nationalistic pride made any willingness to compromise a possible election vulnerability. The army focused its attention away from the border. In China, a new sense of competition with India as emerging economic giants seemed to make Beijing more assertive. China's punitive expedition had halted any Indian grasp for its most extended ideas of where its borders lay in the rugged mountains and bleak plateaus on the roof of the world. What was left was a stalemate.

14

OF ROYALTY AND ROYAL WEDDINGS

"YOU UNDERSTAND," THE COURTIER SAID, "THAT HIS MAJESTY DOES NOT give interviews. He cannot be quoted. This is just an informal conversation for your background information." But, I asked, can't I use indirect quotes to describe what His Majesty said in an informal conversation? Well, yes, this was conceded.

This was a discussion that I had twice just a year apart on the fascinating fringes of the Indian subcontinent, in Nepal and Afghanistan. In both cases, I was, according to royal officials and local journalists, the first foreign correspondent to be granted the privilege of "an informal conversation" with a monarch who had recently assumed direct responsibility for his government. Both kings were seeking foreign understanding of their controversial personal rule. In both Kathmandu and Kabul, I had cultivated enough friendships with royal ministers as well as senior journalists who had palace connections to offer the test case for the kings' new public relations efforts.

The royal conversations came during a couple of years when I also was a personal guest for the weddings of an Indian *maharaja* and a Himalayan crown prince, both of whom I had earlier come to know, on the understanding that I was invited to report the weddings for the Associated Press. And there was a third wedding in this period, with a bride purchased from the United States Educational Foundation in India. It was very royal, too, but someone else reported it.

The first South Asian monarch whom I met was the *druk gyalpo* of Bhutan, Jigme Dorje Wangchuck, at his temporary capital, Paro. I spent more time with him—during interviews, informal chats, archery contests, lama dances, and other events—than the other kings. His story is told elsewhere.

A nearby Himalayan kingdom, Nepal, was more readily and frequently accessible. As the only Western journalist in that period who visited Nepal regularly and took a serious, continuing interest in its affairs, I got to know it fairly well. In the spring of 1962 I sought an interview with King Mahendra Bir Bikram Shah Dev.

I was not very optimistic about getting it. The king did not grant interviews, indeed was a shyly retiring person whose closeted upbringing apparently had left him lacking in self-confidence. He seldom even talked with ambassadors accredited to his court or to other foreigners, and he rarely ventured out of his palace compound. Besides, a number of people in Kathmandu knew that I had been critical of him in the past for having abolished a democratically elected government and imprisoned in 1960 its prime minister, B. P. Koirala, whom I'd gotten to know well in a number of interviews.

Anyway, in April 1962 I asked for an audience with the king. I wanted to ask him about Nepal's relations with India and other subjects. Relations with India were topical at the moment. India controlled Nepal's access to the outside world; trade and communications with the only other contiguous neighbor, across the roadless Himalayas to Tibet and eastern China, were virtually nonexistent. The king had recently visited New Delhi for talks with Prime Minister Jawaharlal Nehru.

For years, Nehru had treated Koirala like a younger brother, helping his Nepali Congress Party grow until it won a 1959 election and then supporting its experiment with democratic government. Angered by the king's abolition of the government and jailing of Koirala, Nehru had secretly authorized support for guerrilla harassment of the royal regime by Nepali Congress members based in India. The king had, in the polite language of diplomacy, discussed with Nehru the subject of stopping "outside interference," which Nehru did not admit existed.

A network of Nepali official and journalist friends helped convince the palace that I would make a good trial effort for the king to reach the outside world. When I was ushered into a small audience building in the royal compound to meet King Mahendra on April 22, one of those officials translated from Nepali into English. The king spoke English well, but he apparently wanted this buffer to give himself time to think and to introduce an element of deniability into anything that I might attribute to royal thinking, however vaguely. Besides, he was fairly stiff. This presumably was a result of having led a cloistered palace existence. Mahendra was, after all, a Hindu deity, so he could not readily go out to talk with farmers and other ordinary people. They held him in too much awe to be able to conduct a meaningful conversation, and he apparently was too shy to know how to draw people out. Life had not required him to sharpen social or political skills.

With me, he talked about trying to clear up "misunderstandings" with India, although making it plain that he had not directly asked Nehru to crack down on guerrilla harassment from there. He also talked about his economic development plans and his scheme for creating an indirectly elected Parliament—not one that risked popular choice. His only reference to Koirala was vague and indirect. It made an interesting story, without direct quotes.

Almost exactly a year later, on April 18, 1963, King Mohammed Zahir Shah of Afghanistan granted me an audience. I had flown to Kabul several weeks after the king had led a royal family decision to oust his first cousin and brother-in-law, Mohammed Daoud Khan, who for a decade had autocratically run the country as prime minister. The king installed Afghanistan's first commoner prime minister and began trying to involve the people of his primitive country in constitutional government. Heavily dependent on foreign aid, the king wanted foreign understanding for his intentions. He was scheduled to visit the United States, so a story reaching AP members there was good advance publicity.

On several previous reporting trips to Afghanistan, I had become acquainted with a few key people. One was Sabahuddin Kushkaki, the American-educated head of the official news agency Bakhtar, editor of the government's English-language newspaper, the *Kabul Times,* and a journalism teacher at Kabul University—as well as AP's Kabul stringer. Another key person was a former Afghan ambassador to Washington, Mohammed Hashim Maiwandwal, who was then a cabinet minister.

When I was escorted into the *Arg,* the large royal compound in the center of Kabul, for tea with the king in one of the compound's four palaces, Maiwandwal was there to help translate. The king spoke English fluently but, like Mahendra, felt safer and more confident using a translator. His Majesty was friendly and hospitable in a somewhat stiff sort of way. But after opening formalities and a discussion of such safe topics as his experimental work to improve Afghan agriculture, in which he did talk with farmers, the king spoke easily about his hopes for public participation in government, his pride in the economic development already achieved, and his ambitions for further progress. The conversation made an interesting article that said what the king was thinking about Afghan ambitions, prospects, and problems.

Zahir Shah was looking forward to the day when the new group of well-educated commoners—mostly Western educated, but some from Soviet bloc schools—would be able to take over the nation's management from the royal family. Unfortunately, this period of royally guided government by an educated elite lasted only a decade. First a Communist period and then Islamic radicals destroyed most economic progress and decimated the educated class.

The first royal wedding that I attended was at Bharatpur, the site of a celebrated bird sanctuary ninety-five miles south of Delhi. The *maharaja* of Bharatpur, Brajendra Singh, now a member of Parliament dutifully elected by his former subjects, was noted for extravagant duck hunts in his marshlands. Being only casually acquainted with him on the Delhi social circuit, I was somewhat surprised when in 1962 I was invited to his wedding. A forty-three-year-old widower, he was going to be married to the young daughter of another member of the old nobility. He obviously wanted publicity. I was willing to give it to him in return for attending a traditional Hindu wedding with royal trimmings. It was held at his palace, which was a large Victorian house with sweeping, well-tended lawns prowled by peacocks that periodically fanned their tails and meowed like loud cats.

The wedding was in several stages of devoutly Hindu proceedings, with Brahmin priests in charge of the chanting, ceremonial walking around in patterns, lighting of incense, and other traditions. I took photographs as well as notes for a feature story. A week or so later, the *Times* of London published a group of my photos. This voice of the British establishment obviously felt there was some nostalgia among its readers for such colorful old Indian traditions as a *maharaja*'s wedding. The publicity made the *maharaja* feel well rewarded for having invited me.

The second time I was a guest of the groom at a royal wedding, it was an international affair. The groom was the *maharajkumar* (crown prince) of Sikkim, Palden Thondup Namgyal. As a widower with two young sons in 1959, Thondup met at the bar in a family-style hotel in Darjeeling, a hill resort near Sikkim, a young American woman inexplicably spending the summer there. She was Hope Cooke, a rich, young college student who was a forerunner of the Western hippies or beatniks who swarmed over the region toward the end of the 1960s and in the early 1970s. Smitten with her, despite her lack of striking physical beauty, he decided he wanted to marry her. Hope later wrote that, during their long courtship, he "sometimes treats me like a sex object—but quite differently, in the nicest way."

The courtship was long because the idea of the crown prince's marrying the American beatnik caused a crisis in Sikkim and consternation in New Delhi. She had been reared as a Christian. He had been proclaimed as a child to be an incarnation of a Tibetan Buddhist lama and had been educated in a monastery in Tibet before the death of his elder brother pulled him back into a secular role to become the heir apparent. The lamas and other elders of Sikkimese society were scandalized by the idea of his marrying a Westerner who could become their queen. The Indian government feared disruptive effects. But Thondup was determined.

I had first met Thondup in early April 1959 on a visit to Sikkim while seeking news of the recent Tibetan uprising in Lhasa. He had given me my first detailed explanation of Tibetan Buddhism while showing me around the Institute of Tibetology that he had recently founded just outside Sikkim's ridgeline capital, Gangtok. After that, I interviewed him whenever I was in Delhi during one of his frequent visits there. He introduced me to Hope Cooke and kept me up to date on his efforts to marry her. When, after a year's delay, he finally got grudging approval for the wedding from Sikkimese elders as well as Indian authorities, he invited me to be one of the palace guests. A handful of other Western journalists were invited, but dozens of others were rebuffed from covering this seemingly fairytale wedding of the New York heiress and the Himalayan prince.

The wedding was performed on March 20, 1963, in the Tsuk Lhakhang, or royal chapel, by Sikkim's senior lamas in accordance with Buddhist tradition. The gods of Sikkim were, no one doubted, looking benignly down from their abode atop the world's third-highest mountain, Kanchenjunga, rising 28,210 feet on the Sikkim-Nepal border. While Thondup's aged and feeble father presided, sitting cross-legged on a platform in an incense-rich temple, surrounded by statues, paintings, and other symbolism of the Tibetan religion, the lamas chanted invocations and blessings. Lamps of yak butter were lit, ceremonial white silk scarves exchanged. Although Hope said later she had not had any rehearsal, she had already settled into a publicly submissive appearance, changing from the boisterous hippy to whom Thondup had first introduced me into the whispery-voiced consort role that she later affected. But there was nothing whispery about the palace party after the wedding. It was a raucous American-style blast, with the U.S. ambassador to India, John Kenneth Galbraith, trying to keep up on the dance floor with Thondup's wild and notorious sister, Pema Tsedeun Yapshi Pheunkhang, known as Princess Coo Coo la.

What happened after that is a sad story. Thondup's father died the following December, and Thondup became the nominal ruler of Sikkim from his palace, a two-story bungalow with a red, corrugated iron roof. But he grew restive under Indian control. When Thondup invited me to have drinks with him and

Hope while they were visiting Hong Kong in 1970, he politely remonstrated over an article on Tibet that I had published in *Foreign Affairs* the year before. It mentioned Sikkim as an Indian protectorate. He wanted to think of his land as being independent and was seeking foreign support for the idea—without success, because no country felt it worthwhile to challenge India's imperial attitude.

While Hope did some useful things, such as encouraging a revival of traditional Sikkimese arts and crafts, she also did things that caused Indian officials to see her as a troublemaker. She was probably a minor factor in a decision by India, under the tough-minded—indeed, dictatorial—Prime Minister Indira Gandhi, to tighten its already strong control of Sikkim. India stirred up Nepali Hindu settlers who had come to outnumber the Buddhist traditional inhabitants. In 1975, the royal system was abolished and Sikkim was annexed as a state of India. The dream of being a Himalayan queen ended, Hope left Thondup, taking their two small children to New York. Thondup spent lonely and frustrated years in Gangtok before going to the United States for cancer treatment. He died there in 1982.

The third very royal wedding lacked meowing peacocks, chanting Hindu Brahmins, or incense-burning Buddhist priests. Instead, it featured sparrows in the eaves and a meek Indian civil servant. But it was special in its own way.

In June of 1963, I was in West Pakistan to cover a visit by President Sukarno of Indonesia and then do some reporting on Pakistani political and economic subjects. I flew back from Lahore to New Delhi on Saturday morning, June 29, and went in to the AP office at 19 Narendra Place to see what had been happening.

In the mail was an invitation for me to attend on the following Tuesday, July 2, the farewell dinner dance of Ambassador Galbraith. I had gotten to know the best-selling author and Harvard economist fairly well during the two years that he had been in India as a political appointee of President John F. Kennedy, whom he had long advised. Galbraith's reading suggestions and discussions with him had given me what I sometimes jokingly described as my graduate education in Third World economic development.

There was also mail from AP headquarters in New York. Stan Swinton, the head of the AP's worldwide business operations, had written on June 21 a short note to enclose a letter that he had received. Stan said the letter was from the man with whom he had shared an apartment when they were young AP newsmen in Detroit in 1940 and 1941. Stan asked me to help his friend if help were needed.

The letter had been written June 19 by Fred J Pannwitt, who was now the chief editorial writer for the *Chicago Daily News*. Fred had written to Stan that his daughter, Monica Jean, had just graduated from Swarthmore College with high honors and a Phi Beta Kappa key. He had put her on a plane June 12 to go to India on a Fulbright program. It was the letter of a proud father, but a father with a certain unease about his daughter's venture into the unknown. Fred said he would appreciate it if the AP bureau chief in India could help her, perhaps by introducing her to interesting people.

I recalled reading an article several years earlier about the Swarthmore honors program. Described as a jewel of American higher education, the program focused on junior- and senior-year seminars. It had impressed me with its rigorous scholastic standards that used outside academics to test a student's broad knowledge at graduation time, instead of simply giving grades for courses that could be quickly forgotten.

On Monday, July 1, I telephoned Galbraith's social secretary, Bimla Nanda, and asked her if it would be all right for me to bring a date to the dinner dance, which was formal, Indian diplomatic life being very formal in those days. She said it would be fine.

Then I phoned the India International Center in New Delhi, where the group of Fulbright scholars was staying during an orientation program before being assigned to educational institutions in India. The group of new bachelor degree holders was scheduled to help improve the standards of English speaking for Indian students who had learned the somewhat peculiar South Asian form of English, while also doing research that would later help in graduate degree work at American universities. Most of the group intended to go home to seek doctorates in South Asian studies after one or two years of firsthand experience in India.

Monica wanted to research the role of journalism written by Indians, rather than British journalists working for the main newspapers in India, in the Indian independence movement between 1890 and 1920, before Mohandas K. Gandhi transformed the movement. She had a scholarship waiting at the University of Wisconsin, a leading American center of South Asian studies, to begin graduate work there, as well as a prestigious Woodrow Wilson grant to help her pay for graduate study at any American university.

When I reached Monica Jean Pannwitt on the phone, I introduced myself as the AP bureau chief, said I'd received her father's letter through Stan Swinton, and asked if she'd like to attend Ken Galbraith's farewell dinner dance the following night—formal. There was a short, shocked silence. Then she agreed.

But she had not come to India equipped for formal dances, she said. No matter, I said, any frock will do. The first time I met Monica, in the lobby of the International Center, she was wearing a simple, lovely dusty-rose dress and had her long blonde hair stacked stylishly atop her head. I was wearing a summer tux—white jacket, black trousers, black bow tie, and a dark red silk cummerbund.

She said later that her mental image of an AP bureau chief had been "short, fat, and fortyish."[1] She therefore approached this moment with some trepidation but didn't want to miss the opportunity to meet Galbraith. I hadn't bothered to conjure up a mental image of a Swarthmore graduate. Anyway, we both turned out to be tall, slender, and not so old—I was early thirtyish. I drove her off in the AP's black Ford, but I had been too conservative in setting a time to pick her up. There was time to kill before arriving at the ambassador's spacious new residence. We drove slowly around Chanakapuri, the diplomatic enclave of New Delhi, while talking. Monica told me about summer jobs as a proofreader of telephone books, a publicity person for local charities, and a reporter for a suburban weekly paper, about an adventurous car trip through the western United States with several college girlfriends in the summer of 1961, and about playing softball and basketball on Swarthmore's girls' teams. I remember thinking as we drove into the traffic circle by the Indonesian embassy that this is not just some good-looking bookworm, this is an interesting woman.

The dinner dance was crowded with senior Indian officials and the diplomatic corps. Ken and Kitty Galbraith welcomed Monica graciously, and several officials and diplomats whom I knew after almost four and a half years in India asked to meet the attractive young lady with me, but most of the time I had her to myself amid the crowd. At the end of the evening, when I drove Monica back to the International Center, I asked if she'd like to go to the Fourth of July evening picnic and sporting events at the American embassy's residential compound, two nights later—I was already committed elsewhere on the 3rd. She accepted.

When I arrived at the International Center on the Fourth, not only was Monica waiting but also a bunch of her Fulbright colleagues. They all wanted rides to the embassy picnic, and maybe also a chance to look me over. A bit surprised, and none too happy, I packed more people into the Ford than it probably had ever carried. But they said they could arrange transportation home, so after the picnic, softball game, and other sports I drove Monica to New Delhi's commercial center, Connaught Place, for coffee and more conversation. Then I took her into a suburb to see the tomb of the sixteenth-century Moghul emperor Humayan, a little-known model for the later, more celebrated Taj Mahal, by the light of an almost full moon. Waking up and tipping a night watchman, we walked around the deserted gardens and tomb, ill-kempt but lovely in the moonlight, still talking.

The next day, Friday, the Fulbright group was going down to Agra to see the real thing, the Taj Mahal, by the light of Saturday night's full moon. I told Monica I'd call her when she got back on Sunday. When I did, she accepted my dinner invitation. After dinner, we drove around as I showed her the magnificent British-built center of the New Delhi capital area. But the Ford had been having some engine trouble, and on that hot night it cut out and would not start again. Monica later said she thought I was faking it—the old "we've run out of gas" routine—but I wasn't. I flagged down one of the tiny, ancient taxis that plied the Delhi streets. In the taxi on the way to the International Center, I kissed her for the first time. She did not resist.

The next night, Monday, July 8, after the office driver had retrieved the car from its overnight parking place and gotten it fixed, I took Monica out to dinner again—our fourth date. We went to a little restaurant overlooking the swimming pool at the Ashoka, a government-owned hotel that was at the time Delhi's best. Over dinner, I told her every cautionary thing I could think of about my family and my personal background that she should know. After this warning preamble, I told her that the following night I was going to ask her to marry me. I was offering her the prospect of the vagabond life of a foreign correspondent, not the stability of some comfortable house in the suburbs.[2] But, no, I was not asking her now, so she did not have to comment. I was just warning her so she would not be surprised when it happened. She should think about it.

When I picked her up for dinner Tuesday evening, July 9, Monica told me that she had hardly slept the night before. In fact, I had been too excited to sleep as well as usual, either. Over dinner, rather than on bended knee, I asked her to marry me. She accepted.

But there were complications. The Fulbright program had scheduled Monica to tutor English and do her research at a women's college in Jaipur. This lovely pink limestone city is in the desert of Rajasthan, 150 miles southwest of Delhi. Monica was due to leave for Jaipur in a few days. We had no desire to be that far apart, the condition of Indian roads making it more than a fair commute. So I went to see Olive Reddick.

A severely prim spinster of mature years, Dr. Reddick headed the United States Educational Foundation in India, which administered the Fulbright program. She knew me because I was on her board of resident Americans who met several times a year to interview and vote on Indian candidates for Fulbright scholarships to the United States. But the connection had no effect. Dr. Reddick reacted with great suspicion when I told her I wanted to marry one of her charges. It was obvious that she felt herself personally responsible for protecting these young students, especially the girls, from the many dangers of India, and I looked suspiciously like a danger. Besides, she said, the U.S. government had paid a lot of money to fly Miss Pannwitt out to India and give her a month of orientation. Miss Pannwitt now had an obligation to fulfill by teaching in Jaipur for at least a year.

Unhappily, I then stopped at the office of Lui Ram. An American, she was the wife of Vernon Ram, one of India's leading sportswriters and a friend whom I occasionally hired to file stories to the AP on important sports events that we could not cover with our normal staff or stringer network. I explained the situation to Lui, who was Dr. Reddick's deputy and office manager. She was delighted to hear that I had found a bride. Don't worry, we'll find a way, Lui assured me.

At the same time, I wrote two letters. The first was one of my very occasional carbon-copy letters to my parents and to my brother, Earl, and sister, Margaret, in the United States. As usual, it started off with the weather: the monsoon had arrived, so daytime temperatures were down to just 95 or so, but there hadn't actually been much rain yet. The letter moved on to describe a recent trip with Nehru and Galbraith to the dedication of the Punjab Agricultural University, built with American help, where I observed the sad decline in Nehru's health. Then I mentioned that this was not the usual season for visitors to India—most came in the delightful winter weather—but that one had come accompanied by a request for me to provide any needed help, I had met her, "and we plan to get married July 25." The second letter was written to Fred Pannwitt. I asked for his daughter's hand in marriage.

Earl lived in New York City, where airmail from India landed, so he got his copy first. Although Earl did not personally know my old boss in Delhi, Wally Sims, who was then the AP World Service editor in New York, Earl knew of him and phoned the news to him. Wally told Stan Swinton. After Wally had given Stan additional background on me, Stan phoned Fred in Chicago. Stan congratulated him on the news and kindly put in a good word for me.

Fred, who had not yet received his letter, was naturally astounded. So was his wife, Barbara, known as Bobbie. They were expecting Nicky, as they called her,[3] to come home in a year or two and begin work toward a Ph.D. in South Asian studies. Early the next morning, before going to work, Fred went down to the post office in Evanston, Illinois, to intercept my letter and letters from Nicky, instead of waiting for them to be delivered. Yes, it was true, I wanted to marry Nicky, and she wanted to marry me. Her parents were invited to the wedding in India. Please reply.

Lui Ram reported that the only way for Monica to avoid the Jaipur commitment was to leave the Fulbright program. But Dr. Reddick was not prepared to let her go unless the money spent on her was repaid. This ransom demand was not an insuperable problem for someone deeply in love and unwilling to be held up by complications. I ended up writing a check to the Educational Foundational for $994. In those days before many rounds of inflation, that was a lot of money—more than I, as a bureau chief paid fairly well by then-current journalistic standards, earned in five weeks. I used to tell people that I bought my wife from the U.S. government.

By the time of the purchase agreement, Galbraith had already left India. Five years later, he wrote one of the recommendations that helped me win a Nieman Fellowship at Harvard University.[4] When Monica and I arrived at Harvard, he and Kitty invited us to dinner, and we told them the bride-buying story. Galbraith was appalled. He insisted that, had he still been there, he would have found a way around Dr. Reddick's ransom demand. Having witnessed Galbraith's self-assured way of ignoring or overcoming bureaucratic rules as a politically appointed ambassador, I did not doubt that he would have.

At Galbraith's farewell diplomatic reception just before he left India, a day or two after Monica had agreed to marry me but before the impasse with Dr. Reddick, the ambassador made a point of introducing Monica to Prime Minister Nehru as my future bride. Nehru knew me, of course. As he extended his best wishes, Nehru graciously shook hands with Monica. This was a rare thing because he normally avoided touching anyone, instead pressing his palms together in front of his face in the traditional Hindu *namaste* greeting.

Once I had arranged to buy Monica, there were still difficulties. One was what to do with her while we arranged a wedding and waited to hear whether her parents wanted to fly out for it. Since Monica had left the Fulbright program, and in fact her group was dispersing from the International Center to its assignments, she needed a place to live.

At the time, I had recently rented the ground floor of a two-story house in a nice, close-in suburb. An Indian family lived upstairs. I was beginning to enjoy a real home after spending my first three and a half years in India living in Room

302 of the utilitarian, government-owned Janpath Hotel, near the AP bureau, and then briefly renting an apartment in the same central area before its owners decided to turn it into an office. Emmanuel George, an Indian Christian whose family lived over the garage, ran my bachelor household. An excellent cook, he supervised a full-time sweeper, or cleaning man and general assistant, and a part-time *dhobi* (laundry man) plus a part-time *mali* (gardener). All I had to do was tell Emmanuel what I wanted and give him money. A dinner party for eight needed only one day's notice, for example, with Emmanuel taking care of everything.

But a temporary place for Monica was a problem. In those days generally, and certainly in the foreign community in India, men and women did not just move in together. Once Monica and I were legally married, she moved into my established household, but not before. Jack Stewart, the American embassy's press attaché, and his wife, Ruth, a childless couple about the age of Monica's parents, volunteered to take Monica in.

During that time, Monica and I went shopping. We had engagement and wedding rings made from the none-too-good quality metals and precious stones available on India's introverted economy. Also, we had tailors make a better wardrobe for her than the student clothes, including a white, street-length, silk wedding dress, and cobblers make new shoes. It was not normal for the groom to buy his bride's trousseau, but this was not a normal situation.

There was also the matter of arranging the wedding. Not having set foot in any churches during my years in India except on reporting assignments or to admire the architecture, I felt it would be hypocritical to seek a church wedding. Monica and I decided on a civil ceremony. Indian law provided for three kinds, for Hindus, Muslims, and Christians. Monica and I went to the Delhi municipal government building in the old part of the capital and filled out long forms to have a civil Christian wedding.

Fred wrote back that he and Bobbie "have tried to give [Monica] an education suitable to her talents, and above all to instill in her a spirit of independence and the ability to make her own decisions. So we couldn't oppose her decision now, even if we wanted to." But, he added, what they'd heard from her and others "helps to convince us that her decision now, speedy as it is, is the right one."[5] We had their blessings. They wrote to Monica that they could not fly out to India anytime soon. We would have to go ahead without them.

The Delhi municipal official designated to perform civil marriages for Christians was J. O. G. Russell, an Indian Christian who was the deputy commissioner for housing, specializing in loans. His office was in a long, thatched-roof temporary building, surrounded by construction materials. Birds flew in and out of the open eaves.

On the hot early afternoon of Thursday, July 25, 1963, we gathered at the dusty, cluttered office of the Delhi Administration's Deputy Commissioner for Housing (Loans). Jack and Ruth Stewart brought Monica. My closest Indian friend and AP colleague, Rangaswamy Satakopan, attended as an official witness and also took photographs. Another friend, Neville Maxwell, also came. A U.S. embassy consular officer, E. Paul Taylor, came to certify that we were married under laws that the American government recognized. Russell read the brief marriage rites, legalistic rather than biblical, that mostly consisted of questions to us. These included my avowing that I did not have any other wives, since in Indian society multiple wives were not uncommon but under Christian law not permitted. Then we signed our names and we were married. It seemed like a royal wedding to me.

The rest is, as they say, history. In fact, it is in the historic record. Satakopan sent the AP a brief news report on the wedding, along lines I had approved in advance. The *New York Times* had a spot to fill on its wedding page the next day, and it published the report.

As a convenient nearby destination, I took Monica back to Agra—not to the somewhat seedy colonial-era hotel where the Fulbright scholars had stayed, but to the city's newest and best. We went to see the Taj Mahal together. With her, with a one-third moon waxing, it seemed even more magical than the dozen or so times I had been there to cover important visitors. Then, after a day or two back in Delhi, we went to Ceylon (now Sri Lanka) for the second part of our honeymoon, driving around that spectacularly beautiful and then peaceful tropical island.

And one year to the day after I first kissed Monica in that taxi, our first son was born in Evanston. Two years to the day after I first talked to her on the phone, our second son was born in Moscow. She never got back to that Ph.D. program, going on instead to other, more influential and original contributions to worldwide education. And life has been pretty royal ever since.

15

ONE HORSE, MANY HORSES

HE LOOKED SO LONELY, OFTEN STANDING OFF ON THE SIDE OF DIPLOmatic cocktail parties by himself. I decided that, between conversations with various Indian officials and foreign diplomats who might yield some useful tidbits of information, I would go over and talk with him.

He was the ambassador to India from the Mongolian People's Republic. India was one of the few nations that had diplomatic relations with the big East Asian country as part of its friendship with the Soviet Union, which so tightly controlled Mongolia that most nations ignored its claim to an independent existence. Mongolia used India as one of the few countries to which it could send students to study English, in preparation for possible wider contacts with the outside world. There was little other business between the two nations on either side of China.

The ambassador's own English was none too smooth, but he seemed flattered to have someone willing to chat briefly with him. His contacts were too limited to provide any information of use to me, as I had suspected. He was, however, eager to praise Mongolia. I politely but vaguely said that I would like to visit his beautiful land some day—unaware that it had something of a complex about how many horses and other livestock it had.

The second or third time that the ambassador and I went through a desultory dialogue, he said I should visit Mongolia. Is that possible? I asked. He could arrange a visa, he said. Suddenly, this sounded interesting. I knew that Mongolia had for decades been virtually a closed country only rarely accessible to Western journalists.

The next morning I sent a cable to the AP foreign editor in New York, Ben Bassett, asking if he was interested in having me pursue this possibility. Yes, by all means, he responded. Although my responsibility was to cover news from South Asia, with Mongolia being considered part of the territory covered by the

AP bureau in the Soviet Union, no one from Moscow had been able to visit it for a very long time. If I could go from India, that would be a good opportunity for the AP to offer clients a fresh look at an isolated land.

The next time I saw the ambassador at a cocktail party, sometime in the summer of 1963, I told him I would love to visit his country. He said he would try to arrange a visa, and he took my card that identified me as the AP bureau chief in Delhi. Some weeks later, he phoned. I should come by his embassy to fill out the paperwork, and the visa would be issued.

During those intervening weeks, the AP had asked me to move from New Delhi to Moscow in early 1964. Bassett agreed that it would be best to try to delay the Mongolia trip until after I had arrived in Moscow. When I asked the ambassador about a delay, however, he said the arrangements were waiting for me in his capital, Ulan Bator. It was that autumn or maybe not at all. Go ahead, Bassett said.

Bookstores in New Delhi had a few books on Mongolia that I eagerly began reading to acquire background. The only one that came close to discussing the contemporary country was *Nomads and Commissars: Mongolia Revisited,* by Owen Lattimore. This American scholar on Mongolia and Chinese frontier regions had ranged that area in the 1920s. In describing Mongolia's relationship with the Soviet Union in the 1930s, he invented the political meaning for the word "satellite," the term applied to East European nations after World War II. Lattimore's latest book was based on a 1961 return to Mongolia.

The American Express office in Delhi found connections to Ulan Bator in the international airline guide. They booked me on an Aeroflot flight from Delhi to Tashkent in Soviet Central Asia and then another flight from Tashkent to Irkutsk in Siberia, connecting there to Ulan Bator. The flight from Tashkent to Irkutsk stopped in several places, including Karaganda. That sounded interesting because I knew Karaganda was a base for Soviet nuclear weapons testing.

By the time I was scheduled to leave Delhi on November 23, four months after Monica and I were married, we had just learned that she was pregnant. She had no problem with my being away for several weeks, however, having known when she married me that mine was a traveling job.[1]

In the early hours of November 23 in India, ten and a half hours ahead of Washington, D.C., time, Monica and I were awakened by a phone call. It was Rangaswamy Satakopan, the AP's Indian reporter who lived by the office. A cable had come in from AP New York reporting that President John F. Kennedy had been assassinated. New York wanted Delhi to get a statement from Prime

Minister Jawaharlal Nehru and any other Indian reaction. I left this in Swamy's very capable hands and caught a bit more sleep before my early morning flight.

When I presented my tickets to Irkutsk and Ulan Bator to Aeroflot officials in Tashkent, they seemed perplexed. After lengthy consultations, they informed me that my connecting flight had been canceled and I would have to wait in Tashkent. For two days, I waited while wandering around looking at the colorful marketplaces in the old part of the city and monumental Soviet buildings in the new area. Finally, I was told that the direct route to Irkutsk was not running, and I would have to go to Moscow to get there—two very long sides of a triangle instead of a short side. It was obvious that foreigners were not allowed to fly through the sensitive area of nuclear facilities and, also around Karaganda, a massive array of forced labor camps forming part of what became known later as the Gulag. I had to buy a ticket to Moscow. The price to Moscow for a one-way ticket, all they would sell me then, was about $60. That turned out later to be the price normally charged to Soviet citizens, not the much higher one that foreigners were required to pay. When I got to Moscow, Aeroflot charged me the high foreigner rate to Irkutsk. I bought a one-way ticket.

Arriving in Moscow for an overnight layover, I went into the city to a prominent hotel and asked for a room. Did I have a voucher? the clerk asked. When I had been in Moscow in 1962 on an Intourist package arrangement required to get a Soviet visa, I had vouchers for an assigned hotel as well as meals. Without them this time, the clerk turned me away. So I went to the AP bureau. Preston Grover, the bureau chief, let me stay in the study of his apartment across the hall from the office—a room that became my children's nursery after I succeeded him six months later.

When I began the flight east, blizzards were swirling across Siberia, forcing us to land several times. Each time, I and a few other non-Soviet passengers were met at the ramp, escorted through blowing snow to a room, and literally locked in until escorted back to the plane when it had been given clearance to leave, sometimes hours later. The towns and airports were closed to foreigners, as was most of the Soviet Union for most of its seventy-four-year existence.

The welcome at Ulan Bator the next day was a bit more relaxed. Two tourist officials escorted me to the Ulan Bator Hotel, recently built by Czechoslovakia as aid to Mongolia, just beyond the eighteen-columned State Theater on the east side of the city's main square. That huge open space, larger than Moscow's Red Square, Mongolians proudly noted, was named for Sukhe Bator. He was in the official history of Mongolia the twenty-eight-year-old leader of local Communists who took power in 1921, although they were only a front for Bolshevik secret police later known as the KGB. Behind this front, what had long been a backward province of China established itself as, in theory, an independent nation, but in fact became a backward province of the Soviet Union.

The government of the Mongolian People's Revolutionary Party (MPRP), the local Communist organization, was initially run by Mongols from the Soviet Union. In the 1930s, warplanes and armored cars of the U.S.S.R.'s Red Army were sent across the border to put down resistance from Buddhist monasteries. Moscow provided some aid to recover from widespread ravages, but it was not until after China became a Communist state in 1949 that large amounts of aid began to flow to Ulan Bator. China began offering aid in 1952, touching off competition between Moscow and Beijing for influence. A railroad built south from the Trans-Siberian line to Ulan Bator in 1950 was extended to the Chinese border in 1955. As Sino-Soviet relations thrived, the new line provided an economically important shortcut from European Russia into China's heartland compared with the tsarist-era Trans-Siberian route that looped east of Mongolia. It also brought some fifteen thousand Chinese laborers into Mongolia to build industrial aid projects in the manpower-thin country. China began to eclipse the Soviet Union in importance to Mongolia, despite the continuing Soviet grip through Moscow-trained Mongolian leaders who had succeeded the Soviet Mongols.

As its big flanking Communist neighbors drifted into open hostility in the early 1960s, Moscow forced Ulan Bator to curtail its ties to Beijing. By the time I got there at the end of November 1963, most Chinese aid projects had been suspended and most laborers were gone. Reduced traffic between the U.S.S.R. and China meant that the rail line across Mongolia had little traffic, sharply cutting transit fee earnings. These things were difficult for me to learn in Ulan Bator.

Shortly after checking into a nice suite of rooms in the hotel, I learned that I was in the hands of Mongolia's nascent tourist efforts rather than any government office responsible for visiting journalists that might answer questions. It turned out that the reason I had been given a visa was so they could try out their tourism facilities on a real, live Westerner, journalist or not. At first, this did not seem to be a problem. The tourist personnel kept me busy enough doing things that would make interesting feature stories. It was only later that I found it impossible to establish myself as a journalist who wanted to interview government officials.

The tourist personnel were a bit uncertain how to handle me. A senior tourism official and an assistant who translated with barely adequate English asked me what I wanted to do. See as much of your beautiful country as possible and learn about it, I said. What do you suggest? Well, how long do you want to stay? As long as possible, to see as much as I can, without mentioning my firm intention to get home to Monica before Christmas.

But, I asked them, how much is it going to cost me for the suite that I had been given in this nice, apparently almost empty hotel? And what will it cost for meals, guides, transport, and other things? I made it clear that I had only a limited amount of money. In those days before credit cards, I had only traveler's checks, depleted by unexpected Soviet air fares. They quoted me a room rate that seemed high. At that rate, I can't afford to stay very long, I said. So they cut the rate. This kind of negotiation continued on other expenses along the way. It was obvious that they wanted to try out as many tourist attractions as possible on me, so they were willing to keep prices down, probably to a level charged Soviets, rather than setting something special for non-Communist outsiders.

The next morning, their unfamiliarity with Westerners became even more obvious at breakfast. What did I want to eat? Well, some eggs and toast would be fine. Do you want caviar for your toast? No, that seemed extravagant. But the translator insisted that caviar went with toast, breakfast or not. In those days, it was still fairly plentiful and relatively inexpensive in the U.S.S.R., and Mongolia probably got it at a low price charged to Soviets. So, after making sure that breakfast would not cost too much, I had caviar that first time. Afterward, I self-consciously insisted that I didn't need it. Various kinds of fruit were also provided. Later meals emphasized mutton, something that may have been beef but also may have been the commonly eaten horse, plus potatoes, cabbage, and other staples served in uninspired ways. In answer to solicitous questions about the food, I politely said it was fine, good, thanks. At least I didn't go hungry.

The tourist office began arranging activities. While my questions about talking to government officials were pleasantly sidetracked, they kept me fairly busy seeing the limited sights of the fairly new, scarcely attractive capital city encrusted with ice and dirty snow in the streets. The average annual temperature in Ulan Bator, from deep winter to somewhat warm summers, is below freezing: 25 degrees Fahrenheit. In December, the thermometer seldom got above zero and usually was well below that.

A first outing was to a museum displaying in best Soviet propaganda style the horrors of Buddhism lama domination before Mongolia's Soviet takeover. A darkened stone building contained various torture devices said to have been used on ordinary people, including a heavy wooden box in which people were locked for long periods without space to sit up or lie down properly. The building was the winter palace of the Jebtsundamba Khutuktu, Mongolia's Tibetan-born senior incarnate lama known as the Living Buddha. He was the country's figurehead monarch when he died in 1924, but the Communists declared that no further incarnations would be found. The palace displayed elaborate clothing and other possessions of him and his wife, as well as things belonging to other lamas, as examples of how ordinary people's wealth was wasted in a feudal society. But what I remembered the most was how cold it was in the unheated building. Another museum, hardly less cold, was devoted to natural history. Its dingy exhibits, badly presented in poor light, included only a few examples of the dinosaur relics for which Mongolia had become famous in the 1920s expeditions of Roy Chapman Andrews from the American Museum of Natural History in New York.

In spare time between planned outings, I went over to the city's main department store west of the square along Peace Avenue. Its offerings were pretty bleak. I wanted heavy boots or at least overshoes to wear with my ordinary leather shoes from India, as well as a thicker overcoat. Alas, Mongolians averaged much smaller sizes than I. No boots or overshoes that would fit. No overcoats, either, although I liked their style of a woven woolen outside with a sheepskin inside: leather against the weave and fleece facing inward. The too-small shoes were made in the capital's small industrial zone, where I was taken through a somewhat grimy but efficient-looking shoe factory with Czechoslovak-made equipment. This was obviously the proudest example of modern industry in a nation whose economy was still almost entirely pastoral.

One outing was to a workers' rest center across rolling, snow-covered hills outside of the capital. In a grim little collection of buildings nestled in a valley, a dozen or so Mongolian men were drinking tea and amusing themselves with a game of chance without any monetary stakes, at least in my presence. It involved rolling a handful of dried sheep vertebra. The vertebrae are so formed that they can come to rest in any one of five (or maybe it was seven) different positions, and the person who rolls the most into the same position wins a round.

The tourist office, obviously trying to keep me entertained, also arranged for me to attend the circus. In addition to some good jugglers and various animal acts, this was most notable for stomach-churning displays by young women contortionists—incredible enough to churn my stomach, aside from theirs. And I went to the opera in the massive State Theater. The mimicry of Soviet culture seemed to require that even the small population of Mongolia, then estimated at about a million, should produce singers, dancers, and musicians capable of presenting classic operatic performances. The most charitable thing one could say about the performance I saw was that they tried hard with their limited resources.

Still unable to get a meaningful answer from the tourist office to my queries about talking to government officials, and knowing that no Western nation had diplomats stationed there whom I might consult, I sought interviews at the Soviet and Chinese embassies in Ulan Bator, hoping to get basic information about aid and other involvement. The Chinese refused to see me at this time when the United States did not have diplomatic relations with "Red China." The Soviets, however, received me at their large compound. The reason, presumably, was that their embassy was curious what an American journalist was doing there. It produced a diplomat who spoke some English and served me tea. When I asked about the volume and nature of Soviet economic aid, he gave only vague generalities. Questions about educational and cultural connections drew equally unsatisfactory answers. Political questions seemed fruitless.

The tourist office suggested that I might want to see some of the countryside. I eagerly agreed. It proposed a trip to Tsetserleg, a town some 275 miles west of Ulan Bator as the Mongolian crow flies. Before setting out, I complained as politely as possible about the translator that I had been using. His English was not really up to handling many of my questions about the things they had chosen to let me see. So they found another young Mongolian who also claimed to speak English. They also found some felt boots large enough to be worn over my shoes, the *valenki* so popular in Russia in frigidly snowy weather.

Four of us—one of the tourist officials, the new translator, a driver, and I—set off across the snow-covered countryside in a Soviet-made military command car with canvas top and sides and a heater minimally adequate for the below-zero temperature. As we bounced across the plains, it quickly became apparent that there were no highway markers—indeed, probably no real highway beneath the snow, just tracks across the landscape. The vehicle had a compass, however, and the driver seemed confident that landmarks told him where he was going.

The first stop was at a collection of yurts. The round yurt, known locally as a *ger,* is made of a wooden lattice circle covered with layers of felt and canvas, with a hole in the center to vent fireplace smoke. Since long before Genghis Khan's time, these easily dismantled and reassembled structures have been the homes of herders as they moved their flocks among pastures. The small core of solid but drab Soviet-looking buildings in Ulan Bator was surrounded by suburbs of yurts, most of them hidden behind fences.

It seemed unlikely that any word could have been sent ahead to warn the pastoral family living in the yurt that my guides approached. It had a motorcycle parked outside, indicating that this was a prosperous family, probably the reason it was picked. We were warmly welcomed in their warm home. Sitting on rugs, we were served Tibetan-style tea—whose salt-and-soda taste I had learned to like in Bhutan—and also *kumis,* the fermented mares' milk that is Mongolia's main alcoholic drink and a quickly acquired taste. The man of the house gave answers to my questions about his herd and other things as I looked around, noting along one part of the circular wall a little collection of pictures featuring the Communist leadership. Such displays had in some Mongolian homes replaced Buddhist shrines, but many still kept religious symbols.

Farther across the rolling, almost featureless steppe, a gas pump and a small restaurant appeared. Then on into the early night, we continued headlong until the headlights picked up the bright eyes of some animal. "Tally-ho!" The tourist official broke out a gun and cranked the windshield up as the driver slipped and swerved in the snow to follow the creature. The official took a couple of shots without hitting it, however, and eventually we lost it. So we stopped, the translator said it had been a fox, and we looked around. The three Mongolians searched the clear night sky, identified some stars to determine which way we wanted to go—this apparently being better than relying on the compass—and we set out again to pick up tracks and landmarks on the usual route.

Late that night we came to some buildings in the Orkhon River valley, where a barracks provided housing. This was a collective farm at Karakoram, the fabled capital of Genghis Khan in the thirteenth-century. The next morning, I could see that the farm, providing basic economic, medical, veterinarian, and educational services for pastoral families, was a bleak group of unpainted buildings. Nearby was a large stone tortoise that is associated somewhat uncertainly with Genghis Khan, the rest of his capital having disappeared. Massive ruins there were of a Buddhist monastery, Erdeni Tzu, built in 1585, shortly after Tibetan Buddhism was introduced into Mongolia. The monastery was razed in the 1930s Stalinist destruction of Mongolia's Buddhist establishment.

That second day we stopped to see men fishing through the thick ice of a small lake. Walking across the ice caused it to crack with the deeply distant sound of plucked violin strings. We also stopped from time to time to see herders on horseback, many of them carrying the long poles with big rope loops at the end that was the Mongolian equivalent of an American cowboy's lasso. Sometimes close to the track were small herds of horses, cattle, and sheep, and a few two-humped Bactrian camels wandered about, but larger herds always seemed to be off toward the horizon.

In addition to writing notes on Mongolian life, I was taking photos to illustrate my reports. I wanted pictures that showed horses and other livestock close up enough to be easily recognizable in a newspaper as well as pictures of the local cowboys. On request, a few cowboys caught cattle for me. Several times, the tourist official asked me why I didn't also take pictures of the large herds in the distance. I tried to explain that they would not show up well in a newspaper photo. But every time we stopped to photograph herders and livestock, the official reiterated that I should focus my little fixed-lens camera on the vast, distant herds.

Finally, Tsetserleg. Its number of unpainted wooden buildings distinguished it as one of Mongolia's more important towns. The tourist official apologized for the primitive little hotel's having only outhouses, a most inconvenient necessity as the temperature plunged much farther below zero. But he arranged there for my first interview with a governmental official. In a small office, I met the mayor, who, naturally, was also the head of the local unit of the Communist party. After preliminary politeness, I began asking questions about how he was selected, the role of the party, how the government was organized, local taxes and budgets, the economy, and similar things. This quickly bogged down. The translator, trained for tourist purposes, did not know the English for governmental or economic terms. I had to abandon the interview.

At least I was able to learn the importance of such towns for supporting herders moving among pastures in their regions. We went out to visit one herder camp west of town in the most mountainous terrain I had yet encountered in Mongolia. The families there, possibly more out of deference to officialdom than natural hospitality to strangers, showed me around and treated me to more *kumis*. They also insisted that I ride one of their two-humped Bactrian camels.

Back in Ulan Bator after I had taken more photos of herders and flocks, the head of the tourist office expressed displeasure that my camera had been trained primarily on closeups of just one mounted herder or a few horses and other cattle. Why hadn't I taken more pictures of the vast herds? The longer he talked, the more unhappy he became. Finally, he accused me of wanting to show the world that Mongolia only had a few livestock, instead of the more than 20 million in official statistics. My attempts to explain the nature of newspaper photography were unavailing. I was clearly suspected of being an anti-

Communist Westerner determined to denigrate the claimed economic success of this wonderful people's democracy.

It was in this unpleasant situation and with time running out on my visit that I resumed efforts to break out of the tourist office cocoon and talk to national government officials: the prime minister, the foreign minister, the agriculture minister, others. Finally, I was asked to provide a list of questions that I wanted to ask the prime minister, Yumjaagiyn Tsedenbal. Also the secretary general of the ruling Communist party, Tsedenbal had long been Moscow's man to run the country (with the presumed help of his Russian wife).

The smart thing would have been to write up politely bland questions about Mongolia's economic progress, its foreign relations, even its attitude toward establishing diplomatic relations with the United States, in order to get my foot in an official door. Unwisely, I instead wrote more specific questions based on what I knew about the country's difficult position between the U.S.S.R. and China, the effects on the economy of winter setbacks to livestock, and similar things. Perhaps because the questions were too specific, perhaps out of general hostility to Western journalists, perhaps because the Soviet embassy had already dropped a blackball on me, I was never given a chance to talk with a national government official.

I did, however, discover an ambassador living in my hotel from Yugoslavia, Tito's Communist nation that was part of the world nonaligned movement rather than being committed to either Moscow or Beijing. Here was someone who did talk with local officials, who had been in Mongolia long enough to know a lot. When I approached him, he invited me to tea. In fluent English, he told me a great deal about Mongolian affairs, answering questions for which I had no other sources. He was invaluable in helping me expand the tourist office's arrangements into a substantive report. Among other things, he confirmed my suspicions that the paucity of traffic on the railroad from the U.S.S.R. to China that ran a few blocks south of the hotel meant the Sino-Soviet rift was exacerbating the financial hardship for Mongolia caused by a halt of Chinese aid projects.

One final outing that the tourist office arranged, responding to my questions about the current status of Buddhism, was to Gandantegchinlen Monastery on the northwest outskirts of Ulan Bator. While a few monasteries had been preserved as museums, Gandantegchinlen seemed to be the only working religious center left from those 580 or so monasteries and temples that existed before the destruction of Mongolia's pre-Communist social and economic system. It obviously existed more to show foreign visitors than for domestic devotions, which were severely restricted. It had about one hundred monks, compared with the estimated ten thousand to twenty thousand who had been in monasteries in the Ulan Bator area before the Communist takeover.

Gandantegchinlen, whose name in Tibetan meant "great place of complete joy," was more a collection of buildings on an open plain than the kind of walled, even fortified Tibetan Buddhist monasteries I had seen in the Himalayas of India, Nepal, Sikkim, and Bhutan. Its golden-roofed temple built in 1838 was impressive with an eighty-six-foot-high golden statue of the figure representing the compassion of all Buddhas, known here as Migjid Janraisig but in Tibet called Avolokitesvara. The senior monk to whom I was introduced seemed less impressive. He professed not to know that the Dalai Lama was no longer in the Potala in Lhasa. Perhaps the Dalai Lama's flight in March 1959 was too political a subject for him to get into, or perhaps Soviet and Mongolian authorities had suppressed news of the Lhasa uprising that caused the escape.

In my last days in Ulan Bator, the tourism director raised again the matter of my not photographing vast, distant herds. Becoming a bit paranoid as I prepared to leave, I took all but two of my many rolls of film out of their yellow Kodak boxes to reduce their bulk and worked them into the lining of my overcoat. I was afraid they might be taken away from me at the airport as I left, and I hoped to have to give up only the two rolls. The boxes were hidden in the hollow arms of a large, overstuffed chair in my hotel sitting room.

Although there was no trouble at the airport, all my film getting out, arrangements to fly home were as curious as those going to Ulan Bator. When I said I did not have a return ticket from Irkutsk to Moscow, tourist officials arranged one at the only price they apparently knew: the cheap internal rate charged to Soviets and loyal satellite subjects. This was about half what I had paid to fly from Moscow to Irkutsk. By contrast, when I got to Moscow and had to buy another ticket to Tashkent to pick up my original ticketing, I was charged the high rate for foreigners, more than double what I'd paid to fly from Tashkent to Moscow. So on four flights within the Soviet Union, I was charged cheap rates twice and high rates twice.

From Irkutsk to Moscow, the TU-104 airliner had to refuel. I forget exactly where, but it probably was Omsk. It was December 21, the shortest day of the northern year, and the route was at a northerly latitude. We landed for refueling in the afternoon. I was met, escorted to a room in the terminal, and served tea. The stuffy room was not locked, however, so I wandered out onto the terrace facing the aircraft ramp and watched the sun set and the sky darken. A minder disapprovingly found me there when it was time to reboard. We took off. As the plane climbed higher and higher on its westward course, the western sky began to brighten. Then, somewhat to my surprise, I could see the sun slowly coming up again, pausing for a while just above the horizon, and then setting for a second time that day.

After another night in Grover's study, I went out to Sheremetyevo airport for the flight to Delhi via Tashkent. Moscow's main international airport had only a large shed as a passenger terminal. When it came time to board at nearly midnight, everyone had to go out into the bitter cold and stand in a flood-lit line while security personnel slowly and laboriously double-checked passports to make sure no unauthorized person escaped the Communist paradise.

Back in Delhi, I finished writing up a number of articles about Mongolia. The film went off to London for developing and selection of those photographs that fit the articles. News agency people rarely know much about how their stories are published in media around the world that get them, but I did find that the *Christian Science Monitor,* then a widely circulated and highly respected newspaper with strong interests in foreign countries, published most of the articles with many pictures.

After Christmas, Monica and I went to Kathmandu and then to Varanasi, the city long known as Benares, where an eclipse of the moon evoked great wailing from multitudes lining the Ganges River. When we got back to Delhi, a world conference on some aspect of Asian political developments was being held there. Among those attending was Owen Lattimore. Monica and I invited him to lunch to talk about what I had seen and what his perspective was on the remote nation. It was a fascinating occasion.

After finishing the AP articles on Mongolia, I wrote an overview and sent it to *The Economist,* to which I had been contributing occasional articles about developments in South Asia. The British magazine published it promptly. Its foreign editor learned in February 1964 that I was in London and invited me to lunch. He also invited Britain's leading historian of Mongolia, C. R. Bawden from the University of London's School of Oriental and African Studies. This was another fascinating lunch. Keeping an eye on Mongolia from afar, after the MPRP's 1971 congress I wrote from Hong Kong about it for the *Washington Star* and then published in *Foreign Affairs* a longer article drawing on my Moscow experience since visiting Ulan Bator, "The Sovietization of Mongolia."

Without pictures of herds of horses or other livestock.

16

DENYING KHRUSHCHEV

FOR A QUARTER OF A CENTURY, THE ONLY WAY TO GET AHEAD IN THE Soviet Union was to please Stalin. The brutal rule of a paranoid dictator, who remained isolated from the reality of personal contact with his people, was implemented by a generation of future Soviet leaders who acquired bloody hands that they later tried to hide in the white gloves of statesmanship. Most of them seemed to have had any humanity crushed in the process. They became such colorless, bureaucratically reclusive success stories as Mikhail Andreyevich Suslov, who was known as an austere Communist ideologist after most people had forgotten his role as the butcher of Lithuania and in other atrocities. For them, the masses were only to be manipulated from afar, to be addressed from a safe distance atop Lenin's tomb or other shielded podiums in controlled situations.

But somehow, one man with hands as bloody as any, with as much ruthless love of power for its own sake as any, with a taste for conspiracy to match the worst of them, emerged differently from the Stalinist pressure cooker. He still retained some sense of human relations, some love of personal contact with the Soviet people, who enthusiastically reciprocated his personal warmth. He knew how to act like a popular politician as well as an unelected ruler.

This was Nikita Sergeyevich Khrushchev, first secretary of the Communist Party of the Soviet Union beginning shortly after Stalin's death in 1953, and also the head of the government after becoming premier in 1958. He was a colorful, dynamic figure who catapulted the U.S.S.R. from its closed, secretive decades of Stalinism into a superficially open, but at heart no less secretive, relationship with the world.

Khrushchev enjoyed strutting the stage as the leader of a nation that had pulled itself up by its bootstraps to become a great power. He began to travel abroad to personify and propagate Soviet claims of world authority and of Communism's political and economic success. He became the chief salesman for the Communist concept of economic growth through Soviet-style central planning. With that concept widely accepted not only in the vast reaches of the world then emerging from colonialism and seeking shortcuts to independent prosperity but also among many Western economists, Khrushchev easily found foreign audiences to give him the personal accolades that he so enjoyed. He traveled abroad frequently, and he entertained a steady stream of foreign leaders in Moscow.

The first time I reported on Khrushchev was when he visited India in February 1960. After talks with Prime Minister Jawaharlal Nehru and other usual events for official visits to New Delhi, Khrushchev went to Bhilai. On a previous visit to India, in December 1955, the Soviet leader had promised aid for the construction of a large steel plant at Bhilai as part of the Indian government's "public sector" industrialization.

Bhilai was in 1955 a village in a remote part of central India where coal and iron ore were found close together. Soviet engineers had by the time of Khrushchev's second visit been working in the new township there for more than three years. It was a hardship assignment under dusty, basic living conditions where daytime temperatures soared above 100 degrees and nights were little cooler for weeks on end in pre-monsoon May and June. The most memorable part of reporting Khrushchev's visit to Bhilai was the tremendous enthusiasm with which the Soviet men, women, and children living there in virtual exile greeted him. He was an obviously popular figure, and he responded with the warm affection of a born politician—as if, contrary to the Stalinist system, he had been seeking votes in public meetings all his life. He seemed genuinely to enjoy shaking hands and even exchanging bear hugs with his adulatory countrymen, kissing countrywomen.

In addition to wanting to see the world on his own foreign trips, Khrushchev invited to Moscow numerous foreign leaders, particularly those from the Third World whom he cultivated in an effort to offset Western influence among newly independent, mostly nonaligned nations. His favorite place for entertaining them, naturally enough, was in the historic Kremlin.

The yellowish Grand Kremlin Palace, built in the 1840s just west of fourteenth- and fifteenth-century churches, stands boldly on a hill above the crenellated red brick walls that define the ancient heart of Moscow, looking out over the Moscow River. Most impressive of the palace's staterooms is the Georgievsky Hall, commemorating the tsarist military order of St. George, the dragon slayer. Along its 190-foot length, under its fifty-five-foot-high arched ceiling hung with five magnificent chandeliers, are marble slabs carved with the names of honored military units and generals. Across the hall's elaborate brown parquet floor of rare woods, polished to reflect the white walls, have walked generations of great Russians and world leaders.

When Stalin ruled from the Kremlin, it was a closed, mysterious place. But, after consolidating his new power, Khrushchev opened up much of the historic citadel so the public could see the churches and museums that inspired pride in Russian history. A high point in state visits to the U.S.S.R. of kings and emperors, of presidents and prime ministers was a formal reception for them in the Georgievsky Hall.

In addition to journalists from a visitor's home country who accompanied him or were resident in Moscow, Soviet authorities invited some Western journalists to these receptions. As representatives of the Western press as a whole, the Moscow bureau chiefs of the four major Western news agencies—the Associated Press, Reuters, United Press International, and Agence France Presse—routinely received calls from the press department of the Soviet Foreign Ministry to pick up invitations. In addition, a rotating selection of individual newspaper and broadcast correspondents was also invited. When I succeeded Preston Grover as AP bureau chief in June 1964, I became a regular on the invitation list.

At the south end of the hall closest to the Moscow River gathered the Soviet leadership and the honored visitor with a few of his senior officials. There was an invisible line that separated them from the lesser Soviet officials, diplomats, and journalists who made up the reception guests. Only on personal invitation could a diplomat cross that line to talk with Khrushchev or his top comrades. We journalists knew that we would be cut off by bodyguards if we had the audacity to move toward the line. Sometimes, instead of having aides bring favored diplomats up to talk with him, Khrushchev would cross the line himself to invite conversation with diplomats and even journalists, with whom he occasionally liked to have verbal jousts.

Among the Kremlin receptions that stand out in my memory was one on September 11, 1964. It was for the president of India, Dr. Sarvepalli Radhakrishnan, a world-renowned philosopher who had in the years around 1920 employed modern scholarly terms to give some coherence to the eclectic collection of ancient myths and beliefs known as Hinduism. Nehru selected Radhakrishnan to become a decorative vice president of India, and in 1962 he moved up to the figurehead position of president. Radhakrishnan made both ceremonial posts influential with his wise counsel to leaders of the ruling Congress Party. More assertive and gregarious, but no less intelligent, was Radhakrishnan's son, Dr. Sarvepalli Gopal. Gopal, an Oxford-educated historian, was the head of the historical section of the Indian Foreign Ministry, a protégé of Nehru's, and a friend of mine.

Radhakrishnan's 1964 visit to the Soviet Union was the occasion—it might even be described as the cover—for Gopal and other government officials accompanying him to conduct sensitive business. After India's Himalayan border war with China in 1962, the Soviet Union halted sales of military equipment to India. At the time of Radhakrishnan's visit two years later, Delhi wanted Khrushchev's government to resume sales. It wanted on long-term barter arrangements new kinds of warplanes, tanks, and other equipment that might be used in the Himalayas, or on the plains facing traditional enemy Pakistan. The Indian press had carried stories about this goal.

Official statements on the beginning of talks between Indian and Soviet officials were as usual opaque. But at the Kremlin reception that night, Gopal took me by the elbow and steered me into the center of hall. As we paced up and down under the chandeliers, he told me in low tones exactly what weaponry the Soviets had agreed to provide and other details of the talks. I had a good story, although not an exclusive one.

By a convention that had developed years earlier out of the competitive rough and tumble of chasing people at large Moscow receptions, the four Western news agencies pooled their news gleanings at the end of such events before going back to their offices to write separate stories. We bureau chiefs would stand near the door as people left and compare notes on what we had learned. Nonetheless, I had the comfort of better background and overall depth on this story. And often the other bureau chiefs were not so interested in a story that they heard secondhand as was the person who talked directly to the source. The trick was for that person to fill in the others in as brief and unexciting a way as possible—yet without being liable to later accusations of cheating on the agreement—so the others would file only scant reports, if anything.

After Gopal's briefing, the best part of the evening was still to come. Radhakrishnan was accompanied from Delhi by a dozen or so senior journalists, virtually all of them representing the English-language media that dominated Indian public discussion. All of them were acquaintances of mine, some good friends. I explained to them the convention that journalists from the honored guest's country could approach the invisible line and ask to talk with Khrushchev, who seemed always to oblige. My friends naturally had questions that they wanted to ask about the official talks, about relations between their two countries in general, and a few other topical but narrowly national points. I, however, had something else in mind.

In 1964, the United Nations was conducting peacekeeping operations in several parts of the world. Some of the operations went against Soviet foreign policy interests in trying to cultivate and win over particular nonaligned nations that objected to them for nationalistic reasons. With political calculation, Moscow opposed them as Western colonialism. To show its loyalty to objecting nations, the Soviet Union refused to pay U.N. assessments for the disputed operations. Its refusal angered a majority in the U.N. General Assembly, where Moscow could not exercise the veto that it had in the Security Council. Over Soviet objections, the assembly voted that a country that failed to pay its peacekeeping assessments would, after a certain deadline, not be allowed to vote in U.N. meetings.

Angered in turn, the U.S.S.R. replied that it would quit the world organization rather than be forced to pay for operations to which it objected. Moscow was daring the rest of the world to bring the assessments issue to a test. It seemed to assume that enough nations would feel the need to keep a superpower in the organization that the U.N. majority against it would wither away. But, going into the summer of 1964, the majority held firm. Soviet officials and propagandists intensified their campaign as a showdown neared when the U.N. General Assembly met in New York in late September. Moscow's position seemed like an unrealistic bluff to most diplomatic and journalistic observers in the Soviet capital, but they heard it endlessly reiterated.

Standing in Georgievsky Hall, I gave the Indian journalists a quick summary of this situation. Go up there and talk to Khrushchev, I said, and, in addition to Indo-Soviet questions, ask him if the Soviet Union would really quit the United Nations rather than be forced to pay the assessments. Don't mention the Soviet propaganda campaign on the subject, I added.

Khrushchev was quite willing to talk to them. India was a major player in the nonaligned world, and its press was therefore an important sounding board. Khrushchev's personal interpreter for English, a smiling but carefully proper man named Viktor Sukhodrev, translated the Indians' questions and his answers, so there could be no question about the accuracy of what Khrushchev said. And the Indian reporters took down the answers in shorthand, so there could be no question about getting a complete account.

They came back across the line and read their notes to me. On the question about really walking out of the United Nations rather than being forced to pay in order to retain a U.N. vote, Khrushchev's answer was something like, "Of course not! We have no intention of leaving the U.N. It's too important an organization for us not to be there."

I dutifully briefed my fellow bureau chiefs on this point, buried in a lot of other material that the Indian journalists had collected from Khrushchev, what Gopal had told me, and my gleanings from various diplomats at the reception. Then I went back to the AP office and wrote one story on what I had learned about Soviet-Indian talks and another quoting Khrushchev on the United Nations. The latter pointed out that he had undercut a months-long Soviet campaign to get the U.N. to back off of the assessments showdown by his determination to stay in the organization. My story received wide notice abroad. The other bureau chiefs apparently had buried the point in general stories, if they reported it at all.

In Moscow there was silence. Then, two weeks after the Kremlin reception and as the U.N. General Assembly was about to open, the Soviet government newspaper *Izvestiya* published on September 26 an article on its international news page entitled "Soviet Position Is Unchanged." After quoting Lenin on the way "the venal capitalist press" was accustomed to lie, it said:

> Speaking about a possible discussion at the forthcoming General Assembly session of the problem of the "financial arrears" of the Soviet Union, the Associated Press implies that the Soviet Union has allegedly changed its position on this question and is willing to remain in the U.N. even if it is deprived of the right to vote in accordance with Article 19 of this organization. The news agency refers to words allegedly heard somewhere to the effect that the Soviet Union "has no intention of leaving the U.N."
>
> Actually, nobody has pronounced these words, and the whole idea about a "new" position of the USSR is pure invention with no basis at all. The position of the Soviet Union on this question is firm and unchanged.

The article went on to reiterate Soviet refusal "to pay the expenses of maintaining U.N. troops that have become an instrument of the colonialists' policy." It concluded:

> That's how it is, gentlemen of the Associated Press. You are free to lie, to make noise, to shout and to repeat the lies about "changes" in the position of the Soviet Union. There is no change, and there will be no change. . . . [T]he Soviet Union will not pay the bills for colonialist adventurers.

Naturally, I wrote a story quoting *Izvestiya*. In it, I explained that Khrushchev had made the statement, without reference to the intricacies of Article 19, through his personal translator and taken down in shorthand by experienced journalists. Significantly, the Soviet Foreign Ministry's press department never chastised me for the original story. It was always quick to complain to Western correspondents who got something wrong in a way that reflected ill on the U.S.S.R. or who otherwise created unwarranted trouble. Sometimes the press department found ways to penalize those who had offended it, and correspondents had even been expelled from the U.S.S.R. for troublesome or erroneous reporting. But I was untouchable on this one. The Foreign Ministry had to have known exactly what Khrushchev had said.

Nonetheless, the ministry—or, rather, the Communist Party's Central Committee Secretariat that controlled it, maybe even Khrushchev himself—decided that the campaign against the U.N. assessment had to continue. The showdown did not come that autumn. A year later, the United States and other Western countries backed down and quit trying to force Moscow to pay.

Izvestiya's retreat from something the Soviet leader had said embarrassingly highlighted Khrushchev's long-established tendency to make bombastic statements without thinking ahead to possible consequences. Four days after the Kremlin reception, Khrushchev was quoted by a Japanese parliamentary delegation as saying Soviet military officials and scientists had shown him a "terrible weapon" of unlimited power, capable of destroying mankind. After worldwide headlines, we journalists asked him about this at a return reception given by Radhakrishnan two nights later. Khrushchev claimed to have been misunderstood. His son wrote decades later that he had seen a new Soviet intercontinental ballistic missile just before meeting the Japanese.

The contradictions were among several signs that the foreign community in Moscow—journalists, diplomats, and others—failed to appreciate as showing the growing vulnerability of Khrushchev's power. We knew that he had stirred displeasure within the Soviet Communist Party with his preemptory ways, but we did not understand how significant this unhappiness was. Within three weeks of *Izvestiya*'s denial, however, Khrushchev had been overthrown by his Communist Party comrades.

17

WRECKING RECEIVING LINES

THIS IS THE STORY OF HOW I THWARTED A SOVIET PRACTICE OF GIVING prominence in Moscow to the Viet Cong early in the Vietnam War period, and as a result caused the Soviet government to abandon its use of diplomatic receiving lines.

Since the development of special rules for the exchange of representatives among medieval Italian city states, diplomacy has become swaddled in ritual. Some of the rules by which diplomats live are codified in international agreements, such as diplomatic immunity. Others are only accepted in practice but nonetheless held almost sacred by most protocol-conscious members of foreign services.

One accepted concept is the ranking of ambassadors for purposes of precedence and ceremony. To avoid controversies among representatives of different countries, ambassadors are ranked by seniority. This has nothing to do with age. Seniority depends upon how long it has been since an ambassador formally presented his credentials from his own country's chief of state to the chief of state of the nation to which he is accredited. The ambassador accredited the earliest among those currently in a capital is the *doyen* of the diplomatic corps there. He is consulted by the host foreign ministry on matters affecting the corps as a whole, speaks for the corps on ceremonial occasions, and organizes farewell parties for ambassadors who leave after a shorter time in residence than his own.

A tradition much cherished by diplomats is the receiving line. The numerous airport arrivals and departures of state visitors, receptions, and other formal occasions of the diplomatic world require some organized way of handling introductions and greetings. Ambassadors therefore line up to shake hands, or press their palms together in front of their faces in the Hindu *namaste* form of greeting, or sometimes among Communist comrades exchange bear hugs, or whatever seems appropriate.

But how to line up? Seniority provides the answer. By diplomatic convention, after the host and senior officials of his country at the head of a receiving line with the chief guest, followed by diplomats of the visitor's country, the line continues with the *doyen* of the diplomatic corps and then other ambassadors according to their time since accreditation.

So it was that, when an important foreign leader came to Moscow in August 1965 and the Soviet leadership gave a reception for him in the Kremlin's magnificent Georgievsky Hall, there naturally had to be a receiving line. There always was such a line when the U.S.S.R. entertained a foreign leader. Sometimes a short line was organized just inside the main entrance to the hall, at its northwest corner. This time, however, Soviet authorities had invited more diplomats than could be conveniently lined up there to shake hands with the honored guest. The receiving line would not fit conveniently into a corner of Georgievsky Hall.

I usually was so busy elsewhere that I arrived at receptions after the receiving lines had broken up. In more than a year of attending several Kremlin receptions a month, I had not noticed how Soviet Foreign Ministry protocol officials handled receiving lines. But this time I was a bit early. The officials were inviting ambassadors who would form the receiving line to walk from the Georgievsky Hall in the nineteenth-century Grand Kremlin Palace through a short passageway and down a few curving stairs into a connecting hall. This was the Granovitaya Palata, built in the fifteenth century for Tsar Ivan III to hold councils of state and receive foreign envoys. The four domed chambers of its ceiling that curve down to a massive central column and the outer walls are decorated in dark murals that maintain the heavy, almost gloomy atmosphere of Ivan the Great and other brutal tsars.

Trailing behind the diplomats, I watched with idle curiosity a procedure to which I had never before paid attention. Soviet protocol officials, lists in hand to be sure they did not slight anyone, were telling the ambassadors where to line up. Since this was by seniority, the longer-resident ambassadors well knew who should be standing on their left and right, and they readily fell into place toward the head of the line. But toward the end of the line, which had some seventy-five diplomats in it, the protocol officers had to steer people. As that went on, I noticed a curious thing: the protocol officers put into line the representative of the National Liberation Front (NLF) of South Vietnam, Dang Quang Minh.

It was then six months after an attack by Communist troops on the American military advisory team's compound at Pleiku in the South Vietnamese highlands had led to the first U.S. air raid on North Vietnam's capital, Hanoi. Soviet premier Alexei N. Kosygin was in Hanoi at the time urging North Vietnam to consider negotiations with the South's American-backed Saigon government, rather than pursuing a war that Moscow feared would worsen the international atmosphere. Ho Chi Minh's Hanoi government was quietly outraged that a fellow Communist country—even worse, a Communist superpower—would seem soft on American causes, so they politely ignored Kosygin's message.

Even more outraged were the Soviets that Kosygin's presence had been ignored in Washington's decision to bomb Hanoi. This escalation of the war was perceived by the Soviet Union, in its competition with China for influence in North Vietnam, as leaving no alternative to giving full public support to Hanoi. That also meant support for the NLF. The NLF, the political aspect of a force referred to as the Viet Cong, at the time claimed to be an indigenous expression of South Vietnamese public opposition to Saigon. Years later it was admitted to have been a creation and fully controlled creature of Hanoi, whose army constituted the core of the guerrilla war against Saigon.

Two months after the Pleiku attack and Kosygin's visit to Hanoi, Dang Quang Minh arrived on April 23, 1965, to take up residence as the NLF representative in Moscow. He was given an official welcome at Vnukovo II, the ceremonial side of the Moscow airport used for special events. A few days later, TASS, which claimed to be a Soviet news agency but was primarily a propaganda outlet and cover for nonjournalistic activities that included espionage, carried a report about Minh. It said he had presented credentials from the head of the NLF to the president of the Soviet Committee of Solidarity with Asian and African Countries. The committee was a group that pretended to be private citizens—in a country where nothing was private because the government and everything else were controlled by the Communist Party and its strong right arm, the U.S.S.R.'s political police, the KGB. The committee was used to maintain ostensibly unofficial relations with the many Third World underground political groups or guerrilla armies that the Soviet Communist Party championed—and, in many cases, secretly financed through KGB channels—while the Soviet government maintained formal relations with the governments that those groups and armies opposed.

The TASS report on Minh's presentation of credentials followed the pattern of the agency's accounts of new ambassadors' presenting their diplomatic credentials to the president of the U.S.S.R. or one of the many vice presidents who stood in for that figurehead. I thought at the time that the report on Minh was curious, mainly because I could not remember any other newly arrived Asian or African liberation group's representative getting the prominence of such a presentation ceremony. Vietnam was obviously special because of its impact on both Soviet-American and Sino-Soviet relations. Moscow wanted to prove its devotional support of Hanoi to Soviet antagonists in Washington and Beijing. The NLF man had become a symbol of this, going through the pretense of representing an authority comparable to a legitimate, recognized government.

As part of that symbolism, the protocol officers at the August 1965 reception were putting him into line just as if he had ambassadorial status. Several ambassadors who had arrived in Moscow after Minh were placed in the receiving line after him. I recognized two of them, the ambassadors of Greece and Turkey, who had recently arrived a few days apart. After the visitor who was being honored with the reception had gone down the line shaking all the hands, and the group had moved back into the Georgievsky Hall, I went up to one of these ambassadors and invited the other one, who was standing nearby, to join us.

"Did you realize," I asked them, "that you were placed in the receiving line after the representative of the South Vietnamese National Liberation Front—who is not an ambassador?" The Greek and Turk were both surprised. They had not been in town long enough to recognize many colleagues in the diplomatic corps. They had just been following the Soviet protocol officials' directions. To be sure my point got across, I vaguely suggested something about how awkward, even embarrassing, this improper positioning in line below a diplomatic imposter who is an enemy of the United States must be for two ambassadors representing American allies.

My self-appointed role as *agent provocateur* was quickly rewarded. The two ambassadors became indignant. Each man's rising concern stimulated the other's further reaction. With a little more encouragement from me, they worked themselves up to declaring that being put below the NLF man was unacceptable. What, I asked them, does that mean for the next receiving line? They agreed that they would refuse to join a line in which the NLF man was placed as an ambassador ranking above them.

In accordance with the conventions of sharing news gleaned from Kremlin receptions, I casually mentioned this to the other Western news agency bureau chiefs who were present. None seemed interested. Then I went back to the AP bureau and wrote a story saying that the new Greek and Turkish ambassadors had declared that they would not stand in any future Soviet receiving line below the NLF representative. The next morning's *International Herald Tribune* in Paris published my story prominently. Virtually the entire diplomatic corps in Moscow received the paper by air mail. In those pre-Internet days it was read as the main source of world news. The gauntlet had been thrown down most publicly.

Within a day or two, Monica and our two babies and I left Moscow for two delightful months of home leave spent visiting our parents in Evanston and Baton Rouge. During my absence, Preston Grover, whom I had replaced as bureau chief in 1964, came back temporarily to fill in for me. Before leaving, I made sure that he understood the receiving line situation. I asked him to watch what happened on future occasions that normally would have receiving lines.

By the time I returned to Moscow in late October, there were no more Soviet-organized receiving lines. The Foreign Ministry had abandoned responsibility for lining people up. Rather than deal with the political problem of either downgrading the NLF's Minh or facing a boycott by some ambassadors, the Soviet government had taken a humiliating third way out. The Foreign Ministry informed embassies that if any of them wanted to have receiving lines when visitors came from their countries, it would be up to the visitor's own embassy to organize the lines. Soviet protocol officials would be glad to assist. But the basic message was that the embassies themselves would have to take responsibility for choosing how to position people.

There continued to be some receiving lines, but not many. So far as I could tell, no embassy in Moscow chose to put Minh in lines for receptions that included non-Communist diplomats. The NLF's man became less prominent on Moscow's diplomatic scene.

18

BLOCKING BLACKMAIL

HE SOUNDED INSISTENT, ALMOST PLEADING. "I MUST SEE YOU," HE SAID on the phone. "Can we have lunch today?" Perhaps he only wanted to repay my hospitality of a couple of weeks earlier when he first came to Moscow. But there was something more urgent in his voice. I agreed to meet him at the Hotel Nacional for lunch in the second-floor dining room that looked out across Manege Square at the Kremlin. It was one of the few restaurants in Moscow easily accessible to Westerners in the 1960s.

He was one of the most prominent journalists in a small West European nation that was a staunch member of NATO. He edited a major newspaper, wrote a popular column, and frequently appeared as a television commentator. Everyone in the country knew him, and he knew everyone, with access to top government circles. Now, in 1966, he was making his first visit to the Soviet Union in order to write a series of articles on the country.

His nation's media had no resident correspondents in the U.S.S.R. He therefore lacked the kind of connections with Western journalists in Moscow that some visiting reporters depend on for guidance and advice on first visits to a new country. So he turned to the Associated Press, the main world agency providing news to his own country, for help in Moscow. Before he arrived, I received a letter from the AP bureau chief in his country introducing the editor and asking me to provide whatever help he needed. It was a normal thing for the AP, something I did for a lot of visiting journalists.

When he came to Moscow, he phoned. His English was fluent. I invited him to visit the AP bureau and have lunch in our apartment across the hall. Monica was used to having luncheon guests as part of my job as bureau chief. Our maid, Svetlana Razuvayeva, fixed such lunches, usually with Monica's help, with our babies sometimes crawling or toddling in from the nursery for cameo appearances.

The visitor and I had a long talk about Soviet politics and economics and living standards, relations with China and wartime Vietnam and other current foreign policy topics, restrictions on foreign correspondents and how to request interviews through the Foreign Ministry's press department, which diplomats were worth talking to besides his own country's ambassador, using the AP's Telex machine if he wanted to send stories back to his paper, and many other things. He struck me as the good, solid reporter that his reputation indicated, a mature professional.

Several times during the next week he came back to see me. He tested various story ideas on me and asked for additional background to put into perspective things he had learned in interviews. Then he set off on a trip to several Soviet cities. He was seeking a feel for the way things worked outside Moscow. Intourist, the official Soviet travel agency that was controlled by the political police, the KGB, had laid out an itinerary for him to travel by himself, with translators and chauffeured cars meeting his plane or train at every stop.

Naturally, I warned him that foreigners were carefully programmed by the authorities. We were supposed to meet only those people and see only those things that had been approved in advance to give us impressions that the Communist regime wanted us to have. The only factories or collective farms that foreigners were allowed to visit, for example, were the showcase ones whose production was good by Soviet standards, and people whom they met knew exactly what the official line was and recited it almost by rote. Questions that came too close to awkward facts were answered with half-truths or not answered at all.

Trips within the U.S.S.R. were thus made so sterile that I never went on the kind of conducted tours of Soviet provincial areas that the Foreign Ministry organized for Moscow-based foreign correspondents. My trips with other American journalists to Central Asia, to the Caucasus, across the length of the Soviet Union to the Pacific on the Trans-Siberian Railway, and to other places were no more successful in shaking official controls, but at least we were—within severe limits—able to choose which places we wanted to visit instead of having an itinerary laid out in advance. But, of course, we were always put into those same hotel rooms that every other foreign visitor seemed to get, the ones that presumably were bugged with concealed microphones and probably had concealed cameras, too. The KGB did not give people any privacy. It was because of the constant problem of the political police that Moscow correspondents tried whenever possible to travel in pairs rather than alone.

The West European journalist's insistent phone call came about two weeks after I had last seen him, before his trip outside Moscow by himself. He was back. And he sounded concerned.

When I met him at the Nacional, he was obviously agitated. We were quickly shown a restaurant table. I was aware that tables assigned to foreigners—maybe *all* the tables—were bugged: microphones in the ashtray, the flower display, whatever. That did not bother me. We lived with surveillance all the time. The Russians who worked in the AP bureau were regularly questioned about what we did. Probably Svetlana, too. It was a KGB condition of being allowed to work for foreigners. My attitude was that there was no use worrying about the bugged phones, the microphones in the walls, and employees' reports on our activities. There was nothing to hide in my private life. Professionally, I collected information in order to publish it, so nothing to hide there, either, except maybe sources. To the limited extent that I had any private sources in Moscow's claustrophobic and sometimes paranoid atmosphere, they were people who recognized the facts of Soviet life. Some of them, such as a *Pravda* editor who talked to me from time to time over lunch or in his office without official interview arrangements, knew the facts.

When we sat down to order lunch, he eagerly, anxiously poured out a story of what had happened to him in Tbilisi, the capital of Soviet Georgia. Ah, yes, I knew Tbilisi. It had been the third stop on a Caucasian trip that Vince Burke of the *Los Angeles Times* and I had taken a year earlier. Vince had picked up some sort of bug at the first stop, in Baku, capital of Soviet Azerbaijan. By the time we got to Yerevan, capital of Soviet Armenia, he was feeling sick and losing enthusiasm. Finally, he decided to fly directly home to Moscow, skipping the third stop, in Tbilisi. But I had forged ahead by myself to interview people on various aspects of Georgia, to visit Stalin's home village of Gori up the valley northwest of Tbilisi and several other places, and to write a few feature stories despite being unable to get meaningful answers to the more probing questions. Nothing untoward had happened, despite my being alone.

The West European editor was not so fortunate.

Intourist had assigned him a translator and a driver in Tbilisi. They had taken him around to see the city, to visit Gori, to talk to a few minor local officials. He had had interviews on such safe subjects as claimed health standards and production of the local wine, which was noted as the Soviet Union's best but wisely was kept out of international wine-tasting competitions. Then, he related, one afternoon his driver said a cousin was having a party that evening at a village near Tbilisi. They were invited. It was a good chance to meet a broad range of Soviet people, the translator explained. The editor accepted the invitation.

In typical Georgian style, there was lots of food, drink, and music, lots of toasts to friendship and long life and other things. He drank a few. The next thing he remembered, he was in bed, nude, in a compromising position with a nude boy. Flashbulbs were going off as people standing around the bed took photographs. Then the boy disappeared, and his clothes were handed to him. He was groggy, but he remembered that on the way back to Tbilisi the translator said he shouldn't worry about this, it was just an unfortunate incident.

But he was worried. He knew a setup for blackmail when he saw it. I confirmed his suspicions. Sometimes the KGB made such setups appear to be heterosexual activity, sometimes homosexual—whatever seemed likely to be the most effective. Either way, such things had been happening in the U.S.S.R. for years with military attaches from Western embassies in Moscow who were drugged while traveling, with diplomats, with foreign businessmen and academics, but rarely with journalists. In the case of military attaches, the purpose usually was to get them withdrawn from the Soviet Union because Soviet authorities had decided on the basis of surveillance that they were too perceptive, too observant, generally too effective to be allowed to practice their authorized job of seeking to learn about the Soviet armed forces. For others, the KGB's goal was blackmail, but most working journalists were not worth blackmailing.

I told the editor about cases of people who had been compromised in the U.S.S.R. and were later blackmailed into providing information, if not becoming fully indoctrinated spies. And about those who had been blackmailed into becoming "agents of influence" by subtly pushing Soviet propaganda lines through their work or personal contacts.

You're right to be worried, I told him. The KGB is obviously working according to a plan that it probably began developing when you applied for your visa. At some time in the future, back home, someone will approach you discreetly. He won't have copies of the photographs with him, not the first time. There will only be an allusion to "that unfortunate business in Tbilisi." But the point will be clear. They may ask you to gather information in your country, or at the least to pass along the kind of inside information that your high-level political contacts can yield. They may try to bring pressure on you to play down in your editing, writing, and television commentary any criticism of future Soviet actions. Or they may want you to give subtle support to some Soviet propaganda campaign against NATO plans.

But you can protect yourself, I told him. Do three things. First, go directly from here to see your country's ambassador in Moscow, whom you already know from interviewing him. Tell him the whole story. He will probably write up a secret record of it. A few people in your Foreign Ministry will see it, but not many. Then, as soon as you get home, tell the whole story to your wife. And tell the publisher of your newspaper. They don't need to tell anyone else.

Then, when some Soviet agent eventually approaches you, tell him politely but firmly that you cannot be blackmailed. You will have nothing to fear. The KGB would only embarrass itself if it tries to make use of the photographs. You could say that you will write a column about any attempt to blackmail you.

He seemed relieved. We finished lunch and parted. I saw the ambassador of his country at a reception that evening and asked if the journalist had talked with him after our luncheon, without asking the subject. He said he had.

That was the last I ever heard of the journalist, except for a letter from the AP bureau chief in his country. He wrote that the journalist had asked that I be told he greatly appreciated my help and advice.

There was, however, an interesting development about a year later. It involved the New York correspondent for one of South America's most respected newspapers. The paper depended on the AP for world news coverage, and its New York man relied on AP copy to help him cover the United States. So when he was planning a reporting trip to the Soviet Union, he got in touch with the editor of AP World Service, my former bureau chief and friend from India, Wally Sims. Wally wrote to me that the correspondent was coming and, as usual, I should extend whatever hospitality the Moscow bureau could offer.

He was a distinguished older man who had prepared himself well for the trip. Not only had he been reading widely on Soviet affairs, but also he had been studying Russian and within a few months had acquired a passably workable knowledge of the language. After the usual lunch and briefings by me, the usual interviews around Moscow, and numerous visits to the AP bureau just to chat, he set off by himself to tour the country with Intourist's help. I gave him the usual warnings. He said he would be back to see me after his tour, and he would want to send some articles from the bureau's Telex machine.

It was only several weeks later that I realized that he was long overdue to return to Moscow, but we had not heard from him. After waiting another week or so, I sent a message to Wally asking if the correspondent had returned to New York. Wally replied that he had. I thought it strange that, after being so affable and somewhat dependent during his earlier stay in Moscow, he had not gotten in touch after his Soviet provincial tour. But then I dismissed it from my mind.

About a year after that, when I was at Harvard, I received a phone call one day from New York. It was the correspondent. Wally had mentioned to him that I was now in the Boston area and, on request, had provided my phone number. He wanted to apologize, the correspondent said. He had felt bad about not getting in touch with me when he returned to Moscow. He had wanted to thank me for the help I had given him. But there had been a problem.

When he was in Tbilisi, he related, his Intourist translator and driver had suggested that they go to a party. After some drinking, the next thing he knew was that he was nude in bed with a nude woman. Photographs were being taken. Later, he was assured that everything was all right, that this was an unfortunate incident.

But, he said, he was told one thing very firmly. "When you go back through Moscow, you must not talk to Mr. Bradsher."

19

STABBED IN THE BACK

THE LAUNCH OF A SPACECRAFT WAS BIG NEWS IN MOSCOW IN 1964 WHEN the space race with the United States was deemed of worldwide importance. Six Soviet space flights beginning with Yuri Gagarin's on April 12, 1961, had each carried one person. Now, Voskhod—the name means "sunrise"—took three men into orbit on Monday, October 12, 1964, for what was proclaimed to be "a long flight."

This meant an even busier time than usual for the Associated Press bureau in Moscow. The three-man bureau was shorthanded. George Syvertsen, the correspondent with the most Moscow experience, was on vacation and about to pick up a new car for the bureau in Helsinki and drive it down to Moscow. Fred Coleman had just arrived on September 15 from AP New York on his first foreign assignment. I had been in Moscow for seven months, the last three and a half of them as bureau chief. In addition, Brian Calvert from AP's London photography staff was in town on a short-term visa.

Fred and I wrote articles on the launching based on reports from the Soviet news agency, TASS, and on watching television, those being our only sources because the Soviets never held briefings or allowed access to launch sites. The leader of the Soviet Union, Nikita S. Khrushchev, appeared on television congratulating the cosmonauts by radiotelephone after they reached orbit, and they replied on television. Khrushchev, the first secretary of the Soviet Communist Party and premier of the government, was at his vacation estate on the Black Sea beach at Pitsunda in the Abkhazia region of Soviet Georgia. With him was a fellow member of the party's eleven-man ruling committee, the Presidium, who was the titular president of the Soviet Union, Anastas I. Mikoyan.

The televised congratulations turned out to be Khrushchev's last public act in the role he had held since 1953 of the Soviet Union's ebullient boss. His next act made Fred and me even busier than the space shot had already done.

It became known later that the Presidium had met in Moscow the day after Voskhod's launch and decided to remove Khrushchev from party and government leadership. He was the victim of a Kremlin *coup d'etat,* stabbed in the back by his comrades and protégés. Leonid I. Brezhnev assumed the top job of party boss. While leading the Soviet Union longer than anyone except Stalin, Brezhnev dragged the country down from Khrushchev's improvement in living standards into an era of stagnation.

Brezhnev had first met Khrushchev, who was twelve years older, shortly after joining the Communist Party in 1931. Khrushchev was already a rising star in the party, which he had joined the year after the 1917 Bolshevik Revolution. On the Ukrainian front in World War II, Brezhnev was a political commissar working under Khrushchev, who was Stalin's senior political commissar in the south making sure soldiers loyally did as they were ordered. From then on, Brezhnev clearly was Khrushchev's protégé.

After six months of political infighting following Stalin's death on March 5, 1953, Khrushchev assumed what had been the old dictator's key job: party leader with the title of first secretary of the Central Committee, the party group that in theory set policies and selected the Presidium, although committee members were actually selected by Presidium bosses in a top-down control system. Khrushchev gave Brezhnev jobs that led to his becoming in February 1956 a candidate, or alternate, member of the Presidium and one of the Central Committee secretaries. After Khrushchev out-maneuvered a Presidium effort to oust him in June 1957 by rallying the Central Committee on his side, he promoted Brezhnev to full membership in the Presidium.

After another protégé of Khrushchev's had fallen by the wayside, in 1960 Frol R. Kozlov won favor as Khrushchev's right-hand man and party second secretary. Brezhnev, who had seemed to be in the running for that job, was sidelined to the powerless honor of chairman of the Presidium of the Supreme Soviet, the nation's rubberstamp parliament. This was the job commonly described by foreigners as president of the U.S.S.R. He kept his Presidium seat but lost his party secretary job. It was in the presidency role that I first encountered Brezhnev, reporting his state visit to India in December 1961. The visit was not memorable.

Kozlov suffered a stroke in April 1963 and never recovered. Some evidence suggested that he had already become the focal point of growing conservative opposition to Khrushchev's policies. Khrushchev turned to Brezhnev as his party deputy, again making him a party secretary in June 1963. When I passed through Moscow on a trip from India to Mongolia in November 1963, journalists said that Khrushchev had recently introduced Brezhnev to a French visitor as his eventual successor.

When I joined the Moscow bureau in early March 1964, Khrushchev seemed to be in unquestioned control of the Soviet Union. A bombastic figure on the international stage, he vied with United States presidents for world prominence. His seventieth birthday on April 17 was marked by celebrations and congratulations from foreign Communist leaders that rivaled the "cult of personality" of Stalin, which he had denounced eight years earlier.

Not until decades later did Soviet memoirs reveal that in March 1964 Brezhnev and Presidium member Nikolai V. Podgorny had begun approaching other Presidium members about ousting Khrushchev. They spent the summer and early autumn secretly securing the support of Central Committee members in order to avoid a repeat of Khrushchev's successful maneuver in 1957. The arguments they used against Khrushchev—in conspiratorial meetings disguised in such ways as hunting trips and soccer stadium gatherings—became clear only later.

Buoyed by the seventieth birthday celebrations, Khrushchev acted as if he were in unquestioned control. He had already diluted the authority of the Central Committee by holding what were called "enlarged plenary sessions." Outside specialists on subjects to be discussed were added to the occasional committee meetings, thus packing them with Khrushchev supporters and denying committee members an opportunity to debate issues in frank privacy. In August 1964, Khrushchev told Soviet media that an upcoming committee meeting would make a particular decision about agriculture, preempting the committee's right to decide.

About this time, the AP's main rival in providing news in the United States and much of the rest of the world, United Press International, published a story about Khrushchev's authority under the byline of its Moscow bureau chief, Henry Shapiro. Shapiro had come to Moscow as a law student in 1933, married a Russian, and stayed on most of the time since then. Living in a nice apartment in a building with Russians, rather than one of the KGB-monitored ghettos to which other foreign journalists and diplomats were assigned, he was widely viewed by Western diplomats and journalists as being heavily compromised. He was reputed to be fed official information favorable to the Soviet Union—he always knew ahead of time when spacecraft were about to be launched, for example—while playing down unfavorable material.

The story, probably written at Shapiro's direction by one of his young reporters because he was noted for his inability to write well, said: "Seldom before has the mantle of supreme Soviet power rested more firmly and securely on the shoulders of one man than it does today on the former coal miner Nikita Sergeyevich Khrushchev. Confident of the loyalty of his subordinates. . . ." In fact, as became known much later, Khrushchev had already received several warnings of plotting to overthrow him, but he dismissed them with expressions of confidence in his lieutenants.

As Brezhnev became busier in his new role as Khrushchev's deputy, his protocol duties as Soviet president increasingly became a nuisance. At the July 14, 1964, Bastille Day reception on the lawn of the French embassy—it was a lovely summer afternoon, and the champagne flowed freely—we journalists and the diplomats puzzled over a rumor that Brezhnev was about to pass the presidency to Mikoyan. A number of guests, including Shapiro, scoffed at the idea. They pointed out that Mikoyan was an Armenian rather than an ethnic Russian, and argued the president had to be a Russian. The next day TASS announced that Brezhnev was giving up the presidency "to concentrate on party matters," and Mikoyan would assume the title.

In the next two months, Khrushchev seemed to become both more bombastic and more erratic. He was obviously enjoying his power and the popularity demonstrated by enthusiastic Russian crowds wherever he appeared. Then he went on vacation to Pitsunda, accompanied by his old friend Mikoyan. From there they congratulated the Voskhod cosmonauts at the beginning of their announced "long flight."

But the next day, Tuesday, October 13, the spacecraft landed after making just sixteen earth orbits in twenty-four hours and seventeen minutes. Fred and I were as surprised as other space-watchers. A purported transcript of the conversation between ground control and Voskhod, published years later, had the cosmonauts arguing unsuccessfully against orders to land. The reason for the short flight was never fully explained. It did become known, however, that the three men were so crowded in the small space that they could not wear spacesuits, and all three suffered from space sickness. The usual Khrushchev congratulations for a successful space flight were not heard—nothing from Pitsunda.

That was the day, it turned out, that Brezhnev, Podgorny, and other conspirators convened in Moscow a secret Presidium meeting—they were always secret—to denounce Khrushchev. Brezhnev telephoned Khrushchev the night before to return to Moscow for a Presidium meeting "on agriculture." Khrushchev was suspicious but decided the next morning to return. The KGB had changed Khrushchev's usual security guards for his escort back to Moscow.

In the Presidium meeting room in the old tsarist Senate building of the Kremlin, Brezhnev began the criticism of his patron. He charged that a 1962 division of the Communist Party into industrial and agricultural wings had "sowed disorganization," although he had slavishly praised it at the time. Khrushchev made decisions unilaterally, without consulting his comrades, Brezhnev said. Others took their turns denouncing their leader. They accused him of packing Central Committee meetings so "no one can speak frankly." One Presidium member said Khrushchev was "unpredictable, arbitrary, and unrestrained." Another said, "Instead of the Stalin cult, we have the cult of Khrushchev." One of his protégés, Aleksandr N. Shelepin, said he was "coarse, erratic, and inclined to intrigues."[1]

The next day, Wednesday, October 14, the Presidium meeting resumed so that other members could voice their complaints about the way Khrushchev had dominated the party. Only Mikoyan defended his friend, weakly. Then the Presidium voted to oust Khrushchev from the party leadership and also to instruct the government to remove him from the premiership. With tears in his eyes, Khrushchev admitted errors. "I'll do what's best for the party." Officially, the Presidium granted Khrushchev's "request" to retire "in connection with his advanced age and deterioration of his health."

With a majority of Central Committee members already lined up in support, Presidium members then went nearby to the Kremlin's Sverdlovsk Hall, where the committee had gathered. Brezhnev opened the meeting with a brief summary of the indictment. Mikhail A. Suslov, the bloody-handed Stalin hatchet man who had become the gray eminence of the party as chief ideologist but had not been a key conspirator, then gave details. Without discussion, the committee voted unanimously—two Ukrainian delegates who might have supported Khrushchev were excluded from the hall—to remove him. Wary of anyone else's gathering both party and government power, it also decided that never again should the posts of first secretary and premier be combined. Brezhnev was named first secretary. Alexei N. Kosygin, Stalin's young production boss in World War II and a deputy premier since 1957, became premier.

All this occurred in the usual secrecy of Presidium and Central Committee meetings. Soviet media had no mention of them the next day, Thursday, October 15. Instead, they were full of congratulations pouring in from satellite countries and other foreign Communists for the Voskhod flight. But the messages published in Moscow were not addressed to Khrushchev, as previous such messages had been. They were addressed to the Central Committee. Only later did we learn that the versions published in media of the East European countries where they originated had Khrushchev as the addressee. Soviet censors had already gotten the word. We had not. Nor did we or other Western journalists find it curious that Khrushchev was not listed as appearing that Thursday for a Presidium luncheon for visiting Cuban president Osvaldo Dorticos Torrado. So far as we knew, he was still in Pitsunda.

Late in the afternoon, AP London sent us a message about a little item in the *London Evening News*. It was from the paper's stringer in Moscow, Viktor Louis. Vitaly Evgenyevich Louis had gone from school to Stalin's prisons for nine years but then appeared in Moscow as a purveyor of information to foreigners. He was widely believed to have been recruited by the KGB while in the Gulag to influence Western journalists, peddling official lines or trying to downplay unfavorable information. His *Evening News* item noted that Khrushchev had not been mentioned in Soviet media since the Voskhod launch. This was suggestive but inconclusive. Viktor, who usually cultivated Western journalists, refused to elaborate when we phoned him.

As rumors swirled through the Western diplomatic and journalistic community in Moscow, there was official silence. Fred and I telephoned everyone we could think might be helpful, but no one we could reach knew anything definite. It was, of course, never possible to reach any official spokesman under the Soviet system of controlling the news. I asked AP London to keep a close eye on the TASS English-language wire that it received, since London's filing an AP bulletin would be quicker than my writing it and sending it on the wire to London for them to refile, and I would then follow up with a comprehensive story. London replied that they were all busy with the British parliamentary election held that day. Early returns indicated that the Labour Party would end thirteen years of Conservative rule. AP's London staff thought this was the biggest story in the world that day. It did not want to be bothered by rumors of an upset in Moscow.

It was a misty evening. I sent Brian out to look for photo possibilities to illustrate whatever was happening. Ever since, I have regretted not telling him to station himself inconspicuously in Manege Square at the northeast corner of the Kremlin, at right angles to Red Square. A three-story-high portrait of Khrushchev on the front of the Hotel Moskva faced the square. The portrait disappeared during the night. A picture of workmen removing it would have been a prize-winning illustration of Khrushchev's downfall. As it was, no one came up with a good photograph to depict the change.

Fred and I kept waiting, writing stories about the rumors and uncertainty. Sometime around midnight AP's foreign desk in New York sent a message that UPI's Shapiro had just reported that Khrushchev was out. We had no way of confirming this, lacking the contacts that fed him information.

Finally, past 2 A.M. on Friday, October 16, TASS carried a brief resolution issued by the Communist Party Central Committee. Using the Presidium wording about advanced age and deteriorating health, it said Khrushchev had resigned and been replaced by Brezhnev as first secretary and Kosygin as premier. That was blandly neutral. A contrastingly sharp editorial from Friday morning's party newspaper, *Pravda,* was then distributed by TASS. It condemned Khrushchev for "subjectivism and drift in Communist construction, harebrained scheming, half-baked conclusions and hasty decisions and actions divorced from reality, bragging and bluster, attraction to rule by fiat, [and] unwillingness to take into account what science and practical experience have already worked out."

This seemed pretty conclusive: the party had reacted against his domineering style, his uninhibitedly personal way of exercising his authority, his preemptory efforts to revitalize a stagnant administrative system with changes that threatened the jobs of his comrades. Yet the world was left wondering. Theories proliferated about the *real* reason for Khrushchev's downfall.

While Soviet media offered no further guidance and officials were reluctant to discuss the situation, Westerners jumped to all sorts of conclusions. Few Western Kremlinologists examined the inner workings of the party to look for the primary reasons for Khrushchev's protégés to stab him in the back. Instead, specialists in Soviet agriculture proclaimed that it was the failure to meet farm targets that had caused the ouster. Some foreign policy experts argued that the humiliation of having put nuclear warhead missiles in Cuba and then pulling them out in the showdown with the United States in October 1962 was what turned his comrades against him. Others focused on problems in relations with Western Europe as the cause.

Some who had watched Sino-Soviet relations deteriorate since 1959 and turn to bitterly open polemics by early 1964 decided that Khrushchev's failure to keep on good terms with China, the other big Communist power, was what had brought him down. There were suggestions that without Khrushchev things would be patched up. This seemed to gain support when it was announced that Chinese premier Zhou Enlai would come to Moscow for the November 7 anniversary of the Bolshevik Revolution. Before he arrived, however, I wrote an analytical piece that examined the dispute and concluded that the nationalistic issues were too basic to be resolved by a change of Soviet leadership. In fact, relations continued to deteriorate to 1969 border clashes followed by Mao Zedong's sloganized advice to his people to "dig tunnels deep and store grain" in preparation for war with the Soviet Union.

What had become of Khrushchev? From being in press, radio, and television many times daily, he had disappeared. Journalists wondered where he was, not knowing that he had lost his large city apartment and spacious dacha outside Moscow. Instead, he was assigned to a smaller dacha in the country near Usovo and a pension then equivalent to $513 a month, four times the average Soviet industrial wage. About two weeks after his ouster, however, UPI created a sensation by reporting that he had been seen driving in the city. This was a UPI invention to liven up a dull day. His memoirs made it clear that he was kept under police watch well away from the city. Several Western correspondents drove around as far outside town as permitted in hopes of finding him, without success.

There was one exception to his being kept out of sight, however. On March 14, 1965, the usual elections for show purposes, rather than offering substantive choices, were held for the Supreme Soviet. Purely on speculation, rather than having any tipoff, I went that Sunday morning to the polling station for Khrushchev's old city apartment. So did a lot of other correspondents. He showed up, shuffling slowly, and cast a ballot. To reporters' insistent questions, he said he was fine but little else. It was the last we saw of him.

The fact that Khrushchev was allowed to retire peacefully, if unhappily, was testimony to the changes that he had brought to Soviet public life. After Stalin had killed off officials whom he removed from power, and later officials had been banished to minor posts far from the capital, the system had been ameliorated.

While Moscow continued to be a major center for news, keeping us journalists busy, we eventually began to miss Khrushchev. The number of foreign visitors, and Kremlin receptions for them, declined. At receptions, Brezhnev did not seek out the verbal jousts with foreign correspondents that Khrushchev occasionally did. Speeches became more boringly formulaic. Moscow became a somewhat duller place.

20

BOMBED IN MOSCOW

IT WAS A DELIGHTFUL CHRISTMAS. OUR SONS WERE AT AGES, THREE AND a half and two and a half, when Christmas is magical, Santa Claus very real, his presents wondrous, and life freshly exciting every morning—an excitement in which parents revel. The pleasant day ended with a warmly friendly dinner across town with another family with small children.

Then the bomb went off.

We had just returned from dinner after 9 P.M. in the light green Volkswagen Beetle in which Monica ran around Moscow with Keith and Neal looking over her shoulder from seats attached in the back. Someone up the one staircase of our large building where apartments were occupied by Western diplomats and journalists (Russians lived up the other staircases) seemed to be having a late Christmas party. As a result, all of the parking spaces carved out of snowbanks were occupied in the illuminated area watched over by the KGB man there to keep check on what foreigners did and block access to them by ordinary Soviet citizens. So I pulled on through the parking area and parked on packed snow just behind the building, out of the illumination and the militiaman's sight.

We had been in our apartment about twenty-five minutes when the bomb exploded under the front right corner of the Volkswagen, five floors below the AP bureau that occupied an apartment across the hall from where we lived. Windows were shattered for several floors up, but none of the Russians in those apartments below the office was hurt.

In the seven-decade history of the Soviet Union, this was the only reported case of a foreigner's car being bombed in Moscow. The U.S. government concluded that the Soviet political police, the KGB, were trying to intimidate me. It was easy to figure out why. I was an inconvenient person to have in charge of the Moscow bureau of the world's largest news agency. I often did not adhere to the polite caution expected of foreign correspondents in the U.S.S.R.—a politeness that, for some, ran through self-censorship to obsequiousness until it fringed on peddling Soviet propaganda.[1] Instead, for almost four years I had been calling things as I saw them. As a result, the Soviet government had six weeks earlier started trying to make life even more difficult for me than its normal treatment of Western correspondents. It sought to isolate and so far as possible ignore me. Now the KGB seemed to be adding intimidation to that pressure.

Western journalists were already pretty isolated. Josef V. Stalin had begun in the late 1920s inculcating the populace with the idea that all foreigners were spies, and any involvement with them would mean serious trouble, even banishment to the Gulag of concentration camps. The only Soviet citizens authorized to maintain contact with resident foreigners were members of a few small, special categories. These included a limited number of government officials and journalists, some artists and writers, and office and household employees hired through a KGB-controlled government agency.

The press department of the Soviet Foreign Ministry was the official point of contact for non-Communist correspondents. It authorized visas for resident journalists, usually on the basis of strict reciprocity. The journalists' home countries had to provide an equal number of residence visas for Soviet correspondents, a significant percentage of whom were actually officers of the KGB or Soviet military intelligence, the GRU.

Requests for interviews with Soviet officials had to be made to the press department, which might—or, usually, might not—do anything about them. From time to time, the press department arranged what purported to be news conferences by government officials but usually ended up being boring lectures on subjects of minor significance, with reporters' followup questions filibustered or completely ignored. Questions about governmental announcements were supposed to be directed to the press department, rather than the part of the government where the announcement originated. Any travel outside a twenty-five-mile radius from the Kremlin had to get the press department's advance approval. Only after it was given could transportation and hotel arrangements be made. As was repeatedly obvious, the KGB then made its arrangements to keep an eye on the traveler.

By Christmas 1967 the press department had a lengthy file on me, stuffed with all sorts of incidents. So did the KGB.

It was probably the lack of any significant file that helped me get to Moscow in the first place. During five years in India, I had known and worked smoothly with Soviet and East European correspondents, including having a TASS correspondent as vice president of the Foreign Correspondents' Association of South Asia when I was president. My record apparently looked harmless to the Soviet authorities who issued me an initial residential visa.

I enjoyed working in South Asia, had no desire to leave, and had just married a young lady who had only recently arrived to learn about India. But when AP asked me to go to Moscow, it was too interesting a challenge to pass up. The Soviet Union's ebullient premier and Communist Party boss, Nikita S. Khrushchev, was making headlines practically every day. With the Vietnam War still a small guerrilla action, Moscow was by far the most important single source of world news after Washington. The Soviet Union was an increasingly significant player in international affairs. Aside from its strengthening armed forces, its claimed economic growth was being used as a model for newly independent nations, with whom it traded on terms that were represented as economic aid but often proved rapacious. While becoming more confrontational with the West, it sought to win over the Third World by impressing its leaders with the supposed benefits of Soviet-style Communism.

My first visit to Moscow had shown me how easy it was to impress them.[2] After more than three years in South Asia, I flew to Moscow in May 1962 for the first stop of a home leave trip around the world. On the circuit of guided tours that one had to buy in advance in order to get a Soviet visa, I had a quick look around in Moscow and Leningrad (now St. Petersburg again). Leaving aside politics and the police state that kept the political scene stable, the comparison with South Asia was strikingly in the Soviet cities' favor: solid, apparently well-constructed buildings downtown, fairly clean, open, and orderly streets, neat and relatively well-dressed people, richly stocked museums. It was not until I came to Moscow with Monica that we understood the consumer shortages or saw the bricks falling from shoddily constructed buildings' facades and other aspects of Soviet reality.

The shortages and other problems affected Monica in particular. With a spirit of adventure rather than complaints, she gave up a comfortable situation with servants in New Delhi for the harder living in Moscow. Although we could import some food and other supplies from Nordic countries in our first two years there, a privilege later denied, decent consumer goods were hard to obtain in Moscow. Monica became adept at improvising for formal dinner parties for ambassadors and other diplomats that were part of the combined social and working scene in Moscow.

She was expecting our first child when we arrived there, and she went home to her parents in Evanston for his birth. After I'd picked them up there and we returned to Moscow, the American embassy doctor diagnosed Keith as having a problem he could not solve and did not think Russian hospitals could handle, either. Monica took him to Stockholm for treatment. When a second child was expected a year later, the embassy doctor took us and some other American couples expecting babies on a tour of the Soviet Union's top maternity hospital. He thought it quite adequate. Only a couple of weeks before the baby was due did we learn that the hospital had closed for the summer, which its administrators had not bothered to mention when showing us around. Too late to fly out, Monica delivered Neal in Moscow's very ordinary Russian-style Birth House No. 13. It was a harrowing experience of basic medicine and primitive facilities.

Monica adapted well. Talking to our KGB-vetted maid, Svetlana Razuvayeva, and our building's janitress who served as a part-time babysitter, Tonya Savina, she acquired fluent spoken Russian, while my language ability was poor. Keith and Neal learned to talk using English with us, Russian with the maid and babysitter.

Soviet authorities probably began to wonder about me soon after I took over from Preston Grover as Moscow bureau chief—at thirty-three, the youngest that AP could remember. Incidents included baiting Khrushchev into a statement that later had to be denied, forcing the abandonment of Soviet diplomatic receiving lines, and thwarting a KGB blackmail attempt—stories told elsewhere.

Soviet authorities may also have been discomforted by my reporting of an incident involving the man who succeeded Khrushchev as Communist Party general secretary seven months after my arrival in Moscow. This was Leonid I. Brezhnev, whom I had first seen in India. Shortly after I arrived in Moscow, I attended a reception at the Romanian embassy to get another look at him, when he was scheduled to be the guest of honor in his role as Soviet president. Brezhnev showed up late and obviously drunk, but I did not write about his condition—in fact, I probably did not write about the reception at all, because it lacked any hard news. But his drunkenness became news once he took over the top job as party boss, while sharing Khrushchev's titles with the new premier, Alexei N. Kosygin.

The incident was at a Kremlin reception. Khrushchev had established a tradition of the Soviet leadership's giving large receptions in the afternoon following the two big annual parades through Red Square: on the November 7 anniversary of the Bolshevik Revolution, and on May Day, the international day for workers that the U.S.S.R. had turned into a major holiday. Brezhnev and Kosygin continued the tradition. In addition to Soviet Communist Party and government officials and any special foreign visitors in town for the celebrations, ambassadors were invited and so were the bureau chiefs of the major world news agencies, plus a few other foreign journalists.

The November 7, 1964, reception came too soon after Khrushchev's ouster for his former comrades who had turned against him to be on anything but their best behavior—especially in the presence of Premier Zhou Enlai of antagonistic China, who had come to size up the post-Khrushchev situation. But by May Day of 1965, Brezhnev felt comfortably in command. And he showed it.

The reception in the large hall at the top of the modern Palace of Congresses building began in the usual way. The Soviet leadership and special guests gathered in the west end of the lower part of the hall, in the invisible bubble of an area ordinary guests understood not to enter without special invitation. The other guests sipped drinks passed out by waiters and nibbled from buffet tables in the rest of the lower center section and up a few steps to two higher rims around the room. About forty-five minutes into the reception, as usual, toasts were made in dully routine forms of self-congratulation. A while later, my fellow Western journalists and I compared notes on what we had picked up in the way of news. Nothing worth reporting, we agreed. With ambassadors and some Russians beginning to drift out, my journalistic colleagues were eager to be gone. Having no reason to rush back to the office to file a story, I told them I wanted to stay a bit longer. I wanted to keep an eye on the leaders, particularly Brezhnev, who seemed to be drinking a lot. My colleagues left.

Brezhnev kept drinking. Then he came out of his bubble area to greet some of the remaining guests. In the best style of Soviet exuberance, he gave bear hugs to some of the men. Then he started giving bear hugs to the women, with kisses. By the time he had worked his way up to the area of the rim where I was standing watching, he had lost interest in greeting the men and the bear hugs of women had turned into pawing. He was obviously drunk, but none of the Soviet officials dutifully trailing behind him had the temerity to try to restrain him. It was quite a spectacle. Eventually, he got to the entrance and left.

Now I had a story worth filing. Without using the word "drunk," which would have been a very non-Communist kind of red flag to the press department, I tried as delicately as possible to convey the atmosphere of the occasion. My story got some notice in the West. It doubtlessly was also noticed by embarrassed officials in Moscow. Never again did I see or hear of Brezhnev's being drunk on a public occasion.

Some other things probably irritated Soviet authorities. There was, for example, my way of reporting unmanned Soviet space launches. In the mid-1960s, the Soviet-American competition in space was big news, so every kind of launch deserved attention. Unmanned Soviet launches were always announced in a stereotyped fashion. TASS would say it had been authorized to report that a rocket had been launched into orbit as part of the U.S.S.R.'s scientific research program in space—making it sound like harmless, even laudable work. Then it would give the parameters of the orbit: apogee and perigee plus inclination to the earth's equator and orbital time. That was all, after saying everything was working well (failed launch attempts were not announced by Moscow but sometimes were reported by Western space-monitoring sources) and a paragraph of fluff about research to benefit mankind. Rarely was there any explanation of what particular research was being conducted.

Because of the importance of space stories, I had begun educating the AP bureau on the subject. I got us on the mailing list for press material from the U.S. National Aeronautics and Space Administration (NASA). More usefully, I also began getting publications of Dr. Charles Sheldon of the U.S. Congressional Research Service. His analysis of space shots showed that particular parameters were used for particular purposes.[3]

One of the politically most sensitive subjects at the time was reconnaissance satellites. Khrushchev had angrily accused the United States of having "spy-in-the-sky" satellites watching his country, a followup to his explosive anger in 1960 over U-2 overflights of the U.S.S.R. The Soviets refused, however, to talk about their own reconnaissance satellites. Yet the parameters for a large proportion of Soviet launches were, according to Sheldon's work that others confirmed, those for such satellites. So, when TASS put out a launch report with the proper parameters, I would write a story starting off with some variation of, "The Soviet Union announced today that it had launched a rocket into an earth orbit of the kind that Western scientists say is used for 'spy-in-the-sky' reconnaissance satellites." This, I heard from East European correspondents who got special briefings from Soviet authorities that were denied to Westerners, was not popular.

The "race for space" raised other problems. Some Soviet claims of planetary probes were contradictory. After the first probe was sent to Venus, officials of the State Committee for Space Exploration announced that it had radioed results down to a certain altitude as it descended into the hot, dense atmosphere that finally caused its equipment to fail. But when a year or so later a second Soviet probe entered Venus's atmosphere, the new, bigger, and better claims made it clear that the first claims could not have been true. When I asked about this at a news conference called to celebrate the latest results, I got sharp looks from the speakers, who then ignored my question.

Although Moscow did not have such revealing documents as telephone books—phone numbers were state secrets—we somehow acquired a phone number for the space committee. When we called to ask for explanation or elaboration of its announcements, the standard reply was, "You know you are not supposed to call here," before hanging up.

The space race created one triumph for the bureau. On March 18, 1965, Soviet cosmonaut Alexei A. Leonov became the first person to go outside an orbiting capsule on a "space walk." Moscow television showed this live. A visiting AP London photographer took pictures of Leonov floating in space from the bureau's television screen. He processed the best few and took them down to Fotokhronika TASS, the photo division of TASS that we had to use for all photo transmissions to AP London and beyond.[4] The Fotokhronika editors were surprised. They had not thought of photographing television images and were just sitting around waiting for the space committee to give them pictures, which they expected then to sell to AP and other photo agencies. But they agreed to transmit our photos, giving us a temporary lead. One of our photos was the cover of the following week's *Time* magazine.

Photo censorship had its odd moments. In 1964, in beginning a campaign to enhance the image of security and intelligence services, the Soviet Union for the first time acknowledged espionage by Richard Sorge. He was a German who worked in Germany and Japan as a journalist while spying for the Soviets. Among other things, from Tokyo he warned Moscow of the coming Nazi German attack on the Soviet Union, a warning that Stalin ignored. Caught by Japanese police in October 1941, he was executed in 1944.

After remaining silent about him for two decades, Soviet authorities recognized Sorge's work by posthumously awarding him the nation's highest honor, a Hero of the Soviet Union medal, and issuing a 4-kopek postage stamp depicting him and the medal. To illustrate our report, the bureau's Russian photographer, Vasily Gritsan, took a photo of a stamp, I wrote a caption, and Gritsan took it down to Fotokhronika to transmit. A little while later they phoned. They could not transmit the photo because the caption identified Sorge as a "Soviet spy."

The Fotokhronika editor said the Soviet Union did not have spies. What are they, then? I asked. The Soviet Union does have agents, I was told. So Gritsan retrieved the photo, I wrote a new caption saying Sorge was a Soviet agent, and the picture went out. The article that it illustrated called him a spy.

Other articles that I wrote, as the bureau's chief reporter and analyst, probably were not popular with Soviet bureaucrats. In late 1965, Kosygin announced a new policy that sought to put some rationality into Stalin's economic system that had become increasingly hidebound, inefficient, and wasteful. It gave industrial managers responsible to Kosygin's government some of the power previously exercised by local Communist bosses. I was skeptical that Brezhnev would accept a reduction in party power. After all, a key reason that Khrushchev had been ousted was his plan to curtail party power and prerogatives.

A year after the changes had in theory been introduced, I reviewed the sparse official evidence and Soviet media reports, and talked to various diplomats, East European journalists, and others about the significance of the reforms so far. The more information I collected, the more I was convinced that Brezhnev was not in fact accepting this shift of power. Therefore, Kosygin's reforms had to fail because politics would continue to interfere with economics.

When I tried my ideas and information out on political and economic experts in several Western embassies, I got hesitant reactions. U.S. embassy officers in particular were not prepared to make any judgment on the first year of the supposed reforms. But, encouraged by a few sources, I wrote my own judgment. It was harsh. I said Brezhnev's party was unwilling to yield power, and therefore Kosygin's reforms were not taking effect. History has borne out this judgment, but at the time it was not one that Soviet authorities appreciated. In fact, Brezhnev gradually whittled down and eventually usurped Kosygin's governmental authority.

Then there was the telephone incident. The AP bureau was a small apartment consisting of three main rooms: the office ,where the reporter on duty sat facing the secretary-translator who monitored radio and television broadcasts while scanning newspapers, a second room with additional work space, and, opening off the second room, a room with the teleprinters on which we sent stories on a wire to AP's London bureau, which relayed them to New York for worldwide distribution. During the day, someone was always in the main office with the telephones, but the only person working at night could not hear the phones while he was sending reports on the teleprinters. The phones had extensions in my bedroom across the hall so that I could pick up calls after the bureau closed about midnight, but, with two infants trying to sleep, I usually kept them switched off when I was home during the evening.[5] So I wanted further extensions, or at least a bell, that the evening reporter could hear in the teleprinter room.

Repeated appeals to telephone authorities got nowhere. Finally, a couple of officials came to the office to discuss the situation. Their first reaction was that nothing could be done. But, I said, how would a person working in the teleprinter room know if someone phoned with something important late at night? I was using one of the bureau's translators, Tamara Devyatkina, for this conversation because that was easier than trying to communicate in my halting Russian. The officials were unimpressed. Then I made the mistake of trying a hypothetical situation to illustrate my problem. Suppose, I said, there is a sudden change of Soviet leadership? This had happened a year or so earlier when Khrushchev was ousted. We would need to hear the phone if another change occurred, I said. The officials reacted sourly. Eventually they left. We never got the extensions or even an extra bell in the teleprinter room.

But I did get a summons to the press department. A junior official gave me a severe dressing down for, according to him, having advocated the ouster of Brezhnev and Kosygin. My request that he ask the office translator what had actually been said was ignored. Of course, I suspected that the KGB had already brought this up with the translator during what foreigners always presumed were regular KGB debriefings of those allowed to work for us.

Another run-in with communications people occurred over adding a Telex machine in the teleprinter room. AP headquarters decided it would be a good idea for us to have a backup for the teleprinters that sent news on a leased line to London. Telex worked more like a telephone, dialing up a temporary connection to another Telex machine that could be anywhere, in order to send written material by the same electro-mechanical means as the teleprinter. It was, in the mid-1960s, state-of-the-art international communications.

One end of the long, narrow teleprinter room had space for a Telex, we thought. But, when a Soviet official came to discuss the installation, he said there was not enough room. Looking around, he declared that the room was already overcrowded with three teleprinters, not to mention the shelves of old Soviet newspapers that we kept for reference. A Telex could not be put in. By law, he said, every machine had to have at least ten square meters (108 square feet) of space. But, I replied, Soviet law only requires eight square meters (86 square feet) of living space for each person, a figure I knew from recent research that was often not honored. How can a machine deserve more space than a person? Abrupt end of conversation. The press department did not summon me this time, however. And, after removing some shelves, we got the Telex, even though the room was not forty square meters in size.

The KGB may also have been unhappy with me for obstructing plans to put another American correspondent on trial, charged with assaulting a militiaman—a KGB officer in a police role. A friend with whom I'd made a trip into Soviet Central Asia, Adam Clymer of the *Baltimore Sun,* was roughed up during a demonstration by Chinese and Vietnamese students against the U.S. embassy on March 4, 1965. When he tried hysterically to push through a militia line protecting the embassy to get in for medical treatment, I restrained him and led him away. Later, he was arrested. I was summoned by a Soviet prosecutor who tried to talk me out of being prepared to testify that I had taken Adam away. Although I could not be certain he had not returned later and gotten in trouble then, I insisted to the prosecutor that I had removed him. The authorities dropped plans to put Adam on trial, instead expelling him. U.S. embassy officers presumed that I had saved him from likely imprisonment.

Another incident might not fit into reasons for the authorities to dislike me, but it probably fit having some KGB enemies.

In the summer of 1967, Monica and I were invited to a party beginning in the late afternoon at the American embassy's dacha, a large old bungalow in the country outside of Moscow that the diplomats used for parties and short vacations. As we were driving home, the light of late northern summer evenings was still in the sky but the ground was darkening, so I had my car lights on.

I was keeping a reasonable distance along the road behind a Moscow taxi. We were the only two vehicles noticeable on the rural highway; no lights behind me. Suddenly, the taxi driver apparently spotted someone who wanted to be picked up along a fairly deserted stretch of farmland. He jerked to a stop without signaling or pulling much off the two-lane road. I swerved left into the other lane, which had no oncoming cars, to avoid hitting the taxi. As I passed the cab, Monica and I heard a crash on our left. We stopped and got out to check; the taxi driver sped away, obviously wanting to avoid trouble. A motorcycle with a sidecar carrying three militiamen—that is, KGB in police uniforms—had crashed into the ditch. It obviously had been following me fairly closely without its lights on so I would not notice it, and when I swerved it swerved even wider and the driver lost control.

One of the militiamen had a bloody and apparently badly broken leg. Monica and I asked if we could help. The militiamen seemed more embarrassed than distressed. No, they had a radio and would call for help. Please leave. So we did. This doubtlessly was another entry in my KGB file.

While I was in Moscow, a dissident movement got going. Until the 1960s, virtually no one had succeeded in publicly challenging the dictatorial, repressive system created by Vladimir I. Lenin and reinforced by Stalin. The KGB and its predecessors clamped down too efficiently and ruthlessly to allow anyone openly to question the Soviet Communist Party's monopoly on truth and wise management. But a few brave souls began to accept the terrible personal risks involved in speaking out about the systemic violation of human rights that were promised in the Soviet constitution and other documents intended to impress the outside world.

In the early spring of 1964, after I'd been in Moscow only a short time, we got word of a news conference by someone who wanted to describe his illegal treatment by the authorities. Several Western correspondents met him in the little park between the Ukraina Hotel and the Moscow River. I was impressed by the man's seemingly rational, calm sincerity as he described having complained publicly about unsafe working conditions as a coal miner. As a result he was arbitrarily declared to be insane and sent to a psychiatric hospital, where he was injected with drugs that gave him painful hallucinations and other suffering. What he said about miners' problems rang true. But could he be believed? We correspondents walked away wondering about the insanity angle. TASS later carried a story asserting that we had been taken in by someone who didn't know what he was talking about because he was crazy.

Only later did we begin to hear so many other, well-authenticated reports that we came to realize the KGB used mental hospitals as severe prisons for people who challenged the Soviet system. The KGB actually ran some mental hospitals itself. Anyone who complained about the dangerous, sweatshop conditions of poorly paid Soviet labor was, by official definition, crazy. Drugs that endangered such prisoners' health, and in some cases permanently crippled them, were forcibly injected into what had been normal, healthy people. They were not normal only to the extent that they were brave enough to try to claim Soviet citizens' theoretical rights that the supposed "workers' state" systematically ignored.

Despite the dangers, dissent grew. More people found the courage to express their opposition to censorship, repression, and unsafe working conditions. As bureau chief, I was responsible for being sure such stories were covered. We did not deliberately play down the dissident story, as the press department doubtlessly wanted and some correspondents did. But the AP was not so successful as some other Western correspondents in establishing productive contacts in dissident circles because neither I nor my reporters were able to develop the kind of contacts with fringe intellectual elements that paid off in news.

Some of our best tips on dissidents and on the occasional small protest demonstrations that they organized came from American graduate students living at Moscow State University. During our years in Moscow, Monica met at the American embassy doctor's office several old high school and college friends who were there researching, within the narrow limits allowed by Soviet authorities, their doctoral dissertations. Some became good friends, but they were cautious about telling us everything they learned from their Russian student contacts.

What finally and quite clearly turned the press department against me, no doubt exacerbating earlier dislike, was my review of changes over half a century of Soviet rule.

November 7 of 1967 was the fiftieth anniversary of the Bolshevik Revolution in what was now named Leningrad. I decided in the summer of 1967 to take advantage of my accumulated background knowledge, good files, and Soviet and diplomatic contacts to write a series of articles summarizing and evaluating the achievements of a half-century of Communist rule in many different fields: industry, agriculture, education, health, science, culture, living standards and consumer goods, armed forces, and others.

It seemed at the time to be a logical, straightforward part of covering the Soviet Union at time when it was loudly trumpeting its achievements. But, in retrospect, trying to assess those achievements was a pretty daring deviation from the normal pattern of journalistic coverage of the Soviet reality. The tradition reaching back to the censorship of Stalin's time was for Western correspondents to wait until their Moscow tours ended and they had left the country to write a series of articles on what the U.S.S.R. really was like—"This Is Russia, Uncensored," as one was titled. I knew this history, which had continued in somewhat diminished form even after formal censorship ended in 1962, but I didn't think much about it.

My anniversary articles, which the AP distributed to newspapers worldwide as a series, were what I considered balanced. I gave the U.S.S.R. credit for its many achievements. The article on Soviet industry, for example, reported the rise to world leadership in steel production and several other kinds of gross output. But it also noted that economic trends under capitalism in the last two tsarist decades, if continued after World War I and despite the setbacks of World War II, would have given Russia as much or even greater industrial strength by 1967—without the incredible hardships of Stalin's industrialization.

The article on agriculture credited the regime with expanding output and beginning to improve diets. It also pointed out the vast gap between the meager output of large, inefficient collective and state farms and the productivity of tiny household gardens. It was from these private gardens that free-enterprise efforts supplied a large proportion of Soviet vegetables, milk, and other kinds of food. The fresh, good-quality vegetables in peasant markets were in notable contrast to supplies in often empty-shelved state stores.

Writing about culture, I described a display at Moscow's international airport on the outstanding ballet troupe, soccer team, educational achievements, and other cultural attractions of Sverdlovsk, a major Siberian industrial city (since returned to its tsarist name, Yekaterinburg). But then I quoted a Soviet newspaper on that city's high rate of drunkenness and "hooliganism"—usually used as a term for riotous behavior or crime—by people who lacked adequate facilities for sports and entertainment.

On health I cited the Soviet Union's virtually eliminating many endemic diseases of tsarist Russia, figures on the number of doctors and hospital beds per person that were among the most impressive in the world, and the advanced research claims of Soviet medical science. The article also mentioned the low training requirements for Soviet doctors, the inadequate supplies of equipment and medicine, and the growing trend for the better-off to pay for private medical care because state medicine was so poor.[6]

Similar articles on other subjects gave the U.S.S.R. credit for achievements, including citing its claims to world leadership in many fields, while trying to give the achievements and claims balance. And I wrote about the "convergence theory" then gaining popularity in some Western intellectual circles. Governmental activism was growing in the West, where new social programs and pension systems were funneling increasing shares of gross national product through official programs. Some relaxation of rigid Stalinist economic systems was supposedly occurring in the East. This caused some Western economic and political observers to write that capitalism and Communism were converging into a similar, middle position.

A few weeks before the fiftieth anniversary, *Newsweek* asked its correspondent in Moscow, Robert "Bud" Korengold, quickly to prepare something similar to what I had long been working on. Bud raced around interviewing people and writing. The magazine came out with a lengthy special anniversary article. I found it to be generally accurate and balanced, different from my articles more in style than general tone. But Soviet officials were irate. *Newsweek* already had a record of run-ins with Moscow censorship and its successor system of trying to guide foreign reporting, and the magazine was prominent enough that the authorities apparently felt it could not be ignored. Pressure was applied through various channels to get *Newsweek* to withdraw Korengold from Moscow. Although not formally expelled, he left because his editors did not want to take the chance of being denied permission to have another correspondent in the U.S.S.R.

The reaction to my articles was more subtle. The reason for this was unclear, but it probably was explicable in several ways. One was that AP feature articles, as distinct from hot current news, are published only irregularly as editors find room. I never heard of any important paper's publishing my whole series. So there was not the prominence and focus provided by *Newsweek*. Another possible reason was that the press department did not want to pick a fight with the AP that might raise questions about TASS's regularly distorted and biased coverage of the United States.

The reaction was so subtle that I did not at first realize that there had been any. The November 7 anniversary approached normally, except for the Soviet media's being even more insistently and excessively self-congratulatory over half a century of Communism than the usual bragging about alleged accomplishments. As usual, the bureau received a pass for the big parade of soldiers, weapons, labor union organizations, and others through Red Square past the Communist leadership standing atop Lenin's tomb. It was a glorious occasion for which the weather cooperated: a cloudless, 68-degree day. After returning to the office to write the wrap-up story on the parade and speeches in Red Square (the running story had been written by a colleague in the office based on television coverage), I realized that I did not have an invitation to the traditional Kremlin reception that afternoon. The parade pass had been for the AP in general, with any staff member able to use it, but Kremlin reception invitations were issued by name. Normally, the bureau received a phone call from the Foreign Ministry to pick up an invitation a few days before an event, and as AP bureau chief I had routinely been invited to all government receptions. Not this time. A British correspondent filled me in on what little news had developed at the reception, so the AP was not left at a disadvantage. But I was puzzled.

On the next working day, I had a secretary phone to ask what had happened to my invitation. She got an evasive reply. Then some days later the Foreign Ministry phoned to say the office driver could pick up an invitation for a Kremlin reception. It was made out for Michael Johnson. Mike was the reporter whom I routinely designated as being in charge when I left Moscow, since the government required that someone be responsible. Now they were deliberately ignoring me. The absence of a November 7 invitation had obviously not been an accident. Soviet officials were mad at me.

Then came the bomb.

It did not destroy the car, but it did blow in the front right corner of the sturdy little Volkswagen. The gas tank, in the front of the rear-engine Beetle, was knocked loose but had not exploded, as some said it might have done had it not been almost full. A special device for warming up the engine in cold northerly climes, which had a reputation for sometimes blowing up, was intact—as was shown by photographs taken by a U.S. consular official who came over to investigate—contrary to rumors that later circulated in someone's apparent effort to make the explosion seem to be my fault. There were also rumors that a gas line underneath the car had exploded, which fit with the fact of an explosion and fire that night in a Russian apartment house a mile or so away that apparently was caused by a natural gas leak. But the bomb blast was visible in the packed snow and pavement underneath the car.

When Monica and I were invited down to the nearby police station that night, the officer asked me if I had any enemies among the foreign community in Moscow. I replied, no, and I certainly hope I don't among the Soviets, either. The stiff, unamused officer said there would be an investigation.

The embassy and the State Department quickly came to the conclusion that the Soviet government was trying to intimidate me, perhaps scare me out of Moscow. At the time, Malcolm Toon headed the department's Soviet desk. He had been the political counselor in Moscow earlier in my time there, so he knew me. A diplomat who believed one had to stand up to the Soviets with all the toughness that they used toward the non-Communist world, which he did later in an outstanding tour as U.S. ambassador to Moscow, Mac Toon gave Soviets in Washington a hard time over my case. When a very small bomb or a large firecracker later went off by a window of the Soviet embassy there without causing any damage, its officials repeatedly demanded that the U.S. government catch the culprit immediately. Mac's standard answer as the investigation dragged on became: We're looking, and, by the way, how are you doing on catching the person who bombed Mr. Bradsher's car?

AP's general manager, Wes Gallagher, was on Christmas vacation. As soon as he got back a few days later, he sent a message asking if I or my family felt unsafe in Moscow, and would we like to leave. I thanked him, but said, after talking it over with Monica, that I saw no need to leave then. I had written to Wes in October, before any trouble began, that I wanted to apply for a Nieman Fellowship at Harvard University for the following autumn but, should I fail to get it, I had no desire to give up what I considered a good assignment. After the bombing, we left it at that.

The Soviets required nondiplomatic foreigners to insure their cars with the government firm Ingosstrakh. After the bombing, I tried to file a claim with Ingosstrakh. Their answer was that they could not consider a claim until they had a police report. But the police told my secretary that a report was not ready, that when it was ready Ingosstrakh would get it, and to stop bothering them. So she called Ingosstrakh regularly, to be told that they were awaiting the police report. This runaround continued for weeks. Finally, one day, well over a month after the bombing, the secretary made another routine inquiry to Ingosstrakh and was surprised to be told, "Mr. Bradsher should file his claim." Ah, did that mean the police report finally had been received, and could we get a copy of it? "File the claim." Nothing further. I never did get a police report, presumably because the police had been told by the KGB not to make one.

Ingosstrakh refused to pay as much as I claimed, but it did cover most of the cost of my having the U.S. embassy's garage replace or repair damaged and missing parts of the car, with new parts having to be imported from Helsinki. The car eventually ran about as well as ever. When we left Moscow, we sold it to an African diplomat who knew its history for not much less than we had originally paid for it.

Busy taking care of infants since shortly after we arrived in Moscow, Monica was eager to see a little of the Soviet Union when the boys got old enough for her to leave them with the maid and babysitter. That meant getting press department permission to go outside the twenty-five-mile circle. When I applied in early 1968 to go on a reporting trip to Siberia accompanied by Monica, I was refused. Trips by myself or with other correspondents, which I'd made many times up to late 1967, were also denied. The authorities even vetoed attempts by a group of wives of U.S. embassy personnel and journalists to visit some famous monasteries and villages noted for their traditional crafts. Only when Monica dropped out of the group were the other women allowed to go. The message was clear.

Incidents kept occurring. About 1966, I had struck up a friendship at diplomatic and government receptions with the kind of person who did not usually talk to foreigners. Or maybe he struck up the friendship with me. Anyway, he was Igor Belyayev, the Communist Party newspaper *Pravda*'s editor for Middle Eastern affairs and a member of the sixteen-person board that oversaw that most authoritative and powerful of Soviet papers.

This was an unusual friendship because *Pravda* editors were part of an inside elite who knew a lot of the regime's secrets. Yet Belyayev was willing to have lunch with me from time to time and even to let me visit him occasionally at his *Pravda* office. "Not accidental, comrade," as we Westerners liked to remind each other, echoing Soviet phraseology, about some of the more peculiar things that happened to us in Moscow. Perhaps Belyayev had been assigned by Soviet media managers to try to influence what I wrote about sensitive areas of Soviet activity. I recognized that possibility and didn't worry about it. We talked about a lot of things, and I found him a cautious but helpful guide to understanding some kinds of events. The fact that he did not break off the relationship after the pressure on me had begun suggested that someone higher up thought it was a useful arrangement.

One lunch with Belyayev was in early 1968, some eight months after the Six-Day War in which Israel destroyed Soviet-trained and -equipped forces of Egypt and Syria, to Moscow's great embarrassment, with Egypt losing the Sinai Peninsula and Syria losing the Golan Heights. Among other things, Belyayev told me that unspecified Soviet authorities were worried that the then current strongman in Syria, Colonel Salah al-Jadid, was beginning to make moves suggesting a willingness to confront Israel again in an effort to regain the Golan Heights. That could lead to another disastrous Middle Eastern war. The Soviets disapproved, hoping Jadid would not try such a doomed enterprise. There was an implication that Moscow was at best worried about another embarrassment, and at worst afraid of having to bail out a wayward client.

After waiting a couple of days in an effort to avoid making my source too obvious, I wrote a story saying what Belyayev had told me about Soviet concern but giving no hint of sources. After all, as the Middle East editor for *Pravda,* Belyayev was an authoritative source, and getting a second confirming source would have been impossible. The story was widely published abroad, particularly making headlines and causing reverberations in the Middle East. This seemed at odds with Soviet efforts to cozy up to Jadid. He apparently complained to Moscow. The Foreign Ministry issued a formal denial that any Soviet authorities were worried about his activities, which the AP dutifully reported.

The press department called me in and accused me of having "repeatedly resorted to such falsifications in your coverage of other Soviet internal and external subjects." But the Foreign Ministry presumably knew exactly where I'd gotten the story. Significantly, when I phoned Belyayev after a deliberate delay of several weeks to ask if I could drop by *Pravda* to talk with him, he welcomed me. Perhaps I had been used to convey a message to Syria that served Kremlin purposes, despite the official denial. Or, less likely, maybe Belyayev had been speculating on his own about Syria and was important enough not to have gotten in trouble for it.

This was about the time that a jet fighter crash killed Yuri A. Gagarin, the first man in space and one of the most celebrated public figures in the Soviet Union. On the morning of March 28, 1968, one of the AP bureau's translators arrived at work before the normal 9 A.M. opening time. He routinely turned on Moscow Radio and a tape recorder to catch whatever was said, just in case we wanted later to go back and check on something. He was just in time to hear a special announcement, ahead of normal newscast time, that Gagarin had died the day before in the crash of a jet fighter he was piloting. We got out a quick bulletin quoting Moscow Radio and then followed it up with details and background. There still was nothing on the TASS wire that normally was the first source of any important news. We heard later that Moscow Radio had broken a rule for letting TASS distribute news on its foreign wires before a broadcast gave Western news agencies a chance to beat TASS. But beat TASS we did, and also other agencies.

Later we got a note from AP New York relaying the displeasure of a newspaper editor in the Midwest. Why, he wanted to know, didn't the AP have the dramatic story that United Press International had distributed later that day? It said Gagarin's MiG-15 trainer had suffered some sort of failure and he had heroically stuck with the plane to keep it from crashing into a village. We replied that we didn't have such a dramatic story because not only we but also every source we knew had never heard such a story. We never knew whether UPI, chagrined by being beaten on the first report, made up the dramatic story in an effort to recover or was fed it by some Soviet source in an effort to enhance Gagarin's reputation. UPI's reputation for hyping stories made us strongly suspect the former.[7]

By the late spring of 1968, demonstrations against Soviet human rights abuses were becoming more common as the still-small dissident movement gathered members and courage. One day the London *Daily Telegraph* correspondent, John Miller, spread the word—on undoubtedly tapped phones, so the KGB knew—that three young British visitors planned to hand out leaflets calling for the release of political prisoners, with some Soviet dissidents present. This would be at the statue of Aleksandr Pushkin, the early nineteenth-century poet who was one of old Russia's most honored cultural figures, in a square on Moscow's main street, Gorky Street (later back to its tsarist name of Tverskaya Street). By this time, I had won the Nieman Fellowship and was scheduled to leave Moscow in August. Already being in trouble and on my way out, I decided to cover the demonstration myself rather than risk one of my reporters getting into the bad graces of the press department.

Pushkin's statue was ringed by militiamen, most of whom probably were actually KGB officers, and by people in civilian dress who had the easily spotted look of plainclothes police or KGB security. But at an agreed time, the three British visitors defiantly stepped forward to place flowers by the statue and to start trying to read a declaration against the abuse of rights theoretically promised in the Soviet constitution. The militiamen immediately began arresting them and supporting Russian dissidents for holding a public meeting without permission. There was some scuffling, some blows struck, some screams. Not all the deliberate roughness of the police, aided by plainclothesmen, was directed at the demonstrators. Western journalists were also targeted. I was roughed up and my camera was seized. While other journalists were allowed to leave, I was detained and taken to a militia station. After some confusion and delay, probably caused by checking for instructions from above, I was allowed to leave after film of the incident had been taken from my camera.

Several days later, on June 21, the government newspaper *Izvestiya,* second only to *Pravda* in importance and authoritativeness, published a lengthy article about the incident, its first mention by Soviet media. It was described as a Western-encouraged provocation. Aside from the British visitors, I was the only provocateur identified by name. *Izvestiya* said my "work as a journalist is mainly devoted to writing slander and seeking sensations."[8] A senior U.S. diplomat commented that my reporting had been complimented. Miller, who had been there and who was also scheduled to end his tour in Moscow that summer, was jokingly mad at me that I had gotten all the credit while he got none. Being denounced by Soviet media was considered something of a badge of honor for a Western journalist. But I suspected that I was singled out more because of accumulated grievances than because of that one episode.

After I left Moscow in August 1968, Soviet authorities did not lift the black cloud they had hung over me. In 1971, while working out of Hong Kong, I applied at the Soviet embassy in Cambodia—the handiest Soviet diplomatic mission for me as I went about my new reporting beat—for a visa to go to Moscow to report a Communist Party congress. The request was refused. In 1974, Monica and the boys and I sought visas to cross the U.S.S.R. on home leave from Hong Kong, stopping in Moscow. At the last minute, these, too, were refused.

In 1978, while I was a diplomatic correspondent in Washington, I was scheduled to accompany Secretary of State Cyrus R. Vance on his U.S. Air Force plane to report his visit to Moscow for arms control talks. According to routine, the State Department sent the passports of Vance's officials, plus those of journalists traveling with him, in one batch to the Soviet embassy in Washington for visas. They came back with visas for everyone except me. People in Vance's office who knew of my earlier Moscow difficulties refused to accept this. They told the Soviets that I was part of the official party and could not be turned down. As a result of their insistence, I got a visa. That three-day visit was my first return after a decade and my last as a journalist.

21

CHINA'S MOST DESPICABLE

THE MESSAGE FROM BEIJING WAS SENT TWICE TO MAKE SURE IT GOT through clearly: "Hong Kong journalists are a despicable bunch, and Bradsher is the most despicable of them all. He will never be allowed to visit China again."

A British Broadcasting Corporation correspondent first brought the message down to Hong Kong in the spring of 1974. A week or so later, a Canadian correspondent brought the same message to the British Crown Colony. Both had heard it from officials of the Chinese Foreign Ministry's press office while on reporting assignments in Beijing.

The press office controlled all of the professional activities and many aspects of the private lives of those journalists who were given visas to live and work in China, or just to make working visits. American correspondents were not then among the chosen few with residential visas, and only rarely were allowed to visit. The reason was that the United States still had diplomatic relations with the Republic of China on Taiwan, where Chiang Kai-shek ruled a remnant regime claiming to represent the mainland that he had lost to the Communists in 1949. For American journalists, and for correspondents from most other countries except for a small group allowed to live in Beijing, Hong Kong was the base from which to try to cover news from the big Communist power.

Officials were angry about my reporting from Hong Kong because it perceived a continuing power struggle in China. They insisted there was no struggle, no questioning of the leadership of Chairman Mao Zedong, no disagreement within the leadership group of Mao and his comrades headed by veteran prime minister Zhou Enlai and a newly promoted young radical who had emerged from "the Great Proletarian Cultural Revolution," Wang Hongwen.

But I had been writing from Hong Kong for the *Washington Star* for eighteen months or so, since the late summer of 1972, that there was a continuing struggle.[1] According to my analysis, there was not yet an end to the Cultural Revolution, which at its violent peak in the late 1960s decimated the ranks of men who had led the Chinese Communist Party for decades and disrupted the country's political, economic, social, and educational life. The infighting had merely gone underground to continue in less public forms. I had interpreted Wang's promotion at the party's tenth congress in August 1973 as confirmation of a revitalized power struggle and had then found mounting evidence of dissention.

Mine was, however, a fairly lonely analytical position that ran contrary to public pronouncements from Beijing and to the overwhelming majority of media and diplomatic reporting, as well as to the U.S. government's position. Most people accepted Chinese claims of calm unity because, they thought, the Cultural Revolution was over.

The message from Beijing was not delivered directly to me. Neither the BBC man nor the Canadian correspondent knew me personally, and neither tried to get in touch with me when he reached Hong Kong. But they quoted the press officials' statements to political officers in the U.S. consulate in Hong Kong. The consulate had the largest staff of diplomatic specialists on Chinese affairs in the British colony, so many correspondents regularly sought their views. A friend who shared my background in both Soviet and Chinese affairs and was the best analyst in the consulate's political section, Sherrod McCall, passed the message along to me.

Sherrod and I agreed that the message was itself a sign of the power struggle. The Chinese Foreign Ministry's press office seemed to be in the hands of radicals aligned with Wang who did not like my calling attention to their efforts to change the policies of the more pragmatic elements in China's leadership associated with Zhou. At the time, the disruptive, destructive, and sometimes bloody struggles of the Cultural Revolution were generally considered to have ended, so any talk of continuing leadership conflict was unwelcome. And I was also unwelcome—for a while. It proved to be a surprisingly short while.

Writing about China from Hong Kong since December 1969, and making two trips there before receiving the message that I would never be allowed to visit it again, was the culmination of more than a decade of fascination with the country, some study of it as a journalist and as a Harvard fellow, and watching it from several perspectives around its periphery.

When I arrived in India in February 1959, India and China were almost a decade into an officially warm and friendly relationship of two old but newly reinvigorated neighbors across the Himalayas. I covered the deterioration of this into their 1962 border war.

After my arrival in Moscow in 1964, the Soviet Communist Party made public on April 3 a long, angry attack on China that the party's ideologist, Mikhail A. Suslov, had delivered to a closed, secret meeting of the party's Central Committee on February 14. The Kremlin's decision to summarize publicly its differences with China marked a break after some six years of growing disagreements between Moscow and Beijing. "The Sino-Soviet dispute," which was long denied both by the parties and by many Western cold warriors, had come into the open. Relations between the two big neighbors were increasingly bitter as they fought in convolutedly ideological terms. With their great-power interests colliding, Beijing accused Moscow of "revisionism" of Marxist doctrine to suit Soviet domestic needs and maintain leadership of the world Communist movement. This was one of the major running stories during my four and a half years in Moscow, which meant paying attention to Chinese affairs.

The deepening American military involvement in Vietnam intensified the Sino-Soviet conflict. When the United States reacted to a February 7, 1965, Viet Cong attack on American military advisers at Pleiku by beginning a bombing campaign against North Vietnam, China started criticizing the U.S.S.R. for failing to give militant enough support to another Communist regime.

On March 4, 1965, a raw but not too cold winter day, Chinese students gathered in Moscow. Some had been studying there, some passing through on the way home as China pulled many of its students out of the Soviet bloc because of deteriorating relations and fear they would be contaminated by Soviet thinking. They demonstrated against the U.S. embassy over American bombing of North Vietnam. Some Vietnamese students joined them in hurling stones and using slingshots to attack the embassy building. The demonstration dragged on for hours, and I kept phoning updates to the AP bureau from a store facing it. The obvious political purpose was to force the Soviet militia to defend the embassy in accordance with diplomatic commitments. Beijing quickly publicized it as an example of wicked Soviet revisionists protecting American imperialists from the righteous wrath of the world's victims.

As the U.S. military involvement in Vietnam escalated in 1965, the question of what the U.S.S.R. and China might do loomed large. At the time the Indian ambassador in Moscow was T. N. "Tikki" Kaul, whom I had gotten to know fairly well because of my India background. Kaul had been a junior Indian diplomat in Beijing in the autumn of 1950. He remembered well that China had used India's ambassador to send warnings to the United States that the People's Liberation Army (PLA) would intervene if American-led United Nations troops advancing northward in Korea did not stop well short of the Yalu River border of China. The warnings went unheeded, and China entered the Korean War. Now Kaul sensed his own place in history. "Tricky Tikki," as I referred to him privately after lengthy exposure to his ways, told me that Soviet leaders had intimated to him that continued American escalation in Vietnam could draw China into that war. Was this a message or just a speculation? It was not clear, but I reported what Kaul said, with some qualifications.

My application for a Nieman Fellowship at Harvard University said that, after firsthand acquaintance with both the Indian and Soviet models of economic development, I wanted to study more generally the problems of economic development in poor countries. During the autumn 1968 semester at Harvard, where Nieman Fellows had the freedom to attend any course they wanted without being required to submit papers or take tests, I was primarily interested in economics and such related subjects as population growth. But, with the Cultural Revolution just past its peak of violence, I attended a weekly graduate seminar on Chinese politics and I frequently dropped in to hear lectures in an undergraduate course on East Asian history. By the second semester, I had become more keenly interested in Harvard's rich offerings on Chinese affairs, and I spent more time on them than on economics. After a decade of circling around China, I was becoming more directly focused on the country.

When I arrived in Hong Kong in the last few days of 1969 to become the *Star*'s Asia correspondent, the understanding with my editors was that I would focus on China while also traveling widely, from Korea around Asia to Afghanistan, but particularly to Indochina for updates on its wars. During slightly over five years of living in Hong Kong I was out of the colony on assignments 40 percent of the time.

This meant that for long periods, sometimes four to six weeks at a stretch, Monica was left on her own, with the help of an excellent young live-in Chinese helper. She had to take care of our boys' educations and other needs while dealing with the new world of the British colony. After the first year, she became an innovative and much-loved teacher of sixth-grade students at the American-run Hong Kong International School. This involved a commute for her and the boys from our harbor-facing apartment over a mountaintop to the school, sometimes on harrowing days when typhoons were sweeping in. While traveling I was seldom in touch, telephone connections around Asia then being poor. Despite the consumer comforts of Hong Kong, so different from Moscow, it was not an easy life for her.

Aside from my reporting away from Hong Kong and time off there with the family and vacations elsewhere, the rest of my time was devoted to what had long been known as "China-watching": reporting and analysis by journalists and diplomats who lacked direct access to the country.

China-watching from Hong Kong depended on a medley of sources. The primary one was English-language reports from China's official agency, Xinhua, known as the New China News Agency (NCNA). Reuters news agency transcribed its radioteletype reports at its Hong Kong bureau and sold to people like me thirty or forty single-spaced mimeographed pages a day. In addition to its own versions of news, which mostly meant official announcements and speeches, the NCNA often carried major articles from Chinese newspapers. Also, the U.S. consulate published periodically and sold to journalists a "Survey of the China Mainland Press" with translations of longer, more significant articles. And a part of the BBC, in cooperation with the U.S. government's Foreign Broadcast Information Service (FBIS), transcribed and translated national and provincial radio broadcasts from China and sold daily bulletins of the texts.

These were the basic sources for China-watchers. Written supplements included dispatches published by the Hong Kong press from the only Western news agency correspondent then in Beijing, the Agence France Presse man, and a free weekly bulletin from a curious little semi-clandestine group of analysts financed by the British Foreign Office. Then there were oral sources. This mainly meant China-watchers of the U.S. consulate as well as a few China specialists in other diplomatic missions, such as Japan's consulate. It also meant businessmen, travelers, and a variety of others, even including a few journalists working for Hong Kong newspapers owned by China who were willing to talk to Westerners. From such people came the rumors that often swept the China-watching community, sometimes correct about things brewing in Beijing but usually frustratingly vague and uncheckable if not plain wrong.

It soon became obvious to me that there were China-watchers and "China-watcher-watchers." This latter category included virtually all the Western journalists writing about China from Hong Kong. Few of them were qualified to analyze Chinese affairs for themselves. For many, Hong Kong was just another assignment in a series of quick moves around the world, and they lacked background knowledge of China or of Communist systems. In some cases, they lacked any real interest in either. For some, China had been a subject of academic study, even language training, but many of these students of Chinese matters were more attuned to the country's history and culture than its politics and economics, and they lacked understanding of Communism or the veiled language used in Marxist infighting. Even the few foreign correspondents then in Hong Kong whose experience went back to the China of World War II and the subsequent civil war that brought the Communists to power, and therefore thought of themselves a quarter-century later as the deans of the Hong Kong press corps, were more noted for picking up others' analysis than doing their own.

Most foreign correspondents in Hong Kong were unwilling to spend the hours needed to winnow through the daily outpouring of NCNA materials, BBC transcripts, and other raw materials. Such reading was necessary not only to learn what was being said in China but also to note what was not being said, or what was being said differently from the week or month before, or differently between Beijing media to which foreigners were known to pay attention and provincial media intended strictly for local audiences, or who was prominent one month but not the next in texts or photographs. This was the art of "Kremlinology" when applied to the Soviet Union.

For these reasons, most journalists were not really China analysts. They were, instead, China-watcher-watchers who depended on people such as the U.S. consulate specialists to guide them, even to lead them, through interpreting events in China. I talked to the specialists and others. But I used my Moscow background, and my willingness to do the daily reading while in Hong Kong and to scan material accumulated while I was traveling, in order to reach my own conclusions. They were sometimes different than, or ahead of, the diplomatic specialists. Kremlinology worked on Chinese Communism, too.

My efforts paid off in a distinctive way in 1971. In mid-September, a few anomalies cropped up in normal patterns of Chinese behavior. China-watchers did not know what to make of them. Then several of us noted that Lin Biao was no longer being mentioned in the media. Our speculations paralleled rumors that began to circulate suggesting the anomalies involved Lin. One of the Communists' most successful military commanders during the long civil war up to 1949, Lin had ingratiated himself with Mao in the early 1960s. It was then that the PLA under Defense Minister Lin sponsored the publication of the "little red book" of Mao's quotations that became the talisman for the Cultural Revolution. During that upheaval, as Chairman Mao and a group of young radicals purged those accused of being insufficiently revolutionary and of placing bureaucratic convenience or administrative efficiency ahead of popular arousal for political goals, Lin had risen to being named in a new Communist Party constitution as Mao's "close comrade-in-arms and successor" as party chairman. That rewriting of the constitution at the party's ninth congress in April 1969 had been considered by most Chinese and foreigners alike to signify the end of the Cultural Revolution.

Alerted by the anomalies, and reading between the lines with particular focus on what was not being said and who was no longer quoted, I quickly came to the conclusion that something had happened to Lin. He had disappeared from the Chinese hierarchy without explanation, which probably meant he had fallen afoul of Mao and been purged. This was soon confirmed by the toasts at a Chinese embassy reception in Hanoi on the eve of China's national day, October 1. When the embassy had given a reception some days earlier for a visiting Chinese delegation, the formalized toasts had started out with the routine honoring of "Chairman Mao and his closest comrade-in-arms, Marshal Lin." But at the national day reception, Mao alone was mentioned. No word about Lin. Nor was there any plausible explanation for the cancellation of the traditional military parade through Beijing's Tiananmen Square on October 1.

At the time, one of the leading young American academic specialists on China, Michel Oksenberg, was in Hong Kong on sabbatical to research documentary materials on China. Mike and his wife, Lois, had been friends of my wife's at Swarthmore College a decade earlier, so I got to know them. Although studying an earlier period in Chinese Communist history, Mike was a good audience off whom I bounced my perceptions of what was happening. So was Pietro Sormani, a friend in Moscow when he was the correspondent there for the leading Italian newspaper *Corriere della Sera*. Recently arrived in Hong Kong, he had not yet developed a feel for Chinese politics. But he accepted my analysis focusing on Lin and wrote it for his newspaper. That made two of us reporting that Lin seemed to have fallen, while the rest of the press corps remained cautiously vague. Journalists without Kremlinological backgrounds did not notice such signals as the Hanoi toasts and, when called to their attention, were reluctant to put much importance on them.

Some days after the Hanoi reception, a Soviet press report from Mongolia said a Chinese plane had crashed there weeks earlier, on September 13, killing all aboard. Sherrod McCall offered me the idea that this might be linked with Lin's disappearance. Obviously, he knew something. At the U.S. consulate he had access to American intelligence reports, including top secret intercepts of Chinese aircraft communications. I speculated in print on a connection between Lin and the crash. The later official Chinese story was more interesting. Lin was accused of having plotted to kill Mao, failed, then fled to seek asylum in the Soviet Union, but there was a gun battle on his plane, which crashed. The story was widely seen as another reason for considering the Cultural Revolution to be over. Lin, who had used control of the PLA to foster and then benefit from the Cultural Revolution, was no more. Things were back to normal, according to the conventional wisdom.

Unexplained abnormalities remained, however. One was notable during President Richard M. Nixon's groundbreaking visit to China in February 1972, which I covered for the *Star.* After flying out to Guam to board Air Force One, I arrived with the president for my first ground-level look at the country. While Nixon was in Beijing, the Chinese government organized a press conference at a nearby PLA base. The commanding general there voiced what was believed to have been one of Lin's positions: that the United States remained China's main potential enemy, and the Soviet Union was not a problem. This was the opposite of the official position then being taken by the main organizer and host of Nixon's visit, Premier Zhou, and implicitly by Mao. After China's 1969 border clashes with Soviet troops, Mao strongly advocated preparations for a war with the U.S.S.R. as he turned to the United States. Internal disagreements obviously remained, as I wrote about the general's remarks. Other correspondents did not pick up the difference.

After a family home leave around the world in the summer of 1972, we returned to Hong Kong at the beginning of September. Setting to work reading some of the main articles that had appeared in the Beijing press during my two-month absence, as well as scanning provincial radio transcripts, I was struck by subtle sniping at the way the Chinese government was being run. Something was amiss.

Without having the opportunity to talk this over with anyone before going off to Indochina, I wrote a two-part series for the *Star* saying that a new round of political infighting seemed to be developing in China. Governmental policies were being criticized in veiled and often indirect ways, implying that Maoist ideology was being slighted if not ignored by officials. Reviewing the Communist Party's tumultuous past, I pointed out that Mao had a history, going back to the 1930s, of turning on his top deputies, blaming them for mistakes usually of Mao's own making, and purging them. In opening stages of the Cultural Revolution in 1966, Mao had purged his long-time deputy and presumed successor, China's President Liu Shaoqi. Then Liu's successor as No. 2, Defense Minister Lin, had fallen. That left Premier Zhou Enlai, the steely but—in internal politics—usually self-effacing government administrator, as the No. 2 man. With Mao as usual letting someone else handle day-to-day affairs, Zhou was running the country. Significantly, he was doing it with the help of many of the government officials who had been criticized and purged in Mao's Cultural Revolution, only to be brought back to power, presumably by Zhou. Now, I wrote, there was no one between Mao and Zhou to take the heat for any perceived failures or be blamed for the government's efforts to maintain the orderliness needed to cope with China's immense problems rather than emphasizing Maoist political slogans. The next time around, the political clash that seemed to be shaping up had to be between Mao and Zhou.

Then I went off to Vietnam and Cambodia. When I returned to Hong Kong several weeks later, Sherrod told me that Japanese consulate specialists on China had queried him, as a leading American specialist and a known friend of mine, on what kind of line he had been feeding me. The insulting assumption of the question was that I was one of those journalists who could only report what my consulate thought, rather than thinking for myself. But the question also showed that the Japanese were concerned. Tokyo was improving political relations with and making large commercial investments in a country that it assumed had returned to rational behavior under Zhou's skillful management. The Japanese government did not want any renewed turmoil in China. No one else was writing about new political trouble. Was there a looming problem?

Sherrod pointed out to the Japanese diplomats that he had also been on home leave for a couple of months, only returning after my articles had appeared, and had not seen me for some three months. But, he informed me later, he also told the Japanese he had no disagreement with my analysis. The rest of the U.S. consulate political staff was more cautiously hesitant.

In the following months, I kept seeing signs that a political struggle was going on behind the Beijing scenes. I wrote occasional articles on aspects of this, but I was in a lonely minority. Finally, in mid-June 1973, I wrote a three-part series for the *Star* pulling the evidence together. The first one pointed out that by receiving foreign visitors Mao was giving his public endorsement to the foreign policy directed by Zhou. But the chairman had for some time not commented on domestic policy, which Zhou was running in many ways that had been ideologically denounced in the Cultural Revolution. "Mao's withholding of personal commitment to domestic policy . . . perhaps indicat[es] he disagrees with policy which he does not control," I wrote. "[I]f another power struggle comes, it will—in oversimplified terms—pit Mao's ideologically inclined followers against Zhou's pragmatic bureaucrats." Officials who had been banished in the Cultural Revolution but now returned to power included Deng Xiaoping, whom Mao had accused of ignoring him while Deng was secretary-general of the Communist Party's Central Committee up to 1967. But people who had denounced Deng and others, such Cultural Revolution firebrands as Mao's wife, Jiang Qing, and her young protégé, Wang Hongwen, remained prominent. With both purgers and their former victims active, "The overall picture, then, is of unstable personal relations within China's leadership," I wrote. ". . . [A] seemingly placid and stable China [is] in a condition of potential internal conflict."

A followup to the three articles noted "conflicting attitudes over Vietnam, [which] involves Zhou Enlai's policy of good relations with the United States. . . . [L]atent opposition to choosing America as a friend, while continuing hostility with the bordering Soviet Union, has now begun to make itself visible in sniping at Zhou's line."

As these articles finished running on June 20, Monica and the boys and I were off to visit China. We had become good friends in Moscow of a young Dutch diplomat and his Danish wife. Now stationed in Beijing, they visited us a couple of times on shopping trips to Hong Kong, and they invited us to visit them. Since the Chinese government still was not issuing visas to American journalists, I asked for tourist visas on the promise that I would not work while in China. Somewhat surprisingly, we got the visas and flew to Beijing for an enjoyable two weeks in Beijing and in Beidaihe, the foreigner-built old seaside resort for the capital where the Communist leadership now spent every August vacationing and discussing policy decisions. With our host, I met and talked with diplomats of a number of countries. All were politely unbelieving of my theory about internal conflict. The Chinese told them everything was fine, and on the surface things looked quiet.

By coincidence, we were in Beijing as the United States was opening its first diplomatic establishment in China since 1949. Called a liaison office, because Washington still maintained diplomatic relations with Chiang's government on Taiwan, it functioned as an embassy. Henry A. Kissinger, the national security adviser who had opened the way for Nixon to visit China and had later become secretary of state, sent to Beijing career State Department officials to support his policy of good relations with China. They were not willing to believe any evidence of a conflict over relations with the United States between Zhou's pragmatic bureaucrats and the ideological young radicals publicly associated with Jiang Qing but undoubtedly backed by Mao.

Over the following months, dispatches from the liaison office to Washington described a calm situation of broad support for Zhou's policies. But from the U.S. consulate in Hong Kong, Sherrod took the lead in forming a consensus that produced dispatches noting signs of trouble. I understood indirectly that the Hong Kong dispatches were somewhat more restrained than what I was writing increasingly strongly, the restraint arising partly from State Department bureaucratic reasons. Nonetheless, there was an interpretive disagreement between American diplomats in Beijing and Hong Kong. The State Department told Sherrod's bosses to quiet him down if he would not support Kissinger's team.

In early August of 1973, an intensification of sniping in Chinese media, along with indications of important high-level meetings in Beidaihe, suggested that the conflict was reaching a turning point. I wrote frequently about this. Then I got a call at home on a Wednesday evening, August 29, from the Reuters bureau. Grabbing my traveling typewriter, I rushed down to the bureau, read NCNA transcripts just coming in, and began writing for my afternoon paper, twelve hours behind Hong Kong time. Beijing had announced that the tenth national congress of the Chinese Communist Party had ended the previous day, after being held in secrecy. The initial reports on the congress gave little indication of what had happened. Over the next few nights, however, as some speeches and new leadership lists were released, it became clear to me that the power struggle had intensified. Finally, on Saturday night the texts of the key speeches were put out. After reading them at the Reuters bureau, I phoned Sherrod at home to tell him that the lonely line he had been taking in the consulate and that I had been pushing in the press had been validated.

Describing the congress on the basis of the speeches and earlier announcements, I wrote that "Zhou won that round against leftist radicals, but their spokesman [Wang Hongwen] served notice that further challenges to Zhou's personal domination of Chinese affairs will be made. One challenge will be to the rapprochement with the United States." Mao had not spoken at the congress, which was unusual and thus a significant point. "But the radical thrust at Zhou seemed unlikely to have been made without his inspiration and support." Wang was promoted to the No. 3 position in the party, after Mao and Zhou.

Most writers on China did not accept what I considered clear evidence of trouble. Instead, they focused on the usual Chinese descriptions of such a meeting having been "a congress of unity." So I decided to reach out to a wider audience with my interpretation. I wrote a lengthy, extensively footnoted article setting forth the evidence for a renewed power struggle up through the results of the congress. The quickest way to reach China scholars was a widely read and respected monthly publication from the University of California at Berkeley, *Asian Survey.* I didn't know anyone there, but I gambled on sending the manuscript to it, along with a carbon copy to Mike Oksenberg, then at the University of Michigan, who was on the publication's board of consultants. To my pleasant surprise, *Asian Survey* quickly revised the edition then going to press, for November 1973, to lead with my article. Mike said later that he disagreed with the article but had thought it a legitimate interpretation that deserved to be read. Several scholars told me in later years that my article, coming as others were emphasizing claims of unity, was the first inkling they'd seen of trouble in China. After later developments recounted below, I was also told, the article was used by some professors as an example of how to analyze Chinese politics.

In the months following the congress, I kept finding and writing about other signs of struggle. Mao was clearly promoting Wang, whose mixture of appearances and failures to appear on public occasions signaled disagreement with Zhou. "The political situation is sharpening as lines are being drawn more clearly between radicals grouped around . . . Mao Zedong and the bureaucracy headed by Premier Zhou Enlai," I wrote November 25. By then esoteric references in Chinese media criticizing the ancient Chinese sage Confucius seemed clearly aimed by analogy at Zhou. A friend heading the FBIS bureau in Hong Kong who was a China scholar, Joe Simon, pointed out these references to me.

By early 1974, Chinese media were asking how allegedly capitalistic policies could have been allowed to reappear. Americans were blamed for some World War II atrocities by Chiang's forces, in effect challenging Zhou's policy of improving relations with Washington. On March 5, I referred in print to "the renewed Cultural Revolution." With the Cultural Revolution generally assumed to be long over, I was still in a lonely minority, however.

What's more, I had become controversial. Not only was the U.S. liaison office in Beijing sending cables back to the State Department insisting that everything was calm and the Chinese leadership was unified, in effect scoffing at the Kremlinological indications that I seized upon, but also most journalists who wrote about China followed that line. One of them, Leo Goodstadt, wrote from the prominent perch of the *Far Eastern Economic Review.* This Hong Kong-based weekly had distinguished itself by perceptive reporting on the Cultural Revolution from 1966 to 1969. But the *Review*'s staff then changed, and Goodstadt had become one of the magazine's main writers on Chinese internal affairs.

When Goodstadt and I were invited to appear together on a Radio Hong Kong discussion program, he angrily denounced my views. His own credentials for understanding how Communist regimes work were exposed by his stating, in a comparison with Chinese politics, that poor health really was the reason Soviet leader Nikita Khrushchev left office in 1964.

Later, as an approaching typhoon was beginning to blow rain, I chanced to meet in downtown Hong Kong the man who had preceded me as the *Star*'s Asia correspondent, Don Kirk. Kirk, who was now a freelance writer living in Tokyo, had focused on Vietnam for the *Star* and never seriously followed Chinese affairs. Nonetheless, standing there in the wind and rain, he proceeded to upbraid me for distorting the situation in China. There was no struggle going on, he declared. The source of his own presumed knowledge of the situation was not clear, but his was the conventional wisdom. Other journalists around the Hong Kong Foreign Correspondents' Club thought I had gone off the deep end.

Curiously, however, the two big English-language newspapers in Hong Kong began occasionally publishing my analytical articles. Both subscribed to the *New York Times* News Service. Beginning about 1971, the *Times* service had begun distributing selected reporting from the *Star* plus a few other American newspapers as part of its package for subscribers around the world. At first, the Hong Kong papers ignored my material. But by late 1973, they had started publishing my iconoclastic version of Chinese affairs, which contrasted with what their own staff people were reporting from Beijing or writing in Hong Kong. I didn't know the editors, but I presumed they just wanted to cover themselves by offering an alternative. Maybe they also wanted to use an outsider to say things that they thought might cause trouble for their own staff writers. Anyway, it meant that I occasionally gained a local audience of people interested in China, even if most people disagreed with me.

In April 1974 the *Star* relayed to me word that I had won a major American journalism prize for my reporting on China. This was the George Polk Memorial Award for foreign reporting in 1973. I was surprised because my editors had not mentioned entering me for the prize.

It was at about this time, as I was writing that "Zhou has been slowly fading as the struggle progresses," that the "most despicable" messages were sent to me from Beijing. When Sherrod relayed them to me, we concluded that the struggle had reached a point at which Zhou's grip on the government was becoming endangered. The radicals were gaining power in parts of the premier's bureaucracy. I was caught in the middle. Curiously, however, the point of saying

I would never visit China again seemed a bit unnecessary. I had made no effort to visit China since the tourist visit with my family almost a year earlier. I knew working American journalists, especially those knowledgeable about Chinese affairs, had little if any hope of getting a visa.

In the summer of 1974, my family went on home leave again.[2] While in Washington, I went to see Richard H. Solomon. As the National Security Council's China expert, this academic specialist on Chinese politics was the U.S. government's key man on policy toward Beijing. He told me flatly that I was wrong in my interpretations. There was no renewed power struggle. In particular, Chinese-American relations were not an issue in Beijing, he insisted. That was certainly what Kissinger and others wanted to believe. About this time, Mike Oksenberg published an article saying it was a mistake to interpret Chinese politics in terms of a simple split between two main factions. He delineated the political inclinations of some ten different groups as playing together in a complex interaction that drove Chinese policies. I thought the article not only amusing but also so academically equivocal—indeed, splitting hairs—as to be very unhelpful in understanding what was going on. It did not explain what I considered to be signs of conflict.

When I returned to Hong Kong at the end of August, I found continued signs of struggle in China. Interestingly, though, they were not so prominent in Chinese media. Some of the fury of the radicals' attacks on Zhou's pragmatists seemed to have subsided. There had been indications of an economic slowdown. This suggested that, just as in the late 1960s, political campaigns had interfered with production, and so politics had to be brought under control. After writing about this, I did something quixotic. I submitted a visa application to the Hong Kong office of the China Travel Service, which handled visas since there was no Chinese diplomatic representation in the British colony. The request was to attend the mid-October trade fair at Canton (now Guangzhou). Canton fairs every April and October were in those years important events, arranging a quarter to a third of all of China's foreign trade. This was the first time I had asked for a visa to go. In earlier years it had not seemed important. Now it was a test. U.S. journalists were unwelcome at the fair, which was attended mostly by Communist and European businessmen. By asking for a visa, I was in effect turning the other cheek to the messages from Beijing.

After making the application, I went off to Indochina. More by chance than design, I returned to Hong Kong about a week before the fair was to open. Just a few days before the opening, I got a phone call from the China Travel Service.

Come pick up your visa and make hotel and travel arrangements for the fair. That was all, no explanation offered. American and other Western journalists who had been making applications for the fair every year were not given visas this year. Just me. I turned out to be the first American journalist allowed to work in China for a year. It was a year in which anti-American radicals had been in the ascendancy.

Clearly, something had happened in Beijing. The muting of the power struggle that I had noted on returning from home leave must have meant that Zhou's bureaucrats had regained their footing after having for a time been knocked off balance by radical leftists' attacks. With a more calm governmental administration returning, the Foreign Ministry chose to send a signal by inviting me. Sherrod and others at the U.S. consulate certainly interpreted my invitation as a signal. It seemed to mean not only that the radical attack had subsided but also that my well-known reporting of that attack was being endorsed as having been correct. The bureaucrats were happy to have had someone recognize their problems, and even happier to signal now that the problems had subsided. The "most despicable" description no longer applied.

So I took the train to Canton. The fair, which opened on October 15, was not in itself very interesting, although it provided material for several articles. Businessmen regulars mentioned to me being struck by the way I was treated at the stylized events associated with the fair. They noted the prominent place I was given at the opening banquet and the good seat at a performance of the latest "revolutionary ballet" that Jiang Qing had fostered.

My visa was good for a week, and after a few days I was invited by China Travel Service to see some of the area around Canton. This led to several outings. One was to a hot springs resort. My hotel room had a sunken bathtub filled with steaming mineral water that was large and deep enough to take two swimming strokes. A more interesting visit was to a rural commune to see an apparently staged example of enthusiastic public participation in building a new irrigation system. I had carefully controlled conversations with former university students and professional people who had been banished to the countryside by the Cultural Revolution's rejection of the supposedly corrupting influences of higher education, which cost China a decade's worth of skilled professionals. The students and older personnel were somewhat listlessly picking tea. I could tell from having watched tea picking in South Asia by women who grew up doing the job that the Chinese were doing it most ineptly. And I could tell from my Soviet experiences that much of what I was allowed to see had been staged for my benefit, particularly an after-lunch rest period that the tea pickers spent in their barracks studying the writings of Chairman Mao with obviously feigned earnestness.

Summing up what I found on that trip, I wrote that Canton "appears fairly calm and relaxed," despite some political messages recently painted on walls. The campaign to use Mao's influence to attack Zhou's bureaucrats continued. "Since midsummer, however, the intensity of radical attacks has at least temporarily declined, and calls from Zhou's moderates for unity have been more prominent." A few weeks later, I noted signs in the media that Jiang Qing had suffered a demotion in status. This round of struggle was subsiding, although not ending.

In February 1975, I closed the *Star*'s Hong Kong bureau. I had for a year or two been the financially struggling paper's last foreign correspondent, and the editors finally decided they could no longer afford to keep me abroad. I moved my family to Washington, where I became a diplomatic correspondent for the *Star.* In that role I wrote occasionally about Chinese affairs, but I no longer had the time to focus closely enough on China's media and other sources to do detailed analysis of continuing trends. But, reporting President Gerald R. Ford's November 1975 visit to Beijing, I picked up enough signals to write that the political struggle continued.

Zhou died in January 1976, and Mao passed away eight months later. Shortly after Mao's death, key leaders whom I had in print associated with Zhou's pragmatic group arrested the leading radicals. These radicals became known as "the gang of four" and were blamed for leading China into destructive internal conflict. The four were precisely the ones whom I had identified in numerous newspaper articles and in my *Asian Survey* article three years earlier as the key radicals, including Jiang Qing and Wang Hongwen.[3] After years of imprisonment, the four were put on trial in 1980–1981 and sentenced to more years. Mao was later blamed posthumously by the Chinese Communist Party for having introduced errors into Chinese policies, but he was never directly accused by the party of what I had written repeatedly: that he was the force and authority behind "the gang of four." That was, however, the inescapable belief of many Chinese and the conclusion of historians. Only Mao had the power to launch attacks on a series of his deputies who were administering the nation.

The Chinese government's official history now dates the Cultural Revolution from 1966 until Mao's death a decade later. The widespread perception in the early 1970s that it was over is ignored. The struggles that I detected are now placed in the overall context of fluctuating clashes between Maoist ideologues and pragmatic administrators.

Even before the historians had made their pronouncements, two people made interesting comments to me on my controversial interpretations. One was Mike Oksenberg. In late 1976, not long before Jimmy Carter became president and Mike replaced Solomon as the National Security Council specialist on China, Mike told me that I had been right about the power struggle. His own convoluted interpretation had missed the basic point of what was happening, he politely conceded. The other person was Jay Matthews. A friend had introduced me to him just before the *Washington Post* sent him out as its Hong Kong correspondent. After Mao died and "the gang of four" was jailed, Jay graciously wrote a note to me. The journalistic community in Hong Kong had come to realize, he reported, that I had been right.

22

BIRTH OF A NATION

THE WAR WAS OVER, THEY HAD WON, AND THE YOUNG GUERRILLA FIGHTER known as "the tiger of Tangail" seemed intent on improving his reputation as part of claiming a political role in his new country.

During almost nine months of struggle against the Pakistani Army and its local supporters, Abdul Quadir Siddiqui had become known as a ruthless, even vicious warrior who took no quarter. The former student leader had headed a band of *mukhti bahini,* as the guerrilla "liberation forces" were named in Bengali, based in the Madhupur Jungle region in Tangail district. The band operated some fifty miles northwest of Dhaka, capital of the area that had been East Pakistan but with victory became independent Bangladesh.

Now, Siddiqui told a Dhaka crowd on December 18, 1971, two days after the Pakistani Army had surrendered to the invading Indian Army, the new nation for which they had fought must be built on a sound basis. After divisive bloodshed, revenge killings must be replaced by judicial processes. Law and order must be restored, he said. As Siddiqui spoke, bodies festered in Dhaka's streets and in dumping grounds on the outskirts of the city. Civil government had not begun to revive.

As an example of restoring order, Siddiqui said he would turn over to the proper authorities for trial three youths sitting on the ground near the crude wooden platform where he spoke. While he was on his way to the rally, Siddiqui said, he had seen the three trying to rob a merchant and kidnap some girls off the street. He and his men had stopped such lawlessness, which must now end. Rifle-carrying followers of Siddiqui guarded the young men, whose hands were tied behind their backs. The three looked worried.

The rest of the mostly young people on Paltan Maidan, the traditional political meeting ground in the heart of Dhaka's new commercial area, were in a celebratory mood. It reminded me of the last time I had watched youths rally here, the previous March 23. Dhaka University student leaders, carrying amateurish weapons, then raised a new flag of green and red with a golden outline of East Pakistan. This, they proclaimed, was to be the flag of Bangladesh, a new nation that they wanted to be independent of West Pakistan. But two days after the rally, the Pakistani Army had thrown off the subterfuge of political negotiations over the East's status. The result was bitter internecine war that finally brought what the youths had wanted.

The cost was high. No one knew how many had died during the nine months. Immediately after achieving independence, many Bangladeshis used a figure of 3 million killed. Although the 3 million figure continued to be used in political rhetoric to emphasize the sacrifices required to escape from control of West Pakistan's Punjabi power elite, more educated guesses were later reduced to 1 million, and the United Nations' World Health Organization published a study in 2008 that estimated the actual figure at 269,000.

Despite the war's end by the December rally, more were yet to die—some before my eyes.

Covering this cycle of violence for the *Washington Star* was the culmination of a dozen years in which I had, off and on, been reporting on Pakistan. During that time, I had gotten to know the differences and divisions between the two awkwardly joined parts of a never really well-unified nation, to understand a little about the regional and linguistic fissures within each part. I had come to appreciate the subtle beauty of the East's delta land with its myriad rivers populated with picturesque big sailing boats, its diverse shades of green as rice crops and jute ripened in flooded fields, its tea-covered northeastern hills and jungled southeastern hills, its swampy riverine coastlines and one long stretch of pristine beach. And the usually quiet, polite, hospitable people—them had I also come to appreciate in a wide range of urban interviews and on numerous trips into the countryside to talk with farmers.

My first visit was in August 1959, when I was a correspondent based in New Delhi for the Associated Press. At the time, East Pakistan was considered a quiet backwater of a nation whose capital was in Karachi, fifteen hundred miles west of Dhaka across the breadth of India.[1] The two parts—or "wings," as Pakistanis called them—were those areas of the old British India where Muslims were in the majority. As the British *Raj* prepared to relinquish power in 1947, Muslim leaders refused to accept minority status in an undivided India with a Hindu majority. They preferred an awkwardly separated nation of their own. Most of those leaders—urban and urbane lawyers backed by prosperous businessmen, all far removed from the ordinary Muslims of British India for whom they claimed to speak—came from the area that became West Pakistan, or moved there from the big cities of India after independence. Few of them were from the small towns and villages of what became East Pakistan or moved there.

The divided and diverse nation never fit naturally together. West Pakistan's languages were Urdu, Punjabi, Pashto, Sindhi, and Baluchi, most of them influenced by Middle Eastern tongues and written in Persian script. Native East Pakistanis spoke Bengali and wrote in a script derived from Sanskrit. The partition of India also brought Urdu-speaking Muslims to the East, where they were known as Biharis because most migrated from the north Indian province of Bihar. Much of the western wing, where 42.9 million people lived in 310,403 square miles, according to the most recent census, in 1961, was desert or bleak hills with too little water. The East, with 50.8 million in just 55,126 square miles, had over much of the year too much water in the monsoon-soaked delta of the Ganges and Brahmaputra rivers. West Pakistan's psychological orientation was toward the Middle East, of which it was a cultural and ethnic extension. The East was climatically and in some ways ethnically part of Southeast Asia. But, almost surrounded by India, it lacked any strong outward orientation except toward Calcutta.

East Pakistan had been the agricultural hinterland of Calcutta, the political capital of British India during the empire's Victorian heyday, its main industrial center, and the urban focus of a rich Bengali culture. Many of the raw materials that fed Calcutta's industries came from this area. Calcutta, a cosmopolitan city of both Muslims and Hindus, was contentiously awarded to India in the 1947 partition. With the economic and cultural connection severed by political hostility, East Pakistan's natural wealth was diverted to Karachi. East wing exports paid for imports needed to begin the industrialization of Pakistan as a whole, but virtually all the new factories were built around Karachi or farther north in Punjab province. The banks and insurance companies that grew with this industrialization and that increasingly controlled the nation's wealth were also in Karachi, new Pakistan's boomtown. While the East provided 50 to 70 percent of the country's export earnings, varying by year, it got only 25 to 30 percent of imports, including those financed by foreign aid that was provided for the nation as a whole. National political power resided primarily with army officers and big landowners in the Punjab.

When Pakistan began economic development planning in 1955, the West got more investments in improving the country's inadequate power, transport, and other infrastructure facilities on the grounds that it had better-prepared projects than were available in the East. More insidiously, the national government professed to try to balance development plan spending between the two wings while creating special programs outside the plans to fund massively expensive projects in the West. These programs for Indus River basin dams and combating salinity in irrigated areas were implemented while the government endlessly studied but did little about the East's huge need for water control and transportation projects. As for building shelters to protect coastal people from storm-driven seawater inundations that historically had taken high tolls of human life, a fatalistic attitude compounded the Punjabi establishment's desire to avoid spending money in the East.

I visited East Pakistan periodically from 1959 into 1963. The primitive rural economy was visible in the straitened lifestyle of almost self-sufficient villages. In Dhaka, independence had brought some new construction to the old British provincial center, but not much. After an initial exploratory visit to the East, my trips there were usually focused on a particular story: the visit of Queen Elizabeth II, the opening of a powerless parliament in the East on a pretense of having some national government functions there from time to time, the aftermath of a hurricane, student riots against domination by the West, or something similar. But whenever I got there, I also took time to interview provincial officials, politicians, journalists, diplomats, and others on economic and political questions. With translation help by university students, I made many trips into villages to find out what ordinary people thought.

While working elsewhere in the world after 1963, I kept up with the region enough to be aware of rising discontent there. And I knew of a growing feeling among the West Pakistani elite that the East, having been economically exploited for two decades, might become a liability if changing political circumstances gave it the political power that its preponderance of population justified.

So I was eager to get back. The second trip I took after arriving in Hong Kong as the *Star*'s Asia correspondent was to India and Pakistan in April 1970. After visiting Calcutta and Delhi, I flew to Karachi and then up to Rawalpindi, the temporary capital of Pakistan as the nearby new capital of Islamabad was being built. Particularly in Karachi, the economic center of the country, I found businessmen muttering about casting East Pakistan off as no longer needed for the prosperity of the West. It had been sucked dry. The possibility of breaking up Pakistan before the East began demanding a reversal of the flow of resources was being discussed quietly, as a subversive thought.

I intended to fly from West Pakistan to Dhaka. However, the *Star* asked me to rush to Saigon to cover American military incursions from Vietnam into adjacent parts of Cambodia from which Communist forces were operating against South Vietnam. Then in November 1970 I was in Saigon on another of my periodic checkups on the Vietnam situation. On the night of November 12 and 13, a devastating storm hit East Pakistan. It was a cyclone, as they are known in the Indian Ocean region, but a hurricane in Western Hemisphere terminology or a typhoon in East Asian usage. As planned, I went on to Cambodia to take another look at the growing war there. Then the *Star* agreed that I should go to Dhaka for two reasons. One was to look at the cyclone's aftermath. The storm continued to be a big story because of the high death toll and the slow relief work and because it now involved an American military relief operation. The U.S. military had been sent to help transport food to cyclone-devastated coastal areas after the scope of the tragedy and the inadequacy of official Pakistani relief work had become clear. My other reason for going was to cover the Pakistani parliamentary elections scheduled for December 7.

The storm had swept up to the north end of the Bay of Bengal, where the combined Ganges and Brahmaputra dumped silt, building up fertile but flat islands. An already high tide was heightened by a full moon. A wind-swept wall of water lashed across the islands and far into coastal areas. Villages of poor farmers, who had flocked to coastal margins and new delta islands because of overpopulation and land hunger throughout East Pakistan, were swept away in the darkness. No one knew how many people lived in constantly changing delta coastal areas, so there was no accurate toll, but a figure of three hundred thousand deaths was later generally accepted.

After a cyclone had hit the East Pakistani coast south of Chittagong on May 28–29, 1963 (they seemed usually to come at night, adding to the terror), I had rushed there from New Delhi to cover the aftermath for the AP. Bloated bodies were still being fished out of coastal swamps when I went out in the steamy sunshine with recovery teams and talked with surviving villagers. But that storm killed *only* 11,520 persons, according to dubiously precise later records, and I was the only foreign journalist who bothered to go see what had happened. I wrote then about vague government plans to build storm shelters of concrete blocks on the higher bits of ground to provide havens for people who lived in vulnerable bamboo and thatch houses. Few areas had them by the end of the 1960s, when the decade's death toll from cyclones was officially listed as 52,410.[2]

When I got to East Pakistan in late November 1970, I caught rides on U.S. Army helicopters that were taking food to storm-wrecked offshore islands, so I could interview relief workers and, with their help, survivors. And I talked with officials in Dhaka about complaints of slow and inadequate relief efforts by a government in West Pakistan that seemed to treat this monstrous storm with the fatalistic attitude that it was just another of the East's periodic cyclones, another disaster.

Then I turned to the election campaign. I had covered several Pakistani elections in the early 1960s, but they were rigged affairs to choose "basic democrats" as local leaders and to select tame parliamentarians during President Mohammad Ayub Khan's authoritarian rule. The situation in 1970 was wholly new.

For almost a decade, Ayub ran the country with a firm military hand. But by February 1968, when he had become seriously ill and political, economic, and social pressures were building against him, his government was beginning to lose confidence in itself. Ayub began negotiating with various political elements in a way he had not had to do earlier. On February 22, 1969, he ordered the parole from prison of Mujibur Rahman.

Known as Sheikh Mujibur Rahman from a minor inherited title, the man popularly referred to as Mujib was the leader of East Pakistan's Awami (People's) League. His oratorical power and common touch made him a Bengali politician whom the West Pakistani establishment particularly feared. An imposingly large man with a splendid moustache, he had been jailed on various political charges off and on for almost ten of the twenty-two years since independence in 1947. The combination of his leadership and the East's population preponderance were seen as a growing problem by the western establishment. The one earlier time I had been in East Pakistan when he was out of jail, in 1963, Mujib complained to me about discrimination against his region on foreign aid and said he was not afraid to consider autonomy for the East within Pakistan or even independence. The Punjabi army cannot hold down the East, he said then.

Beset by failing health and failing policies, Ayub in effect abdicated on March 25, 1969, with a declaration putting the nation under martial law. The commander in chief of the Pakistani Army, General Agha Mohammad Yahya Khan, became the chief martial law administrator. He also assumed the vacated presidency on April 3, 1969. Yahya was a simple, hard-drinking soldier without the political sophistication of Ayub. But he took a simple, honest step: he abandoned the old system of rigging the political process so that West Pakistan with its smaller population could dominate the East. After conceding that "the people of East Pakistan did not have their full share in the decision-making process on vital national issues," he announced on November 28, 1969, that elections would be held for a new national assembly with equal weight for every individual's vote. That meant the East would elect 162 members of the new assembly, the West only 138. Another 13 seats were reserved for women.

The assembly elections were set for October 5, 1970. However, unusually bad seasonal flooding of East Pakistan in August provided an excuse to postpone them until December 7. The real reason for the delay reportedly was that by August Yahya's regime thought the appeal of Mujib's Awami League had peaked and was declining. Although regime officials were convinced that no one political party would dominate the election in either wing, they wanted more time in which Mujib might lose votes. Mujib had directly challenged the western establishment with a six-point program saying Pakistan should be "a federation granting full autonomy" to the provinces, with the East handling its own affairs except for national government responsibility for defense and foreign relations.

The cyclone became a political factor. The government's failure to respond quickly and fully to the tragedy was widely seen in the East as confirming Mujib's message. As the leading voice of eastern complaints, Mujib gained political strength. He was a powerful advocate in my interviews with him after the storm, not to mention bombastic and egotistical. Everywhere I went talking to people, in Dhaka, in smaller East Pakistani towns, and out into villages, the overwhelming message was strong support for Mujib and the Awami League. Local journalists whom I had known for a decade reported the same. I wrote in the *Star* of December 4, 1970, that Mujibur "Rahman is riding toward an expected sweeping victory . . . on an emotional wave of support for regional autonomy. . . . It is uncertain just how much autonomy would be allowed by the Western-based central government," but the situation "could be reaching some sort of climax [with the vote on] Monday, perhaps a violent one. . . . [T]he eventual result of Rahman's East Pakistani autonomy drive could be to split two widely separated parts of Pakistan into separate nations."

Then I flew to West Pakistan, where the new Pakistan People's Party (PPP), created by Zulfikar Ali Bhutto, was gaining attention. I had gotten to know the Berkeley-educated Bhutto well in the early 1960s, when he was Ayub's young deputy for some domestic and foreign problems and then became foreign minister. Bhutto liked to talk, and he used to give me a lot of time for what were not so much interviews as discussions, sometimes trying out ideas on me. Bhutto came from the feudal landowning class that, together with senior military officers, had run Pakistan since 1947. But as a politician this aristocrat began preaching a populist message of nationalization that promised prosperity to western farmers, whose per capita income was less than $100 a year. With a translator, I went out into Punjab villages and found virtually everyone entranced by Bhutto's vague concept of "Islamic socialism." I wrote that despite the unrealism of the PPP platform, it might win strongly in the West. The resulting split between the Awami League and the PPP, I wrote two days before the election, meant that "[t]he potential for chaos—and even bloodshed—over the issue of keeping Pakistan united must be rated significant."

While Bhutto's PPP won 86 assembly seats in the West, Mujib's Awami League was supported by 72 percent of the eastern electorate and gained control of 167 seats. This gave the league a solid national majority with which to control the assembly's writing of a new constitution and claim full autonomy within a weak nation. "But there is a question as to whether the army leaders like the choice" of the voters, I wrote in the December 8 *Star,* because the generals considered themselves the guardians of national unity.

As the scope of Mujib's victory in the East—indeed, his victory in the nation as a whole—and Bhutto's control of the West became clear, Bhutto was holed up at his large agricultural estate at Larkana in southern West Pakistan, not talking to the press. I went down to Larkana with a British and a Japanese journalist. Bhutto gave us a two-hour interview beginning at 10 P.M. Listening quietly was his daughter, Benazir, at seventeen his eldest child, who had taken a vacation from Harvard University to be home for the elections. Bhutto explained that he wanted her to hear the conversation as part of learning about Pakistani politics—which she later mastered as prime minister twice before being murdered in 2007 by Islamic extremists.

Although Mujib was making post-election speeches in Dhaka saying his six-point program had to be "implemented in all its aspects," Bhutto said that night the six points were constitutionally impractical. "If they are implemented, Pakistan cannot survive for long" as a unified nation, he said. I reported that "Bhutto agreed with the general assumption in West Pakistan that it would be difficult if not impossible for the army to try to keep East Pakistan in a united nation against its will." Before leaving Pakistan, I wrote a wrap-up story for the *Star* of December 13. "Pakistan has experienced a social upheaval by the peaceful use of the ballot box," I began. "The possibility of further, less peaceful, upheavals remains."

In late February 1971, I returned to South Asia, first to cover a parliamentary election in India and then to report the worsening political confrontation in Pakistan. From Karachi, I wrote for the March 3 *Star*: "The inability of the two parts of Pakistan to agree on their future relationship has produced an explosive crisis for this huge underdeveloped nation. The split into two nations, toward which political intransigence has long been moving Pakistan, now looms as a larger possibility. But before it comes, there might be a bloody effort by the Pakistani army, essentially a force from the western part of the divided nation, to keep the eastern part from breaking away. . . . Foreign observers feel such an effort, which could turn the lovely East Pakistan delta into an area like the Mekong Delta at the worst of the Viet Cong days, would in the long run fail." I was, of course, the primary foreign observer who felt that, although some diplomats were beginning to agree.

Flying to Dhaka, I entered a political caldron stirred by a general strike. Mujib had called it to protest Yahya's postponement of the national assembly's opening as a constitutional convention. Yahya wanted time to seek some compromise between Mujib, who insisted on full autonomy for the East, and Bhutto and army leaders, who wanted to keep a strong central government and hoped somehow to limit the power of Mujib's parliamentary majority. But the crowds that rallied around Mujib were in no mood for compromise.

After writing more dire stories of impending trouble, I bought a seat on a British Royal Air Force evacuation flight from an airport crowded with people waiting desperately for regular commercial flights to flee feared trouble. Following a few days in India to wrap up the election victory by Prime Minister Indira Gandhi's Congress Party, I returned to Dhaka. Flying in was easy. Planes were going almost empty to pick up those trying to leave—foreign correspondents rush into places where everyone there is trying to get out.

Tension was building, the strike partially continued, and the government was censoring or "losing" foreign correspondents' stories given to the telegraph office for cabling abroad. I gave one story with a grim interpretation of the situation to a friendly German businessman who was flying to Bangkok, and he delivered it to the AP's bureau there for transmission to the *Star.*

Yahya was holding desultory talks with Mujib in Dhaka, and Bhutto arrived to join them. No constitutional formula was in sight that would satisfy the two political leaders and the army. I reported ominous rumors that the army was flying in troops from West Pakistan late every night at the military side of the airport, but armed guards there made it impossible to confirm what the planes were carrying. Also ominous was Yahya's replacement of the army commander for East Pakistan, who apparently was not tough enough for him. The new man was Lieutenant General Mohammed Tikka Khan. Tikka had earned a reputation for brutality in dealing with tribal efforts to maintain autonomy in the Baluchistan province of West Pakistan. One afternoon, in a discussion with some Bengali political leaders—at the home of Kamal Hussain, a leading lawyer who was also a top aide to Mujib and publisher of the East's best political weekly, *Insight*—I invented the deliberately derogatory label for Tikka of "the butcher of Baluchistan." After I had used the label in several *Star* reports, over the next few weeks the term became widely used by people who had no idea where it had originated. Soon it became sadly more appropriate to call Tikka "the butcher of Bangladesh."

As the stalemate continued, both *Star* editors and I became impatient, and I thought of leaving. Then early in the evening of March 25, most of the twenty-five or so foreign correspondents and photographers then in Dhaka were having dinner at the Inter-Continental, the city's one modern hotel. Finishing dinner and drifting out into the night air, we discovered armed soldiers around the hotel, facing inward with rifles at the ready. A Pakistani Army officer told us we could not leave. He refused to give an explanation.

We began trying to phone people we had been interviewing around town, but many lines had been cut. All international calls were blocked. Several of us gathered in a top-floor hotel room overlooking the main road into the city from the army cantonment and airport. About 11 P.M. we began to hear sporadic firing of automatic weapons and either artillery or recoilless rifles from somewhere up the cantonment road. A Bengali living near the cantonment reported by phone that unarmed local youths were putting up roadblocks to try to stop truckloads of Pakistani soldiers who were moving out to seize control of the city. One truck stopped within our view, and troops used gunfire to clear an alley to the office and printing plant of a Bengali nationalist newspaper, the *People*. Soon the troops came running back, firing into the air as the newspaper premises burned, shouting, "*Allah e Akhbar*" ("God is Great"), the battle cry throughout the Muslim world—no matter that they were savaging fellow Muslims.

In the dim light, we saw about fifteen youths running toward soldiers, shouting defiant slogans. A machine gun was turned on them. Two fell as the others scattered, but the two later got up and left, perhaps wounded. When people in the second floor of a shopping bazaar across the street from the hotel shouted "Bengalis unite," soldiers fired a heavy machine gun mounted on a jeep into the building. As the sounds of shooting intensified about 1 A.M., fires sprang up in the direction of dormitories at Dhaka University, which was a center for Bengali nationalism, and of a police headquarters. Heavy firing could be heard from the direction of the headquarters of the East Pakistan Rifles, a Bengali force that combined police and army duties. The firing began to subside around 4 A.M. About an hour later six T-54 tanks rumbled down the road and took positions in front of our hotel. In the dawn at 6 o'clock a barber came to shave the soldiers as they squatted on the hotel lawn, where the soldiers later burned new Bangladesh flags that they had collected. Sporadic firing could be heard during the day and more smoke seen.

When some of us tried to leave the hotel to see what was happening, an officer on the lawn who turned back one reporter told him, "If we can shoot our own people, there certainly is no reason why I can't shoot you."

Trapped in the hotel, unable to communicate with the outside world, I got together with personal friends who represented the *New York Times*, the *Baltimore Sun*, and *Newsweek*. The *New York Times* News Service distributed *Washington Star* articles as part of its package for newspapers around the world, so we were not competitors, and neither the *Sun* nor *Newsweek* competed directly with either of us. We four agreed to write one joint story and cooperate in trying to get it out whenever the opportunity arose, pooling our efforts to inform the world. Listening to the BBC on my little shortwave radio, I knew the only news that had gotten out so far was a distorted Pakistani government account of "restoring order" plus vague diplomatic reports.

At dusk on March 26, a colonel appeared at the hotel and ordered the foreign correspondents to pack for departure. "You are being advised to leave," he said. But what if we did not want to leave? "Some advice is obligatory," he declared. His aides were more blunt about forcing us out at gunpoint. After dark, we were loaded into army trucks and driven to the airport. Not everyone was on the trucks, however. One of the missing was Arnold Zeitlin, chief of the AP bureau for Pakistan and Afghanistan that had been opened in Rawalpindi since I had once been responsible for all of South Asia from AP's Delhi bureau. Arnold had been visiting Bengali acquaintances in the suburbs when the army cracked down. I phoned him to tell him not to return to the hotel. The AP had also sent in a photographer, Michel Laurent, a Frenchman who at the age of twenty-five had already earned a reputation for skill and courage, to work with Zeitlin. Laurent was unwilling to leave without him, so he hid on the roof of the hotel from the soldiers who searched the rooms for journalists. Zeitlin, Laurent, and a British correspondent left the day after we were deported.

As we were trucked to the airport, we saw at least five places where roadblocks of old cars, fallen trees, concrete pipes, and paving slabs had been cleared away. At the airport, we were told to relinquish all our written material, including notes, and all film. Belongings were searched and most of those items seized, although some of us managed to hide some materials, including the joint story the four of us had written. Then we were loaded onto a Pakistan International Airlines (PIA) plane, accompanied by some armed guards. As the plane finally took off well after midnight, we could see major fires raging in the old section of Dhaka and at several other points around the city. We learned later that Mujib and Kamal Hussain, who was the de facto foreign minister in Mujib's brain trust, had been arrested by Pakistani troops at the beginning of the crackdown and flown to house arrest in West Pakistan.

Two months earlier, on January 30, an Indian passenger plane had been hijacked to Pakistan by supporters of Kashmir's independence from India. India, blaming Pakistan for the incident and particularly angered by the joyful reception the hijackers received in Pakistan, had banned Pakistani planes from Indian air space. This closed the direct routes between East and West Pakistan and forced Pakistani planes to fly around the southern tip of India, doubling the distance between Dhaka and Karachi and almost tripling the trip from Dhaka to Islamabad. The Boeing 707s being used by PIA had to refuel at Colombo, the capital of Ceylon (later renamed Sri Lanka).

When our planeload of hijacked journalists landed at Colombo around 4 A.M. on Saturday, March 27, we roused ourselves sleepily, not having slept much for almost two days. But as we sat there during refueling, several of us began to awaken to the situation. Finally, John Woodruff of the *Baltimore Sun,* Sydney Schanberg of the *New York Times,* and I—maybe the *Newsweek* man, too, but I don't remember him—brushed past the sleepy guards and got off the plane. Sidney and I, and maybe John, too, said we wanted to leave the flight there rather than go on to Karachi, where we apprehended that more trouble and delay awaited us in sending stories. We wanted to get to a cable office in Colombo and file the first eyewitness stories of what we had seen in Dhaka, the first uncensored account of the crackdown.

PIA officials and the now-alert Pakistani guards said we could not stay in Colombo. We appealed to the surprised and bewildered Ceylonese junior officials on duty at the airport at that hour. The PIA officials argued that their airline did not have traffic rights in Colombo allowing passengers to disembark there; it was only a refueling point. Caught in the middle, the Ceylonese did not want to make a decision. While this argument was going on, Schanberg phoned the *New York Times*' stringer in Colombo and asked him to come out to the airport.

The plane was refueled and ready to leave. But we continued to argue. Desperate, I declared to airport officials that I was being held prisoner on the PIA plane, having been put aboard at gunpoint, and appealed for political asylum in Ceylon. The flustered officials did not know how to react to this. We phoned the American embassy in Colombo, waking up a duty officer, and asked for his help. Eventually, about 6 A.M., airport officials awakened the Ceylonese minister of transportation, who was responsible for the airport. Refused permission to talk directly with him by phone, I relayed my appeal for political asylum, but my dramatic version of the situation probably lost something in the relay. I undoubtedly sounded like trouble. The minister did not want trouble, and some cautious U.S. foreign service officer didn't either. We got no help. The ruling was that PIA had no traffic rights, and we had to get back on the plane.

But the delay had gained time for the *New York Times* stringer to get out to the airport. Sid gave him the pool story that the four of us had written in Dhaka. Knowing that it would be transmitted, we finally accepted our fate and left for Karachi about 7 A.M. I happened to note that an Air Ceylon flight to Bombay (now known as Mumbai) and Karachi was leaving Colombo about the same time. In the years since then, whenever I meet Sri Lankan diplomats I tell them theirs is the only country ever to refuse me political asylum (not mentioning that I never sought it elsewhere).

When we landed at Karachi, the authorities put us through another, even more rigorous search for written material and film, confiscating whatever they found. I maneuvered to get near the head of the slow line, not knowing what would happen next but trying to be ready for whatever opportunity might arise. Just behind me, Ted Koppel from the ABC television bureau in Hong Kong and a French television crew cooperated to kick the crew's small chest along the floor past the customs counter where we were being frisked and our luggage searched on raised tables. I helped by raising a fuss to divert attention, and the searchers did not notice the chest. Later, Ted flew to Paris with the French crew and got to use their film on ABC. This greatly angered the filmless CBS and NBC correspondents who had been in Dhaka. They and Ted had made an agreement before leaving there to cooperate in trying to smuggle their film out and then share use of it, similar to my newspaper story pool arrangement. Accused of breaking his word, Ted insisted that the French film was not part of the deal.

After that second search, Pakistani authorities said we were now free to go. Out a window, I had seen the Air Ceylon flight land. At that point, I would have taken the first flight to anywhere outside Pakistan with a cable office. Air Ceylon was just closing the flight back to Bombay as I ran up to its ticket counter, and I managed to get aboard. On the plane I started typing a story from memory—it was all too fresh in my mind to need the confiscated notes. The Bombay airport had a small branch cable office. For hours I sat in a little waiting room there typing and filing "takes" (sections) of stories.

The first take included two notes to the *Star*'s editors. One said our pool story should have reached the *New York Times* from Colombo, and the other asked them to notify the AP that its man was stuck in Dhaka and unable to file. My editor at the *Star,* Burt Hoffman, phoned the *Times,* which had received the pool story but had not planned to pass it on to the other three pool members until time to publish the Sunday *Times.* Burt talked them into passing it to him in time for our second Saturday afternoon edition, so the *Star* was the first to publish an eyewitness story. The AP, lacking its own coverage, distributed a story crediting the *Star* and quoting me, based on the pool piece and the Sunday stories that I sent from Bombay.

Since the pool story had laid out the basic facts as we knew them, I wrote at the Bombay airport more graphic, detailed accounts of what had happened. My main story started simply, "Dhaka is burning," and, in addition to giving the highlights, explained the background to the crackdown. A sidebar gave a chronology of what we had been able to observe and learn from the Inter-Continental. Then, having been away from home for thirty-nine days, I caught an Air India flight leaving for New Delhi, Bangkok, and Hong Kong. I was so exhausted that I slept through the landing and takeoff at Delhi.

Within days, correspondents based in the area began reporting a savage Pakistani Army campaign to suppress any opposition in the East and to drive into India those Hindus who had remained in the Muslim state—what would later come to be known as "ethnic cleansing." Many Bihari settlers in the East were helping army actions against Bengalis, taking revenge for two decades of having been treated as outsiders by eagerly seizing the jobs and property of those displaced.

An official investigation report by Pakistani justice Hamoodur Rahman on the loss of East Pakistan, written in 1972 but not made public until twenty-eight years later, attempted to justify the March 25 crackdown and the following savagery by asserting that "the initiative in resorting to violence and cruelty was taken by the militants of the Awami League." It said killings by the Pakistani Army were acts of "anger and bitterness" caused by cruelties inflicted by Bengali nationalists. The army "acted under the influence of revenge and anger." This was an essentially dishonest effort to absolve the government, which had taken the initiative, of its crimes. Little or no "violence and cruelty" was reported before the crackdown. After the initial effort to terrorize the people of East Pakistan stimulated guerrilla resistance, some army killings were driven by revenge and anger, but that failed to account for what the army and its local supporters did.

For the next three months after the crackdown, I was busy in Vietnam and Cambodia in addition to reporting on China from Hong Kong. It was early July before I could get back to South Asia. When I arrived in Delhi, Kuldip Nayar, the editor of the Delhi edition of the *Statesman* and an old friend whom I had recruited to file an occasional story as a *Star* stringer, invited me to Sunday brunch. He had gathered a group of senior Indian government officials.

They were convinced that India could not indefinitely accept the situation in East Pakistan because it was creating an intolerable burden of Hindu and Muslim refugees escaping into India. Refugees were then estimated at 7 million, ultimately said to be 10 million. I later saw in the Calcutta area squalid, monsoon-soaked camps of refugees, many living in large concrete sections of pipe stockpiled for a drainage project, whom the Indian government was feeding with its scarce emergency food supplies. The unofficial message of the brunch guests was that India might be forced to intervene directly to resolve an intolerable situation that otherwise had no end in sight. There was a tacit admission that India was already intervening indirectly by training, equipping, and generally supporting the growing guerrilla resistance against the Pakistani Army. But the guerrillas showed no sign of being able to shake the army's grip. Only the Indian Army could do that. I wrote about this overview of the situation without any direct attribution.

After going from Delhi to sample opinion in Rawalpindi and Islamabad, I flew to East Pakistan. The martial law regime was eager to convince Western journalists that reports of its atrocities were inaccurate, despite numerous first-person accounts. One day several of us were taken by helicopter on a tour that included Rajshahi, near the Indian border. The apparent intention of a quick drive around the town, with no chance to interview its inhabitants, was to make us disbelieve reports that its predominately Hindu population had been driven out—with many killed—and replaced with Muslims, mostly Biharis. In addition to stops in other towns, the helicopter touched down briefly in Gopalganj, the home village of Sheikh Mujib. A delegation of barefoot local officials informed us, under the watchful eye of our escorts, that they supported Pakistan's government and rejected Mujib's separatist views. But I managed to edge far enough into the crowd to find someone who whispered to me that this had all been stage managed by the authorities, and the villagers supported Mujib.

My village informant's reference to "the authorities" meant the army, but it had created a civil facade to run East Pakistan. A few Bengali political opponents of Mujib whose lack of popular support had been revealed by the December elections opportunistically seized the chance to obtain the appearance, though not the substance, of power. More numerous were Biharis who rallied to the military regime in hopes of entrenching their political and economic positions despite their minority status. Sharing the Urdu language with the army, and in some cases feeling a stronger Islamic faith than they credited Bengalis with having, many Biharis became devoted supporters of the army. Some joined an army-backed civil guard called the *razakars* that participated enthusiastically in the dirty work of killing or expelling East Pakistan's residual Hindus. They also attacked Bengalis who were known to support autonomy, who were more westernized than traditional Muslims, or who simply held jobs that they wanted.

In Dhaka, a Bengali government official broke down and cried as I interviewed him in the privacy of his home. "I don't know how we can go on. None of us Bengalis know when the army might decide to pick us up. Seventy government officers have disappeared, we don't know where, and we are all afraid." Many prominent nongovernmental Bengalis, such as the head of a gasoline distribution network, had also disappeared. Most other officials, and many private citizens, were intimidated by the military regime from talking with the few Western reporters who tried to cover the situation. The most talkative people were those Biharis and others, including some roguish politicians, who tried to rationalize their support for the military crackdown. They did not want to talk about well-authenticated reports of army reprisal killings in areas of guerrilla sabotage. At the same time, collaborators with the army also feared for their lives. Members of many of the rural "peace committees" set up by the martial law regime were assassinated by the *mukti bahini*.

On trips into the countryside with translators, I found farmers and villagers less willing to talk than in earlier years. When I went up to Tangail to seek more information on Siddiqui's *mukti bahini* operations there, few people wanted to go beyond vaguely general comments. But several Bengalis reproached me over American policy.

At the time, Pakistan was helping the United States make contacts with China, which led to President Nixon's path-breaking February 1972 trip there. As a cynical result, Washington did not cut off planned military aid shipments that arrived in time to help Pakistan's army. U.S. spokesmen muted their voices over the atrocities in the East. This outraged American diplomats at the consulate in Dhaka. A story I wrote for the July 22 *Star* disclosed that the consulate staff had revolted—within diplomatic limits. They had protested to the State Department that the U.S. government had too complacently accepted the bloodshed and repression while trying to do business as usual with Pakistan. Such a policy protest by professional diplomats was unusual enough to emphasize the emotional strain of being helpless witnesses to bloody repression.

Before leaving South Asia, I filed from Calcutta a story for the *Star* of July 26 that began, "India is deep into a dangerous game of supporting—in fact, making possible—an effort to overthrow the rule of West Pakistan over East Pakistan." It was arming, training, and providing border sanctuary to some twenty thousand *mukti bahini* guerrillas. This was being done at the risk of having Pakistan stir up retaliatory guerrilla opposition to Indian rule in the long-disputed Vale of Kashmir, I wrote.

In early November I was back in Dhaka again. Ordinary Bengalis were even more terrorized by the army and their auxiliaries, the *razakars.* More people were disappearing, and villages near *mukti bahini* attack sites were being burned in retaliation. Guerrilla activity was reaching into Dhaka itself. After cautiously asking around, I was put in touch with someone who gave me an address in a congested slum area of old Dhaka, near where the army had burned and killed hundreds on March 25. Someone at that address passed me to someone else, who took me on a circuitous walk to a waste-strewn alley and into a mildewed house. There I was left alone in an empty room. Soon, a young man appeared. He said he had been a graduate student at Dhaka University in March and then had been trained in India to handle explosives. Now he was paid 125 rupees ($27) a month as a guerrilla fighter, but he wasn't clear on the money's source. His group had been bombing non-Bengali businesses in Dhaka "to try to bring business to a halt here, because that will hasten the downfall of the government." He added, "They'll never capture me. I'll get a lot of them before I'm killed. . . . Besides, I carry potassium cyanide, and I'll take that, if necessary."

On November 22 I reported from Delhi, "India's attitude is that it cannot wait much longer to solve the problem which the refugees create," and there was an "implicit threat that India will do something to free East Pakistan" if the turmoil did not soon end. "The mood in New Delhi clearly is one of willingness for a war which India feels sure it can win." Then to Calcutta to report on increasing border clashes. The Indian Army was backing *mukti bahini* incursions from sanctuaries in India across the ill-defined and undefended border into East Pakistan, supporting and supplementing guerrilla groups operating deep inside the region. Indeed, some sources dated the unofficial, covert beginning of the invasion of East Pakistan by Indian army units as November 23, but Indian officials continued denying any aggressive actions.

On December 3, I was in Calcutta to report Mrs. Gandhi's provocative speech to a large crowd. She vaguely threatened increased military pressure on Pakistan to halt its atrocities. The speech had just ended when word came that warplanes from West Pakistan had bombed several Indian military installations northwest of Delhi. Goaded to the limit by India's undeclared war in the east, Yahya had struck back in the west. This irrational act gave Mrs. Gandhi the excuse she wanted to begin an open war to liberate East Pakistan while fighting a holding action along the western border. Early the next morning, the Indian Army's invasion of East Pakistan became a full-scale, openly admitted attack.

Cut off from the primary official sources on the war, I took a flight early that morning from Calcutta to Delhi. Indian Airlines' new Boeing 737 flew about five hundred feet above the ground for the first one hundred miles because of concern about Pakistani jet fighters from Dhaka. Delhi was blacked out at night for fear of Pakistani air raids.

The war was brief. In the East, the outnumbered and outgunned Pakistani Army, cut off from resupply, was easily pushed back by the Indian invasion. In the West, where the main forces of the Indian and Pakistani armies faced each other on the Punjab plains, the maneuvering repeated an indecisive war that Bhutto had provoked over Kashmir in 1965.

An international effort quickly developed to arrange a cease-fire. It was sparked by Nixon's national security adviser, Henry A. Kissinger. He put out the word that the Soviet Union was encouraging India to seize the opportunity to invade West Pakistan in an effort to destroy the government and turn the country into an Indian satellite. Years later I learned that the State Department knew the falsity of Kissinger's line, which apparently was motivated by a desire to help Pakistan as a reward for its role in his China policy. Frustrated foreign service officers had tried unsuccessfully to correct the record. But at the time, I had my first of three experiences of writing what I found to be the truth on the spot that disagreed with Kissinger's politically motivated distortions from Washington. He tried unsuccessfully to talk my editor out of publishing my reports.

At the time the Delhi bureau chief for the official Soviet news agency, TASS, was Vladimir Matyash. A decade earlier, he had been a young correspondent in the TASS bureau there. In mid-1962, I was elected president of the Foreign Correspondents' Association of South Asia and, in accordance with the tradition of the organization's having a Western head and a Soviet bloc deputy, Matyash had become the vice president. As the spokesman for foreign correspondents during the India-China border war in late 1962, I coordinated closely with him.

Now, nine years later, Matyash readily agreed to talk with me several times, although the Soviet embassy in Delhi probably knew how displeased Soviet officials had become with my reporting from Moscow during the intervening years. Perhaps the Soviet embassy wanted to send through me a message to counter Kissinger's distortions. Quoting "informed Communist sources," I wrote that the Soviet Union was "unhappy that its support for India has placed it in the position of opposing the worldwide call for a cease-fire and [the Soviets had] no desire to escalate or enlarge the scope of the conflict." This went against the Kissinger line but has stood the test of historical studies.

The Indian government had for some months been covertly supporting in Calcutta a supposed Bangladesh exile government, whose officials I had talked with, down an uncomfortably dark alley one night, and written about in July. With the war now on, India officially recognized its creation as the legal government for East Pakistan. Foreign governments and Western journalists in Delhi to cover the war just yawned. So, at a press briefing, India's foreign secretary—its top career diplomat, Tikki N. Kaul, whom I knew from Moscow when he was ambassador there—announced that the exile regime was winning new support: it had been recognized by Bhutan. Kaul undoubtedly did not expect any of the reporters to challenge this, but I immediately asked, "Since the 1948 treaty between India and Bhutan specifies that Bhutan 'agrees to be guided by the advice of' India in foreign affairs, does this recognition really show any new support" for the exile regime? Clearly displeased, Kaul changed the subject. No other country recognized the exiles.

As the war in the West was obviously stalemated and India's invasion of East Pakistan made rapid headway, I returned to Calcutta. The Indian Army's

Eastern Command had begun briefing journalists there. On December 15 the army announced that it could arrange to take into East Pakistan a few of the many Indian and foreign correspondents covering the war from Calcutta. It held a lottery, and I won a place on the trip.

The next day, we flew around to the east side of East Pakistan, to Agartala in the Indian state of Tripura. From there, the army took us in trucks to join its forces in East Pakistan. Late that afternoon, Thursday, December 16, word came that the Indian Army had just reached Dhaka and the Pakistani Army had surrendered. We naturally wanted to get to Dhaka, but bridges were out because of earlier fighting. So we were taken to Chandpur, on the main channel of the combined Ganges and Brahmaputra rivers downstream of Dhaka, and put on a commandeered river freighter. While we tried to sleep on the steel deck of the small vessel during the overnight trip up the broad stream, someone began shooting at us from the east bank—without effect, but nonetheless an indication of a still-disturbed situation.

Dhaka was chaotic. Indian troops and *mukti bahini* forces appeared irregularly in streets on which a number of bodies lay unattended. The Indian Army was unprepared for administering the city, which for the time being lacked any recognizable governing authority. Civilians milled about, both happy and nervous.

In the misty morning, I went out to the golf course at the old British-built military cantonment on the north edge of town in time to see the Pakistani officer corps gathered there formally turn over their revolvers to Indian officers in a brief ceremony. It was a modern version of surrendering one's sword, conducted with civility and even a touch of friendliness and mutual respect among men who had a common heritage of British Indian Army traditions.

Then a Bengali journalist whom I'd known for a dozen years took me out to the Palpar wastelands on a riverine edge of Dhaka. This was a place where civility had been sickeningly absent, where hatred and jealousy and revenge had vented primitive rage. There was a large pit from which clay had been dug near a brick kiln. Now it was filled with rainwater and with bloated, putrefying bodies. Someone had just discovered what had become of many of East Pakistan's leading Bengali intellectuals who had disappeared in recent days: doctors, lawyers, university professors, accountants, editors, civic leaders of many types.

Since March 25, educated Bengalis had lived a precarious existence. Not only were they not supporters of West Pakistani rule, but also this group with westernized educations did not accept a fanaticism about Islam that most Pakistani soldiers and Biharis came to believe held the country together. Many of them had disappeared, others had fled to the shelter of villages. As the Indian Army neared Dhaka, as Biharis and other Pakistani collaborators saw their world crumbling, the *razakars,* working with a secret unit of the Pakistani Army, rounded up as many important Bengalis as they could find. About 125 of them had been shot at the brick kiln pit. As we stood on the edge of it in the midday sun and the stink, the local journalist pointed out to me the disfigured bodies of a prominent professor, a noted ophthalmologist, a chartered accountant, and others, both men and women. The *razakars* had vindictively singled out for death the kind of trained, talented people whom an independent Bangladesh would need. If these Biharis were not to control the land and prosper in it, they did not want anyone else to prosper here.

Then I went to the rally at Paltan Maidan. "The tiger of Tangail," his hair wild, his beard curly, spoke in high-pitched Bengali, with another local journalist friend giving me a running summary in English. Claiming control of twelve thousand *mukti bahini* fighters, Abdul Quadir Siddiqui said they would attack West Pakistan unless it freed Mujibur Rahman by December 31.

After the speech, several Western and Indian correspondents went up to Siddiqui to talk to him. We asked how he expected a working government to be established and law and order restored. He talked calmly and reasonably in English. We asked about the murders of many Bengalis by the Pakistani Army and the *razakars.* As in any civilized country, Siddiqui said, "we will give guilty persons legal trials when we catch them. We will punish anyone who takes law and order into his own hands."

As we stood in a little cluster talking, the three prisoners who Siddiqui had said at the beginning of the rally had been caught committing crimes were some twenty feet away, lying on the ground with their hands still tied behind their backs. I noticed that their guards were beginning to abuse them. A fourth youth was being held by the hair and arms on the edge of the circle. As a few hundred people from the dispersing crowd gathered to watch, the guards started kicking the three prisoners. When I saw one guard jump with both feet on a prisoner, I broke into the interview with Siddiqui to call his attention to this. From what he had said to the crowd about turning the prisoners over to proper authorities and had just said about fair trials, I assumed he would stop the abuse.

"Siddiqui walked over," my report in the *Star* said. It continued:

> The guards drew back. Siddiqui waved his swagger stick at the three, then hit two of them with it and made a brief speech to them in Bengali.
>
> The sickened translator was unable later to recall what Siddiqui said, but apparently it was an execution order.
>
> Bayonets on the ends of the guards' rifles were unsheathed.
>
> A youth in a white tee shirt who appeared to have been badly injured by stomping was the first to be bayoneted repeatedly.
>
> He said nothing throughout, no pleading, no prayers. He just lay there and was stabbed and bled.
>
> Then the *Mukti Bahini* went to work on the second youth, bayoneting him on the ground.
>
> The third one, the one in a flowered shirt, was hauled up onto his knees to make a better target. Siddiqui took a rifle from one of the guards and ran at the youth, vigorously thrusting the bayonet into his stomach. Then others struck him.
>
> With those three finished, the fourth youth was thrown into the grassy circle. They were beginning to bayonet him as I walked away.
>
> A single shot rang out that someone said must have been the *coup de grace* for one of the four who had not been very efficiently bayoneted.
>
> The rally was over. Youths who had gathered there with such optimism early on a spring morning nine months ago, who had been so eager to tell me then of their hopes and dreams for Bangladesh, had come back to Dhaka.
>
> But, a civil war later, things were different.

Horst Faas and Michel Laurent were there for the AP taking a series of photographs of these murders that conveyed to the world the savagery of the situation. They shared a Pulitzer Prize for the pictures.[3]

There were other murders. The next day, various *mukti bahini* fighters and mobs of other Bengalis attacked areas where Biharis lived, seeking out members of the *razakars*. Someone on the edge of one angry crowd explained that one focus of attention was a *razakar*. I reported:

> He lay in the dust in the bright sunshine in a suburb northwest of Dhaka.
>
> He was kicked and stomped. Both arms were broken. Then the knives went to work. One leg was hacked almost off. Then the bayoneting began. He did not die quickly.

These reports and others were sent from Calcutta after I caught an Indian military flight there on Sunday, December 19. Public communications from Dhaka had been broken after the Indian invasion began. The U.S. consulate allowed the handful of American journalists who had been penned up in the Dhaka Inter-Continental during the invasion and those of us who arrived immediately afterward to send short, jointly written daily summaries of events that the State Department distributed to the correspondents' publications. But from Calcutta I could cable my accumulated stories. Also, Faas and Laurent began sending photographs by the Indian government's radiophoto service in Calcutta. After the first few bayoneting photos had been sent, however, the Indian government blocked transmission of any more of these scenes that discredited its Bengali protégés and its own ability to maintain law and order in the newly conquered province. The AP flew additional photos to London for worldwide distribution.

Disgraced by the defeat, Yahya resigned the Pakistani presidency under army pressure. Justice Hamoodur Rahman's 1972 investigation urged a court-martial for Yahya and several top generals, whom it accused of a shameful surrender. "They brought defeat and disgrace by their subversion of the constitution . . . and their criminal and willful neglect of duty." Rahman's report was kept secret, however, its recommendations not implemented, and by the time the report was declassified in 2000 almost all the principals were dead. The report added, correctly, that India had interfered in Pakistan's internal affairs, and without its support the secessionist movement would not have succeeded.

After Yahya stepped aside, Bhutto flew home from the United Nations, where Yahya had sent him to plead Pakistan's case against the Indian invasion. By a procedure unauthorized by any constitutional provisions, but justified by his leadership of the largest political party in West Pakistan, Bhutto was sworn in on December 20 as the new president of Pakistan—which now meant just the West, although it took time for his government to admit this. Bhutto did the honorable thing by ordering the release of Mujibur Rahman, who flew home in triumph to become Bangladesh's first president. Bangladesh eventually repatriated the captured Pakistani soldiers, but Pakistan did not want the Biharis. Many of them and their descendants were still living as virtual prisoners in squalid refugee camps in Bangladesh four decades later despite various international efforts to resettle them.

By the time I visited Bangladesh again in 1973, Mujib had followed the route of so many Third World leaders who had been dynamic and inspiring in achieving independence but incompetent and dictatorial in power. I was received then as an honored journalist for having reported the independence struggle, and Mujib was warm and friendly in an interview. But what I then wrote about Mujib's increasingly paranoiac outlook and his inefficient, corrupt regime cost me any official favor.

By the next time I returned, in December 1975, Mujib and almost all his large family had been assassinated by military officers in a coup attempt that led to years of military government. Although the country had crawled painfully out of Kissinger's curse of being "a basket case" economically, narrow-minded political infighting kept it from prospering the way its hard-working, sometimes peaceful people deserved.

23

REPORTING VIETNAM

DUSTY, VERY DUSTY, AS THE ARMORED PERSONNEL CARRIERS CHURNED through the ill-kempt trees of an abandoned rubber plantation and out into fields where rice would be planted when the monsoon rains soon arrived. Truckloads of American soldiers followed them, together with a gaggle of journalists.

We were looking for Communist forces fighting the American-backed South Vietnamese government. Units of the North Vietnamese Army, known as the NVA and sometimes mixed with or disguised as indigenous southern Viet Cong guerrillas, were known to be operating from here in northeastern Cambodia. We had just crossed the border into a country that theoretically was neutral in the Vietnam War but in fact had been dragged by geography into a key wartime role.

Instead of enemies to fight, however, all we saw as we plowed through the countryside and small villages were peaceful peasants. They greeted us with palms pressed together in front of their faces, the *namaste* welcome showing that we had left the cultural area of Vietnam's Chinese-influenced Buddhism and entered a land of Indian-influenced Buddhism. The enemies had withdrawn before this American incursion. Although they had taken with them much of the military supplies brought down the Ho Chi Minh Trail and stockpiled here to support Communist warriors in Vietnam, some munitions were captured.

After two early May 1970 days with the U.S. 11th Air Cavalry Division, walking and hitching rides to interview ordinary soldiers and their officers, I caught a military plane back to Saigon to send several reports to the *Washington Star*. Then, after I had spent several more days of reporting from Saigon on what was officially termed an "incursion" into Cambodia, my editors asked me to go down to Indonesia to cover a diplomatic gathering on the Cambodian situation.[1] Thus ended another of what became numerous reporting visits to the Vietnam War between January 1970 and November 1974.

When the *Star* hired me in May 1969 to become its Hong Kong correspondent, the understanding was that my reporting would primarily focus on China, then in the throes of the "Great Proletarian Cultural Revolution." I was, however, also expected to provide periodic reporting on the Vietnam War and also the less-noted conflict in Laos between the American-backed government and the North Vietnamese-backed Pathet Lao. Although I was several times in jungles where there was some shooting in my general direction, I was not expected to be out with troops covering day-to-day combat. Instead, my job was to provide broad perspective on the changing Vietnamese situation in terms of military, political, and economic developments, while sometimes also writing daily stories on major events.

The *Star* had received reporting from Vietnam in the 1960s from two successive correspondents, Dick Critchfield and Don Kirk. In the aftermath of the Communists' January 1968 Tet Offensive and the beginning of President Richard M. Nixon's drawdown of U.S. forces in Vietnam, however, the editors decided to realign coverage by their single correspondent in Asia. Don was unwilling to return to Washington to work for the paper and quit to become a freelance journalist while working on a book.

After I had worked for the *Star* in Washington for five months, getting to know the paper and its personnel, Monica and our sons and I arrived in Hong Kong at the end of 1969. We were still getting settled, and I was beginning to explore the resources in the British colony for reporting on China, when my editors had a panic attack about Vietnam. Coming up on January 30, 1970, was the second anniversary of the Tet Offensive, which had shaken the American position there and eroded U.S. determination to keep trying to build up a South Vietnamese government able to resist North Vietnam's military determination to reunify the country under its control. Apprehensive that something dire might happen on the anniversary, the editors asked me in late January to go report on the situation in Saigon.

It had been seven and a half years since my first visit to Saigon. On the way back to India in July 1962 from a home leave, I had stopped there out of curiosity about the small-scale guerrilla war. As it mounted in intensity, it was beginning to attract attention because of the growing role of American advisers to the South Vietnamese Army, known as ARVN.

Walking along peaceful, uncrowded streets lined with shops and sidewalk cafes in the former French colonial capital, I found the AP bureau near the old French governor's palace, then being demolished after two rebel South Vietnamese pilots had bombed it five months earlier. The American bureau chief, Malcolm W. Browne, and his newly arrived colleague, Peter Arnett of New Zealand, were in the office.

I found them speculating about the VC, as the Viet Cong were called. How long would it be before the VC began recognizing what kind of places U.S. Army helicopters were using to drop ARVN troop reinforcements near rural clashes? Mal and Peter thought that, before long, the Communists would ambush helicopters coming into a landing zone. They were right. Their grisly view of the conflict was reflected by a wall decoration: the burned hand of a VC or NVA fighter caught in an American napalm attack. Their reporting of the escalating conflict later won each a Pulitzer Prize.

When I returned to Saigon in January 1970, it had changed. No more sidewalk cafes. They had proven too vulnerable to hand grenade-throwing VC youths on motorbikes. Hoards of motorbikes and scooters, some incredibly carrying families of five or six people, crowded the streets. American soldiers, camp followers, and prostitutes. Sleazy and sexy souvenirs at street stalls. Guards at a hotel that had been taken over by U.S. Army officers and the combined U.S. embassy and Army information office—and had been bombed. For good reason, the city had a wartime air.

In a week or so in Saigon, I established press credentials, engaged a part-time translator and general-purpose guide, Hoang Ngoc Nguyen, and met old acquaintances from India who were now key American officials in Vietnam: Ellsworth Bunker and Barry Zorthian. Bunker had been the ambassador to India and was seventy-three years old when President Lyndon B. Johnson twisted his arm to take up the difficult ambassadorship to South Vietnam. Zorthian, the former head of the U.S. Information Agency office in New Delhi, became the public face of the American political and military effort in South Vietnam as head of the U.S. embassy and military command's Joint Public Affairs Office. He established what became known as "the five o'clock follies," an afternoon briefing for journalists on military, government, and, sometimes, diplomatic developments. By the time I began visiting Vietnam regularly, the briefings had developed into contentious affairs, often confrontations between briefers and skeptical reporters.[2]

After sizing up the Saigon situation, I set out to see something of the country, hitching rides on helicopters and supply planes to military bases in various parts of South Vietnam. Then I went to Bangkok to begin to familiarize myself with Thailand's political situation as well as its hosting American military bases supporting the wars in Vietnam and Laos. And on north to Vientiane, the Mekong riverside administrative capital of war-torn Laos, where the *Star* had a Scottish stringer, Tammy Arbuckle. He gave me an introduction to the politics and military aspects of efforts to contain the Pathet Lao.

By chance, I arrived in Vientiane at a time when the government was arranging to fly several visiting journalists on a look around the country. From Savannakhet on the Mekong River in the Lao panhandle we went in dangerously worn-looking Lao Army helicopters up into the hills to a mud-and-bamboo fort, part of a chain of defenses to discourage the North Vietnamese from expanding into Lao lowlands from the Ho Chi Minh Trail, their supply route along the jungled, mountainous spine of eastern Laos into Cambodia.

Then we flew north to Luang Prabang, the royal capital higher up the Mekong, for more military briefings.

The problem was that the briefings just covered the meager efforts of the Royal Lao Army. The real war with the Pathet Lao was being fought by Hmong tribesmen armed and directed by the U.S. Central Intelligence Agency in the mountains of northeast Laos. Tammy had cultivated relations with many of the CIA people running the war from a compound on the outskirts of Vientiane. That, and the kind of gossip that naturally spread around town, gave him a good general knowledge of the war. Getting directions from him, I walked alone into the CIA compound to see what would happen. Someone intercepted me before I got to the huge Quonset hut-style main building, gave me bland answers to a few questions, and then ushered me back onto the street. But across the Mekong at the American air base at Udorn, Thailand, I was able to walk into the command center for the CIA planes and helicopters that supported the Hmong army. The surprised people working there offered more bland answers as I looked around at the maps and charts on the walls. Combined with what I'd known before leaving Washington, what I'd picked up in Vientiane, the bland answers, and observing the general setup and atmosphere, I had another story.

Shortly after I returned to Hong Kong, Cambodia's Parliament voted on March 18 to oust Prince Norodom Sihanouk from the position of head of state. My analytical article noted his long history of deft diplomatic maneuvering and said his role in Cambodian affairs could be expected to continue in new ways.

The next visit to Indochina was to report the incursion into Cambodia, an indirect result of Sihanouk's overthrow. President Nixon announced the incursion on April 30—it was already May 1 in Vietnam, and some twelve thousand U.S. troops were moving—by saying its objective was capturing "the headquarters of the entire Communist military operation in South Vietnam." However, a Communist directive dated March 17—curiously, the day before Sihanouk's ouster—and captured during the incursion ordered NVA and VC forces to "break away and avoid shooting back. . . . Our purpose is to conserve forces as much as we can."

Which they did, moving their headquarters to Kratie, deep in Cambodia, but losing to the Americans some munitions and supplies. Nixon later proclaimed the incursion to have been "the most successful military operation of the entire war." But it had no significant lasting effect.

In June 1970, I made my first visit to Phnom Penh to survey the deteriorating Cambodian situation. Then my editors asked me to fly over to Manila to cover a meeting of the Southeast Asia Treaty Organization (SEATO) on the

Indochina situation. I had by then been traveling around Asia for a bit over six months. In those days, entry to most Asian countries required a current cholera inoculation. Such inoculations were only good for six months, and I had not noticed that mine had expired. The health officer at the Manila airport stopped me. The law said he had to give me a shot then and quarantine me for a week, he declared while implying that something less obstructive might be possible. That became the only occasion in decades of international living and travel when I knowingly paid a bribe. I managed to fight off numerous other attempts to get them in other parts of Asia and Africa.

After the Manila meeting, I caught a ride back to Saigon with Secretary of State William P. Rogers. His visit to South Vietnam included the dedication of an American aid project in a village in the Mekong Delta. With him was the assistant secretary of state for public affairs, Michael Collins. A year earlier, this astronaut had been the pilot of the Apollo 11 command module circling the moon while the first men walked on it. Speaking to the villagers, Rogers praised U.S. efforts to use modern technology to improve rural life. As an example of wonderful American technology, he introduced Collins as a man who had been to the moon. With the translation help of a Vietnamese employee of the aid project, I began on the side of the crowd to ask people what they thought of the project and of Collins's having been to the moon. The project was fine. But about that man having been to the moon, well, we may be just ignorant farmers, but we're smart enough not to be fooled by that!

Over the five years that I repeatedly visited Vietnam and Cambodia, with only one more visit to Laos, I averaged about sixty days a year in Indochina. On some visits I went out into the field. The U.S. military made this easy. All a correspondent had to do was sign up the night before in downtown Saigon and report to the big American air base, Tan Son Nhut, at a specified early hour. Hitchhiking back from such places as Danang could get a little dicey, but I never got stuck when trying to get back to Saigon to send my report.

One trip was to a U.S. Army firebase near the Demilitarized Zone along the 17th parallel, which separated South Vietnam from the North. I went out to the jungle base on the early morning helicopter flight to bring the troops hot breakfasts. The heavily armed base, built up into a hilltop and surrounded by concertina wire, sent out patrols to look for Viet Cong—or actually, NVA—activity that might indicate a coming attack through its area. After spending the day interviewing soldiers about their lives and concerns, I returned to the main base on the evening meal helicopter.

Another trip was to visit Christopher Squire, an American diplomat whom

I'd known in Moscow. In the late 1960s, the State Department had begun drafting diplomats into provincial advisory jobs in Vietnam. Chris was stationed in Pleiku in the highlands not far from the Lao border, the place where a VC attack in 1965 had caused an escalation of American involvement. Showing me the military situation and various economic aid projects in the area, Chris also made a point of introducing me to John Paul Vann. A legend in Vietnam, Vann had served as a U.S. Army adviser to the Vietnamese military in 1962 and 1963 but left the army in disgust with what he considered to be inadequate policies for fighting guerrillas. Back as a civilian adviser, he held the unprecedented power of running all U.S. government operations, military as well as civilian, in his region when I met him. He was respected for working at his headquarters during the day but helicoptering out every evening to inspect a field position and spend the night, the time when VC or NVA attacks were most likely. Shortly after I talked to him, he was killed on June 9, 1972, in a helicopter crash on the way to the field.

That was a busy year in Vietnam, and I spent more time there than in other years. In the spring, the NVA launched a major offensive. In the autumn, as part of his reelection effort, Nixon sought to get the United States out of the war. Despite his having been elected in 1968 claiming to have a secret plan to end the war—a false claim, it turned out—more Americans died in Vietnam during his presidency than in the previous decade.

The spring offensive kept me in Saigon, and occasionally in the field, for several weeks. Much of this reporting was on daily military developments, rather than my usual focus on broader military trends and political and economic developments. Most military coverage was from "five o'clock follies" briefings supplemented by talking with military attaches in several embassies, plus daily visits to the AP bureau, where I had several friends from my own AP time and many new ones, and tapping other sources. My AP time had given me the skills to send my own reports by Telex, the then-latest method of transmitting stories by Teletype directly from a machine in Saigon to one at the *Star.* In the crush of the many extra journalists in town to cover the offensive, the little Telex office was overcrowded with correspondents waiting in line for the Vietnamese operator to punch their stories into the tape used to run the transmitters. I jumped the long queues by punching my own tape on a spare machine and then sending it. Because of the time difference between Saigon and Washington, I could write and send a story in the early evening and get it into editions of my afternoon newspaper that closed in the morning.

Nguyen, my translator-guide, had ARVN contacts that gave him some military information, and he enabled me to interview Buddhist monks and others who opposed the government without supporting the Communists. The recently arrived CIA station chief in Saigon, Tom Polgar, began inviting a small group of American journalists to meetings in a clear attempt to get us to view the war his way, but nonetheless he was a source of some useful information. Those meetings introduced me to a bright young deputy of his, Frank Snepp, whom I later would see separately to get a more skeptical version of events. I also got to know James Haley, a Vietnamese-speaking former U.S. Army officer working for a little contracting firm doing consulting for the Americans in Saigon. He shared useful insights from the Vietnamese media, both North and South, as well as his local contacts.

On one occasion, the U.S. Air Force invited me to interview its general commanding in Vietnam. He wanted the *Star* to report what a wonderful new weapon the "smart bomb" was, guided to its target by a television camera in its nose. I wrote something that added a note of skepticism, being aware of the oft-troubled history of new military devices. Sure enough, a year or so later the "Mark-II" version of this bomb was introduced with explanations of how wonderful it was in solving deficiencies of the original.

More diplomatic than military was the coverage of Nixon's effort to bring the American involvement in the Vietnam War to an end in time to help his 1972 reelection bid. Formal negotiations between North Vietnam and the South and U.S. officials had been going on sporadically and unproductively in Paris since 1968. By late 1972, however, the North, disappointed with the results of its spring offensive, reevaluated its prospects for winning against American firepower. It was also concerned that Nixon's visits to China and the Soviet Union in February and May 1972 might lessen vital armaments support from the Communist giants. As a result, secret negotiations between Nixon's national security adviser, Henry A. Kissinger, and Ho Chi Minh's political and military deputy, Le Duc Tho, that had been going on since August 1969, reached a breakthrough on October 8, 1972.

The North dropped its insistence that the United States replace South Vietnamese president Nguyen Van Thieu with someone more acceptable as part of an American withdrawal. By October 17, agreement had been reached in the secret talks on terms that included a withdrawal and Hanoi's return of American prisoners of war. But when Kissinger flew to Saigon to tell Thieu, who had been kept in the dark about the secret negotiations, Thieu angrily rejected the terms. He felt Kissinger had betrayed him by accepting Communist conditions that he had already rejected, including his having to share authority with the Viet Cong and a vague "third force" in arranging new elections. Kissinger's stormy session with Thieu was naturally held behind closed doors. Journalists, and therefore the public, did not know what was happening. Then, despite his inability to get Thieu's cooperation, Kissinger told a news conference in Washington on October 26 that "peace is at hand." This statement, political rather than factual, gave strong support to Nixon's reelection twelve days later.

In Saigon, I knew something was wrong. My translator, Nguyen, picked up indications of trouble, and so did I. When not out in the field, I made regular morning visits to the U.S. Information Agency library in order to read transcripts from the Vietnamese-language press and government statements put out only in Vietnamese. These were translated by the Saigon office of the U.S. Foreign Broadcast Information Service and sent to Washington for worldwide Teletype transmission. Now the South Vietnamese media showed strong official displeasure with the Kissinger-Tho deal, displeasure that was not being expressed openly. Talks with various Vietnamese observers and diplomats from countries other than the United States confirmed my findings.

My reporting of resistance to his deal distressed Kissinger for obvious political reasons as the election neared. He telephoned the *Star*'s editor, Newbold Noyes, telling him I was wrong, my stories should not be published, or, at least, they should be moved from the front page deep into the paper. Noyes rightly and honorably rebuffed him, as he had a year earlier rejected Kissinger's efforts to censor my reports on the Bangladesh conflict. Readers of the *Star* learned more directly and pointedly that peace was not at hand than those depending on most other media.

As a result of South Vietnam's refusal to accept Kissinger's deal, his talks with Hanoi broke down. Nixon ordered the heaviest bombing of the North yet carried out, Operation Linebacker from December 18 to 29, in an attempt to bludgeon Hanoi into accepting lesser terms. Then in early January negotiations resumed. An agreement was signed in Paris on January 27, 1973, by the United States, North and South Vietnam, and Hanoi's Viet Cong front, the Provisional Revolutionary Government of the Republic of South Vietnam (PRG).

It provided for a cease-fire to be supervised by an International Commission of Control and Supervision (ICCS), withdrawal of all foreign military forces from South Vietnam, limitations on military assistance to forces in the South, and an exchange of prisoners of war. On later visits to Saigon, I went out several times to the ICCS compound to talk with military and civilian members. They were drawn from four nations: Hungary and Poland from Communist countries, and Canada and Indonesia from supposedly neutral countries. Canada withdrew after six months—to be replaced by Iran—during which the U.S. military departed and prisoners were returned. In that six months there were eighteen thousand cease-fire violation reports, in which more than seventy-six thousand people were killed, wounded, or went missing. The war went on.

One of my Saigon visits was to accompany Crosby Noyes, a columnist for the *Star* whose family owned part of the newspaper company. The paper was considered by the South Vietnamese government to be a strong supporter. Thieu granted an interview to Noyes and me that produced little hard news. Then ARVN provided a helicopter for we two to visit Vietnamese military and civilian officials, who would claim good government control of the Mekong Delta southwest of Saigon. By that time I had made many trips into the Delta, in both U.S. Army and ARVN helicopters flying several thousand feet over the riverine terrain. On this occasion, I was surprised when, only a short distance out of Tan Son Nhut, our chopper dropped to within fifty feet of palm trees and rice fields to skim along parallel to main roads. The pilot later explained that Viet Cong or NVA units in the Delta were reported to have hand-held ground-to-air missiles.

During 1973 and 1974, my survey visits to Vietnam produced reports of a deteriorating situation. American aid to Thieu's government fell well short of what Nixon had promised but Congress refused to finance, while the assault directed from Hanoi did not let up. Putting together bits and pieces from military reports with a study of maps, I wrote that the North was also developing a network of roads and trails to bring troops and munitions down the mountainous western edge of Vietnam, supplementing and shortening the heavily bombed Ho Chi Minh Trail. After a reporter for United Press International later heard about "the new Ho Chi Minh Trail" from me, a UPI story got more attention than my own reports. The new route was later confirmed by ARVN intelligence.

In the autumn of 1974, the financially fading *Star* decided that it could no longer afford to keep me as its last foreign correspondent. I was asked to return to Washington the following February to become a diplomatic correspondent based there. So I made one last survey trip of Indochina. The articles that I wrote in late November and early December from South Vietnam, Cambodia, and Laos were so pessimistic about prospects for non-Communist governments in the three countries that they got a lot of attention in Washington.

Five months later, as all three governments were falling to the Communists, I proposed to the *Star*'s editors that I fly out to report the situation. They preferred that I cover that sad period from the State Department and Pentagon.

24

RIDING THE DANGEROUS ROADS

IT SEEMED TO BE A GOOD OPPORTUNITY TO SEE HOW THE WAR AGAINST the Khmer Rouge was going in a part of the country not normally accessible to outsiders. The Cambodian general's plan was to drive up there in a military convoy to survey the situation, talking to his local commanders and maybe looking at fighting in the area, and then return to Phnom Penh the same afternoon.

The handful of Western correspondents who lived in Phnom Penh and covered the war full-time for news agencies and a few newspapers rarely ventured outside the capital unless protected by accompanying military convoys. Too many journalists had been killed or had disappeared on Cambodian highways. One never knew when a roving band of Khmer Rouge fighters might shoot up passing vehicles or simply stop traffic and take away into the rice fields or jungle any foreigners they found. So several correspondents decided to accept the general's invitation to accompany him up on a day's expedition to Kompong Thom.

I was in Phnom Penh on one of my periodic visits to evaluate the Cambodian military, political, and economic situations for the *Washington Star.* On earlier visits I had already seen a little of the fighting, going out from Phnom Penh to where Cambodian Army units were firing artillery somewhat haphazardly into bits of jungle while guerrillas peppered them with sniper fire. But going to one of the few known frontline positions was different than driving in search of action. The uncertainty of guerrilla dangers always limited travel around Cambodia. Talking with the resident correspondents, I decided to join them in one of two journalists' cars in the general's convoy. This would give me a somewhat different view of the war.

It turned out to be a different view than the one I expected. It gave me a taste of the tensions of reporting the guerrilla war that ravaged Cambodia from 1970 until the Khmer Rouge victory in 1975. In that period, thirty-four foreign journalists were killed or disappeared and were presumed dead, one more than died in the much longer Vietnam War, and thirty more than died in Laos. Most were lost on Cambodia's dangerous highways.

Then, after its 1975 victory, the Khmer Rouge began ravaging the country in a different, more horrible way. In less than four years, before they were driven from power in 1979 by a Vietnamese invasion, the movement led by Pol Pot murdered, worked to death, or starved to death an estimated 1.7 million Cambodians, more than a fifth the nation's population.[1] This figure included my excellent translator on visits to Cambodia.

The general's convoy, armored personnel carriers leading the line with command cars and ordinary sedans behind them, left Phnom Penh well after daybreak. No one wanted to travel the roads just at sunrise. Experience had shown that then and late afternoon into dusk were the times that black-clad Khmer Rouge fighters were most likely to emerge from the treelines behind rice fields along roads. Learning the hard way, journalists had developed some criteria for judging road dangers. People working in the fields and looking relaxed in villages were good signs, as was oncoming traffic. But empty fields, tense or empty villages, and no approaching vehicles indicated danger and good reason to race toward the relative safety of a government-controlled town.

The ride up to Kompong Thom took about three hours, including a stop at a smaller crossroads town so the general could talk to a local commander. It all looked peaceful. Kompong Thom itself was a major farming and livestock center. A rice mill stood near the local administrative headquarters, now taken over by the army. Crowded along the embankment-raised roads were stilted open-front businesses, selling groceries and hardware and agricultural supplies, fixing cars and little farm tractors. The general arranged briefings for us journalists on the local situation. These claimed that a Khmer Rouge force had moved toward the town a few days earlier but been repulsed. We talked to some local people to get a feel for their concerns.

Then we developed concerns of our own. A military aide told us that the general had changed his plans, deciding to stay in the area for a day or two. The correspondents, however, needed to get back to Phnom Penh because most of them were one-man bureaus responsible for reporting news from other parts of Cambodia as well as this particular battlefield. It was already mid-afternoon. Little more than three hours of daylight were left, and even less than that before the late afternoon-into-dusk period when the Khmer Rouge liked to come out. Without a military escort, the drive back to Phnom Penh was a fast one, nervous even for the resident correspondents who had hazarded Cambodian roads before. Anxiously scanning the road and fields ahead as we rushed along, we knew that twelve journalists had died or disappeared on the roads in just the first eight weeks of the war.

This war in Cambodia was unleashed as a direct result of North Vietnam's campaign to take over South Vietnam. In 1959, the North's Communist leader, Ho Chi Minh, decided to begin trying to capture the South. To supply Communist fighters there, what became known as the Ho Chi Minh Trail began to be carved from the North through the jungled mountain "panhandle" of southern Laos, bypassing South Vietnamese territory just to the east, and into bleak northeastern Cambodia, a rugged and thinly populated area outside effective control of Phnom Penh. The long, difficult trail could not, however, carry as much munitions and other war supplies as the North wanted. The Cambodian government led by Prince Norodom Sihanouk provided an alternative.

Sihanouk was caught in a dangerous game, but he was used to living by his wits. He had been doing so since he was selected at the age of eighteen by the French rulers of Cambodia in 1941 as the presumably most pliable of several cousins to become the country's figurehead king. Caught between neighbors that were American allies and that had historically nibbled at Cambodian territory, Vietnam and Thailand, Sihanouk labeled his a nonaligned nation. Responding to Chinese sympathy and pressure, however, he turned to Beijing for support. The Chinese Communists arranged in the spring of 1965 for military supplies from China to be trucked, over a highway built by American aid, from Cambodia's only deep-water seaport to North Vietnamese bases established in northeastern Cambodia. This route soon carried 80 percent of North Vietnamese military supplies reaching the bases, the Ho Chi Minh Trail only 20 percent. The Chinese ships were supposed to return carrying Cambodian rice for which China paid inflated prices. As most of the rice crop fell into Communist hands and prices dropped, however, conservative elements in Cambodia became increasingly unhappy with their leftist prince. At the same time, North Vietnamese-backed Cambodian radicals, who became known as the Khmer Rouge, challenged the royal government's control of rural areas.

In March 1969 Sihanouk publicly acknowledged the presence of North Vietnamese bases on his soil. He did not comment publicly when the United States began bombing them as part of its support for Saigon. But it was too late. North Vietnam had effectively taken control of large parts of the country adjacent to South Vietnam. With a combination of military pressure and bribery, Hanoi's tentacles had penetrated deeply into the bureaucratic and economic structure throughout Cambodia. This became intolerable to such conservative Cambodian politicians as Sisowath Sirik Matak and Lon Nol.

A member of Cambodia's extensive royalty, Sirik Matak had had as good a family claim to the throne in 1941 as his cousin Sihanouk but was passed over by the French. Sirik Matak served in various ministerial and diplomatic positions while often opposing Sihanouk's policies, especially allowing North Vietnamese inroads. Lon Nol had grown up in the same Phnom Penh elite circles as Sihanouk and Sirik Matak, had become a bureaucrat, then chief of national police, then, after brief military training, defense minister under Sihanouk. As a political leader, he won parliamentary elections in 1969 and became prime minister, with Sirik Matak as his deputy.

When Sihanouk went abroad for medical treatment, Lon Nol and Sirik Matak organized a National Assembly vote on March 18, 1970, to depose him as head of state. The pretext was riots against ethnic Vietnamese residents in Cambodia, which the two men may have instigated or at least encouraged. Later, many long-term Vietnamese residents in the permeable border area of eastern Cambodia were killed in pogroms that the government did nothing to prevent or halt. Lon Nol's new government ordered Vietnamese Communists based in Cambodia, both regular NVA troops and Viet Cong guerrillas, to leave the country. It had no power to enforce the order, which was ignored.

A short time after his ouster, on May 5, Sihanouk proclaimed from Beijing the establishment of a royal Cambodian government in exile, with himself as its head. With quick recognition by Communist governments and some neutrals, this soon became a façade for the Khmer Rouge. Sihanouk was gradually reduced to a vocal but powerless front man.

One of Cambodia's nonaligned friends, Indonesia, convened a foreign ministers meeting in an attempt to get some agreement that would preserve the country's neutrality. After reporting an American invasion of northeast Cambodia to try to capture Communist supplies, I rushed from Saigon to Jakarta to report this meeting on May 16 and 17. Only Western-oriented countries sent their foreign ministers, and the conference accomplished nothing. It did, however, provide Lon Nol's spokesmen an opportunity to tell other countries the extent to which the North Vietnamese had assumed control of a large part of Cambodia.[2]

The conference did not focus on the other threat to Cambodia, the growing strength of the indigenous Khmer Rouge. This strength partly depended on weapons provided by the North Vietnamese. Ironically, it also benefited from rural respect for Sihanouk, who had earlier opposed them. The Khmer Rouge used his ouster as a recruiting argument for opposition to Lon Nol's government.

The journalists who rushed to Phnom Penh after the ouster, mostly from news bureaus in Saigon, quickly learned of Khmer Rouge strength. Trying to find out what was happening outside the capital, they hired cars to drive out to provincial areas. In just four days, April 5 through 8, 1970, nine foreign journalists disappeared along Route 1 southeast of Phnom Penh in Svay Rieng province, a part of Cambodia that projected into Vietnam toward Saigon. They presumably were killed by the Khmer Rouge. By the end of the year, twenty-five journalists had lost their lives reporting the Cambodian conflict. By the time of the Khmer Rouge victory over four years later, another nine had died. And tens of thousands of Cambodians had lost their lives, even before the Khmer Rouge slaughtered another 1.7 million.

Some journalists were captured not by the Khmer Rouge but by North Vietnamese troops operating in Cambodia, either in support of the Khmer Rouge or to protect their own bases and supply lines. They were more fortunate. On May 7, 1970, amid the deaths and disappearances attributed to the Khmer Rouge, three journalists on a reporting trip from Washington were captured in Svay Rieng by North Vietnamese troops. They were released forty days later. In April 1971, six journalists were captured by the NVA. A body was identified as that of the one woman among them, but twenty-three days later she turned up alive. The North Vietnamese had released her, something the Khmer Rouge had never done with a Western correspondent.

During the war I visited Phnom Penh periodically. Sometimes I went to report particular news events, but more often as part of my evaluations of the Indochina situation. These were attempts to give readers a broader perspective on daily developments reported by news agencies.

On my third visit there, in late 1970 or early 1971, a young man was waiting for me one morning in the high, dark wood lobby of the old Hotel Royal, now renamed Hotel le Phnom. I had used him as a translator on earlier visits. When he approached me this time, I told him that I did not want to hire him again. His English was not adequate, I told him. He argued; I was firm. He got mad and left. A gray-haired man sitting quietly in the lobby approached me politely, handed me his card, said he had worked for a *Los Angeles Times* correspondent and others who visited occasionally, and asked if he could help me. Ang Kheo could and did. A soft-spoken, courtly former English teacher and tourist guide, he had grown up with many who became key players in Cambodian affairs in the Lon Nol period. He proved to be an invaluable guide.

As a translator, he was one of the best with whom I worked in my many years of wandering around a Babel of nations.[3] In an interview with a Cambodian speaker—or speaker of the former colonial language, French, too, since my French was rudimentary—Ang Kheo kept the translation flowing so promptly and smoothly that I could have a virtually direct conversation with my subject. Then, later, if he felt it was needed he would offer explanations of background information and the subject's probable assumptions that he thought might have affected the interview. I always found these to be objective rather than attempts to shade my impressions.

The Western journalists who lived in Phnom Penh during the war both worked and played hard. The dangers contributed to a fatalism that enhanced desires to live life to the fullest. Among transgressions, a minor one was to have races back to the Hotel le Phnom after late, alcohol-saturated dinners in the wide variety of cafes. This meant hiring bicycle rickshaws, peddled by poorly fed and over-worked peasants desperately trying to make a living, and using loud, inebriated exhortations to get them to strain to victory.

Imitating the late afternoon U.S. military and diplomatic briefings in Saigon, the Cambodian government began regular briefings. They were usually conducted by an official with the readily parodied name of Am Rong. There was seldom much substantive news to offer. Foreign journalists depended on what they could get from often-frustrating interviews with Cambodian politicians and officials or could observe for themselves—within the danger limits of leaving Phnom Penh—or could learn from foreign embassies, especially the American embassy, which channeled weapons, money, and other support to Lon Nol's war effort.

Interviewing around the capital turned up a number of interesting characters. One of the most memorable was In Tam. Sihanouk's interior minister from 1964 to 1966, he had been the speaker of the National Assembly when it deposed Sihanouk. I went to see him when he was running against Lon Nol in the 1972 presidential elections, after Lon Nol had changed his prime minister's role into a presidency. The dubious official election result gave In Tam only 24 percent of the votes. I saw him again when he was Lon Nol's prime minister for seven months in 1973. In Tam was one of the few Cambodian politicians whom I found that I could respect as a man of the people rather than a capital-bred aristocrat. He seemed to be almost the only one with a common touch that appealed to villagers. His simple house with chickens wandering around bespoke his honesty compared with other Cambodian leaders, who had inherited semi-feudal estates or who had gotten fat on American-aid corruption and then built mansions. Although he could inspire ordinary Cambodians in a way that might compete with the Khmer Rouge, he never had a fair chance to become an alternative to the inefficient, corrupt Lon Nol leadership.

Then there was Son Ngoc Thanh, who had briefly been Cambodia's prime minister at the end of the Japanese occupation in World War II. A right-wing opponent of Sihanouk, he became the head of the Khmer Serai guerrilla organization, most of whose members came from the Cambodian community in southwestern South Vietnam. Many suspected it of being funded by the Central Intelligence Agency as an American hedge against Sihanouk's turning too far toward the Communist world. As the Vietnam War accelerated, U.S. Special Forces trained Khmer Serai troops to try to block North Vietnamese operations across the Cambodian border. Thanh became a minister in Lon Nol's first post-Sihanouk government. Going to interview him, I found him surrounded by crisply efficient, English-speaking young Cambodians in American-style camouflage uniforms. The atmosphere in his bungalow seemed less military or political than CIA—part of the oft-mysterious aspects of Phnom Penh in that period.

But undoubtedly the most interesting character of them all was Lon Nol, and he did not give interviews. He lived behind a screen of aides plus an astrologer or two, sending out instructions through his brother or others. Some of his orders suggested that his touch with reality was tenuous. Among other things, he advocated various Khmer magical practices as ways of defeating the Khmer Rouge, or at least of protecting government soldiers from bullets.

The hasty trip to Kompong Thom came during one of my later visits to Cambodia. By then the first U.S. ambassador to Lon Nol's government, a friend from my Moscow days, Emory Coblentz "Cobey" Swank, was no longer in Phnom Penh. After the United States withdrew its troops from South Vietnam in accordance with a January 27, 1973, cease-fire agreement with Hanoi, America warplanes no longer bombed Vietnam and Laos. Instead, Operation Arc Light intensified attacks in Cambodia to support Lon Nol's soldiers.[4] The U.S. Senate voted on May 10 to cut off funds for Indochina military operations, so the bombing was an official secret, an illegality not disclosed to the American public.

Swank named his deputy, the big, imposing Thomas O. Enders, to head an embassy committee handling Cambodian requests for bombing support.

Swank's discomfort with the bombing led the chief war hawk in Washington, Kissinger, to ruin his career by banishing him to a minor job as political adviser to the North Atlantic Treaty Organization's Atlantic Command. This left Enders as the acting ambassador for a while. The impression among diplomats and journalists in Phnom Penh was that Enders had undercut his boss by catering to what Kissinger wanted. In addition, Enders misled Senate investigators sent to Cambodia to look into what was happening. They were enlightened by American journalists. The reporters had learned that they could use specialized pencil-like radio receivers bought in Hong Kong to listen in Phnom Penh to controllers in the U.S. embassy giving instructions to planes high overhead. The secret bombing was widely reported. It lasted from January to August 1973. It was finally halted after misdirected bombs killed 137 Cambodian civilians at Route 1's Mekong River crossing at Neak Luong.

As the war continued, sporadic reports started reaching Phnom Penh of Khmer Rouge atrocities not directly related to fighting Lon Nol's forces. In March 1974, the Communist guerrillas captured the old Cambodian capital Odongk, north of Phnom Penh. Led by Pol Pot, they executed civil servants and teachers and drove the twenty thousand inhabitants into the countryside. In Ang Snoul, a village west of the capital where a Muslim minority lived, they murdered the residents. Sixty people, including women and children, were slaughtered in a small village near the ancient Angkor Wat temples in northwestern Cambodia. Refugees fleeing into Phnom Penh or across the Thai border described indiscriminate terror.

What happened to Odongk and other places was not fully known until much later. At the time it was impossible to confirm such reports, however, because no one—journalists or diplomats or other independent observers—was prepared to risk a visit to the sites. I heard such reports on visits to Phnom Penh, but in what I wrote I mentioned them only briefly and cautiously as being unconfirmed. I was not the only one who remembered the way the media had been used in past wars to spread falsehoods designed to denigrate an enemy. Skepticism merged with wariness of being used again. Unfortunately, we were wrong not to believe the reports. We did not know that a French anthropologist with long experience in Cambodia had acquired in 1972 a Khmer Rouge plan to empty the nation's cities and begin rebuilding society from an agrarian base, without the educated middle class that was blamed for corrupting society. What we did know was that the Khmer Rouge had proclaimed that "seven traitors" leading Lon Nol's government would be executed.

While the Khmer Rouge strengthened, the government army withered from low morale and corruption. The army's numbers were impossible to ascertain because so many commanders claimed far more troops than they had, in order to pocket extra pay for phantom soldiers. Slowly, the Khmer Rouge encircled Phnom Penh. During one of my later visits, their rockets hit in the city's business district in midday. Another time, I was having dinner with other journalists when a rocket hit the top of a many-story apartment building nearby. We raced up the stairs to see the damage and check on casualties, discovering that the smashed-in top floor had been a dingy brothel.

The city was becoming panicky as people seeking to avoid the fighting, the bombing, and the Khmer Rouge terror poured into the sprawling urban area. A large stadium built by Chinese aid to Sihanouk became a squalid refugee camp. So did the skeleton of a hotel on the Mekong River left unfinished by the war, the Cambodiana Hotel that much later was finished as a luxury resort and casino.

The military situation was obviously deteriorating by my last visit, in November 1974, before the *Star* recalled me from Asia. By then, the U.S. Congress had voted to cut off all military aid to Lon Nol's government. Officials whom I interviewed tried to sound optimistic, but they clearly were worried about the survival of any non-Communist government.

By January 1975, the Khmer Rouge had isolated Phnom Penh. With American military support cut off by Congress, the most that the United States could do was fly food into the city. The airlift was unable to provide enough for the 2 million or more people now crowded into it. Without adequate supplies or leadership, government forces began to fall apart. Lon Nol, crippled by minor strokes and a nervous breakdown, fled to Hawaii on April 1. On April 12, U.S. ambassador John Gunther Dean and his staff were helicoptered to American naval vessels in the Gulf of Thailand.

Dean offered also to evacuate key government officials. Some accepted. Three men on the "seven traitors" list did not. They included Sirik Matak. He wrote to Dean, thanking him for the offer:

> I cannot, alas, leave in such a cowardly fashion.
>
> As for you and in particular for your great country, I never believed for a moment that you would have this sentiment of abandoning a people which has chosen liberty. You have refused us your protection, and we can do nothing about it. You leave us, and it is my wish that you and your country will find happiness under the sky.

> But mark it well that, if I shall die here on the spot and in my country that I love, it is too bad because we are all born and must die one day. I have only committed the mistake of believing in you, the Americans.

On April 17, Khmer Rouge troops, many of them rural youths who had never seen a city, marched unopposed into central Phnom Penh. They were greeted with celebrations that the war was over. Celebrations soon turned to horror, however, as the Khmer Rouge ordered residents to leave the city. Even the hospitals were emptied. Forced marches scattered hungry people into unprepared fields and jungles to work under armed guards. Sirik Matak and the two other "traitors" who had stayed were killed a few days later. Reports varied on whether he was decapitated or shot in the stomach and left to die in pain.

One day soon after, I happened to meet by an elevator in the State Department a diplomat whom I'd known in Phnom Penh. He hurriedly, quietly told me that intercepted Khmer Rouge radio traffic—such intercepts were classified top secret by the U.S. government—showed that the victors were systematically killing officials and bureaucrats throughout Cambodia. Without indicating my source, I wrote in the *Star* that the feared purge had started. This was the first published confirmation that the Khmer Rouge were living up to the worst expectations and fears. It was also the first report on what later became known as "the killing fields" of Cambodia.

The Khmer Rouge were destroying the educated element. Their leader, Pol Pot, whose original name was Saloth Sar, was a poor student in Cambodia who got a scholarship to study in France, where he failed. This apparently created an anti-intellectual attitude that poisoned his country's future as he became a radical Marxist.

I continued to monitor Cambodian affairs, reading the unclassified translations of Khmer Rouge media, keeping in touch with Cambodian exiles, and from time to time writing about the country. And I wondered what had become of Ang Kheo.

One day I heard that In Tam, who had gone into exile in Thailand and tried to lead opposition to the Khmer Rouge from there, was going to visit Washington. Arranging with exile spokesmen to interview him on his efforts, I drove out to an address in the Washington suburbs. A young woman welcomed me and said he was running late. In the conversation while waiting for him, I discovered that this woman was Ang Kheo's daughter who broadcast for the Voice of America. She related what escapees from Khmer Rouge "killing fields" had reported about her parents.

Force-marched from Phnom Penh to a labor camp in a primitive part of Cambodia, they had been put to work in the fields on a starvation diet. Ang Kheo had hidden or thrown away his spectacles because the Khmer Rouge considered eyeglasses to be a sign of education and killed their wearers. They wanted to rid the country of an educated class that they said stood in the way of building a pure, clean, new agriculture-based Cambodia. A new generation nurtured on a fanatical belief in peasant ways, under a dictatorial leadership, would be raised to remake the country from the ground up.

Although he tried to act like a peasant, Ang Kheo was soon identified in the camp as an educated man. He was taken out to a ditch and killed by the blow of a hoe to the back of his neck, a common method that saved bullets. His wife was so distraught that she could not stop crying. So they killed her, too.

The tragedy of Cambodia did not end when a Vietnamese invasion at Christmastime of 1978 brought to a close in early 1979 the fanatically bloody Khmer Rouge rule. The Vietnamese installed in power a man who had deserted from the Khmer Rouge early in the "killing fields" period, probably not out of principle but out of fear of getting caught up in the Khmer Rouge leadership's own internecine purges. This was Hun Sen. Despite his political group's coming in second to a royalist party in elections under United Nations auspices in May 1993, Hun Sen used his control of the army and bureaucracy to push the winners aside and hang on to power. Opposition politicians, human rights activists, labor union organizers, and others were murdered without any significant investigations or prosecutions.

Cambodia became a nasty dictatorship. A peaceful, pleasant, pastoral land of smiling Buddhists had been changed by war and its awful aftermath into a place of impoverished peasants exploited by Hun Sen's greedy men with weapons and the power to make and use laws for their own benefit. Tourists, including Monica and me in 2006, saw the smiling Buddhists who had survived and were building new lives in straitened circumstances. But it was hard for Cambodia's people or us to forget their incredible suffering.

25

SHOESHINES AT JAFFA GATE

IT GOT TO BE A FAMILY JOKE AT HOME IN ARLINGTON, VIRGINIA: EVERY time I needed a good shoeshine, I would fly to Israel to visit an elderly Muslim man sitting just inside the Jaffa Gate of Jerusalem's walled old city. He gave excellent shines. I needed a lot of shines from 1977 to 1980, one of the times when the United States was deeply involved in trying to bring peace to the Middle East.

As the diplomatic correspondent of the *Washington Star,* I made numerous reporting trips to the region. Some were exploratory trips on my own, some to report specific developments plus adding background articles, and some were covering visits by U.S. officials: in the press plane accompanying President Jimmy Carter, and traveling on U.S. Air Force planes with Vice President Walter F. Mondale and Secretary of State Cyrus R. Vance.

These American officials were hopeful of being able to reduce, even overcome, Arab-Israeli differences and resolve the long-standing Palestinian problem. Their success was quite limited. After talking with many Israelis during the period when Carter worked out a 1979 peace treaty between Israel and Egypt, I concluded that the treaty's parallel understanding on autonomy for the West Bank would not be fulfilled by Israel, thus thwarting the broad goal of achieving Arab-Israeli peace. The Carter White House did not appreciate my pessimistic analytical articles for the *Star.* They did, however, prove sadly correct. The attitudes in Israeli political circles that I perceived then continued into the next century to trouble—in fact, to obstruct—international efforts to resolve the Arab-Israeli conflict.

After tourist stops in Beirut and Tehran in 1959 and then coming close to becoming an Associated Press special correspondent in the Middle East beginning in 1969,[1] the first time I visited Israel was as a tourist with Monica, Keith, and Neal in June 1974. Not until late 1977 did I begin what turned into an intensive period of reporting from Israel and its Arab neighbors.

The 1977 start was a survey trip after first reporting the opening in Belgrade on October 4 of a conference on implementation of the 1975 Helsinki agreement on security and cooperation in Europe, the signing of which I had reported. Then I flew to Cairo, which my family had visited as tourists in 1972. My get-acquainted reporting on political, economic, and military conditions in Egypt was followed by similar inquiries in Riyadh, Saudi Arabia, then in Beirut, Lebanon, in Damascus, Syria, in Amman, Jordan, and finally down into the rift valley north of the Dead Sea to cross the River Jordan to Jerusalem and Tel Aviv, Israel.

The River Jordan marked the border between Jordan and the river's West Bank that Israel had captured from Jordan in the Six-Day War, June 5 to 10, 1967. This included East Jerusalem, the location of the Temple Mount sacred to both Jews and Muslims. Israel had also captured the Golan Heights from Syria and the Sinai Peninsula from Egypt. Arab neighbors tried to recover this territory in a war from October 6 to 26, 1973, known in Israel as the Yom Kippur War for the Jewish religious holiday. The 1973 war moved the cease-fire line with Egypt back from the Suez Canal to a position in the bleak Sinai desert but left Israel with the West Bank, Gaza Strip, Golan Heights, and most of the Sinai. Positions were frozen when Jimmy Carter became president of the United States in 1977 with hopes of ending the Middle East confrontation.

Shortly after I returned to Washington from that tour of the Middle East, the Arab-Israeli situation was transformed by an unprecedented visit by Egyptian president Anwar Sadat to Jerusalem on November 19 and 20, 1977. Sadat's reaching out to the new hard-line Israeli government of Menachem Begin's Likud Party broke years of armed hostility, punctuated by war, between the two nations. Widespread hopes of real progress toward Middle Eastern peace raised by Sadat's initiative were gradually cooled, however, by a marked reluctance in Arab capitals and Israel to make concessions—especially in Israel. On a visit to Washington in early 1978, Prime Minister Begin was adamantly opposed to accepting suggestions from President Carter for phased agreements with Israel's Arab neighbors that would mean giving up conquered territory.

In late June 1978, Carter sent Vice President Mondale to Jerusalem and Alexandria, where Egyptian officials often spent time at Mediterranean beach houses, to try to overcome the impasse. Flying on Mondale's Air Force Two, I reported the tour. It failed to break the deadlock, however. Reporting on such official trips, I usually either went ahead early to report on the background and setting for the visit, or I stayed behind when the officials went home to follow up on their results and do other reporting. Sometimes I did both, just joining the official party while it was in its target area.[2]

After Mondale flew home on July 3, I stayed on in Alexandria and then went down to Cairo. Amid interviews with the usual suspects—government officials involved in foreign, economic, and military affairs (no significant political affairs in Sadat's tightly run Egypt), diplomats of several nations, various international aid groups, and academics—I hired a car to take me over to the Suez Canal, took a boat across, and was picked up by American contractors working for the United Nations Emergency Force. They drove me into the Sinai desert to the bleak encampment of air-conditioned trailers from which they monitored a neutral buffer zone established after the 1973 war by a 1975 disengagement agreement between Egypt and Israel. Their focus was on the Gidi and Mitla passes. Deep sand and rugged terrain elsewhere made these the only points in the Sinai between the Mediterranean and the Red Sea where heavy armor, such as tanks and artillery, could readily pass from east or west. This made an interesting feature story, as did Egypt's growing population and resulting congestion and land-use problems. Another hired car took me back to Alexandria to interview at his coastal villa Egypt's foreign minister, Muhamed Ibrahim Kamel, on prospects for some agreement with Israel. He was guarded on possibilities, as were Israeli officials when I then went back to their country.

After reporting from Geneva on arms control talks between Vance and Soviet foreign minister Andrei A. Gromyko and a few weeks at home, I was back in Jerusalem on August 5 accompanying Vance for another effort to get Israeli-Egyptian talks going.[3] The secretary of state talked with Begin, and then we flew to Alexandria, where Vance met with Sadat. This resulted in an announcement in Washington on August 8 that the two Middle Eastern leaders would meet with Carter on September 5 to seek a framework for a peace agreement. The meeting would be at Camp David, the presidential retreat seventy miles north of Washington in the mountains near Thurmont, Maryland.

As a hoard of us reporters waited at a press center set up in the American Legion hall in Thurmont, the conference proved to be difficult. Carter's briefers passed along little real news. Egyptian and Israeli officials usually met separately with journalists from their countries, who passed along tidbits to the Americans. The main news was no news, continuing stalemate. But Carter was determined not to give up as days passed and speculation mounted that he would not be able to achieve anything significant.

Finally, after eleven days, the participants agreed to end the conference. Facing that deadline of failure, the public learned much later, Carter met for two and a half hours with Sadat. The Egyptian president wanted East Jerusalem with its Muslim holy places included in an autonomous West Bank for the Palestinians. This, he argued, should accompany any peace treaty between his country and Israel. Then Carter met for four and a half hours with Begin, who demanded that Jerusalem be the undivided capital of Israel. Carter asked the Egyptian and Israeli leaders each to give him a letter stating their positions, and he would give Sadat a letter stating American opposition to Israeli annexation of East Jerusalem. This would thinly paper over the disagreement.

Carter's separate meetings ended at 12:25 A.M. on Sunday, September 17. With U.S. Sunday papers having early deadlines and no more Saturday evening television news reports, other American correspondents had written pessimistic stories and gone to dinner and bed. I hung on in the press center, where remained a few Egyptians and Israelis reporting on their different Middle Eastern time schedules. Then an Egyptian editor told me, I reported, "that there had been 'a dramatic development' that had saved the talks from collapse." A short time later, the few Israeli correspondents hanging on to file stories for their Sunday afternoon papers began to get phone calls from Begin's aides. I phoned the late editor at the *Star,* Gus Constantine, to stand by for putting a new top on my pessimistic story already out in early editions. The Israelis told me at 1:24 A.M. that there was now "cautious optimism." Gus took dictation, got the mechanical staff to replate the presses, and this ran in final editions circulated in the inner Washington metropolitan area. No other American paper had any indication that a deal was coming.

Told later that Sunday morning that there would be an afternoon announcement in Washington, we rushed down to the Old Executive Office Building by the White House. In its auditorium, joined by Begin and Sadat with Vance and National Security Adviser Zbigniew Brzezinski nearby, Carter announced two agreements. One of the agreements created a framework for negotiating a peace treaty between Egypt and Israel after some thirty years of intermittent war. Supposed to be signed within three months, the treaty would return the Sinai Peninsula to Egypt by April 1982. The second agreement had a framework for autonomy for the 1.1 million Palestinians living in the Israeli-controlled West Bank and Gaza Strip. Three years into a five-year transitional period of autonomy, negotiations were supposed to begin between Israel, Jordan, Egypt, and Palestinian representatives to determine the final status of these areas.

Not knowing what had been the sticking points at Camp David, but knowing what the most sensitive issue was, I asked Carter, "What provision is there for Jerusalem?" Vance came to the microphone. It wasn't possible to work out all the details at once, he said, without mentioning the standoff and the exchange of secret letters. So, he added, some things had to be left for later. It turned out to be much later. Claims to the Holy City of both Judaism and Islam, as well as Christianity, remained controversial many decades later.

Two days after the announcement, Vance left for a tour of the Middle East to seek political understanding and support for the Camp David results, with several of us correspondents on his plane. First stop: Amman, Jordan, to explain the agreements to King Hussein bin Talal. He was miffed about not having been consulted on provisions for the West Bank, which had been part of Jordan before the 1967 war. Then to talk to Saudi Arabia's King Khalid in Riyadh. The plan was then to see President Hafez Assad in Syria, but Assad put Vance off in order to meet with fellow hard-line Arab leaders who were skeptical about, if not outright opposed to, the Camp David results. Vance's party, including us journalists, used up several heel-cooling days being shown Saudi oil facilities at Dhahran, the center for the world's richest oil fields, and a new industrial port being built at Al Jubayl on the Persian Gulf.

When Vance flew home from Damascus, I stayed on to interview several officials. They included a Syrian cabinet minister who was bitter that American efforts made no provision for returning the Golan Heights to Syria. Then I went down to Amman for more Jordanian reaction and on to Jerusalem for the Israeli attitude—and another shoeshine at the Jaffa Gate.

Arab countries were displeased with Egypt, which they suspected of selling out the Palestinian cause in order to get a separate peace with Israel, the return of Sinai, and more American aid. And Arabs were uncertain that Israel would relinquish its grip on the West Bank and Gaza, an uncertainty well justified by later developments. At a November conference in Baghdad of most Arab nations, the Camp David accords were denounced and Egypt ostracized. Additionally, the Palestine Liberation Organization of Yasser Arafat opposed the Camp David idea of West Bank mayors' electing new representatives as a step toward autonomy. He feared this would undercut his claim to speak for the Palestinians from exile in Tunis.

In Israel, too, political and religious opposition to any granting of self-rule in the West Bank was building rapidly. With growing political strength, conservative Jews insisted on holding on to the area, which they said Jehovah had given to the Jewish people as Samaria and Judea. Several thousand Orthodox Jews had built settlements in the area since its capture from Jordan in 1967. Begin had agreed at Camp David to halt new settlements for a time, but for how long became a contentious issue.

The Israeli opposition, as well as Sadat's hesitancy over promising never to fight Israel again, were problems that I continued to report from Washington and that took me back to the region on several more reporting trips. The next one was in December 1978, again with Vance. The Camp David agreements had envisaged the signing of an Israeli-Egyptian peace treaty within three months, by December 17. Nearing that deadline, we arrived in Cairo on December 10 for Vance's talks with Sadat in an effort to break the stalemate. On this trip, while the reporters had little to do during closed-door talks in Cairo, I went with Mrs. Grace Vance to visit the step-pyramids at Saqqara, south of the later-built and more famous pyramids at Giza. Escorted by Egypt's leading archaeologist, we were able to go where few were allowed, including deep inside the main pyramid to see rare, only recently discovered wall paintings.

The weather turned chilly and rainy, unusual for that time of year. One day we handful of reporters traveling with Vance sheltered from the rain outside a suburban Cairo palace of Sadat's, waiting for him and Vance to come out and tell us something about their talks. As we waited, we joked about what we wanted to do when we grew up. Standing around dodging raindrops and waiting for important people to drop a few words didn't seem much like an adult occupation, even if it did provide elements of news stories.

Vance interrupted his Cairo talks to represent the United States at the funeral in Jerusalem on December 12, 1978, of former Israeli prime minister Golda Meir, who had died after a long struggle with cancer. On this cold, rainy day, it was Vance who got wet. The Israelis did not make room at the funeral for the journalists traveling with him. We wrote reports based on watching television.

Vance returned to Cairo, then back to Jerusalem. While in Cairo, I found time for interviews about Egypt's complex and changing military situation and its need for new armaments, partly based on information that I had gotten from a high-ranking civilian source in the Pentagon, and related problems of its lagging economy. Then Vance and I shuttled back to Jerusalem—though I didn't really need another shoeshine—because of growing controversy there over the agreements. Opposition to loosening any control over Samaria and Judea was growing more vocal, becoming more of a drag on any intention Begin may have had of carrying out the West Bank part of the Camp David agreements. Doubts that he really intended to follow through were increasing in Washington, and my interviewing in Israel made me more doubtful.

When Vance flew home on December 14, I remained in Jerusalem for more interviewing there and in Tel Aviv, the commercial and media capital. The next day, I reported that the Israeli cabinet had rejected Egypt's insistence on linking a peace treaty firmly to a West Bank settlement for Palestinians.

That same day, the White House made the surprise announcement that the United States would establish diplomatic relations with the People's Republic of China. Carter's National Security Council specialist for China, my old friend Michel Oksenberg, had worked this out. It meant recognizing the Communist regime as the lawful government after refusing to do so in the twenty-nine years since Mao Zedong proclaimed victory over the Chiang Kai-shek regime that had retreated to Taiwan. This required converting relations with Taiwan from full recognition to a quasi-diplomatic but still substantial connection. A cable from *Star* editors asked me for an analytical report on this. I wrote an article calling it a psychological victory for China because the United States had dropped its insistence that Beijing renounce the use of force against Taiwan before being recognized. The Israeli military censors, who had to approve any press material cabled from their country—which they normally did quite readily, so long as military matters were not discussed—seemed bemused to clear a piece about Chinese-American relations.

After daytime interviewing in Israel, I spent evenings writing and sending the *Star* a two-article package from my Egyptian interview notes. Then I began a similar package on long-term problems for Israel. Then my editors cabled that Vance was on his way to Geneva for another round of talks with the Soviet Union on nuclear arms controls. The editors asked me to go to Geneva. Because of delays in finding space in the paper for the Egypt and Israel packages of analytical articles that were not spot news, the editors were still publishing my earlier stories while I was beginning to file daily reports from Geneva. For two consecutive days, the *Star* ran my byline from three different continents, Africa, Asia, and Europe. After the arms talks, once more flying on Vance's plane and making a stop in Brussels for his meetings with NATO officials, I got home, exhausted, late on a rainy Christmas Eve.[4]

The Camp David agreements were still bogged down. The three-month period specified for completing a peace treaty had expired. Sadat knew it would be politically damaging for him to sign a treaty with Israel, recovering the Sinai, without obtaining the second part of the package, autonomy for Palestinians in the West Bank and Gaza, including East Jerusalem. He was also reluctant to sign an Israeli treaty that specified its precedence over other treaties, meaning Egypt could not fulfill treaty obligations to help Arab nations in case of their war with Israel. Begin was under strong political pressure not to yield on the West Bank and Jerusalem (Gaza was a lesser issue in Israeli politics, and the Golan Heights were not part of the Palestinian package). He also face pressure not to remove those Israeli settlers who had built new communities in the West Bank and Sinai. Many of the settlers were dedicated Zionists from the United States. Answering a call from Orthodox enthusiasts, they had moved to Israel and on into territory captured in 1967. One of the largest settlements was the town of Yammit on the Sinai's Mediterranean coast just west of Gaza, with a cluster of fourteen villages on its periphery.

Carter decided that he needed once again to intervene personally. That meant a week-long trip to Egypt and Israel beginning March 7, 1979, for presidential arm-twisting. I flew to Israel ahead of him to sound out his prospects. They did not look good, I reported. Then, shuttling between Jerusalem and Cairo on the press plane accompanying Carter, I wrote of the difficulties he encountered. Once again, as at Camp David, a stalemate loomed. But then, at Israel's international airport near Tel Aviv, as journalists waited on the morning of March 13 for Carter's departure for a farewell visit to Cairo on the way back to Washington, I spoke to several State Department officials whom I knew well from covering their work. One of them told me a glimmer of hope had appeared. Carter would take to Cairo some complex language that obscured the point about a treaty with Israel taking precedence over Egypt's other obligations. Begin's cabinet was willing to live with that, so the question was whether it might be acceptable to Sadat. Middle East time was far enough ahead of Washington that I was able to get off a brief report for early editions of the afternoon *Star* indicating that morning papers' pessimism might yet prove wrong.

In Cairo later in the day, Sadat accepted the modification. A basis for signing a peace treaty had appeared. This was announced in time to make most *Star* editions with my story. Carter flew back to Washington, accompanied by the press plane, while I stayed in Cairo. Yet, although Sadat could commit an Egyptian government that he controlled dictatorially, the problem remained of getting Israel's argumentative and divisive parliament, the Knesset, to ratify Begin's final agreement. My editors asked me to fly back to Jerusalem to cover the Knesset's reaction. After writing a final wrap-up Cairo story for the next day's paper, exhausted after long working days and short nights, I collapsed into the only hotel room with an empty bed. It was lent to me by the U.S. Information Agency, which had been using the room for briefings. Up a few hours later, I was asleep again when my plane took off for Athens on the roundabout route for regular commercial connections between Egypt and Israel, which were, technically, still at war.

Public discussion in Israel was heated, keeping me busy reporting the ebb and flow of opinions in Jerusalem and making car trips down to Tel Aviv. Then, after several days, the Knesset began its debate. Told it would end in the evening with a decisive vote on accepting the peace agreement, I checked out of the American Colony Hotel but stored my luggage there before going off to the Knesset press gallery. However, the debate dragged on and on. Small Orthodox Jewish factional parties argued strongly against yielding anything on the West Bank, making the outcome uncertain. Factions that had planted settlements there, intending further to expand their territory at the expense of Palestinian farmers and villagers, strongly opposed allowing local autonomy. Begin wearily tried to answer criticisms, to argue that the overall gain of peace with Egypt was worth some sacrifices, without, however, promising to block West Bank settlements.

Finally, about 3:15 A.M. on March 21, the vote was taken. The agreement was narrowly endorsed. After talking with a few parliamentarians in the lobby, I raced off in a taxi to get my luggage at the hotel and then to the airport. I was just in time to catch the early morning Swissair flight to Zurich, writing my story on the plane. I was enough hours ahead of Washington time that I knew I could still make all editions of that day's *Star*. At the Zurich airport I Telexed the report to the *Star* and then caught flights to New York and Washington. Walking out of National Airport, I passed displays of the *Star* with my story as the banner headline.

The Egyptian-Israeli peace treaty, signed by Sadat and Begin with Carter presiding on the White House lawn on March 26, was the key part of a package that included extensive American aid. Israel was promised $3 billion a year in grants and military aid. Egypt was promised $1.3 billion annually in aid to modernize its armed forces, now cut off from the Soviet armaments on which it had depended for a decade, plus economic development aid. These payments continued for decades, becoming subsidies that could not be cut for both American domestic political reasons and for regional stability.

Just two months after signing the treaty, Begin approved two new settlements on the West Bank. His government also established regional councils for Jewish settlements and prepared autonomy plans that gave Israel exclusive control over West Bank water, communications, roads, public order, and immigration. The negotiations between Israel, Jordan, Egypt, and Palestinian representatives that were supposed to begin in three years never got beyond preliminary talks, as Israel insisted on different interpretations of what had been agreed than others believed. Neither Jordan nor the Palestinians ever became involved.

While the Israeli withdrawal from the Sinai and the question of West Bank autonomy remained, I went back to the Middle East. In Jerusalem, another visiting American correspondent and I rented a car to go see the situation in the Sinai. We drove down to the Gaza Strip, then a tightly policed but peaceful area densely populated by Palestinians and some Israelis. Then on along the Mediterranean coast to Yammit, where three thousand of its seven thousand settlers in the Sinai lived in homes built more like wartime desert bunkers than the American residences they'd left behind. Already aggrieved at the prospect of being uprooted from the place for which they'd uprooted their previous lives, they did not want to talk with us. Eventually, at the April 1982 deadline set at Camp David for the completion of Israel's evacuation of the Sinai, the Israeli Army had to force them to leave Yammit—which it bulldozed rather than leave to the Egyptians—and move inside Israel's borders or to new West Bank settlements.

We reached El Arish, the most important old town in a Sinai inhabited mostly by Bedouins. Egyptian shop owners expressed concern about a drop in business with the departure of the Israelis, who maintained 170 military installations in the Sinai and used the region to exploit oil fields. In El Arish we watched the first stages of the withdrawal.

Vance returned to the area for a ceremonial meeting at Beersheba on the edge of Israel's Negev Desert to complete plans for the withdrawal. After the meeting, I caught a ride back to Jerusalem on a bus with Israeli officials. One was Ariel Sharon, a military hero controversial because of his involvement in the slaughter of Palestinians in 1953 and of his ignoring orders in leading his troops against Egyptians. By then, as minister of agriculture in Begin's government, Sharon supported an expansion of Jewish settlements in the West Bank and Gaza, an expansion contrary to the agreement that Carter thought he had obtained at Camp David. Sharon was happy to talk with me about his hard-line views, and he and some of his colleagues discussed the situation most of the bus ride back to Jerusalem. It was obvious that strong elements within

Israel's ruling Likud Party and its Orthodox factional party supporters had no intention of accepting autonomy for the West Bank.

From Jerusalem, Vance's plane with journalists aboard went to Rome. When he then went elsewhere on other business of less interest to the *Star,* his Middle Eastern team and I left his Air Force plane to take a commercial flight back to Washington. On the trans-Atlantic flight, squeezed into a middle seat between people who did not appreciate my clacking away on my little travel typewriter, I wrote an analytical overview of what had been accomplished—or, actually, what had not been accomplished. I wrote that Israel had gotten the part of the Camp David agreement that it wanted, the peace treaty with Egypt, but that there was little or no reason to expect it to carry out the other part by allowing the West Bank autonomy under its own Palestinian leaders. Therefore, I wrote, the basic reason for tensions in the region, the Arab-Israeli conflict, would continue.

Sitting near me on that flight was William B. Quant, Carter's National Security Council specialist for the Middle East and a key player in all of Vance's negotiations. We had seen a lot of each other during various trips. When I finished writing, Bill asked to see my article. Normally, journalists do not allow people involved in their stories to read them before they appear in print, but I somewhat reluctantly passed it across the aisle to him. He read it, sighed, and said he didn't agree. It did not give enough credit for the successes in bringing Israel and Egypt together. I said that wasn't the point; the point was that the region's basic problems remained because the West Bank situation was unresolved.

Bill did not argue further. History was not on his side.

26

HAZARDS OF JOURNALISM

SABAHUDDIN KUSHKAKI WAS BANNED FROM JOURNALISM IN AFGHANI-stan and later cast into prison with other prominent Afghans, few of whom survived. Jan Petranek was banned from Czechoslovak journalism, banished to a menial job, and badly injured in an apparent assassination attempt. Armando Doronila was banned from journalism in the Philippines and forced to emigrate. George Syvertsen was killed by a Khmer Rouge rocket in Cambodia, and Welles Hangen was captured by the Khmer Rouge and later beaten to death. Larry Burrows was photographing from a helicopter shot down in Laos. Michel Laurent was the last journalist killed in the Indochina wars. My Cambodian translator, Ang Kheo, was killed by a Khmer Rouge hoe to the back of his neck. A Vietnamese journalist who was also my translator, Hoang Ngoc Nguyen, was sent to a primitive jungle camp for years of Communist re-education.

They are some of the people with whom I worked in various parts of the world. For them, journalism was a dangerous profession. So has it been, and remains, for others throughout the world. Many journalists have been persecuted and killed for the audacity of working to tell their neighbors what was going on around them.

The work of a war correspondent can obviously involve danger. In Iraq in just one year, 2007, by one count 107 journalists and their assistants were killed, by another count 171—several international groups come up with different counts. But wars are only part of the danger. The New York-based Committee to Protect Journalists (CPJ) found by mid-2012 that 926 journalists had been killed since 1992. Of them, 34 percent were covering wars, and overall only 13 percent of the deaths were foreign correspondents. By CPJ listing of other deaths in overlapping categories, 41 percent were reporters covering politics, 21 percent reporting on corruption, 15 percent on human rights, and 14 percent on crime. The committee listed 151 deaths in Iraq during these two decades, 72 in the Philippines, 53 in Russia, 43 in Colombia, 42 in Pakistan, 42 in Somalia, and 24 in Afghanistan. Drug trafficking made Mexico probably the most dangerous place for journalists; its governmental human rights commission said in July 2012 that 82 journalists had been killed since 2000 and 16 were missing. Many of the deaths worldwide were victims of malign governments, political bosses, insurgents, drug barons, local gangsters, and others who feared having their activities examined or exposed. Few of the killers were ever identified. Even fewer were ever prosecuted.

For a few of those I've known who suffered for their work but survived, the eventual outcome—after years of oppression—was good: returning as nationally recognized and honored journalists, respected for honest reporting and well-informed, objective commentary. Both Petranek and Doronila achieved such comebacks. But others who survived the hazards of journalism were never able to regain the distinction that they had earned in their chosen careers.

In the 1950s, Kushkaki was selected on the basis of secondary school achievements and family connections in Kabul to be sent by the Afghan government to study journalism in the United States. This was a time when the royal government of Afghanistan was trying to modernize the nation with predominately Western methods but also some Soviet training for its youth. Kushkaki earned a bachelor's degree at the University of Nebraska and then a master's in journalism at another American university. On return to Kabul, he soon became the head of the official Bakhtar news agency, founding editor of the government's English-language daily *Kabul Times,* and a journalism instructor at Kabul University. Juggling several jobs, he also became in 1960 the AP stringer in Kabul. I came to know him on my own reporting trips to Afghanistan and also saw him in Moscow when he visited there in a new capacity, as head of the official Radio Kabul.

Kushkaki quit government work in the late 1960s to establish his own newspaper, *Caravan.* It quickly became recognized as the nation's best, most honest and independent paper, standing above a number of other papers noted for politicized and often corrupt reporting. His reputation earned him a place in 1972 as minister of information and culture in a reformist government. But when Mohammed Daoud Khan overthrew his brother-in-law and first cousin, King Mohammed Zahir Shah, and the reformist government in 1973, Kushkaki was banned from journalism. Daoud did not want honest, penetrating reporting of his regime. Kushkaki turned to trade to support his family. When I made a reporting trip to Kabul shortly after Daoud's coup, I phoned Kushkaki. He embarrassedly said it would be difficult for him to talk with me, making it clear that he was apprehensive of further trouble.

Daoud was overthrown and murdered by a military coup d'etat in 1978 that quickly gave way to a pro-Soviet Communist leadership. The Communists crowded most of the Westernized leaders of the democratic period into Pul-i-Charki prison. Kushkaki's name soon appeared on Amnesty International's list of "prisoners of conscience." When the Soviet Union invaded Afghanistan on December 27, 1979, to murder the Communist leader and install its own favorite, it made a few moves intended to show good intentions. Pul-i-Charki's gates were opened for political prisoners. Among the few who emerged was Kushkaki. Most had been murdered, among eleven thousand political prisoners that a later Soviet stooge in Kabul said were killed by his predecessors.

Kushkaki returned to the trading business that his daughters had kept running. Within a few weeks, however, a neighbor with government connections warned him that he was likely to be arrested again as the new regime tightened control. He fled over the mountains to Pakistan, and his family soon followed. After several years of struggling to survive there, he wrote to me. I suggested that he apply for a fellowship at the U.S. government-sponsored Woodrow Wilson International Center for Scholars, where I had written my first book on Afghanistan. I used my connections at the center, playing on the "prisoner of conscience" angle, and he was awarded a fellowship. It paid for him and his wife to fly to Washington, D.C., in 1983, first staying with Monica and me and then settling in an apartment for six months while he wrote at the center an account of recent Afghan events.

After later editing Afghan news for the Voice of America, Kushkaki returned to Pakistan to work with the Afghan resistance to the Communist regime and Soviet occupation. He became the head of the Cultural Council of Afghan Resistance, which operated with money that Monica helped obtain from the American government-funded National Endowment for Democracy and some private organizations. (I was by then working for the U.S. government and did not feel that I should get involved in trying to obtain government money.)

The council documented the resistance struggle. It also wrote and published elementary school textbooks that were smuggled into Afghanistan to provide alternatives to official textbooks heavily laden with Communist propaganda. However, Islamist groups in the resistance, created and supported by Pakistan's Inter-Services Intelligence Directorate (ISI), disapproved of Kushkaki's politically neutral approach, making his work difficult. The Islamists assassinated a number of neutral and monarchist elements of the Afghan resistance movement based in Pakistan. The Pakistani government did nothing.

Eventually, Kushkaki returned to the United States, where he had helped his children and their families settle. This outstanding journalist was a taxi driver in the Washington area for the last years of his life, during which he turned increasingly to his Islamic faith for solace.

During my five years in Hong Kong as Asia correspondent of the *Washington Star,* I made repeated trips to Saigon to report on the Vietnam War situation. On the first of these trips, in late January 1970, I sought out someone who could translate for me and help me understand local politics. There were two little English-language daily papers being published at the time. I went into the newsroom of one of them, introduced myself, and asked if anyone wanted to work for me part-time. No one responded. So I went to the second paper, up a steep flight of stairs near the old French opera house. No response there, either, but I left my calling card. Shortly after I had returned to the Caravelle Hotel, there was a knock on my door. A small, unimpressive-looking young man introduced himself as Hoang Ngoc Nguyen. Explaining that he had been in the second newsroom when I was there, he offered to work for me so long as I did not tell his paper.

Nguyen (pronounced "win," his personal name because Vietnamese are rarely identified by the family names that come first) turned out to be impressive in ways other than appearance. He was an enterprising person who had a foot in virtually every camp around the wartime capital. After studying economics in university, he was working on his second master's degree in order to keep an educational deferment from the draft. No leftist himself, he knew fellow students in the leftist opposition to the American-backed government. He knew Buddhist leaders also opposing the Catholic-oriented government. And he knew a wide range of government people. Not only did he know where to find virtually anyone I wanted to interview, but also he came up with good suggestions of other people from whom I could get useful insights into South Vietnamese affairs.

Nguyen was helpful not just to me. The British embassy arranged for him to attend a course of several months at Oxford. This puzzled me. Eventually I realized from some of the information he passed along to me that his varied journalism sources included some at that embassy. It, too, valued his wide-ranging information. On at least one occasion, in 1974, Nguyen passed along to me some useful facts and a very pessimistic British evaluation of South Vietnam's situation that none of the British embassy officers with whom I talked from time to time would have admitted or the American embassy approved. It was a well-justified pessimism, as I had already realized.

Eventually the draft caught up with him. Nguyen got himself assigned to the short, intensive officer training program for the Rangers, one of Vietnam's toughest military branches. But once he had his second lieutenant's commission, he seemed to have used his educational qualifications as well as pulled some strings to get himself assigned to work in the Ministry of Finance rather than go fight.

Nguyen's placement there once led to a classic journalism case of using sources to expose lies, or at least half-truths. When the United States withdrew from Vietnamese combat under a 1973 truce agreement, it promised the South extensive economic aid. In his Finance Ministry post in 1974, Nguyen saw correspondence from the U.S. embassy saying that various aspects of the promises could not be fulfilled. He told me, and I asked the embassy about the situation. Its spokesman denied that there was any problem, and embassy finance officers would not talk directly to me. Nguyen then gave me photocopies of some of the embassy's letters to the ministry. Without disclosing my possession of them, I began to ask the spokesman more specific questions. He continued to issue denials. Finally, when I asked about specific phrases that had been written to the ministry, his bosses realized that they could not continue to deny that the United States was backing away from some promises. It made an important story for the *Star.* The U.S. Congress and the Ford administration in Washington were already disassociating themselves from South Vietnam's fate, however, so my specifics did not surprise anyone.

The *Star* pulled me back to Washington some six weeks before Saigon fell to the North Vietnamese. Nguyen's sister had married an American serviceman and was working for a trucking line in Salt Lake City. Phoning her from time to time, I learned that Nguyen had been sent to a Communist "re-education camp" along with other South Vietnamese military officers and government employees. He was held in the hardships of such camps for a couple of years, after which the sister moved and I lost touch. But in the early 1990s I began seeing the name Hoang Ngoc Nguyen on English-language articles about the booming Saigon economy. He had survived, as I should have known that such a spunky, enterprising person would. For a while he was editing a small, Australian-backed economics magazine in Saigon. Then his name disappeared from media that I could access.

When Monica and I visited Saigon in 2006, I asked about Nguyen. No one seemed to know him or the magazine. I asked others to look later, but extensive inquiries failed to find him. I hope he prospered to the end of a difficult career.

At least he survived the Indochina wars and their aftermath. My Cambodian translator did not survive, as told earlier, nor some other friends and acquaintances.

One was George Syvertsen. He was in the AP bureau in Moscow when I became bureau chief in 1964. A good, hard-working reporter who spoke basic Russian and Polish, he seemed to resent my taking over with little Russian speaking ability, despite a longer resume as an AP foreign correspondent and the experience of having run a bureau. Nonetheless, we worked well together, I thought. One night a year later, however, he sent a report saying a Soviet Communist Party congress would be held on schedule that year. I mildly reprimanded him for failing to mention my recent reporting of a postponement or explain the difference so readers might not be confused. In a huff, George said he was quitting, a decision that he may long have been brooding about. He had left the AP by the time the congress was postponed.

In the late 1960s, CBS News sent George to Saigon as a junior reporter, and when the Cambodian war erupted in 1970 he went to Phnom Penh. Driving south on May 31, 1970, looking for the elusive war with Khmer Rouge guerrillas, his jeep was hit by a B-40 rocket. It killed him, another former AP reporter turned CBS producer, Gerald Miller, and a cameraman from India, Ramnik Lekhi, whom I had know in New Delhi, plus their Cambodian driver. A five-person NBC camera crew in a car following them, led by Welles Hangen, whom I had known in Delhi and then in Hong Kong, was seized by black-clad Khmer Rouge fighters and led away. Villagers later said Hangen and his crew were beaten to death three days after their capture.

In Vietnam and while at home in Hong Kong, I got to know one of the most celebrated combat photographers of the war, Larry Burrows of *Life* magazine. We occasionally played tennis in Hong Kong in a foursome that included a friend of his, Prince Peter of Greece and Denmark, a noted anthropologist who wintered in the British colony. Larry had become famous for his bravery in capturing pictures of the hazards and casualties of helicopter assaults. On February 10, 1971, he and three other photojournalists were working from a helicopter shot down during a South Vietnamese attack on the Ho Chi Minh Trail in Laos.

Michel Laurent, alongside whom I'd worked in the Bangladesh war, was killed while photographing a battle near Saigon on April 27, 1975, just before the city fell to the North Vietnamese Army.

The story of Jan Petranek is one of those harrowing examples of how journalists can be victimized, yet an encouraging one of survival and recovery. Petranek was the Delhi correspondent of Prague Radio during much of the five years I was in India. A pleasant, well-educated Czech, he seemed more gregarious than the average Communist-bloc journalist reporting from South Asia. He also seemed more open-minded and inquiring. Although there was little social contact between Western and bloc correspondents in Delhi, I got to know Jan when we were covering events away from the capital. He was always likeable and friendly.

He moved to Moscow not long after I did. The atmosphere was more restrictive than India in the Soviet capital under Khrushchev and later Brezhnev, but we saw each other from time to time. His office across town from the AP bureau was papered with references on Soviet space achievements, a major story in the mid-1960s. While cautious about passing along information from the special briefings that Soviet officials gave to journalists from satellite countries, he was occasionally helpful in my understanding events. In 1967 he was recalled to Prague Radio's headquarters in the Czechoslovak capital.

The next time I saw Jan was in Hungary at a major conference of world Communist parties. He came to Budapest in February 1968 as part of the Prague media group covering the new Czechoslovak Communist Party's first secretary, Alexander Dubcek. In talking to me, Jan was positively aglow with enthusiasm for Dubcek and what he represented: a fresh look at the way their country was being run. Jan conveyed an overwhelming aspiration that Moscow's dictation could be lessened and the Czechoslovak people allowed to experiment with a more progressive system. A month after the Budapest meeting, Dubcek introduced "socialism with a human face" to begin the "Prague spring" of new hope for his nation. He abolished censorship, allowed artistic freedom, and permitted new civic movements to be created instead of having the Communist Party control all organizations.

But the "Prague spring" was strangled when Soviet-led Warsaw Pact nations invaded Czechoslovakia on August 21, 1968, to reimpose Kremlin rules on the country. All I could learn at the time was that Petranek and other liberals had been ousted from Prague Radio and banned from journalism. When I visited Prague on a reporting trip in September 1975, I inquired about Jan with caution, not wanting his old connections with Western journalists to cause him any further trouble. The Czech assistant to the Reuters correspondent told me Jan had been assigned to maintain furnaces in an apartment complex on the outskirts of Prague. Curious, I rode a city bus out to look at the complex, a typical Soviet-style grim housing area, but did not get out, not wanting to risk an accidental meeting that might cause him trouble.

After democracy returned to Czechoslovakia in 1989, I began to see Petranek's name in translations from Prague media. He was back. Monica looked him up when she went to Prague in August 1991 to attend an academic meeting on behalf of the National Geographic Society. He told her of having been severely injured in what he believed was a traffic accident arranged with the intention of killing him, long a Soviet way of silencing inconvenient people. While tending furnaces, he had taken out his journalistic frustration in the politically safe way of writing children's books under an assumed name. Now he had become the editor of one of Prague's most respected newspapers.

When I was in Prague in January 2000 he told me of his misfortunes and his new successes. After helping several newspapers get established as liberal voices of the new democracy, he was concentrating on television commentary in Prague while also broadcasting for the BBC to Russia. After dinner together one snowy evening, Jan and I were standing at a trolley stop. Several times people passing by glanced at us, did a double take on recognizing him, and tipped their hats to him. After returning the courtesy, Jan told me he did not know the people. But, he added diffidently, "It happens all the time. They know me from television." Obviously, they not only knew him but also respected his honest, objective journalism.

Armando Doronila was the editor and a columnist of one of the Philippines' leading newspapers, the *Manila Chronicle,* when I started visiting his country for the *Star* in 1970. He had for several years also been the *Star*'s stringer for the Philippines. A few years earlier, North Vietnam had invited him and several other prominent Filipino journalists to see its side of the war against the South and its American backers. Armando sent the *Star* a valuable series of articles on the visit at a time when few American correspondents could visit the North.

It did not take me long in Manila to understand the respect with which Doronila was regarded by other journalists. He was considered to be a fearlessly honest writer in a political situation noted for deviousness and corruption. Sadly, but not surprisingly, when President Ferdinand Marcos proclaimed martial law on September 21, 1972, Doronila was one of the people arrested as newspapers were closed. Using dictatorial powers to benefit himself and his political cronies as they amassed great wealth at the expense of poor farmers, Marcos did not want honest reporting.

Upon release from prison, Doronila was banned from journalism. The government also refused to issue a passport enabling him to seek a job abroad. It was only through the intervention of the Australian ambassador that he was finally allowed to leave the country and take a job with a newspaper in Australia. In February 1986, Marcos was forced by "the people power revolution" of popular uprisings to flee into exile. Doronila returned to Manila to resume his role as a leading journalist, becoming first the editor and then editorial consultant and columnist for the *Philippines Inquirer.* He also wrote a book surveying developments in his country and contributed thoughtful reports to the Philippines Institute for Development Studies. A mild stroke in 2005 at the age of seventy-seven caused him to remove himself from consideration for becoming the Filipino ambassador to Belgium and the European Union. But he continued to epitomize the best of journalism in a nation where big landowners and local political bosses were blamed—but seldom prosecuted—for the Philippines' having one of the world's highest rates of reporter murders. Doronila was still writing blunt columns about political shenanigans well into his eighties.

Others whom I knew over the years suffered for being faithful reporters of things that powerful or unscrupulous men did not want reported.

V. Tarzi Vittachi was the editor of the *Ceylon Observer* in Colombo long before his country became known as Sri Lanka. The *Observer* was the leading English-language newspaper from Lake House, a publishing establishment that also put out newspapers and magazines in the island nation's other main languages, Sinhalese and Tamil. Lake House's owners were close to the United National Party that had led Ceylon to independence from Britain in 1948 and continued to govern until upset in 1956 elections by the Sri Lanka Freedom Party. The *Observer* was critical of the religiously and racially divisive politics by which the SLFP won and which helped create a civil war decades later. As a price for peace with the new government, Vittachi was fired by Lake House's owners.

He was succeeded by Denzil Peiris, another talented, straightforward journalist whom colleagues later described as being a "legendary" editor and the country's "greatest all-round editor." Denzil was an excellent AP stringer in Ceylon during the years when I visited there from New Delhi, 1959 through 1963. He, too, however, later fell afoul of political trends and was relieved of his duties.

At least Vittachi and Peiris were able to go on abroad to new careers in journalism and related work after political pressures ended their early successes. And Petranek and Doronila survived banishment to return to well-deserved prominence in their professions. Even Nguyen was able to make something of a comeback as a writer for English-language publications on business in Vietnam in the early 1990s. But many other journalists have not been so fortunate. Too many have paid with their lives—from Mexico to Pakistan to many other countries—for giving the public information essential for good government and economic honesty.

POSTSCRIPT

THE DARK-PANELED LOUNGE OF AN ELITE MEN'S CLUB IN LONDON'S PALL Mall, with sherry offered by quietly discreet servants, was the classic setting in olden days for recruiting an Englishman for Her Majesty's Secret Intelligence Service. The whoops and hollers of a children's swimming meet that I was timing on a rainy Saturday morning in August 1981 was the setting for my unexpected recruitment by the U.S. Central Intelligence Agency.

The latest owner of the *Washington Star,* the Time Inc. media empire, had just announced that it would close the money-losing paper in two weeks. Under other owners for a century, the *Evening Star,* as it was long known, had been a pillar of the Washington establishment and one of the most respected newspapers in the nation. In the 1930s and 1940s it carried more advertising than any other paper, minting money. When I started reporting for it in 1969, it was a financially troubled but still major, respected voice in the nation's capital.

Troubled by three things that caused it, as well as virtually all big-city afternoon papers across the country, to fail by the 1970s. One was the changing nature of employment. Fewer people got up early for manual or service jobs that ended by 4 or 5 P.M., when they would go home and read the day's news. Second, worsening traffic made it harder for papers to get early afternoon news into print and delivered to suburbs by late afternoon, forcing deadlines earlier and earlier until there was little time to publish domestic news that had not already been in morning papers. And, the crowning blow, evening television news that could report up-to-the-minute developments became a more popular respite from a working day than reading.

So, suddenly, I was about to be out of a job that morning when I was timing at the Arlington Forest Club pool. Neal was an AFC star in the breaststroke and freestyle. Keith was off alone that summer he turned seventeen, touring British and French castles by bicycle and train on a grant he'd won to study their architecture.

There were opportunities for me to take a new reporting job. Among them, a major Midwestern newspaper asked me to become its Washington bureau specialist in foreign and defense affairs, but it seemed in danger of closing, too. (It survived.) The *New York Times* asked if I wanted to be considered for an opening as its Southeast Asia correspondent. After living for six and a half years in the Washington area, however, my desire to move abroad again was constrained. Monica had recently left teaching to become an educational media editor for the National Geographic Society, where she later won American prizes for developing materials used by millions of schoolchildren worldwide. Keith and Neal were getting excellent educations at a leading prep school, St. Albans.

The CIA job offer was intriguing. With an exception in Saigon mentioned earlier, I had had little to do with the agency. It had a strict policy against employing or otherwise using American journalists to help it collect information. I had kept my distance from agency people, not making efforts to find out who they were, hidden in U.S. embassy and consular jobs in such places as New Delhi, Moscow, and Hong Kong. In this I was different from a number of correspondents, especially in Southeast Asia, who seemed to believe CIA people were the only really good sources. Some of these correspondents did not bother to develop many contacts among political and economic officers in diverse countries' embassies, as I did, to supplement information from local officials and media, aid organizations, and other sources. Instead, they chased after CIA officers in American diplomatic missions.

The swimming meet approach was surprising for another reason. I had on several occasions apparently discomforted the agency with my reporting. One mentioned earlier involved the Tibetan guerrilla force in Nepal. My challenging the U.S. government's interpretation of Chinese politics had not sat well, either. Nor, probably, did my writing about a Cambodian group apparently run by the CIA. On another occasion, I reported on curious characters supposedly seeking investment opportunities in the Azores if those Atlantic islands should react to a Communist takeover in Portugal by declaring independence. The Maryland company listed on the calling cards that the characters gave me in Ponta Delgada, the Azores' administrative center, disappeared immediately after I wrote about them in the *Star.* When I broke a story that Soviet military spending was a several times higher percentage of the U.S.S.R.'s gross national product than the U.S. government estimated, I carefully concealed the source. It turned out that my asking questions around Washington made the CIA worried that I would reveal the existence of its Soviet defector source for the information. I didn't, but three months later a nationally syndicated columnist did in recycling my story.

Such things did not seem to matter. In 1981 the Reagan Administration was expanding the CIA. Among other recruiting, it was looking for people with good backgrounds on foreign affairs to analyze the information that it and other American agencies collected. One of its top analysis officials had teenagers in that swimming meet, and he approached me. That led to offers of senior analytical positions in several different areas of the agency. After a delay to get security clearances, during which I wrote encyclopedia yearbook articles, I chose one of them, later moving to broader responsibilities. The result was interesting and challenging work not only in Washington but also in extensive travel on six continents, mostly for consultations with other nations' intelligence services.

My journalism career had ended. It had been a fascinating and enjoyable career.

NOTES

1. A GUBERNATORIAL PUSH

1. Extensive digging in library files of the League of Nations, British parliamentary debates, newspapers, books, and magazines produced "The Ethiopian Crisis 1934–1936."

3. KILLING THE LONG-HAIRED LAMA

1. Pant expected the Chinese soon to build an already-announced railroad into Tibet from the north, and then flood it with ethnic Chinese migrants who would change the character of the long-isolated land. His prediction for the railroad was off, because the cost of the difficult railroad delayed its opening until 2006, but by the beginning of the twenty-first century Tibet had been so flooded with Chinese that its cities had lost their historic character. Tibetans were turned into a minority in many areas.

4. THE DALAI LAMA'S TREASURE

1. Chinese records that became available decades later showed that Mao Zedong advocated reforms in Tibet with the belief that stirring up rebellion there would enable Chinese authorities, in crushing it, to eliminate the traditional power structure. Mao told meetings of his Communist leadership in Beijing that if the Dalai Lama tried to flee from Tibet he should not be stopped because it would be good to be rid of him. But Chinese soldiers did try to stop him in 1959; see "Killing the Long-Haired Lama."

5. BEHIND THE HIMALAYAS

1. John Kenneth Knaus, *Orphans of the Cold War: America and the Tibetan Struggle for Survival* (New York: Public Affairs, 1999), 235.

2. When word reached Delhi, I immediately flew to Kathmandu to take over reporting of the story from the AP's stringer there. I got no inkling of Tibetan guerrillas in Mustang, and the clash was attributed to the lack of clear border definition. After returning to Delhi, I wrote an article summing up the Nepali situation and sent it off to *The Economist,* a publication that I had been reading since 1954 but to which I had previously contributed only a letter. It published the article, beginning a freelance connection that lasted for several years with articles based on my AP report-

ing trips to Pakistan, Afghanistan, and Mongolia in addition to another on Nepal. *The Economist* had a regular contributor in India, so I never tried to write for them about that country.

3. In the 1980s, Nepal opened up the Muktinath region to tourism. Its spectacular scenery quickly made it the most popular part of the Himalayas to visit. By the 1990s a reported thirty thousand people a year were visiting it (a figure that may have included the usual Hindu pilgrims). Some walked from Pokhara up the Kali Gandak, some made the nineteen-day "Annapurna circuit" trek counter-clockwise to approach Muktinath from the 17,769-foot-high Thorung La (by 2008, some ten thousand tourists a year were reported on the circuit) and some simply flew from Pokhara up to Jomsom, where they could hire a helicopter to go up to Muktinath rather than taking the time and trouble of walking. In what had been simple, primitive villages in 1961, hotels, restaurants, and various other tourist facilities sprang up. Jomsom acquired eleven restaurants, thirty-one guest houses and campgrounds, ten government offices, and three schools. The owner of a new hotel in Kagbeni sent his daughter to a hotel management school in India. The trails became littered with refuse, some of the environment was despoiled, and in general "tourist pollution" set in. By 2008, jeeps could drive all the way up the Kali Gandak to Jomsom, with a few breaks to ford not-yet bridged parts of the river, and then up to Muktinath.

6. CLIMBING CHO OYU

1. Mallory and a companion, Andrew Irvine, were last seen alive on June 8, 1924, climbing strongly near the summit before clouds swirled around them. Mallory's frozen body was found seven decades later high on the mountain. He seemed to have fallen some distance. Whether he had reached the top remains unknown. Irvine's body was not found.

9. INTO BHUTAN BY MULE

1. A teenage girl who watched a performance of traditional lama dances in 2004 was quoted in Bhutan's national newspaper as saying, "When we die, we meet the characters that we see during the [dances], and if we do not recognize them we will see them in a state of anger and fury. My mother told me this, and since then the [dances] have meant something different."

2. A census in 2006 put the population at 635,000.

3. The decrepit monastery that we visited—age uncertain, but probably a reconstruction of the original 1694 monastery at that perilous site—was restored beginning the following year, 1961, but it burned in 1998. It was rebuilt, using modern architectural methods to attach it more securely to the cliff face, and rededicated on March 26, 2005. Considered a sacred site, it is no longer open to tourists.

10. MAIL FROM THE NAGAS

1. The origin of the word Naga is unclear. It may simply be a use of the Sanskrit word for mountain, *naga*; it may come from a Kachari word for young man or warrior; or it may have a Tibeto-Burman language source.

2. The Russian advance into Central Asia and some of the European powers' carving up of Africa were other nineteenth-century examples.

3. Later, after leaving the *Times*, he wrote in 1973 for the London-based Minority Rights Group a paper on "India and the Nagas" that is the source for some of the background given here.

11. LEFT OFF THE EARTH

1. About 1965, while reporting on a Communist-front world youth congress in Moscow, I was in the grandiose lobby of the Kremlin's Palace of Congresses when I recognized Keuneman, then forty-eight years old. I asked how things were in Ceylon. He was greatly embarrassed to be recognized. Knowing how the Soviet Union subsidized and directed such foreign Communist parties as his, I suspected he was in town for more than the youth congress. His party had split into pro-Moscow and pro-Beijing factions as the Sino-Soviet rift widened, and Keuneman was probably discussing that with his Soviet handlers.

2. These included Indira Gandhi, daughter of Jawaharlal Nehru, in India; Benazir Bhutto, daughter of Zulfikar Ali Bhutto, in Pakistan; in Bangladesh both Sheikh Hasina Wazed, daughter of Mujibur Rahman, and Khaleda Zia, widow of Ziaur Rahman; Corazon Aquino, widow of Benigno Aquino Jr. in the Philippines; and Megawati Sukarnoputri, daughter of Sukarno, in Indonesia. Sirimavo Bandaranaike's daughter, Chandrika Kumaratunga, later became executive president of Sri Lanka. A similar case of family connections was Yingluck Shinawatra, who became prime minister of Thailand in 2011 because of support from her exiled brother, former prime minister Thaksin Shinawatra.

12. TIGER HUNTING WITH QUEEN ELIZABETH

1. Sources vary a bit on the bag, and it is not clear that this was the number killed by the king himself, while others in his party killed more.

13. PUNITIVE EXPEDITION

1. Quoted from *India's China War* (London: Cape, 1970), 97, by my friend Neville Maxwell, the *Times* of London correspondent in Delhi from 1959 until 1967. His 1970 book showed how obdurate Nehru had been during China's efforts to reach a diplomatic settlement, and how India had then provoked the border war. This reversed prevailing Western interpretations of the situation, which had accepted India's version of being the victim of Chinese aggression. The Indian government was greatly angered by the book, which remains the definitive account of this dispute and is the source of some details in this chapter.

2. The Indian defense ministry's history of the war said Krishna Menon "has been held guilty, and rightly so," for what it called "the debacle." It accused him of putting pliant, rather than competent, officers in charge of the armed forces while sidelining the experienced old guard. Placing primary blame on Krishna Menon, however, obscures other factors, such as Nehru's focus on economic development while curtailing defense spending.

14. OF ROYALTY AND ROYAL WEDDINGS

1. Her father's newspaper, the *Chicago Daily News*, for a couple of years spanning this period had a correspondent based in New Delhi. He had invited Monica to dinner with his family shortly after she arrived there. She found him to be short, overweight, a heavy smoker, and generally not very interesting, she said later.

2. As it turned out, after a dozen years of living in eight different apartments in New Delhi, Moscow, the Boston and Washington, D.C., areas, and Hong Kong, we settled for a quarter-century

into a nice suburban house in Arlington, Virginia, that Monica had found, and when I retired we moved to another suburb in Baton Rouge, Louisiana. The Baton Rouge house is a nice one that we bought on her recommendation while I was temporarily working in Myanmar (Burma), and I did not see it until we had owned it for three months.

3. I started off calling her Monica—even when I later learned of the nickname Nicky, I did not like it—so that became the name by which everyone except old family and school friends knew her. The 1960s being an era when women still took their husbands' names when marrying, she used to say that she lost not just one name but two, giving up Nicky Pannwitt for Monica Bradsher.

4. Monica took advantage of our presence at Harvard to attend its Graduate School of Education, where she earned a master's degree. This meant that she had to work very hard at her courses, while I had a more relaxed time because my fellowship did not demand any particular course work. I helped by taking part in caring for our young sons, retyping the final versions of her class papers, and, while she studied at night after the boys went to bed, cleaning up the kitchen of our rented house, which lacked a dishwasher. So, not only did I buy my wife from the U.S. government, but also, I used to tell people, I then had to wash dishes to put her through Harvard.

5. Monica had written to her parents about the Galbraiths' dinner-dance, but her letter apparently was as much about meeting me as the party itself. After receiving her next letter saying she planned to marry me, her father wrote: "You were right in believing that your first letter about Henry had set our antennae quivering. It had all the hints we needed to surmise that our girl was in love. But one letter was hardly adequate preparation for what followed."

15. ONE HORSE, MANY HORSES

1. With the adventurous spirit that had taken her to India as a Fulbright scholar, Monica did not just sit home waiting for me to return. She set out alone by bus to see some of her Fulbright friends who had dispersed to their teaching and research assignments. First she went to Jaipur, where the Fulbright program had scheduled her to work. She visited the woman who had taken her place and a second Fulbright woman in Jaipur. Then she went to Chandigarh to visit other young scholars from the program. She was beginning to experience morning sickness but gamely carried on with lengthy rides on none-too-comfortable buses, meeting interesting people along the way.

19. STABBED IN THE BACK

1. While this material comes from a wide variety of sources to supplement my memory, the details in this paragraph and the next two are from William Taubman's excellent book, *Khrushchev: The Man and His Era* (New York: Norton, 2003).

20. BOMBED IN MOSCOW

1. The Kennan Institute of the Woodrow Wilson International Center for Scholars in Washington, D.C., commissioned an American scholar about 1977 to study American reporting from Moscow in the Soviet period. Then it convened a seminar of several dozen former Moscow correspondents to discuss the results. The meeting devolved into such hostile denunciations of slav-

ishly pro-Kremlin reporting by Henry Shapiro of UPI—who, having retired, was present—that the moderator felt it necessary to intervene, cutting off the attacks.

2. Not all of them. In 1965, an important Pakistani political leader whom I had known for several years visited the U.S.S.R. as the head of a parliamentary delegation. At the Pakistani embassy's farewell reception for the group, he took me aside. The delegation had been taken on a tour through Soviet Central Asia, the historically Islamic area to the north of Pakistan that Moscow claimed was an example of happy cooperation among various ethnic groups in "building Communism." The Pakistani said, "I grew up under British colonialism in India, and I know colonialism when I see it. That's Russian colonialism in Central Asia."

3. This was part of my effort to build up background material for the bureau. Amazingly, Grover (and apparently several bureau chiefs before him) had kept no files, and the only ones in the office were a decade or more out of date. When, shortly after I arrived, something came up about Soviet military aid to Algeria, Grover brightly said, oh, yes, he had a clipping across the hall in his (later my) apartment from a London newspaper that listed the amounts and types of Soviet arms deliveries to Algeria up to then. But the bureau had no such regular resources. This was a ridiculous, if not criminal, lacuna in a situation where Soviet media rarely offered background, often changed their story from one week to the next, and seldom explained facts essential to understanding new developments. I began subscribing to some of the rich resources of Western research on Soviet affairs and keeping subject files.

4. By this time Soviet authorities had dropped decades of censorship of outgoing news stories, allowing us to file directly onto a Teletype line to London whatever news we could collect from their censorship-at-source system of denying us access to most types of news. They could and did deny inconvenient or embarrassing stories. But an inconvenient or embarrassing photo could hardly be denied in those days before computer alteration of pictures. Therefore, censorship of outgoing photos was maintained by having Fotokhronika decide what to transmit.

5. Just before turning our apartment phones on as we went to bed, Monica or I would put fresh diapers on the soundly asleep babies—cloth diapers, the only kind then available. I would then go across the hall to check on what had been happening before the night reporter closed up. This became known as "diapering the office."

6. Monica's bad experience with a Moscow maternity hospital was not mentioned, but we knew of other examples of bad medicine. When my dental bridge broke, I was told that Soviet dental clinics did not have the quality of metals needed to repair a routine Western fixture. A Russian working for the AP bureau got a prescription for new spectacles, only to learn that they were unavailable in Moscow. During a family vacation on a lake in central Finland, I went into a small town shop with the prescription and was told that it was for one of the most common types of glasses, which the shop quickly supplied.

7. Russian documents declassified in 2003 showed Gagarin and a flight instructor had been given outdated weather information and that the weather had deteriorated significantly by the time of their flight. Their plane went into a spin, possibly because another jet fighter passed too close to it in bad visibility conditions, although this was never certain. Spinning down through multiple cloud layers that kept them from seeing the ground, Gagarin and the instructor misjudged their altitude and could not recover in time. The official reports made no mention of a village.

8. The *Izvestiya* account said that I fled the scene and invented a frightened comment by me, hiding the fact that the police had held me for a while.

21. CHINA'S MOST DESPICABLE

1. During my Nieman year at Harvard, I intended to return to work for the AP in June or July 1969. Beginning that January, I asked AP's personnel chief, Keith Fuller, to tell me where he planned to assign me as an AP foreign correspondent so I might take some spring semester courses as background on the area. I kept asking and getting put off. In early May, the *Washington Star* offered me a job as its Asia correspondent specializing in Chinese affairs. Still unable to get anything out of Fuller, I accepted. When I stopped in New York to tell the AP I was quitting, the foreign editor, Ben Bassett, told me they had been thinking of creating a new position for me as senior roving correspondent in the Middle East but had not yet gotten around to anything definite.

2. When a friend of my mother's in the United States ended a casual conversation with ten-year-old Keith by saying he'd see him again, Keith said he would not see the man for two years. He earnestly explained, to the man's and my mother's great amusement, that "We only go around the world every two years."

3. The other two were Zhang Chunqiao and Yao Wenyuan.

22. BIRTH OF A NATION

1. The common joke was that Pakistan owed its existence to three men: the Prophet Mohammed and the Wright Brothers.

2. Later, independent Bangladesh did better. Its government program of building two-story storm shelters and an early warning system of village radios was credited with keeping the death toll from an unusually severe cyclone on April 30, 1991, to *just* 138,866—another suspiciously precise official figure—and two major cyclones in 1997 killed fewer than a thousand people.

3. The Pulitzer Prize for international reporting in 1971 also went to coverage of the final days of the Bangladesh struggle, by Peter Kann of the *Wall Street Journal*. Peter, a friend who lived in Hong Kong, had not been in East Pakistan on March 25 but later visited there at least once and was in Dhaka during the Indian invasion. He published a first-person, two-part diary of sentence fragments about events, rumors, and anecdotes from December 3 to 18. The panel of Pulitzer judges for international reporting selected both Peter's and my coverage to share the prize, as it had often been shared over the years, according to Newbold Noyes, a long-time member of the top Pulitzer board as editor of the *Star*. This final review board decided, however, to give the prize to Peter alone. Noyes said members told him the *Journal* had lobbied strongly against Peter's having to share the prize. Peter had already been designated as a future leader of the *Journal*. He became its publisher in 1988.

23. REPORTING VIETNAM

1. When the Cambodian incursion began, I had for several weeks been on my first reporting trip to India and Pakistan since leaving South Asia in 1964. My editors asked me to rush to Vietnam to cover the story. By the time I got to Indonesia, I had been away from Hong Kong for well over a month. In that first spring in Hong Kong, five-year-old Keith came down with several medical problems. Monica had to hospitalize him while also taking care of four-year-old Neal when our Chinese helper was away. In response to her appeal, I got home from Indonesia within a few days, but this was another of the trying times for her as the wife of a foreign correspondent.

2. Zorthian recalled years later, "We reached a stage where the government's word was to be questioned until proven true, whereas in the past it had been the government's word is valid until proven to be wrong."

24. RIDING THE DANGEROUS ROADS

1. This has become the consensus figure among Western scholars, after earlier estimates ranged as high as 3 million deaths.

2. The speech on this was given to a closed session, and at the end we reporters got only snippets of what had been said. I then trailed the Cambodian speaker back to his hotel, knocked on his door, and asked for a copy of his speech. This gave me the only detailed account of the charges against North Vietnam, but I later shared the copy with an Associated Press correspondent, so other newspapers also received the details.

3. Deserving mention in a different context, two other outstanding translators worked for the Associated Press in Moscow when I became bureau chief there in 1964. Both these women, Mila Taubkina and Tamara Devyatkina, could smoothly handle simultaneous translation, for example, of broadcasts of a rambling speech by Soviet boss Nikita S. Khrushchev. By contrast, I suffered from some terrible translators in various places. Two were in Mongolia. Another was a Nationalist government translator in Taiwan for an interview with the official responsible for Tibet and Mongolia, which the Nationalists claimed as part of China. This translator turned my questions into long discussions with the official and then gave me short accounts of how the official had supposedly replied—answers obviously concocted to present an approved version of a sensitive subject.

4. The argument was made by some critics of Kissinger that the intensified bombing radicalized the Khmer Rouge in a way that led to the horrors of their rule after defeating Lon Nol. This was denied by Swank and others. It also goes against evidence available later on Khmer Rouge intentions since long before 1973.

25. SHOESHINES AT JAFFA GATE

1. As mentioned earlier, the AP had thought of sending me there, but, frustrated by its failure to decide, I accepted a China assignment from the *Washington Star.*

2. Among many examples: before reporting President Gerald Ford's July 26–August 4, 1975, visit to West Germany, Poland, Finland, Romania, and Yugoslavia, I went to West Germany, and after Ford left Belgrade I reported from Czechoslovakia and Portugal (then in the throes of a Communist takeover attempt); before Ford's December 1–5, 1975, trip to China, I went to South Korea and Japan, and after covering his following visits to Indonesia and the Philippines I stayed in Manila for additional reporting and then returned home after reporting from Bangladesh, Nepal, India, and Pakistan; after covering President Carter's visits to Venezuela, Brazil, and Nigeria, March 28–April 3, 1978, I stayed in Nigeria and then went on to Kenya, Zambia, Tanzania (joining there a separate trip by Secretary of State Vance), South Africa (with Vance and again after he left), Rhodesia (now Zimbabwe), and Southwest Africa (now Namibia). On Carter's trip, I had agreed with *Star* editors beforehand that I would leave the presidential press party in Lagos, Nigeria, to do other Africa reporting. When I returned to Washington more than a month later, I learned that the editors had rewritten news agency reports to publish under my byline a story from Monrovia,

Liberia, where Carter stopped for a few hours on the way home after leaving Lagos, but where I had never been. I complained strongly about this dishonest use of my name.

3. While I was in Jerusalem on this occasion, I was standing with Israeli journalists outside Prime Minister Begin's office waiting for a briefing on results from a cabinet meeting. While we waited, the Israeli reporters, who were in touch with their offices by phone, began speculating on who would represent the government at the pope's funeral. It was August 6, 1978, and the death of Pope Paul VI had just been reported. On another trip to Israel a month and a half later, I was again standing outside the prime minister's office with Israeli journalists on September 28, waiting for a spokesman to appear, when they began speculating on who would represent the government at the pope's funeral. That's long past, I said. No, they said, the death of Pope John Paul I had just been announced.

4. Before leaving on that trip, I had been alone in reporting from Washington that a new treaty between Vietnam and the Soviet Union seemed intended to gain Soviet protection from China so that Vietnam could move against the Chinese-aided Khmer Rouge regime in Cambodia, whose forces were harassing Mekong Delta areas of Vietnam that historically had been ethnic Khmer. Vietnam invaded Cambodia about Christmastime, but this was not noted in the outside world until a week later—while I was on vacation, not doing my usual reading of radio transcripts from the area that might have given me an exclusive on the invasion.

INDEX

ABC network, 126, 232
Abernathy, Ralph D., 9, 11
Abkhazia, Soviet Union, 175
Adeane, Michael, 114
Aeroflot, 146–47
Afghanistan, *ix*, 6, 18, 64, 86, 92, 125, 132, 134–35, 206, 230, 277–79, 280, 292; king of, 134–35, 278
Africa, 249, 272, 292, 297
African guerrillas, *ix*
Agartala, India, 239
Agence France Presse (AFP), 29, 159, 207
agents of influence, 172
Agra, India, 67, 111, 140, 144
Air Ceylon, 232–33
Air Force One, *ix*, 210
Air Force Two, 267
Air India, 233
Air University, Maxwell Air Force Base, 18–19
Akihito, 109
Aksai Chin, 119–25, 128–29, 131
Alexandria, Egypt, 267–68
Algeria, 295
Am Rong, 260
Amerasinghe, Hamilton Shirley, 103
American Colony Hotel, Jerusalem, 274
American Express, 146
Amman, Jordan, 267, 270
Amnesty International, 279
Andrews, Roy Chapman, 150
Ang Keo, 259–60, 264–65, 277
Ang Snoul, Cambodia, 262
Angami Nagas, 91–92
Angkor Wat, Cambodia, 262
Annapurna mountain, Nepal, 43, 45, 49, 292
Ao, Imkongliba, 95
Ao Nagas, 91
Ao, Shilo, 99
Apollo 11, 249
Aquino, Benigno, Jr., 293
Aquino, Corazon, 293
Arab-Israeli conflict, 266, 276
Arabs, 267, 270, 273
Arafat, Yasser, 270
Arbuckle, Tammy, 247–48
Arg, Kabul, 134
Arlington, Virginia, 266, 294
Arlington Forest Club, 287
Armenia, Soviet, 171, 178
Arnett, Peter, 246
Arrowsmith, Marvin L., 64, 67
Ashoka Hotel, 140
Asia, 206, 246, 249, 263, 272, 280
Asian Survey, 214, 218
Assad, Hafez, 270
Assam Rifles, 93
Assam state, India, 25, 27, 58, 74, 91, 94, 114, 117, 120, 126, 129
Associated Press (AP), 4, 31, 50, 99, 107, 109–12, 117, 126–27, 132, 134, 146, 159, 162, 169, 173, 183, 194, 196, 199, 221, 224, 230, 233, 241–42, 250, 266, 278, 282, 285, 291, 296–97; London bureau, 20, 30–31, 60, 117, 122, 126–27, 175, 180, 189–91, 242, 295; Moscow bureau, 146–47, 168, 171, 173, 182, 190–94, 205, 282–83, 295; New York headquarters, 6,

Associated Press *(continued)* 122, 129, 137, 145–46, 175, 181, 190–91, 200; Rawalpindi bureau, 230; Saigon bureau, 246, 250; World Service, 141, 173, 185
Athens, Greece, 274
Atkinson, Larry, 27, 56–57
Atlanta, Georgia, 6, 12
Australia, 281, 285
Avolokitesvara, 155
Awami League, 225–27, 234
Ayub Khan, Mohammad, 64, 109–10, 225
Azerbaijan, Soviet, 171
Azores, 288

Baghdad, Iraq, 270
Bahadur, Sawai Man Singhji, the second, 111
Bakhtar news agency, 134, 278
Baku, Soviet Union, 171
Baltimore Sun, 192, 230–31
Baluchi language, 222
Baluchistan, West Pakistan, 229
Bandaranaike, Sirimavo Ratwatte Dias, 106, 293
Bandaranaike, Solomon West Ridgeway Dias, 56, 102, 104–6
Bangalore, India, 112
Bangkok, Thailand, 59, 233, 247; AP bureau, 228
Bangladesh, 30, 220–21, 230, 238, 240–42, 252, 282, 293, 296–97; army, 243; death toll, 221. *See also* Pakistan, East
Barber, Noel, 26–27, 61–62
Bassett, Ben, 145–46, 296
Baton Rouge, Louisiana, 9, 13, 294
Bawden, Charles R., 156
Bay of Bengal, 58, 74, 224
Beersheba, Israel, 275
Begin, Menachem, 267–69, 271, 273–75, 298
Beidaihe, China, 212–13
Beijing, *x*, 59, 119, 121, 125, 131, 148, 154, 167, 203–5, 207–18, 257–58, 272, 291
Beirut, Lebanon, 266–67
Belgrade, Yugoslavia, 267, 297
Belyayev, Igor, 198–200
Benares, India, 156
Bengal, Bengalis, 58, 91, 233, 235–36, 239–42
Bengali language, 60–61, 220, 222, 240–41
Bernheim, Roger, 94
Bharatpur, India, 135
Bhilai, India, 158
Bhutan, 23, 41–42, 71–87, *photos following page 100*, 120, 125, 130, 155, 238, 292; Bhutan National Congress, 84; borders, 76, 83; Dzongkha language, 72, 80, 86; economy, 75–77, 81, 83, 85; education, 83; gross national happiness, 85; history of, 75–77; international status, 83; Nepalis in, 83–84, 86; political changes, 73, 76–77, 86; population, 75, 292; relations with India, 25, 76, 82–83; roads, 77–78; tourism, 85–86; *tsongdu* (assembly), 73, 77, 82–84
Bhutto, Benazir, 227, 293
Bhutto, Zulfikar Ali, 226–28, 237, 242, 293
Biharis, 222, 233, 235, 240–42
blackmail, Soviet, 169–74, 186
"boat people," Vietnamese, *ix*
Bolsheviks, 148; Bolshevik Revolution, 176, 186–87, 194, 196
Bombay (Mumbai), 112, 232–33
bombing, Moscow, 183, 197–98
Bonham-Carter, Christopher, 114
Bose, Delip, 22–23
Bradsher, Augusta S., 141, 296
Bradsher, Earl L., 141
Bradsher, Earl L., Jr., 141
Bradsher, Keith Vinson, 144, 183, 186, 198, 206, 212, 246, 266, 287–88, 296
Bradsher, Margaret (Day), 141
Bradsher, Monica Pannwitt, 53, *photos following page 100*, 107, 144, 146, 149, 156, 169, 183, 185–86, 197–98, 206, 212, 246, 265–66, 279, 282, 284, 288, 294–96. *See also* Pannwitt, Monica Jean (Nicky)
Bradsher, Neal Clifton, 144, 183, 186, 198, 206, 212, 246, 267, 287–88, 296
Brahmaputra River, India, 26, 58, 91, 94, 120, 126, 129, 222, 224, 239
Brahmins, 135, 137
Brannon, Lynn, 13

Brezhnev, Leonid Ilyich, 176–79, 181–82, 186–88, 190–91, 283
Britain, 111, 285, 287–88, 291; Foreign and Commonwealth Office, 207; Secret Intelligence Service (MI6), 287
British Broadcasting Corporation (BBC), 127, 203–4, 207–8, 230, 284
British embassy, Saigon, 280–81
British India, 21, 24, 58, 71, 75–77, 88, 110, 112, 120–21, 221–22, 239, 295
Browne, Malcolm W., 246
Brzezinski, Zbigniew, 269
Budapest, Hungary, 26, 283
Buddha, 45, 84, 107; *bön* (pre-Buddhist), 84; Buddhism, 45, 72–73, 91, 136–37, 148–50, 152, 154–55, 244, 251, 265, 280; dances, 72–73; Gelugpa and Nyingmapa, 35–36; Himalayan history, 72–73, 120; Theravada, 101
Bunker, Ellsworth F., 247
Burke, Vincent, 171
Burma (Myanmar), 88, 90–91, 294
Burrows, Larry, 277, 282
bus boycott, 7–15

Cairo, Egypt, 59, 267–68, 271, 273
Calcutta, India, *x*, 22–23, 27, 29–32, 34, 36, 38–39, 55, 58–62, 68–70, 75, 77, 91, 98–99, 112, 222–23, 234, 236–39, 242
Calvert, Brian, 175, 180–81
Cambodia, 211, 224, 234, 244, 247, 248–49, 254–65, 277, 282, 288, 296–98; army, 255–56; parliament, 248; racial strife, 258; Vietnamese invasion of, 256, 265
Camp David, 268–73, 275–76
Canada, 203–4, 253
Canton, China, 216–18
Caravan, 278
Carter, Jimmy, 219, 266–70, 272–76, 297–98
Caucasus, 170–71
CBS network, 232, 282
Central Intelligence Agency (CIA), 25, 39, 41, 47–48, 50
Ceylon, 56, 101, 144, 231, 285, 293; history, 101–3, 107; National Planning Council, 103; parliament, 101, 105; population, 107
Ceylon Observer, 285
Chakravarti, Subhash, 55–56, 60–61, 77
Chandigarh, India, 294
Chandpur, East Pakistan, 239
Chhukha Dzong, Bhutan, 79
Chiang Kai-shek, 34, 121, 203, 212, 214, 272
Chicago Daily News, 138, 293
Chimborazo, 51
China, 33, 76, 83, 100, 114, 119–20, 129, 133, 145–46, 148, 154, 166, 170, 181, 187, 192, 203–19, 234, 236, 245–46, 251, 257, 288, 291, 293, 298; civil war, 208; foreign aid, 148, 154, 263; Foreign Ministry press office, 203–4, 217; People's Liberation Army (PLA), 45, 47–48, 117–18, 124–25, 128–31, 205, 208, 210, 291; U.S. diplomatic relations with, 151, 210, 212, 216, 236–37, 272. *See also* India-China border war; China, Republic of (Nationalist China)
China, Republic of (Nationalist China), 121, 203, 297. *See also* Taiwan
China Travel Service, 216–17
China-watching, 207–8; China watcher-watchers, 207–8
Chinese embassy, Hanoi, 209
Chinese embassy, Ulan Bator, 151
Chittagong, East Pakistan, 224
Chitwan National Park, Royal, 112
Cho Oyu mountain, 52–53, 55–57
Chowringhi Road, Calcutta, 58, 60
Christian Science Monitor, 156
Christians, 143–44, 270
Christmas, 3, 18, 90, 97–98, 129, 149, 155, 183–84, 272
Chumbi valley, Tibet, 23, 34, 74–75
Clymer, Adam, 192
Coleman, Frederick, 175, 178, 180–81
Collins, Michael, 249
Colombo, Ceylon, 101, 105, 231–32, 285
Columbia Missourian, 3–4
Committee to Protect Journalists, 277
communications, *ix–x;* Teletype, 13, 127, 250, 252, 295; Telex, *x*, 20, 170, 173, 191–92, 250, 274

Communist Party
—Ceylon, 104–6, 293
—China, 204, 208, 210, 212; 9th congress, 209; 10th congress, 204, 213–14; constitution, 208
—Czechoslovakia, 283
—India, 60, 65–66
—Nepal, 54, 115
—worldwide, 283, 293
—Soviet Union, 157, 163, 166, 175–81, 185–87, 193, 202, 205, 282; Central Committee, 176–77, 179–81, 205; Presidium, 175–81
Congress Party, India, 60–61, 65–66, 127, 130, 160, 228
Connaught Place, 65, 68, 110, 139
Connery, Don, 39–40
Conservative Party, Britain, 180
Constantine, Gus, 269
convergence theory, 195
Cooke, Hope, 135–37
Corea, Gamani, 103
Corriere della Sera, 209
cosmonauts, 175, 189
Critchfield, Richard, 246
Cuban missile crisis, 119, 181
Cultural Council of the Afghan Resistance, 279
cyclones, 223–26, 296
Czechoslovakia, 147, 150, 277, 283–84, 297

Dahanayake, Wijayananda, 105–6
Daily Express, 26, 54–57
Daily Mail, 26–27, 54, 56–57, 61–62
Daily Telegraph, 22, 200
Dalai Lama, Tenzin Gyatso, 24–31, 33–39, 41–42, 47, 61, 74, 77, 121, 126, 128, 155, 291
Damascus, Syria, 267, 270
Daniel, AP driver, 122–23
Daoud Khan, Mohammed, 134, 278–79
Darjeeling, India, 21–23, 33, 36, 77, 135
de Silva, Colvin R., 104–5
Dean, John Gunther, 263
Delhi, New and old, India, 20, 32, 63, 65, 68, 73, 75, 98, 109–11, 117–21, 123–25, 129–31, 133, 135–37, 140, 146, 156, 158, 185, 221, 223–24, 230, 233–34, 237–38, 247, 282–83, 285, 288, 291, 293
Delhi municipal government, 143–44; deputy commissioner for housing (loans), 143–44
Demilitarized Zone, Vietnam, 249
Deng Xiaoping, 212
Devyatkina, Tamara, 191, 297
Dexter Avenue Baptist Church, 9–10, 17
Dhaka, *x*, 112, 220–21, 224, 226–37, 239–42, 296
Dhaka University, 221, 230, 236
Dharamsala, India, 37
Dhaulagiri mountain, Nepal, 45, 49
dissidents, Soviet, 193–94, 200–201
Dixon, Margaret (Maggie), 2, 4–6
Doig, Desmond, 39–40
Dorje, Jigme Palden, 75–78, 81, 83, 85, 87
Dorje, Tessla, 81, 85
Dorje, Ugyen, 83
Doronila, Armando, 277–78, 284–85
Dorticos Torrado, Osvaldo, 180
druk gyalpo of Bhutan. *See* Wangchuck, Jigme Dorje
Dubcek, Alexander, 283
Dum Dum Airport, 22, 29–30, 39, 68–69
Dunn, Cyril, 104
Durdin, F. Tillman, 104

East India Company, 58, 91
East Pakistan Rifles, 230
economic planning, 158, 194–95, 206
Economist, The, 156, 291–92
Egypt, 199, 266–70, 272–76
Eisenhower, Barbara, 63
Eisenhower, Dwight D., 47, 63–65, 67–69, 109–10
El Arish, Egypt, 275
elephants, 108–9, 113–14
Elizabeth II, 68–70, 103, 108, 110–13, 115–16, 223
Enders, Thomas O., 261–62
Erdeni Tzu monastery, 152
Evanston, Illinois, 142, 144, 186
Evening Star. See *Washington Star*
Everest, Mount, 51–53
Exercise Sagebrush, 5–6

Faas, Horst, 241–42
Far Eastern Economic Review, 214

"five o'clock follies," 247, 250, 260
Folsom, James ("Kissin' Jim"), 12
Foothills, India, 28–29
Ford, Gerald R., *ix*, 218, 281, 297
Foreign Affairs, 137, 156
Foreign Correspondents Association of South Asia, 117, 128, 185, 238
forward policy, India, 124–25, 128
French embassy, Moscow, 178
frontier guards, Chinese, 129
Fulbright program, 138–42, 144, 294
Fuller, Keith, 296

Gagarin, Yuri Alekseyevich, 175, 200, 295
Galbraith, Catherine (Kitty), 139, 142
Galbraith, John Kenneth, 128, 136–39, 141–42, 294
Gallagher, Wes, *photo following page 100*, 197–98
Gandantegchinlen Monastery, 154–55
Gandhi, Indira, 137, 228, 237, 293
Gandhi, Mohandas K., 11, 18, 61, 93, 138
"gang of four," China, 218–19
Ganges River, India, 44, 58, 222, 224, 239
Gangtok, Sikkim, 24–25, 33–37, 74, 77, 136–37
Gaza Strip, 267, 269–70, 273, 275
Geneva, Switzerland, 268, 272
Genghis Khan, 151–52
George V, 108, 110–11, 113, 293
George VI, 32
George, Emmanuel, 143
Georgia, Soviet, 171, 175
Georgievsky Hall, 158, 161, 165, 167
gho (garment, also *kho*), 24, 71, 79, 82
Gidi Pass, Sinai, 268
Golan Heights, 199, 267, 270, 273
Goodstadt, Leo, 214–15
Goonetilleke, Oliver, 103–4, 106
Gopal, Sarvepalli, 123, 130–31, 160, 162
Gopalganj, East Pakistan, 235
Gori, Soviet Union, 171
Graetz, Robert, 16
Gravina, Dorothea, 55
Gray, Fred, 9, 14
Great Leap Forward, China, 48
Great Proletarian Cultural Revolution, 203–4, 206, 208–12, 214, 217–18, 245; little red book, 208
Grimes, Paul, 78, 94, *photo following page 100*
Gritsan, Vasily, 189–90
Gromyko, Andrei Andreyevich, 268
Grover, Preston, 147, 156, 159, 186, 295
Guangzhou, China, 216
Gulag, Soviet, 147, 180, 184
Gupta, M. M., 53, 55
Gurkhas, 39, 44, 119

Haley, James Michael, 251
Hampta La (pass), 42
Hangen, Welles, 277, 282
Hanoi, North Vietnam, 166–67, 251–53, 257, 261
Harper, Steve, 54–57
hartal, 59–62
Harvard University, 142, 174, 198, 204, 206, 227, 294, 296; Graduate School of Education, 294
Hassimara, India, 78
Hawley, Elizabeth, 50
Heck, L. Douglas, 54
Helsinki agreement of 1975, 267
Hevajra, 84
Hillary, Edmund, 52
Himalayas, 23, 33, 42, 51, 56, 58, 73–74, 108, 117–20, 128–31, 133, 155, 160, 204, 292; geology of, 44, 78; pronunciation, 23
Hindus, 45, 90–91, 133, 135, 143, 159, 221–22, 233–35, 240, 292; Vaishnava Hinduism, 49
Hmong, 248
Ho Chi Minh, 166, 251, 257
Ho Chi Minh Trail, 244, 247, 253, 257, 282
Hobrecht, Earnest, 29
Hoffman, Burton, 233
Home, Alexander Frederick Douglas-Home, 113–14, 116
Hong Kong, 137, 156, 201–3, 206–16, 218–19, 223, 232–34, 245, 248, 262, 280, 282, 288, 293, 296
Hong Kong Foreign Correspondents' Club (FCC), 215
Hong Kong International School, 206

Hooghly River, India, 58
Hotel Moskova, Moscow, 180–81
Hotel le Phnom, Phnom Penh, 259–60
Howrah, India, 58, 60–62
Hubbard, Hillman H., 9, 11
Humayan's tomb, 139
Hun Sen, 265
Hungary, 26, 253, 283
hurricane. *See* cyclones
Hussain, Kamal, 229, 231
Hussein bin Talal, 270
Hyderabad, India, 93

In Tam, 260–61, 264
India, 83, 89–90, 92, 99, 108–12, 120–21, 125, 131, 133, 136, 138, 145–46, 155, 158, 169, 176–77, 184–86, 204–5, 221–23, 228, 231, 236–37, 242, 246–47, 282–83, 292–94, 296–97; Air Force, 129, 242; Army, 45–46, 88, 93, 117–18, 124–26, 128–31, 220, 234, 237–41; Army Border Roads Organization, 78, 82; External Affairs Ministry (Foreign Ministry), 37–38, 95, 119, 126, 160; Intelligence Bureau, 23; parliament, 21, 25, 73, 90, 93, 122–23, 126–27, 135; Press Information Bureau, 117; Republic Day, 32–34, 129–30; State Bank of India, 37, 39, 129; Survey of India, 51
India International Center, 131, 138–40, 142
India-China border war, 36, 48, 117–31, 160, 204, 238; eastern sector of border, 121; maps, Indian and Chinese, 119–21, 125–26, 128; U.S. military aid to India, 128–29; western sector of border, 121
India-Pakistan wars: Kashmir, 120, 124; East Pakistan, 220–43
Indian Airlines, 231, 237
Indian journalists, 160–62
Indochina, 206, 210, 216, 248–49, 253, 259, 261, 277, 282
Indonesia, 137, 244, 253, 258, 293, 296–97
Indonesian embassy, New Delhi, 139
Indus River, 124, 223
Ingostrakh, 198
Insight, 229
Institute of Tibetology, Gangtok, 136
Inter-Continental Hotel, Dhaka, 229–31, 233, 242
International Commission of Control and Supervision (ICCS), 252–53
International Commission of Jurists, 37
International Herald Tribune, 168
Intourist, 147, 170–71, 173–74
Iraq, 6, 277
Irkutsk, USSR, 146–47, 155
Irvine, Andrew, 292
Islam. *See* Muslims
Islamabad, Pakistan, 105, 223, 231, 234
Israel, 199, 266–76, 298; Israeli army, 272, 275
Israeli-Egyptian peace treaty, 268, 271
Izvestiya, 162–63, 201, 295

Jadid, Salah al-Jadid, 199
Jaffa Gate, 266, 270
Jaipur, India, 111, 140, 294
Jakarta, Indonesia, 59, 258
Janpath Hotel, 122, 142–43
Japan, 211, 297
Japanese consulate, Hong Kong, 207, 211
Japanese parliamentary delegation, 163
Jayewardene, Junius Richard, 106
Jebtsundamba Khutuktu, 150
Jelep La (pass), 23, 74
Jemison, T. J., 9–10
Jerusalem, 266–76, 298
Jews, 267, 270–71; Orthodox Jews, 271, 273–74, 276
Jiang Qing, 212, 217–18
Johnson, Frank M., Jr., 14–15
Johnson, Lyndon B., 109–10, 247
Johnson, Michael R. (Mike), 197
Joint Public Affairs Office, Saigon, 247
Jomsom, Nepal, 45–46, 48, 50, 292
Jordan, 267, 270–71, 275
Jorhat, India, 94, 98
journalists' deaths, 255–57, 259, 277–82, 286

Kabul, Afghanistan, 125, 132, 134, 278
Kabul Times, 134, 278
Kabul University, 134, 278
Kagbeni, Nepal, 48, 292

Kalam, Pakistan, 53
Kali Gandak River, Nepal, 41–45, 48–50, 292
Kalimpong, India, 23–25, 33, 74, 77
Kamel, Muhamed Ibrahim, 268
Kanchenjunga mountain, 136
Kandy, Ceylon, 106–7
Kann, Peter, 296
Karachi, Pakistan, 64, 105, 109, 221–23, 228, 231–33
Karaganda, USSR, 146–47
Karakoram, Mongolia, 152
Karakoram mountains, 119–20
Kashmir, 53, 93–94, 120, 126, 231, 236–37
Kathmandu, Nepal, 41, 43, 47, 50, 53, 57, 112, 115, 123, 132–33, 156, 291
Kaul, T. N. (Tikki), 205–6, 238
Kennan Institute for Advanced Russian Studies, 294
Kennedy, Alan, 126
Kennedy, John F., 109, 119, 137, 146
Kennedy, Lillian, 1
Kennon, Robert F., 1, 5–6
Kerala state, India, 60, 65–66, 103
Keuneman, Pieter, 105, 293
Khalid bin Abdul-Aziz Al Saud, 270
Khampas, 24, 46–47
Khmer Rouge, 255–59, 261–65, 277, 282, 298; deaths caused by, 259, 264
Khmer Serai, 261, 288
Khrushchev, Nikita Sergeyevich, *photo following page 100,* 109, 157–63, 175–82, 185–88, 190–91, 215, 283, 297
"killing fields," Cambodia, 264–65
King, Martin Luther, Jr., 7–18
kira (garment), 71
Kirk, Don, 215, 246
Kissinger, Henry A., *ix,* 212–13, 216, 237–38, 243, 251–52, 262, 297
Knesset, 273–74
Knox, Rawle, 94, 97
Kogan, Claude, 52, 56–57
Kohima, Nagaland, 88, 95–96, 98–99
Koirala, Bishweshwar Prasad, 53–54, 115, 133–34
Kompong Thom, Cambodia, 255–56, 261
Konyak Nagas, 91
Koppel, Edward James (Ted), 232–33
Korean War, 2, 4–5, 119, 205–6
Korngold, Robert (Bud), 195–96
Kosygin, Alexei Nikolayevich, *photo following page 100,* 166, 179, 181, 186–87, 190–91
Kozlov, Frol Romanovich, 176
Kratie, Cambodia, 248
Kremlin, Moscow, 158–60, 165, 167, 169, 179–80, 182, 184, 186, 196–97, 200, 205, 283, 293; Grand Kremlin Palace, 158–59, 165; Granovitaya Palata, 165; Palace of Congresses, 187, 293
Kremlinology, 181, 208–9, 214
Krishna Menon, V. K., 125, 127–28, 293
Ku Klux Klan (KKK), 13
Kulu Valley, India, 42
kumis, 152–53
Kunlun mountains, 120
Kushkaki, Sabahuddin, 134, 277–80

Ladakh, India, 120, 124–26, 128–29
Lagos, Nigeria, 59, 297–98
Lahaul, India, 42, 53
Lake House, Ceylon, 285
Lambert, Raymond, 52
Lancashire, David, 126, 129
Lanka Sama Samaja Paksava (LSSP), 104, 106
Laos, *ix,* 245, 247–50, 254, 256–57, 261, 277, 282; army, 247–48
Lattimore, Owen, 146, 156
Laurent, Michel, 230–31, 241–42, 277, 282
leeches, 74, 85, 119
Leh, India, 124, 126, 129
Lekhi, Ramnik, 282
Lenin, Vladimir Ilyich, 162, 193
Leningrad, Soviet Union, 185, 194
Lenin's tomb, 157, 196
Leonov, Alexei Arkhipovich, 189
Lewis, Rufus, 10–11
Lhasa, Tibet, 20–21, 23, 34–35, 37–38, 41, 47–48, 74, 76, 120–21, 155
Lhotse, mountain, 52
Life, 282
Likud Party, 267, 276

Lin Biao, 208–10
line of actual control, 128–29
Liter, C. P., 2, 4–5
Liu Shaoqi, 210
Living Buddha, Mongolia, 150
Lok Sabha. *See* India: parliament
Lon Nol, 258–63, 297
London Evening News, 180
Los Angeles Times, 171, 259
Lotha Nagas, 91
Louis, Viktor (Vitaly Evgenyevich), 180
Louisiana State University (LSU), 1
Luang Prabang, Laos, 247

Macdonald, Victoria (Vicky), 23–24
Madhupur Jungle, East Pakistan, 220
maharaja: Bharatpur, 135; Rajasthan, 111; Sikkim, 136
maharajkumar. See Thondup, Palden Thondup Namgyal
Mahendra Bir Bikram Shah Dev, 43, 53, 112, 115–16, 133–34
Maiwandwal, Mohammed Hashim, 134
Makalu (mountain), 52
Mallory, George Leigh, 51, 292
Manege Square, Moscow, 169, 180
Manila, Philippines, 248–49, 284–85, 297
Manila Chronicle, 284
Mao Zedong, 34, 48, 121, 125, 182, 203, 208–14, 218–19, 272, 291
Marcos, Ferdinand, 284–85
Marxism, 205, 208
Matthews, Jay, 219
Matyash, Vladimir, 238
Maxwell, Neville, 78, 94, 99, 106, 144, 292–93
McCall, Sherrod, 204, 209, 211, 213, 215, 217
McMahon Line, 120–21, 123–25, 128, 131
Mehta, Jagat, 37–38, 119–20
Meir, Golda, 271
Mekong Delta, 228, 249, 253, 298
Mekong River, 247–48, 262–63
Menon, P. N., 95
Middle East, 199, 222, 266–70, 275–76, 296
Middle East negotiations, 266–76
middle sector, India-China border, 121
Migjid Janraisig, 155
Mikoyan, Anastas Ivanovich, 175, 178–79
Miller, Gerald, 282
Miller, John, 200–201
Minh, Dang Quang, 166–68
Mitla Pass, Sinai, 268
Mondale, Walter F., 266–68
Mongolian People's Republic, 145, 156, 177, 209, 292, 297; ambassador to India, 145–46; circus, 150; history, 147–48, 152, 154–55; livestock, 152–153; opera 150–51; state theater, 147, 150
Mongolian People's Revolutionary Party (MPRP), 148, 153–54, 156
Montgomery, Alabama, 6, 7–19, 67; bombings, 7–8, 12, 15–17
Montgomery Advertiser, 13, 15–16
Montgomery Improvement Association (MIA), 10–11, 13–15
Morning Advocate, Baton Rouge, 2, 4–6
Moscow, 127, 144, 146–47, 154–56, 158, 161, 164, 167–71, 173–75, 177, 179–86, 188–89, 192, 194, 196–97, 199–202, 205–6, 208–9, 238, 250, 261, 278, 283, 288, 293–94; Moscow Radio, 200; Moscow television, 189
Moscow River, 158–59, 193
Moscow State University, 194
Mujib. *See* Rahman, Mujibur
mukhti bahini, 220, 234–37, 239–41
Muktinath, Nepal, 43, 46, 48–49, 53, 292
Mumbai. *See* Bombay (Mumbai)
Muslims, 91, 102, 143, 221–22, 229, 234–35, 262, 266–67, 269–70, 279–80, 295
Mussoorie, India, 37
Mustang, Nepal, 43, 47–48, 291
Myanmar. *See* Burma (Myanmar)

Nacional (hotel), Moscow, 169, 171
Nagaland, 88–100, 115; atrocity allegations, 88–90, 93, 95–96, 98–99; Christianity, 90, 92–93, 97; geography, 90–91; guerrilla war, 93–94, 96; history, 91–94, 99–100; Naga Home Guard, 93–94; Naga National Council (NNC), 93, 95–96; Naga People's Convention (NPC), 94–95

Nagas, 88, 91–92, 292
namaste, 142, 164, 244
Namche Bazaar, Nepal, 53, 55, 57
Nanda, Bimla, 138
Nasser, Gamal Abdel, 109
Nathu La (pass), 34–36, 74, 131
National Assembly, Cambodia, 258, 260
National Association for the Advancement of Colored People (NAACP), 8–9, 11, 14
National Geographic Society, 284, 288
Nayar, Kuldip, 234
Nayar, V. M., 94
NBC network, 232, 282
Neak Luong, Cambodia, 262
NEFA. *See* Northeast Frontier Agency (NEFA), India
Nehru, Jawaharlal, 21–23, 25, 27, 32, 36–38, 60, 63, 65–66, 74, 93–94, *photo following page 100*, 110, 121–23, 125–31, 133–34, 141–42, 146–47, 158–60, 293
Nepal, 41–42, 47, 51, 54, 86, 92, 94, 108, 112–16, 119, 121, 123, 132–34, 136, 155, 288, 291–92, 297; adjectival form, 54; ethnic group, 83–84, 86, 137; parliament, 53, 115, 134. *See also* Bhutan: Nepalis in
Nepali Congress Party, 53, 115, 133
Neue Zürcher Zeitung, 94
New China News Agency (NCNA), 207–8, 213
New Delhi. *See* Delhi, New and old, India
New York Post, 14
New York Times, x, 70, 78, 94, 104, 144, 230–33, 288
New York Times News Service, 215, 230
Newsweek, 16, 195–96, 230–31
Nguyen, Hoang Ngoc, 247, 251–52, 277, 280–82, 286
Nieman fellowship, 142, 198, 200, 206, 296
Nixon, Edgar Daniel, 8–11, 15, 18
Nixon, Richard M., *photo following page 100*, 210, 212, 236–37, 246, 248, 250–53
North Atlantic Treaty Organization (NATO), 169, 173, 262, 272
Northeast Frontier Agency (NEFA), India, 25–27, 121, 123–29
Noyes, Crosby, 253
Noyes, Newbold, 252, 296

Observer (Colombo), 103
Observer (London), 94, 104
Odongk, Cambodia, 262
Oksenberg, Lois, 209
Oksenberg, Michel, 209, 214, 216, 219, 272
Old Executive Office Building, Washington, 269
Operation Arc Light, 261
Operation Linebacker, 252

Padma Sambhava (Guru Rimpoche), 49, 84
Pakistan, 49, 64, 92–94, 105, 108–12, 131, 137, 160, 228, 230–31, 236–37, 278–79, 286, 292–93, 295–97; army, 220–21, 225, 227–30, 233–37, 242; economic development, 222–23; elections, 224–27; Inter-Services Intelligence Directorate (ISI), 279. *See also* Pakistan, East; Pakistan, West
Pakistan, East, 30, 55, 58–59, 112, 220–22, 223–28, 229, 231, 233–39, 242, 296; description, 221–23. *See also* Bangladesh
Pakistan, West, 221–28, 231–32, 236–40, 242; description, 222
Pakistan International Airlines (PIA), 231–32
Pakistan People's Party (PPP), 226–27
Palestine Liberation Organization (PLO), 270
Palestinians, 266, 269–70, 272–76
Palpar, Dhaka, 239
Paltan Maidan, Dhaka, 220, 240
Pandatshang, Ragpa and Togbye, 24
Pannwitt, Barbara (Bobbie), 141–43
Pannwitt, Fred J, 138, 141–43, 294
Pannwitt, Monica Jean (Nicky), 138–43, 293–94
Pant, Apa, 24–25, 33–38, 291
"parachute journalism," *ix*, 128
Parks, Rosa L., 9–10, 14
Paro, Bhutan, 71, 73–74, 79–82, 84; *dzong*, 71, 80–82, 84–87
Paro River (Pachu), 71, 79, 84, 86
Pathet Lao, 245, 247–48
Patterson, George, 22

Peiris, Denzil, 103, 105–7, 285
Pentagon. *See* United States: Defense Department
People, 229
Perera, N. M., 104–5
Peter, Prince of Greece and Denmark, 282
Petranek, Jan, 277–78, 283–85
Pheunkhang, Pema Tsedeun Yapshi (Princess Coo Coo La), 136
Phi Beta Kappa, 12, 138
Philip, Prince, 111, 113–14
Philippines, 277–78, 284–85, 293, 297
Philippines Inquirer, 285
Philippines Institute for Development Studies, 285
Phizo, Angami Zapu, 93–95, 99
Phnom Penh, Cambodia, 248, 255–65, 282
photography, problems of, 110–13, 153–55
Phuntsholing, Bhutan, 78–79, 85
Pitsunda, USSR, 175, 178, 180
Pleiku, South Vietnam, 166, 205, 250
Podgorny, Nikolai Viktorovich, 177–78
Pokhara, Nepal, 43, 48–49, 292
Pol Pot, 256, 262, 264
Polgar, Thomas, 251
Polk, Camp, 5–6
Polk, George Polk Memorial Award, 215
Portugal, *ix,* 288, 297
Potala, 34–36, 155
Prague, Czechoslovakia, 283–84
Prague Radio, 283
Prague spring, 283
Pravda, 171, 181, 199–201
Provisional Revolutionary Government of the Republic of South Vietnam (PRG), 252
Pul-i-Charki prison, Kabul, 279
Pulitzer Prize, 241, 246, 296
Punjab, Pakistan, 221–23, 225, 227, 237

Quant, William B., 276

Radhakrishnan, Sarvepalli, *photo following page* 100, 159–60, 163
Radio Hong Kong, 215
Radio Kabul, 278
radiophotos, 29–31, 242
Rahman, Hamoodur, 233–34, 242
Rahman, Mujibur, 225–29; nine-point program, 226–28, 231, 235, 240, 242–43, 293
Rajasthan state, India, 111, 113, 115, 140
Ram, Lucille (Lui), 141–42
Ram, Vernon, 141
Ram Lila grounds, Delhi, 63, 65–68
Ramadan, 111–12
Ramparts, 50
Rana, K. B., 43–44, 46, 48–50
Rana prime ministers, 55, 108, 115
Rashtrapati Bhavan, 33, 65
Rawalpindi, Pakistan, 105, 223, 234
razakars, 235–36, 240–41
Razuvayeva, Svetlana, 169, 171, 186
receiving lines, 164–68, 186
reconnaissance satellites, 188
Red Square, Moscow, 147, 180, 186, 196
Reddick, Olive, 140–42
Reuters, 20–21, 29, 50, 70, 94, 112, 115, 127, 159, 207, 213, 283
rhinoceros, Asian, 108–9, 114–15
Riyadh, Saudi Arabia, 267, 270
rockets, journalistic, 20, 31, 127
Rogers, William P., 249
Route 1, Cambodia, 259, 262
Rowley, James J., 63–67, 69
Roy, Bidhan Chandra, 61
Royle, Don, 27, 30–31, 126, 129
Russell, J. O. G., *photo following page 100,* 143–44
Russia, 178, 278, 284, 292. *See also* Soviet Union

Sadat, Anwar, 267–69, 271–74
Saigon, 109, 166, 224, 244, 246–47, 249–53, 257; description, 246–47, 258–60, 280–82, 288
Saloth Sar (Pol Pot), 264
Samara and Judea, 271
Sanskrit, 101, 222, 292
Satakopan, Rangaswamy ("Swamy"), 20, 22, 27, 126, 144, 146
Savannakhet, Laos, 247
Savina, Antonina (Tonya), 186

Schanberg, Sidney H., 231–32
Scopes, Leonard A., 115–16
Sema Nagas, 91–92
Sen, Sarendranath, 27–30
Senanayake, Don Stephen, 102–3
Senanayake, Dudley S., 101–2, 106
"seven traitors," Cambodia, 262–64
Seventeen-Point Agreement, Tibet, 29, 35
shabdrung, 76, 82, 87
Shakabpa, Wangchuk Deden, 24
Shapiro, Henry, 177–78, 181, 295
Sharon, Ariel, 275
Sheldon, Charles, 188
Shelepin, Aleksandr Nikolayevich, 179
Sheremetyevo airport, Mosocow, 156, 195
Sherpas, 52–53, 56–57
Siberia, 146–47, 198
Siddiqi, Zamir, 64
Siddiqui, Abdul Quadir, 220, 236, 240–41
Sihanouk, Norodom, 248, 257–58, 260–61, 263
Sikkim, 23–25, 33, 35, 37, 86, 131, 135–37, 155; *chogyal*, 24, 35
Siliguri, India, 22, 30, 84
Simon, Joseph J., 214
Sims, Watson S. (Wally), 20, 22, 25, 27–31, 53, 64, 94, 105–6, 112, 122–23, 141, 173–74
Sinai Peninsula, 199, 267–70, 272–73, 275
Singh, Brajendra, 132, 135
Sinhalese, 101–4, 106, 285
Sino-Soviet relations, 148, 154, 167, 181–82, 205, 293; border clashes, 182, 210
Sirik Matak, Sisowath, 258, 263–64
Six-Day War, 199, 267, 270
"smart bomb," 251
Smiley, Glenn E., 15
Snepp, Frank W., III, 251
Solomon, Richard H., 216, 219
Somarama, Talduwe, 105
Sorge, Richard, 189–90
Sormani, Pietro, 209
South America, *ix*
South Asia, 62, 64, 101, 104, 108–9, 118, 126, 138, 142, 145, 156, 185, 217, 228, 230, 234, 236, 283, 296
Southeast Asia, 109, 222, 288
Southeast Asia Treaty Organization (SEATO), 109, 248
Southern Christian Leadership Conference, 18
Soviet embassies: New Delhi, 238; Phnom Penh, 201; Ulan Bator, 151, 154; Washington, D.C., 197, 202
Soviet Union, 119, 124, 145–48, 154, 157, 159–66, 169, 172–73, 176, 182–83, 185–88, 194–96, 200, 202, 205, 208, 210, 212, 217, 237–38, 251, 274, 278–79, 288–89, 293, 295, 298; agriculture, 177, 179, 181, 195; army, 148; censorship, 189–90, 295; Central Asia, 146, 170, 192, 292, 295; Committee of Solidarity with Asian and African Countries, 166–67; economic reforms, 190; Foreign Ministry, 165, 168, 196, 199; Foreign Ministry press department, 159, 163, 170, 184, 187, 191, 194, 198–201; GRU (military intelligence), 184, 189–90; KGB (Committee for State Security), 148, 166, 170–71, 172–73, 177, 179–80, 183–84, 186, 191–93, 198, 200–201; medicine, 186, 195, 295; pay scales, 182; State Committee for Space Exploration, 188–89; Supreme Soviet (parliament), 176, 182; Ukraine, 176, 179. *See also* Communist Party: Soviet Union
Soviet-American relations, 167, 188, 268; arms control negotiations, 202, 268, 272
space race, 175, 188, 188–89, 283
Spiti, India, 42, 53
Squire, Christopher A., 249–50
Sri Lanka. *See* Ceylon
Sri Lanka Freedom Party (SLFP), 102, 105–6, 285
Srinagar, India, 126, 129
St. Albans, 288
St. Louis Post-Dispatch, 3
St. Petersburg, Russia, 185
Stalin, Josef Vissarionovich, 104, 157–59, 171, 176–77, 179–80, 182, 184, 190, 193–95
Statesman, 21–22, 39, 234
Steward, Jack, 143–44
Stewart, Ruth, 143–44
Straten-Ponthoz, Claudine van der, 52, 55–57
Suez Canal, 267–68

Sukarno, 109, 137
Sukhe Bator, 147–48
Sukhodrev, Viktor, 161
Survey of the China Mainland Press, 207
Suslov, Mikhail Andreyevich, 157, 179, 205
Svay Rieng, Cambodia, 259
Swank, Emory Coblentz (Cobey), 261–62, 297
Swarthmore College, 138–39, 209
Swat, 49, 53
Swinton, Stanley M., 137–38, 141
Syria, 199–200, 267, 270
Syvertsen, George, 175, 277, 282

Taiwan, 119, 203, 212, 272, 297
Taj Mahal, 67, 111, 139–40, 144
Taksang monastery, 84–85, 292
Tamils, 102–3, 106–7
Tan Son Nhat airport, Saigon, 249, 253
Tangail, East Pakistan, 220, 235, 240
Tashkent, USSR, 146–47, 155–56
TASS agency, 127, 166–67, 175, 178, 180–81, 185, 188, 193, 196, 200, 238; Fotokhronika TASS, 189–90, 295
Tatopani, Nepal, 44
Taubkina, Mila, 297
Tawang, India, 27, 120, 128–30
Taylor, E. Paul, *photo following page 100*, 144
Tbilisi, USSR, 171–72, 174
tea, Tibetan, 82, 152
Tel Aviv, Israel, 267, 272–74
Tenzing Norgay, 52
Terai, Nepal, 108, 112
Tet offensive, 246
Tezpur, India, 26–30, 33, 35, 39, 61–62, 126, 128–30
Thag La ridge, 125
Thailand, 247, 257, 262, 293
Thakkhola district, Nepal, 43, 45–46
Thanh, Son Ngoc, 261
Thapa, Nar Pratap, 42–43, 50
Thieu, Nguyen Van, 251–53
Thimphu, Bhutan, 82, 87
Third World, 158, 166, 185, 242
Tho, Le Duc, 251–52
Thomas, Rex, 7, 12–16, 18–19
Thondup, Gyalo, 38–39, 47
Thondup, Palden Thondup Namgyal, 35–36, 132, 135–37
Thorung La (pass), 292
Thurmont, Maryland, 268
Thyangboche monastery, Nepal, 53
Tiananmen Square, Beijing, 209
Tibet, 34, 73–74, 77, 83, 100, 117–19, 131, 155, 29, 297; Chinese invasion of, 22, 24, 34, 38, 73, 121, 124–25, 133, 137; refugees from, 33, 37, 126; revolt in, 20–24, 38, 41–42, 46–47, 74, 77, 121, 136, 155. *See also* Khampas; Tibetan guerrillas
Tibetan guerrillas, 22, 24–25, 39, 41–42, 45–48, 50, 288, 291
"tiger of Tangail," 220
tigers, 108–9, 111, 113–15, 119
Tikka Khan, Mohammed, 229
Time, 39–40, 189, 287
Times (London), 78, 94, 135, 292–93
Times of India, 38–40, 77
Tito, Josip Broz, 154
Tokyo, 127, 215
Toon, Malcolm S., 197
Trans-Siberian railway, 148, 170
Tripura, India, 239
Tsangpo River, Tibet, 48
Tsedenbal, Yumjaagiyn, 154
Tsetserleg, Mongolia, 151, 153
Tukuche, Nepal, 48
Tuskegee, Alabama, 17–18
typhoon. *See* cyclones

U-2 planes, 188
Udorn, Thailand, 248
Ugyen Pelri Palace, Paro, 80
Uighurs, 100
Ulan Bator, Mongolia, 146–51, 153–56
Ulan Bator Hotel, 147–49, 154–55
United National Party (UNP), 101–2, 106, 285
United Nations, 83, 86, 95, 103, 120, 125, 161–63, 205, 242, 265; Article 19, 162–63; Emergency Force, 268; Office of the High Commissioner for Refugees, 86; peacekeep-

ing, 161–63; World Health Organization (WHO), 221
United Press, 3–4
United Press International (UPI), 29–31, 110–11, 159, 177–78, 181–82, 200, 253, 295
United States, 119, 134, 167, 183, 196, 203–5, 210, 212, 236, 251–52, 257, 261, 263, 266–67, 270–75, 278–81, 289; Air Force, 4, 129, 202, 251, 266, 276; Army, 126, 224–25, 244, 246, 249–51, 253; Army's 11th Air Cavalry Division, 244, 258; Army Special Forces, 261; Central Intelligence Agency (CIA), 248, 251, 261, 287–89; Congress, 263, 281; Congressional Research Service, 188; Defense Department, 254; Educational Foundation in India, 132, 140, 142; Foreign Broadcast Information Service (FBIS), 207, 214, 252; Information Agency, 30, 247, 252, 274; National Aeronautics and Space Administration (NASA), 188; National Endowment for Democracy, 279; National Security Council, 216, 219, 272, 276; Navy, 263; Senate, 261–62; State Department, 197, 202, 212, 214, 236–37, 242, 250, 254, 264, 273
University of California, Berkeley, 214, 226
University of Missouri, School of Journalism, 2–4
U.S. consulates: Dhaka, 236, 242; Hong Kong, 204, 207–9, 211, 213, 217
U.S. embassies: Colombo, 232; Moscow, 186, 190, 192, 194, 197–98, 201, 205; Moscow embassy dacha, 192; Phnom Penh, 260–62; Saigon, 281
U.S. liaison office, Beijing, 212–14
Usovo, Soviet Union, 182
U.S.S.R. *See* Soviet Union

Vance, Cyrus R., 202, 266, 269–72, 275–76, 297
Vance, Grace S. (Gay), 271
Vann, John Paul, 250
Victoria, 110
Vientiane, Laos, 247–48
Viet Cong (VC), 109, 164, 166–68, 205, 224, 228, 244, 246, 248–50, 252–53, 258
Vietnam, North, 109, 166–67, 192, 205, 245–47, 249, 251–52, 257–58, 261, 281, 284, 297–98; North Vietnamese Army (NVA), 244, 248–50, 253, 258–59, 282
Vietnam, South, 109, 166, 211, 224, 234, 244–54, 257, 259, 261, 277, 280–82, 286; Army of the Republic of Vietnam (ARVN), 246, 250–51, 253, 281; Ministry of Finance, 281; National Liberation Front (NLF), 166–68
Vietnam negotiations, 251–52, 261, 281
Vietnam War, 6, 67, 164, 170, 185, 205–6, 212, 215, 224, 244–45, 247, 251, 253, 256, 280–81, 296
Vittachi, V. Tarzi, 285
Vnukovo II airport, Moscow, 166
Voice of America, 264–65, 279
Volkswagen, *photo following page 100*, 183, 197–98
Voskhod, 175–76, 178, 180

Wang Hongwen, 203–4, 212–14, 218
Wangchuck, Jigme, 76, 83
Wangchuck, Jigme Dorje, 71–73, 75–78, 80–83, 85, *photo following page 100*
Wangchuck, Jigme Khesar Namgyel, 86
Wangchuck, Jigme Senge, 85–86,
Wangchuck, Ugyen, 76, 80, 83
Washington, Booker T., 17
Washington, D.C., 146, 166–67, 185, 202, 212, 214, 216, 218, 236, 238, 246, 248, 250, 253–54, 259, 264, 267–69, 271–74, 276, 279–81, 287–89, 293–94, 297
Washington Post, 219
Washington Star, 156, 203, 206, 210–11, 215, 218, 221, 223–24, 226, 227–29, 233–34, 236, 238, 240, 244–47, 250–55, 263–64, 266, 269, 272–74, 276, 280–81, 284, 287–88, 296–98
Weiland, Sidney, 112–15, 127, 196
West Bank, 266–67, 269–76
West Bank settlements, 271, 273–75
White Citizens' Council, 13
White House, Washington, 269, 272, 274
Woodrow Wilson International Center for Scholars, 279, 294
Woodrow Wilson scholarships, 138

Woodruff, John, 231
World War I, 194
World War II, 1, 5, 146, 176, 195, 208, 214, 261
Wyllie, Irvin G., 2

Xinjiang province, China, 119–21

Yahya Khan Qizilbash, Agha Mohammad, 225–26, 228–29, 237, 242
Yalu River, 206
Yammit, Sinai, 273, 275
Yao Wenyuan, 296
Yatung (Yadong), Tibet, 34–35
Yeshe, Gyen, 46–48
yeti ("abominable snowman"), 55–57
Yom Kippur War, 267–68
Yugoslavia, ambassador to Mongolia, 154
yurts, 151–52

Zahir Shah, Mohammed, 134–35, 278
Zeitlin, Arnold, 230–31, 233
Zhang Chunqiao, 296
Zhou Enlai, *x*, 36, *photo following page 100*, 109, 121, 123–24, 128–29, 182, 187, 203–4, 210–18
Zorthian, Baryoor (Barry), 247, 297